THE FREER BIBLICAL MANUSCRIPTS

Society of Biblical Literature

Text-Critical Studies

Sidnie White Crawford,
Series Editor

Number 6

THE FREER BIBLICAL MANUSCRIPTS
Fresh Studies of an American Treasure Trove

THE FREER BIBLICAL MANUSCRIPTS

Fresh Studies of an American Treasure Trove

Edited by

Larry W. Hurtado

Society of Biblical Literature
Atlanta

THE FREER BIBLICAL MANUSCRIPTS

Library of Congress Cataloging-in-Publication Data

The Freer biblical manuscripts : fresh studies of an American treasure trove / edited by Larry W. Hurtado.

p. cm. — (Text-critical studies ; v. 6)

Includes bibliographical references.

ISBN-13: 978-1-58983-208-4 (paper binding : alk. paper)

ISBN-10: 1-58983-208-6 (paper binding : alk. paper)

1. Bible—Manuscripts. 2. Freer Gallery of Art. 3. Bible—Criticism, interpretation, etc. I. Hurtado, Larry W., 1943– II. Series.

BS4.F74 2006

220.4—dc22 2006016865

14 13 12 11 10 09 08 07 06 5 4 3 2 1

Printed in the United States of America on acid-free, recycled paper conforming to ANSI/NISO Z39.48-1992 (R1997) and ISO 9706:1994 standards for paper permanence.

Contents

Abbreviations

AJA	*American Journal of Archaeology*
AJT	*American Journal of Theology*
Bib	*Biblica*
CLFP	Freer, Charles Lang. Charles Lang Freer Papers, Freer Gallery of Art and Arthur M. Sackler Gallery Archives, Smithsonian Institution, Washington, D.C. Gift of the Estate of Charles Lang Freer.
FMP	Freer Minor Prophets
FWKPapers	Kelsey, Francis W. Francis W. Kelsey Papers, Bentley Historical Library, University of Michigan, Ann Arbor.
FWKRecords	Kelsey, Francis W. Francis W. Kelsey Records, Kelsey Museum Archives, Bentley Historical Library, University of Michigan, Ann Arbor.
HTR	*Harvard Theological Review*
JBL	*Journal of Biblical Literature*
JEA	*Journal of Egyptian Archaeology*
JSNTSup	Journal for the Study of the New Testament Supplement Series
JTS	*Journal of Theological Studies*
Neot	*Neotestamentica*
NovT	*Novum Testamentum*
NTS	*New Testament Studies*
NTTS	New Testament Tools and Studies
RB	*Revue biblique*
SBLDS	Society of Biblical Literature Dissertation Series
SBT	Studies in Biblical Theology
TLZ	*Theologische Literaturzeitung*
ZNW	*Zeitschrift für die neutestamentliche Wissenschaft und die Kunde der älteren Kirche*

Acknowledgements

The completion of the Freer manuscripts project and the publication of this volume allow me the opportunity to acknowledge the contributions and assistance of a number of others. Perhaps foremost is Kent Richards (Executive Director of the Society of Biblical Literature), who from my earliest emailed communication about the project endorsed it enthusiastically and has provided constant encouragement and practical support across the years from late 1999 onward.

With Kent's endorsement, other members of the staff in the Atlanta office of the SBL also merit my hearty thanks. Patrick Durusau was particularly influential and crucial in the cognate project of producing new color, digital photographs of the Freer biblical manuscripts. Frank Ames, and then particularly Bob Buller, were wonderfully cordial, efficient, and supportive in the planning and production of this volume. Matthew Collins graciously took the lead in arranging and scheduling the special session to feature presentations from some of the contributors to this volume in the 2006 Annual Meeting of the SBL in Washington, D.C.

At the early stages of my contacts with the Freer Gallery in 1999–2000, Dr. Thomas Lentz (then Deputy Director) and Dr. Dehejia (his successor until 2002) responded cordially and enthusiastically. Dr. Milo Beach (then Director) and some of his staff met with me in my visit to the Freer in the summer of 2000 and encouraged me to proceed with a proposal for a scholarly project focused on the Freer codices. I would also like to thank other members of the Freer Gallery staff, including Dr. Ann Gunter (Chief Curator), Timothy Kirk, Beth Duly, Tara Coram and Susan Kitsoulis (in the Collections Department), and Colleen Hennessey (Freer and Sackler Gallery Archives). I also acknowledge Dr. Julian Raby (current Director), who met with representatives of the SBL and me in March 2003 for further discussions about the project and other matters, including an exhibition.

Bruce Prior brought to my attention the fact that 2006 would be the centenary of Freer's acquisition of the first four of the biblical manuscripts and suggested that I might approach the Freer Gallery with some plan for recognizing this. Bruce's enthusiasm for the Freer manuscripts is infectious, and at this point of writing I look forward to seeing his own labor of love, a full and careful transcription of the Gospels codex.

I also acknowledge gratefully a travel grant awarded by the University of Edinburgh Development Trust, which covered my air fare to Washington in the summer of 2000 for that crucial first meeting with the Freer Gallery administration and staff. We scholars do our work "on a shoestring," so I also want to thank Frank Matera for providing me lodging in guest facilities of Catholic University of America during that visit, when I emailed him with my plaintive appeal.

Introduction

Larry W. Hurtado

The Freer Biblical Manuscripts

Among the many thousands of precious objects held by the Freer Gallery of Art are six biblical manuscripts that comprise one of the most important collections of such items in the world. Yet, although they initially generated enormous popular and scholarly excitement internationally at the time of their acquisition and publication in the early twentieth century, in the subsequent decades they have received only sporadic serious attention from biblical scholars, and the general public today scarcely knows of them. The ten contributions to this volume are intended primarily to help redress the unjustified scholarly neglect, and they will illustrate for any interested reader the insufficiently explored significance of these manuscripts. This centennial year of the acquisition of the first four of them is an appropriate occasion to publish a fresh set of studies of what amounts to a small but highly valuable treasure trove of biblical manuscripts that now belong to the American people thanks to the generosity of Charles Freer.

Freer purchased four of the six manuscripts in December 1906 from an Egyptian antiquities dealer in Cairo. These four Greek parchment manuscripts include a codex of the four Gospels commonly dated to the early fifth or late fourth century, an early fifth-century codex containing Deuteronomy and Joshua (which likely once contained the whole of Genesis through Joshua), an early fifth-century codex of the Psalms, and remnants of a heavily damaged, sixth-century codex of the Pauline Epistles (which originally also contained the Catholic Epistles and Acts).[1] Subsequently, Freer also purchased a fifth-century Coptic codex of the Psalms (in 1908) and a fragmentary third-century papyrus codex of the Minor Prophets (1916–20), these, too, from Egypt. For a much fuller account of Freer and the fascinating story of his acquisition of these manuscripts, I refer

1. These are the dates now commonly assigned in standard handbooks. But note Ulrich Schmid's reopening of the question of the dating of the Gospels codex that appears in this volume.

readers to Kent Clarke's appreciative and thoroughly researched study that follows this introduction.

To be sure, a few decades after the acquisition of the Freer codices, further and earlier biblical manuscripts came to light, in particular the Chester Beatty biblical papyri, the Bodmer New Testament papyri, and, of course, the phenomenal find at Qumran so important for Hebrew Bible/Old Testament studies.[2] Granted, the successive appearances of these remarkable bodies of material may provide one reason why the Freer manuscripts fell into comparative neglect, as scholars turned their attention to more recent discoveries.

But in the time when news of their acquisition was first announced, none of these finds was even imagined. The earliest and most valuable manuscripts for tracing the history of the biblical text (especially in Greek) were the extant great parchment codices dated variously between the mid-fourth and sixth centuries. These manuscripts included Codex Alexandrinus (a fifth-century, four-volume copy of the entire Bible in Greek), Codex Bezae Cantabrigiensis (a fifth-century codex of the Gospels and Acts notable as a bilingual manuscript, with Greek and Latin on facing pages), the great Vatican codex (Codex Vaticanus, a mid-fourth century manuscript of the Old and New Testaments), and, the then-most-recent major manuscript discovery, Codex Sinaiticus (a mid-fourth century codex brought to light by Tischendorf near the middle of the nineteenth century, likewise containing substantially the whole Christian Bible).

It is in the context of this body of manuscript evidence that we have to see the impact of news about the Freer manuscripts. The acquisition of any one of the Freer codices, dating variously from the mid-fourth through the sixth centuries, would have been an notable development. To have four manuscripts of such antiquity announced together, however, comprising early codices of the Gospels, the Pauline Epistles, Joshua and Deuteronomy, and the Psalms was simply breathtaking news.

As described in fascinating detail by Kent Clarke, after purchasing these four manuscripts in December 1906, Freer brought them to Michigan and sometime in 1907 drew them to the attention of Francis Kelsey, a senior academic figure in the University of Michigan. In turn, Kelsey quickly obtained Freer's agreement to put them into the hands of a young assistant professor of Latin, Henry A. Sand-

2. Frederic G. Kenyon, ed., *The Chester Beatty Biblical Papyri: Descriptions and Texts of Twelve Manuscripts on Papyrus of the Greek Bible* (16 vols.; London: Emery Walker, 1932–58). Key biblical manuscripts among the Bodmer papyri are the following: Victor Martin and Rodolphe Kasser, eds., *Papyrus Bodmer XIV–XV: Evangiles de Luc et Jean* (Cologny-Genève: Bibliotheca Bodmeriana, 1961); Victor Martin and J. W. B. Barns, eds., *Papyrus Bodmer II: Evangile de Jean* (Cologny-Genève: Bibliotheca Bodmeriana, 1962). On the many manuscripts of biblical texts from Qumran, see, e.g., Eugene Ulrich, *The Dead Sea Scrolls and the Origins of the Bible* (Grand Rapids: Eerdmans, 1999).

ers, who took on the onerous but exciting tasks involved in making these valuable items available for scholarly investigation. Sanders obviously threw himself into this work with all his might, seeking as quickly as he could to give sufficient attention to all four manuscripts to offer a confident view of them. In a letter to [illegible] to Sanders [illegible] that "he has not previously over-taxed his vision with parchment." Kelsey clearly expected Sanders to make rapid progress in the succeeding months after being given access to the manuscripts, for in that same letter Kelsey already goes on to ask Freer's consent for Sanders to present a public report to scholars on the manuscripts at the general meeting of the Archaeological Institute and the American Philological Association later that year (December 1907 in Chicago).[3]

Clearly, a great deal rested on this presentation, for which Sanders had only a few months to prepare, and he poured all his energy into readying himself for it. Kelsey opens a subsequent letter to Freer, dated 11 December 1907, with a reference to the program of the forthcoming Chicago meeting, which included a notice of the paper to be given by Sanders, and Kelsey mentions that Sanders had just returned to Ann Arbor (from concentrated work on the manuscripts) "hardly able to see on account of the strain of three days of continuous work, but happy as a king!" This intensive work allowed Sanders and Kelsey to confirm to Freer their initial estimate of the high importance of his manuscripts, and Kelsey praised the young Sanders as "one of the three or four men in the United States to whom so important a piece of investigation could be entrusted."[4]

Based on his report at the Chicago meeting, Sanders quickly wrote a scholarly article that was published early in 1908 in which he described the four manuscripts, provided several photographs (of a page of the Deuteronomy-Joshua manuscript, the painted covers of the Gospels codex, a page of Mark, and a page of the Psalms codex), and also gave a transcription of the remarkable and distinctive insertion in the Freer Gospels Codex after Mark 16:14, subsequently known as "the Freer Logion."[5] Thereafter, immediately there followed an excited flood of notices and observations about the manuscripts by an international galaxy of major scholars, including E. J. Goodspeed, C. R. Gregory, Adolf Harnack, Hermann von Soden, Carl Schmidt, and Frederic Kenyon, as well as the

3. Francis Kelsey to Charles L. Freer (31August 1907), courtesy of the Freer Gallery Archive.

4. Francis Kelsey to Charles L. Freer (11 December 1907), courtesy of the Freer Gallery Archive.

5. Henry A. Sanders, "New Manuscripts of the Bible from Egypt," *AJA* 12 (1908): 49–55. It is puzzling that in this article (49) Sanders refers to Freer's purchase of the manuscripts "early in 1907" and says that "Early in December, 1907" he was invited to examine and report on them, when all the correspondence and other materials clearly indicate a purchase in December 1906 and that Sanders was hard at work on the manuscripts in the autumn of 1907.

many reports of a more popular nature in newspapers in Europe as well as North America.[6]

Over the next twenty years after that first formal report on the Freer manuscripts in Chicago, Sanders devoted himself to preparing facsimile volumes and major monograph studies of these codices, beginning with the two volumes on the Deuteronomy-Joshua codex, which appeared in 1910, and on through to the facsimile volume and critical edition of the Minor Prophets codex in 1927.[7] As detailed by Kent Clarke, Freer generously financed all this and took an enthusiastic interest in the work and the finished products. Among their notable features, these facsimile volumes employed what was then the most advanced technology in photographic processes, providing scholars thereafter with incredibly clear images of the manuscripts.[8]

The Gospels Codex

Although each of the Freer biblical manuscripts was, in its own right, a major contribution to the available pool of textual evidence (especially when they first appeared), it was doubtless the Gospels codex that received the most attention

6. Sanders noted fifteen scholarly notices and articles that appeared in 1908–1909 alone. For details, see Henry A. Sanders, *The Old Testament Manuscripts in the Freer Collection, Part I: The Washington Manuscript of Deuteronomy and Joshua* (University of Michigan Studies, Humanistic Series 8/1; New York: Macmillan, 1910), 1.

7. In addition to the critical edition of the Deuteronomy-Joshua manuscript (see n. 6), Sanders produced the following volumes in this period: *Facsimile of the Washington Manuscript of Deuteronomy and Joshua in the Freer Collection* (Ann Arbor: University of Michigan, 1910); *Facsimile of the Washington Manuscript of the Four Gospels in the Freer Collection* (Ann Arbor: University of Michigan, 1912); *The New Testament Manuscripts in the Freer Collection, Part I: The Washington Manuscript of the Four Gospels* (University of Michigan Studies, Humanistic Series 9/1; New York: Macmillan, 1912); *The Old Testament Manuscripts in the Freer Collection, Part II: The Washington Manuscript of the Psalms* (University of Michigan Studies, Humanistic Series 8/2; New York: Macmillan, 1917); *The New Testament Manuscripts in the Freer Collection, Part II: The Washington Manuscript of the Epistles of Paul* (University of Michigan Studies, Humanistic Series 9/2; New York: Macmillan, 1918); (with Carl Schmidt), *The Minor Prophets in the Freer Collection and the Berlin Fragment of Genesis* (University of Michigan Studies, Humanistic Series 21; New York: Macmillan, 1927); *Facsimile of the Washington Manuscript of the Minor Prophets in the Freer Collection and the Berlin Fragment of Genesis* (Ann Arbor: University of Michigan, 1927).

8. It is to be hoped that the new color, digital photographs of the Freer biblical manuscripts will be made available soon for general usage. The members of the team project reflected in the contributions to the present volume join with me in expressing our thanks to the Freer Gallery of Art for allowing us to use CD copies of these wonderful images and to the Society of Biblical Literature and the Institute for the Study of and Preservation of Ancient Religious Texts for their initiative and sustained efforts in seeing that the images were produced.

and that played the largest role in scholarly discussion. At the announcement of its acquisition (and based on Sanders's dating of the scribal hand to the early fifth or late fourth century), the Freer Gospels manuscript was taken to be the third oldest codex containing all four Gospels, only Codex Vaticanus and Codex Sinaiticus surpassing it in age.[9] Moreover, th[illegible] particular to the Freer Gospels codex that immediately fascinated scholars and the general public.

There is the unusual order of the four Gospels, the so-called "Western" order: Matthew, John, Luke, and Mark.[10] It appears that the logic of this arrangement is that the two Gospels ascribed to one of the apostles are placed first, in descending order by length, followed by the two Gospels ascribed to nonapostolic authors, again in descending order by length.[11] The Freer manuscript was the earliest known instance of this arrangement among Greek codices of the Gospels.

Still more intriguing was (and remains) the so-called "Freer Logion." This addition after Mark 16:14, unique to the Freer Gospels manuscript, relates a dialogue between the risen Jesus and his disciples, in which they ascribe to Satan and the unclean spirits their own unbelief and ask about the immediacy of the *parousia.* In response, Jesus answers that the time of Satan's power was ended but warns that certain "fearful things draw near" that will all serve to turn sinners to repentance and salvation.

> And they excused themselves with the words, "This age of lawlessness and unbelief is under Satan, who by the unclean spirits does not permit the truth and power of God to be comprehended." They [the disciples] said to Christ, "Therefore, reveal your righteousness now." And Christ replied to them, "The measure of the years of Satan's authority has been filled up. But other dreadful things are coming. And for those who sinned, I was given over to death that they might turn back to the truth and sin no longer, that they might inherit the spiritual and incorruptible glory of righteousness in heaven."[12]

---

9. Depending on the dating of Codex Bezae Cantabridgiensis (D), fifth or perhaps late fourth century, the Freer Gospels codex was either third oldest or tied with Codex Bezae for that spot.

10. This Gospels order was already known from Codex Bezae Cantabridgiensis (D) and Codex Monacensis (X) and subsequently was attested also in 𝔓[45] (Chester Beatty Papyrus I).

11. In the more familiar order the first and fourth Gospels are those ascribed to apostles, Matthew coming first as the most widely copied and familiar Gospel. The second position held by Mark likely reflects an ancient Christian view that it was an abbreviated version of Matthew. Luke is actually the longest of the four, but its position within this ordering probably reflects the ascription of it to a nonapostolic figure. This order is reflected in Irenaeus, *Haer.* 3.1.1 (ca. 180 C.E.). For a recent discussion, see Martin Hengel, *The Four Gospels and the One Gospel of Jesus Christ* (trans. John Bowden; London: SCM, 2000), 34–47.

12. The Greek text is given among the variants in Mark 16:14 shown in the textual apparatus of the Nestle-Aland Novum Testamentum Graece. Jerome (*Contra Pelagius* 2.15) cites the Latin equivalent of the first three lines of the variant.

Scholars rightly judge this material self-evidently an insertion, not original to the Gospel of Mark. But from where does it come, and when and why did it first come to form part of the ending of Mark in the textual tradition reflected in Codex W? In his 1908 article based on his Chicago presentation, Sanders intriguingly commented that this passage probably derived from "the lost Gospel, which was used by some early Christian editor to complete the Gospel of Mark."[13] Jeremias judged the piece as very ancient on account of "the highly eschatological tone" and "its Jewish-apocalyptic terminology."[14] Indicative of the excitement generated by the passage (which Sanders transcribed and commented on in the 1908 article), the celebrated Caspar R. Gregory quickly produced a small booklet on it, some four years before Sanders published the critical edition of the Freer Gospels codex![15] Other scholars as well immediately addressed the passage.[16] Indeed, it was the focus of a doctoral thesis in 1959 and as recently as 2002 was still receiving the intensive attention of major New Testament scholars.[17] In the most recent analysis, Jörg Frey judges the Freer Logion to have been composed specifically as an edifying expansion of the "long ending" of Mark (16:9–20), and he dates its insertion into this material sometime in the latter half of the second century.[18] Whatever the case, it remains remarkable that, of the several thousand Greek manuscripts of the Gospels, only the Freer Gospels codex preserves this curious reading.

There are other variant readings in this codex that, although scarcely to be considered as part of the "original" text, are very interesting as indications of how

13. Sanders, "New Manuscripts of the Bible from Egypt," 54. In the next sentence Sanders went on to suggest that this passage was subsequently omitted (I presume that he meant from copies of Mark) "because it referred to the destruction of the world as *near at hand*." It is not clear, however, that the statement "The measure of the years of Satan's authority has been filled up" would have been taken as referring to the world's destruction. Moreover, Mark 9:1 much more clearly makes a chronological claim that could well have proven embarrassing, but there is no indication that it was excised in the textual transmission of Mark.

14. Joachim Jeremias, "The Freer Logion," in *New Testament Apocrypha* (ed. Wilhelm Schneemelcher; trans. R. McL. Wilson; rev. ed.; 2 vols.; Louisville: Westminster John Knox, 1991), 1:248.

15. Caspar René Gregory, *Das Freer-Logion* (Leipzig: Hinrichs, 1908). Gregory was unsuccessful, however, in obtaining Freer's financial support to produce an English translation of this booklet. See also Clarke's reference to the matter.

16. E.g., Adolf Harnack, "Neues zum unechten Marcusschluß," *TLZ* 33 (1908): 168–70; Carl Schmidt, *TLZ* 33 (1908): 359–60; Hermann von Soden, *Christliche Welt* 22 (1908): 482–86; Henry Barclay Swete, *Zwei neue Evangelienfragmente* (Bonn: Marcus & Weber, 1908).

17. Eugen Helzle, "Der Schluss des Markusevangeliums (Mk. 16:9–20) und das Freer-Logion (Mk. 16:14 W), ihr Tendenzen und ihr gegenseitiges Verhältnis: Eine wortexegetische Untersuchung" (Ph.D. diss., Tübingen University, 1959); Jörg Frey, "Zu Text und Sinn des Freer-Logion," *ZNW* 93 (2002): 13–34.

18. Frey, "Zu Text und Sinn des Freer-Logion," 24–25.

the text of the Gospels was transmitted and why this transmission could involve a readiness to make insertions and other changes in the text. To cite another example from Mark, at 1:3 the dominant reading is a citation of Isa 40:3, but Codex W here has the whole of Isa 40:3–8.

A smaller but even more striking unique variant appears in Mark 3:21. In the opening words of this verse, according to most witnesses, we have ἀκούσαντες οἱ παρ᾽ αὐτοῦ, "those associated with him [which here likely refers to his family] having heard [about his actions described in the preceding verses]," and the passage goes on to say that they went out to take Jesus in hand ἔλεγον γὰρ ὅτι ἐξέστη, "for they [his family or others?] were saying, 'He is mad.'" In both the Freer Codex and Codex Bezae, however, instead of the reference to "those associated with him," the opening of the verse says, "The scribes and the rest heard about him" (ἀκούσαντες [ὁτε ἤκουσαν, Codex D] περί αὐτοῦ οἱ γραμματεῖς καὶ οἱ λοίποι, and the Freer Codex then has a unique variant in what follows. In place of ἐξέστη ("he is mad!"), Codex W has the scribes and these other unnamed others complain, ἐξηρτηνται αὐτοῦ ("they [the crowds seeking Jesus] have become his adherents!"). Clearly, some early Christian readers of Mark were uncomfortable with what was almost certainly the original readings in this verse, and Codex W uniquely preserves one attempt to soften the verse by removing the reference to the allegation that Jesus was mad.

There are also significant readings in the other Gospels as well. To cite one important example, at the time of its publication, it was very noteworthy that Codex W lacked the pericope of the adulterous woman (which appears in the majority of later manuscripts as John 7:53–8:11). But this is not the place to do anything more than provide some illustration of the matter, and the examples that I have given here will have to do to make the point that the Freer Gospels codex has much to offer the student of textual variation.

Another curious feature of the Gospels codex is the apparent shift in its textual affiliation at several points. Such shifts can be demonstrated in some other manuscripts, but Codex W is noteworthy in the number of them.[19] In Matthew and in Luke 8:13–24:53, the closest allies of Codex W are the Byzantine-text witnesses. In Luke 1:1–8:12 and John 5:12–21:25, however, the codex aligns more closely with Alexandrian-text representatives. The text of the replacement quire of John (1:1–5:11) has some Alexandrian readings and some readings of the so-called "Western" text-type. In Mark 1–4 Codex W agrees more closely with Codex Bezae and other "Western" witnesses. But at some point in Mark 5, the textual affiliation shifts markedly, and throughout the rest of Mark Codex W cannot be tied to any of the major text-types. In this main part of Mark, however, W was

---

19. E.g., Gordon Fee showed such a shift in the text of John in Codex Sinaiticus. See Gordon D. Fee, "Codex Sinaiticus in the Gospel of John: A Contribution to Methodology in Establishing Textual Relationships," *NTS* 15 (1969): 23–44.

later shown to exhibit a very interesting alignment with the Chester Beatty Gospels codex (𝔓45).[20]

Sanders noted these shifts in Codex W and suggested that they reflected "the patchwork character of the parent [manuscript]," which had been prepared after the cessation of the violent persecutions of Christianity under Diocletian (begun in 303 C.E.), who sought to destroy all copies of Christian scriptures.[21] Essentially, Sanders proposed that the parent of Codex W had been copied from whatever damaged and assorted copies of the Gospels were still available where it was produced. In effect, Sanders's theory means that the shifts in textual affiliation in Codex W are residual textual scars of Diocletian's savage pogrom.

Another set of curious features of Codex W that has received scant attention (so far as I know) are the scribe's decorative devices at the conclusion of each Gospel.[22] In W, these are a simple design running down the left/outer margin of the final several lines of text, intersected at right angles by a horizontal line of interlacing design placed between the last line of the Gospel and the title. Moreover, at the endings of Matthew, John, and Luke, the decoration running down the margin includes a simple stylized bird (see example in fig. 1). At the end of Mark, however, there is a somewhat different and more elaborate decoration that runs down the left/outside margin of the last eight lines, with another decorative design running perpendicular across the page below "AMHN," which is written one line below the last line of Mark. And there is no bird!

Figure 1: Freer Gospel manuscript, end of the Gospel of Matthew. Freer Gallery of Art, Smithsonian Institution, Washington, D.C.: Gift of Charles Lang Freer, F1906.274 pg. 112. Used by permission.

20. I return to the textual relationship of Codex W and 𝔓45 in the next section.

21. Sanders, *Washington Manuscript of the Four Gospels,* 139.

22. These are referred to as "tailpieces" and are common in manuscripts of the fourth century and later.

So far as I can judge, these decorations and the AMHN at the end of Mark were the work of the original/main scribe of Codex W, which makes them all the more interesting as to their possible meaning and function. Obviously, at a basic level they function in the same way as such "tailpiece" decorations serve on other biblical manuscripts of this period, to mark off formally the end of a given text with a certain flourish. But what does the little stylized bird signify? Perhaps this is another question for some other scholar to explore, who is better versed than I in such matters.[23]

But on one feature of these decorations, I do offer a view. I contend that the change in the tailpiece for Mark, together with the AMHN, functioned to signal the end of the codex, not simply the end of Mark. If, thus, as seems to be the case, these decorations are from the original scribe, then they further support the conclusion that the present order of the Gospels in W was the original order when the codex was first produced.

Codex W and the "Caesarean Text"

In addition to all its other interesting features, the Freer Gospels codex also became highly important in early twentieth-century efforts to reconstruct the early textual history of the Gospels. In particular, Codex W became for a while the key early witness of a supposed "Caesarean" text-type, which was newly proposed in the early years of the twentieth century.[24] Building on the work of earlier and contemporary scholars, especially the several studies by Kirsopp Lake and his associates, B. H. Streeter coined the term "Caesarean text." Moreover, and still more importantly for this discussion, he claimed emphatically that in Mark Codex W was "far the oldest, and much the purest, authority for this ancient and interesting type of Eastern text—so old and so pure that it makes the existence of such a text no longer an hypothesis but as ascertained fact."[25] Although he was

---

23. A key study of the general phenomenon is Carl Nordenfalk, "The Beginning of Book Decoration," in *Essays in Honor of Georg Swarzenski* (ed. Oswald Goetz; Chicago: Regnery, 1951); see also Carl Nordenfalk, *Studies in the History of Book Illumination* (London: Pindar, 1992).

24. In what follows I focus very selectively on the place of Codex W in scholarly discussion. See also Larry W. Hurtado, "Codex Washingtonianus in the Gospel of Mark: Its Textual Relationships and Scribal Characteristics" (Ph.D. diss., Case Western Reserve University, 1973), esp. 13–43; for a more abbreviated treatment focused on the significance of Codex W in the theory of the Caesarean text, idem, *Text-Critical Methodology and the Pre-Caesarean Text: Codex W in the Gospel of Mark* (SD 43; Grand Rapids: Eerdmans, 1981), 1–13. See also Bruce M. Metzger, *Chapters in the History of New Testament Textual Criticism* (NTTS 4; Leiden: Brill, 1963), 42–72 ("The Caesarean Text of the Gospels").

25. B. H. Streeter, *The Four Gospels: A Study of Origins* (2nd impression, London: Macmillan, 1926 [orig. 1924]), 599. See also idem, "The Caesarean Text of the Gospels," *JTS* 26 (1925): 373–78; idem, "The Washington MS and the Caesarean Text of the Gospels," *JTS* 27 (1926):

challenged by the great F. C. Burkitt, who insisted that the textual witnesses of the supposed Caesarean text did not cohere sufficiently to justify the claim, Streeter repeatedly (and for most scholars thereafter, persuasively) asserted that there was in fact a Caesarean text-type and that Codex W was its earliest representative.[26] In 1933, Frederick G. Kenyon referred to Streeter's proposal as a "turning point" and allowed "the assured place in textual criticism" of the Caesarean text.[27] So, within a little over a decade after Sanders published the facsimile and monograph on Codex W, it had become the center of major debate about the textual transmission of the Gospels.

As I noted earlier, the publication of the Chester Beatty biblical papyri (beginning in 1933) in one sense may have drawn such attention that in general the Freer manuscripts suffered some neglect thereafter. But this was not the case for the Freer Gospels codex, for when the Chester Beatty Gospels codex ($\mathfrak{P}^{45}$, paleographically dated ca. 250 C.E.) was studied, scholars noted a particular affinity between its text of Mark and the Markan text of Codex W.[28] So, in Mark at least, $\mathfrak{P}^{45}$ was seen immediately as confirming that Codex W represented in fact a kind of text that went back far earlier than the fourth or fifth century date ascribed to this manuscript. Moreover, because of the very fragmentary nature of $\mathfrak{P}^{45}$, the affinity with Codex W in Mark meant that it served as the more extensive witness to this early kind of Markan text of Egyptian provenance.[29]

In the years after the publication of $\mathfrak{P}^{45}$, although some scholars disputed the claim that this manuscript and the Codex W really were witnesses in Mark to the "Caesarean text," all were agreed that these two manuscripts exhibited a close textual relationship to each other. The Spanish scholar Teofilio Ayuso contended that $\mathfrak{P}^{45}$ and Codex W were an early subgroup or early stage of the Caesarean text-

144–47. Especially significant for Streeter was Kirsopp Lake and R. P. Blake, "The Text of the Gospels and the Koridethi Codex," *HTR* 16 (1923): 267–86. In turn, Streeter's theory was taken up in the major study by Kirsopp Lake, R. P. Blake, and Silva New, "The Caesarean Text of the Gospel of Mark," *HTR* 21 (1928): 207–404.

26. Burkitt argued that Codex W and Codex Koridethi (Θ) were simply witnesses to the considerable diversity in the so-called "Western" text-type: "W and Theta: Studies in the Western Text of St. Mark," *JTS* 17 (1916): 1–21, 139–52. For Burkitt's critique of Streeter's claim, see his review of *The Four Gospels* in *JTS* 26 (1925): 278–94; idem, "The Caesarean Text," *JTS* 30 (1929): 347–56.

27. Frederic G. Kenyon, *Recent Developments in the Textual Criticism of the Greek Bible* (London: Oxford University Press, 1933), 47.

28. E.g., Frederic G. Kenyon, *The Gospels and Acts, Text* (fasc. 2 of *The Chester Beatty Biblical Papyri;* London: Emery Walker, 1933), xv, xvii.

29. In an earlier essay I discussed the impact and significance of the publication of $\mathfrak{P}^{45}$: Larry W. Hurtado, "P45 and the Textual History of the Gospel of Mark," in *The Earliest Gospels: The Origins and Transmission of the Earliest Christian Gospels—The Contribution of the Chester Beatty Gospel Codex P45* (ed. Charles Horton; JSNTSup 258; London: T&T Clark, 2004), 132–48.

type (the later stage represented crucially by Codex Θ and the “minuscules” 565 and 700).[30] A similar view was offered by others subsequently, including Kirsopp and Silva Lake, and thereafter this became widely (though not universally) held.[31] In a later article Ayuso went so far as to claim that the only two “pre-recensional” types of texts of the Gospels were the “Western” and the “pre-Caesarean” text-types (𝔓[45] and Codex W the two leading witnesses of this latter category), and the witnesses to these two text-types were thus the two *most valuable* tools for reconstructing the original texts of the Gospels.[32]

In my 1973 doctoral dissertation, however, I showed that by any standard of objective measurement 𝔓[45] and Codex W did not exhibit any particular affinity for the so-called “Caesarean text” witnesses. But, equally importantly, I confirmed that in the Gospel of Mark these two manuscripts do have a significant level of agreement with each other, such that they must be seen to witness to a shared textual tradition whose roots go back to Egypt at least as far as the early third century and probably earlier.[33] In short, neither 𝔓[45] nor the Freer Gospels codex tells us anything about a supposed “Caesarean” text-type, but they do jointly witness to an early and interesting textual tradition, at least in the Gospel of Mark.[34]

These remarks will suffice to make the point that the Freer biblical manuscripts were, and remain, historically significant artifacts for tracing the early history of the transmission of the writings that make up the New Testament and the Christian Old Testament in Greek (“Septuagint”). The scholarly neglect of them is unjustified, and the central aim of this collection of studies is to bring them forward for renewed attention by scholars and to illustrate their importance to a wider public.[35]

---

30. Teofilio Ayuso, “¿Texto cesariense o precesariense? Su realidad y su trascendencia en la critica textual del Nuevo Testamento,” *Bib* 16 (1935): 369–415.

31. Kirsopp and Silva Lake, “De Westcott et Hort au Pére Lagrange et au-dela,” *RB* 68 (1939): 503 (497–505). See also Kirsopp and Silva Lake, *Family 13 (the Ferrar Group): The Text according to Mark* (SD 11; London: Christophers, 1941), 7–8. Cf., however, P. L. Hedley, “The Egyptian Texts of the Gospels and Acts,” *CQR* 118 (1934): 23–39, 188–230, esp. 32–35; M. J. Lagrange, “Le papyrus Chester Beatty pour les Évangiles,” *RB* 43 (1934): 5–41.

32. Teofilio Ayuso, “¿Texto arrecensional, recensional o prerecensional?” *Estudios Biblicos* 6 (1947): 35–90, esp. 79–89.

33. Hurtado, “Codex Washingtonianus,” esp. 184–93; idem, *Text-Critical Methodology,* esp. 63–66.

34. Cf. Christian-Bernard Ampoux, “Le texte évangélique de Césarée et le type de texte ‘Césaréen’ des Évangiles,” *Filologia Neotestamentaria* 12 (1999): 3–16.

35. As illustration of the comparative neglect of the Freer manuscripts, I note that so far as can be ascertained, my 1973 Ph.D. dissertation and the monograph that issued from it comprise the only book-length studies of the Gospels codex since Sanders’s classic facsimile edition and monograph.

This Volume

The origins of the present volume lie several years earlier and involve the contributions and cooperation of a number of people. In the summer of 1999, Bruce Prior visited Edinburgh and made an appointment to get acquainted and to discuss his plan to carry out a full transcription of the Freer Gospels codex. During this visit he observed that the centenary of the first purchase of the manuscripts would come in 2006, and he suggested that I consider proposing to the Freer Gallery some way of marking this. After his departure, I gave the matter some thought and shortly thereafter wrote to the Deputy Director of the Freer and Sackler Galleries suggesting an exhibition (to my knowledge, the manuscripts had never been put on formal exhibit) and a scholarly conference focused on the manuscripts, perhaps to be held in Washington in 2006. I also indicated that this conference might be linked with the 2006 Annual Meeting of the Society of Biblical Literature, if this were acceptable to the SBL. Finally, for the conference I offered to recruit a group of scholars to conduct fresh studies of the manuscripts, with a view toward publication of these studies in a multiauthor volume.[36] At about the same time, I also approached Kent Richards about the possibility of scheduling the 2006 Annual Meeting of the SBL/AAR in Washington and was delighted when he reported back early in 2000 that he had been successful in making this arrangement.

In the summer of 2000, I visited the Freer Gallery for discussions with the administration (including Dr. Milo Beach, then Director, and Dr. Vidya Dehejia, then Deputy Director) and key curatorial staff, and I was invited to submit a formal exhibition proposal. I submitted this proposal in January 2001 and was also able to indicate at that point that the SBL had expressed a strong interest in working with the Freer Gallery in producing a new set of color, digital photographs of all the biblical manuscripts (a spin-off project sponsored by the SBL and using the expertise of the Institute for the Study and Preservation of Ancient Religious Texts [ISPART], Brigham Young University).[37] Patrick Durusau (in the SBL office at that time) was particularly active in promoting this photographic project. From November 2000 onward, I also began to recruit scholars willing to commit to producing something for publication in a volume to be published by the SBL.

My aim was to recruit a team who would address in some way all of the six Freer biblical manuscripts, and it is a disappointment that several colleagues who initially offered to produce contributions for this volume have been prevented by various circumstances from doing so. I lament in particular the absence of any

---

36. Larry W. Hurtado to Thomas W. Lentz (20 July 1999).

37. Staff from ISPART commenced this work in the summer of 2002 and returned for further work in March 2003.

studies of the Deuteronomy-Joshua manuscript, the Greek Psalms codex, and the Coptic Psalms codex. I also sought unsuccessfully to recruit some competent art historian to make a fresh study of the important color paintings of the four Evangelists on the wooden covers of the Gospels codex.[38]

The Contributions in This Volume

The ten essays in this volume are a notable collection of fresh scholarship on the Freer manuscripts, notwithstanding these unfortunate gaps in coverage. Individually, they advance discussion in their respective topics, and collectively they are a substantial body of work that is an appropriate reflection of the importance of these important artifacts of early Christianity.

Kent Clarke's lead essay, "Paleography and Philanthropy: Charles Lang Freer and His Acquisition of the 'Freer Biblical Manuscripts,'" is a fascinating account of how Freer obtained these codices and his subsequent enthusiastic support for the preparation of the classic volumes by Sanders. Clarke has studied closely a great body of unpublished material in the Freer Gallery archive (made much easier thanks to permission given to Timothy Brown to photograph relevant material and make it available to Clarke on several CDs), and he brings the people, circumstances, and events to life vividly. He explores the limits (and the frustrations) of what we can know about the real provenance of the manuscripts, when exactly they might first have come to light, and how they came to Freer's attention. Clarke offers a deeply informed and also candidly appreciative discussion that gives the historical and human dimension to these valuable manuscripts.

The Freer Minor Prophets codex is known among specialists on the textual transmission of the Greek Old Testament (Septuagint) as an important textual witness, with a number of readings that raise intriguing questions about their significance and derivation. It is, in fact, the earliest of the Freer manuscripts (third century C.E.) and until the discovery of the Qumran scrolls was the earliest Greek manuscript of the Minor Prophets known. It remains very important for tracing the transmission of the Greek version of these writings. But does this codex reflect the influence of "pre-Hexaplaric" translations of the Hebrew Bible (i.e., prior to the second century C.E., often referred to as the "Old Greek")? Does it, instead, evidence the influence of Hebraizing Greek versions (e.g., those ascribed to Aquila, Symmachus, and Theodotion)?[39] Kristin De Troyer engages these questions in a careful and detailed analysis of the readings of the Freer codex in the

38. To my knowledge, the only substantial study of these paintings is Walter Dennison and Charles R. Morey, *Studies in East Christian and Roman Art* (New York: Macmillan, 1918), 63–81 ("The Painted Covers of the Washington Manuscript of the Gospels").

39. For a recent and general introductory discussion, see Karen H. Jobes and Moisés Silva, *Invitation to the Septuagint* (Grand Rapids: Baker, 2000).

book of Jonah, concluding that these readings show that the manuscript "firmly stands in the tradition of the Old Greek."

Another unresolved puzzle connected with the Minor Prophets codex is the unidentified and fragmentary text that appears at the end of the manuscript. Malcolm Choat's major study will now likely be the starting point for all future discussion of the matter. He has done original work in attempting to assemble some of the fragments and proposes a fresh reconstruction of the extant text of this writing, with detailed commentary on it. But, in addition, Choat gives an expert review of questions about the provenance of the manuscript itself, provides a description of the manuscript and the scribal hand, and discusses the curious marginal glosses and notes. As to the text appended to the Minor Prophets, Choat concludes that it could be the work of Clement of Alexandria, or Origen, or, just as plausibly, could be commentary notes from some other, unknown Christian of the early centuries.

Bruce Prior focuses on the use of the interesting abbreviations of certain words, known (since the pioneering study by Ludwig Traube in 1907) as the *nomina sacra,* with special reference to the text of Matthew in the Freer Gospels codex. He carefully notes all uses of the words in question, identifying places where they are abbreviated and where they are written in full, seeking to find any patterns that might signal what the scribes intended. Prior offers a meticulous and data-focused study that contributes to our continuing quest to understand these fascinating abbreviated forms. He confirms that there are subgroupings of words, some subgroups much more regularly (and probably much earlier) abbreviated than others, and he adjusts some previous discussions in light of his empirical study.

Jean-François Racine's essay is likewise focused on the text of Matthew in the Freer Gospels codex, analyzing its textual affinities and quality. Building on his earlier study of the citations of Matthew in Basil of Caesarea, Racine deploys a sophisticated and multistage method. From a careful quantitative analysis of agreements in variant readings, he concludes that the Freer text of Matthew exhibits a clear affinity with other textual witnesses identified with the "Byzantine" text-type. He also shows that the Freer Matthew exhibits a text with an appreciable level of "textual cohesion," that is, evidence of scribal concerns for a text that is clear, readable, and intended to be edifying to readers.

In a creatively designed study, Dennis Haugh attempts to determine whether the original scribe of the Freer Gospels codex was "slavishly faithful to a number of exemplars" or was "a self-conscious redactor, modifying all the Gospel texts to suit the needs of the community who supported the scribal work." That is, Haugh seeks to establish whether the scribe of Codex W was simply a copyist or exercised a certain level of freedom in modifying the texts that he copied. To address the question, Haugh compares "unique" variants across the four Gospels that are likely intentional changes, seeking to determine whether they exhibit common concerns (which would suggest that they all derive from the scribe) or vary in kind from one Gospel to another (which would suggest that they reflect the effects of the textual transmission of the individual Gospels and are scribal changes made prior to the scribe of Codex W). Acknowledging the limits of our certainty in the matter, Haugh proposes that the data are more consistent with the latter view. In short, the unique variants in Codex W do vary from one Gospel to another such that it is more likely that they reflect changes made in the Gospel texts prior to the copyist of this manuscript.

James Royse provides an amazingly thorough analysis of all the scribal corrections in Codex W, the first such thorough-going study since Sanders's 1918 volume. In all, Royse studies 179 corrections, classifying them as to the several scribes involved. With considerable care, Royse discusses the individual corrections, providing a study of the Freer Gospels codex that will surely be required reading for any subsequent study of this manuscript and that will also feed important data into the wider study of ancient Christian scribal practices and preferences.

In a controversial discussion, Ulrich Schmid reopens the question about the correct dating of Codex W, suggesting that it may have to be assigned to the sixth century instead of the now commonly echoed dating to the early fifth or late fourth century. Crucial to Schmid's argument is the recently revised dating of the Mani Codex, whose hand is widely regarded as closely similar to the hand of the Freer Gospels. Schmid acknowledges that his study is preliminary and will have to be assessed by others with expertise in Byzantine hands, but he has certainly given reasons to reconsider our previously confident dating of Codex W.

Thomas Wayment focuses on variants in the Freer Pauline codex that may result from a scribe copying out what is read by a lector in a scriptorium. In particular, Wayment probes "itacisms," variant spellings of words, and homonyms accidentally written in lieu of the correct word. As with others in this collection, Wayment's essay shows how an intriguing and plausible wider inference can be built on careful analysis of quite specific data.

Finally, Timothy Finney takes readers into the world of "markup," the transcription of manuscripts into machine-readable form. Finney, an expert in the matter and a contributor to the continuing international discussions toward agreed standards for this work, offers examples drawn from his doctoral work on manuscripts of the Epistle to the Hebrews, with special concern for the Freer Pauline codex.

In sum, I reiterate my judgment that each of the essays that follows is a significant contribution in its own right. As a collection they comprise a notable body of work with long-term value for the study of the Freer biblical manuscripts and for the several disciplines that they represent. We offer them also as a tribute especially to Charles Freer's generosity and vision in acquiring the biblical manuscripts that bear his name and to Henry Sanders's prodigious work in putting them at the disposal of all subsequent scholars.

Paleography and Philanthropy: Charles Lang Freer and His Acquisition of the "Freer Biblical Manuscripts"*

Kent D. Clarke

Introduction

"Mr. Freer's splendid collection at Washington," wrote the eminent textual critic Sir Frederic G. Kenyon (1863–1952) in his 1932 Schweich Lectures, "has given America an important standing in respect of Biblical manuscripts."[1] Kenyon's words, recorded some twenty-six years after the original discovery, aptly summarize also the current significance of what has come to be known as the Freer or Washington Manuscripts. But the story of Charles Lang Freer's philanthropic life as it especially relates to the events surrounding the "bringing to light" of these ancient texts has never been told in detail. Although more technical paleographical discussions of the "Freer" or "Washington Manuscripts" are available, no in-depth presentation of the events surrounding their discovery and their purchase by Freer in Egypt has ever been provided. Even in the authoritative critical editions, facsimiles, and journal articles dealing with these manuscripts, a significant number of the pragmatic details were, for various reasons, never formally presented but rather with the passing of time have become "lost" within the archival material. This seems an odd oversight when, for example, Constantine von Tischendorf's 1844 discovery of Codex Sinaiticus in St. Catherine's Monastery is echoed in many of the handbooks introducing New Testament textual

* I would like to thank my colleagues T. A. E. Brown and J. Bruce Prior for their generous provision of much of the archival material included in this essay. On behalf of them and myself, we would also like to express our sincere gratitude to the staff at the Freer Gallery of Art and Arthur M. Sackler Gallery Archives, Smithsonian Institution, Washington, D.C., for the exceptional assistance and open access they have provided.

1. Frederic G. Kenyon, *Recent Developments in the Textual Criticism of the Greek Bible* (Schweich Lectures of the British Academy 1932; London: Oxford University Press, 1933), 94.

criticism,[2] or when the story of a young bedouin shepherd who, when searching for his lost sheep in the northwestern region of the Dead Sea in 1947, happened upon a cave containing ancient scrolls is continually met with popular interest,[3] or even when Morton Smith's purported finding of Clement of Alexandria's "Secret Gospel of Mark" at the monastery of Mar Saba in 1958 engenders ongoing and heated debate.[4] That the story of Freer and his manuscripts has been told only in summary fashion is even more remarkable considering the unparalleled mass of archival resources available for research purposes. Indeed, the personal papers of Freer consist of approximately 145 linear feet of material dating from the years 1876–1931 and include his correspondence, diaries, art inventories, scrapbooks, press clippings, vouchers recording purchases, and vintage photographs. In marking the centenary of Freer's 1906 acquisition of what comprises one of the oldest collections of ancient Greek biblical manuscripts written on vellum, this essay is offered to redress to some small degree the absence of a story that should have been told long ago.

---

2. See such examples as Bruce M. Metzger and Bart D. Ehrman, *The Text of the New Testament: Its Transmission, Corruption, and Restoration* (4th ed.; Oxford: Oxford University Press, 2005), 62–65; Frederic G. Kenyon, *Our Bible and the Ancient Manuscripts* (New York: Harper & Row, 1958 [1895]), 191–93; idem, *Handbook to the Textual Criticism of the New Testament* (2nd ed.; London: Macmillan, 1912), 60–63; Eberhard Nestle, *Introduction to the Textual Criticism of the Greek New Testament* (trans. W. Edie; London: Williams & Norgate, 1901), 53–54; and Frederick H.A. Scrivener, *A Plain Introduction to the Criticism of the New Testament* (4th ed.; 2 vols.; London: Bell & Sons, 1894), 1:90–91. For accounts by Tischendorf himself, see Constantine Tischendorf, *When Were Our Gospels Written? An Argument by Constantine Tischendorf with a Narrative of the Discovery of the Sinaitic Manuscript* (new ed.; London: Religious Tract Society, no date); idem, *Codex Sinaiticus: The Ancient Biblical Manuscript Now in the British Museum* (8th ed.; London: Lutterworth, 1934).

3. Among the many accounts relating the story of the discovery of the Dead Sea Scrolls, see John Allegro, *The Dead Sea Scrolls: A Reappraisal* (2nd ed.; Harmondsworth, U.K.: Penguin, 1964), 17–51; J. T. Milik, *Ten Years of Discovery in the Wilderness of Judaea* (trans. J. Strugnell; SBT 26; London: SCM, 1959), 11–19; and more recently James C. VanderKam and Peter Flint, *The Meaning of the Dead Sea Scrolls* (New York: HarperCollins, 2002), 3–19.

4. See Morton Smith, *Clement of Alexandria and a Secret Gospel of Mark* (Cambridge: Harvard University Press, 1973); and the more popular account in idem, *The Secret Gospel: The Discovery and Interpretation of the Secret Gospel according to Mark* (New York: Harper & Row, 1973); Stephen C. Carlson, *The Gospel Hoax: Morton Smith's Invention of Secret Mark* (Waco, Tex.: Baylor University Press, 2005); Scott G. Brown, *Mark's Other Gospel: Rethinking Morton Smith's Controversial Discovery* (Waterloo, Ont.: Wilfred Laurier University Press, 2005); and for fuller bibliography, see H. Merkel, "Appendix: The 'Secret Gospel' of Mark," in *New Testament Apocrypha* (ed. W. Schneemelcher; trans. R. McL.Wilson; 2 vols.; rev. ed.; Louisville: Westminster John Knox, 1991), 1:106–9.

A Brief Biography of Charles Lang Freer[5]

Charles Lang Freer (1854–1919) was born the third of six children in the river-port town and growing transportation hub of Kingston, New York. In 1868, when Freer was fourteen years old, his mother passed away; a short time later his father was struck with a debilitating paralysis that had also affected and led to the death of his grandfather. With his father unable to provide financially for the family, Freer was forced to leave school and begin work at the local Newark Lime and Cement Manufacturing Company. In 1893 Freer's youngest brother would be doubly stricken by the same paralysis that had earlier affected his father and grandfather, as well as by a severe nervousness disorder. By 1902 a second brother would pass away, while two other siblings would be diagnosed with serious illnesses.[6] Arising from these humble origins, overcoming considerable personal grief, and encumbered by the possibility of his own premature mortality in light of the fate of his parents and siblings, this future Detroit industrialist would ultimately become both a self-made millionaire and a largely self-taught and internationally recognized connoisseur of American and Asian art.[7]

---

5. In constructing this biography, I am deeply indebted to Ann C. Gunter's *A Collector's Journey: Charles Lang Freer and Egypt* (Washington, D.C.: Freer Gallery of Art, Smithsonian Institution, Arthur M. Sackler Gallery, 2002), as well as Thomas Lawton and Linda Merrill's *Freer: A Legacy of Art* (Washington, D.C.: Freer Gallery of Art, 1993). While Gunter's work deals more specifically with Freer's Egyptian travels and purchases (including brief discussions of the Washington Manuscripts), the work of Lawton and Merrill deals more broadly with Freer as an international collector of art. Both volumes serve as fine, and beautifully illustrated, biographies of Freer and his collection.

6. Helen N. Tomlinson, "Charles Lang Freer: Pioneer Collector of Oriental Art" (Ph.D. diss.; 4 vols.; Case Western Reserve University, 1979), 161, 271. Also cited in Kathleen Pyne, "Portrait of a Collector as an Agnostic: Charles Lang Freer and Connoisseurship," *The Art Bulletin* 78/1 (1996): 77.

7. Lawton and Merrill (*Freer,* 8) note that "Freer eventually obtained virtually every work on Asian art published in English during his lifetime. He also acquired all existing books on Whistler and the other American artists represented in his collection, with many of the editions inscribed by the authors; and he retained most of his exhibition and sales catalogues, some of which have his own comments and reflections noted in the margins." This collection of materials served as the initial core of the Freer Gallery's research library, which currently consists of over fifty thousand volumes and four hundred periodical titles, thus making it one of North America's more comprehensive libraries relating to Asian art and turn-of-the century American painting. Tomlinson ("Charles Lang Freer," 79) also notes that Freer possessed a significant collection of Romantic and Aesthetic literature, including works by William Wordsworth (1770–1850), John Keats (1795–1821), Thomas Carlyle (1795–1881), Ralph Waldo Emerson (1803–1882), Henry David Thoreau (1817–1862), Walt Whitman (1819–1892), John Ruskin (1819–1900), Matthew Arnold (1822–1888), Dante Gabriel Rossetti (1828–1882) and Christina Rossetti (1830–1894), William Morris (1834–1896), Algernon Swinburne (1837–1909), Walter Pater (1839–1894), William E. Henley (1849–1903), Oscar Wilde (1854–1900), Harriet Monroe (1860–1936), Bliss

While working as a clerk in the Kingston General Store of John C. Brodhead, Freer made the acquaintance of Frank J. Hecker (1856–1972), who, after serving briefly as a colonel for the Union Army in the Civil War, became the superintendent of the New York, Kingston, and Syracuse Railroad—a local railway that crossed the scenic Catskill Mountains from Kingston Point on the Hudson River to Oneonta in the Susquehanna Valley.[8] At Hecker's invitation, Freer soon joined the company and served most effectively as its accountant and paymaster. In 1876, when Hecker relocated to Logansport, Indiana, to oversee the newly formed Detroit, Eel River, & Illinois Railroad, Freer followed and assumed a role similar to that which he had previously held under Hecker. Upon the merging of the Detroit, Eel River, & Illinois Railroad with the Wabash Railway Company in 1879, Hecker and Freer found themselves without employment. Due in large part to the stress of this situation, Freer became ill and traveled to the quietude of the Canadian wilderness to convalesce. Amid a time of unprecedented railway expansion, Freer and Hecker moved in 1880 to Detroit, where, underwritten by the previous owners of the Detroit, Eel River, & Illinois Railroad, they co-founded the Peninsular Car Company, which would become the second largest wooden rail car manufacturer in the city. In 1884, after its foundry building was destroyed by fire, the Peninsular Car Company constructed a new and more efficient plant on a twenty-five-acre lot at Ferry Avenue. Following Hecker's retirement in 1888 due to ill health, the Peninsular Car Company merged in 1892 with four other competitors to become the Michigan-Peninsular Car Company.[9] Persevering through the harsh economic depression of 1893–1895, and after helping to orchestrate the consolidation of thirteen other car-building companies (including the Michigan-Peninsular Car Company) into the American Car & Foundry Company in 1898, Freer once again became ill and sought temporary respite in Hot Springs, Arkansas. In the spring of 1899, at the age of forty-five, Freer formally retired from active business and gave much of his time and passion to collecting works of art.

Carmen (1861–1929), Maurice Maeterlinck (1862–1949), Arthur W. Symons (1865–1945), and William Vaughn Moody (1869–1910).

8. Originally chartered in 1866 as the Rondout & Oswego Railroad, it became the New York, Kingston, & Syracuse Railroad after reorganization in 1872 and in 1875 was named the Ulster & Delaware Railroad.

9. Despite his retirement, at the outbreak of the Spanish-American War in 1898, Hecker was appointed head of the Division of Transportation, Quartermaster's Department. His main responsibility was to supervise all rail and water transportation for the army in Cuba and the Philippines. After being made a member of the Isthmian Canal Commission in 1904 (an American body of seven members appointed by President Theodore Roosevelt to oversee the construction and maintenance of a canal joining the Atlantic and Pacific oceans across the Isthmus of Panama), Hecker resigned amid allegations that he had mishandled lumber contracts for the canal. Hecker remained, however, a prominent figure in Michigan financial and industrial circles until his death in 1927.

"Art is properly concerned with the living of our lives," wrote Freer in his later years, adding that there existed "an instinctive sense that there must be some way through it to reach an understanding that redemption does exist."[10] Further to this was Freer's belief that there also existed within art—for those individuals with the eyes to see it—a [illegible], or in the words of Lawton and Merrill, "a common artistic impulse."[11] Writing late in 1904 to the secretary of the Smithsonian Institution, astronomer and aeronautical engineer Samuel P. Langley (1834–1906), Freer asserted, "My great desire is to unite modern work with masterpieces of certain periods of high civilization harmonious in spiritual suggestion, having the power to broaden esthetic culture and the grace to elevate the human mind."[12] It has also been noted that Freer's personal and discriminate collecting was not carried out for the purpose of amassing materials in the self-interested pursuit of wealth. Instead, and in keeping with Romanticism's aesthetic of the transcendent, Freer sought through his collecting to encourage a sensitivity of "the beautiful" that would arrest the materialism of the Industrialist Age:

> To be sure, the Detroit industrialist Freer utilized both Paterian aestheticism [English essayist and critic Walter H. Pater, 1839–1894] and Morellian connoisseurship [Italian art critic Giovanni Morelli, 1816–1891] to define himself as an initiate into the upper reaches of American social space. Freer's collecting activity provided an alternative avenue of self-definition apart from his role as

---

10. File entitled "Miscellaneous—From: Charles L. Freer." Contained in Charles Lang Freer Papers, Freer Gallery of Art and Arthur M. Sackler Gallery Archives, Smithsonian Institution, Washington, D.C. Gift of the Estate of Charles Lang Freer (hereafter cited as CLFP). Also cited in Pyne, "Portrait of a Collector," 77. Freer's concept of "redemption" should not be misunderstood as traditionally Christian. In terms of religious convictions, Freer was likely an agnostic who had read widely in mysticism, Theosophy, and Buddhism—the latter having a particularly strong influence upon him. For one view of Freer's religious and broader philosophical convictions, see once again Pyne, "Portrait of a Collector," 75–97, esp. 76–77 and 79–80.

11. Lawton and Merrill, *Freer,* 7.

12. Charles Lang Freer to Samuel P. Langley, December 27, 1904, CLFP. Also cited in Lawton and Merrill, *Freer,* 10; Gunter, *Collector's Journey,* 25. Freer often echoed this unifying ideal, as he does again in a further letter to Langley dated several weeks later: "I regard my collections as constituting a harmonious whole.... They are not made up of isolated objects, each object having an individual merit only, but they constitute in a sense a connected series, each having a bearing upon the others that precede or that follow it in point of time" (Charles Lang Freer to Samuel P. Langley, January 18, 1905, CLFP). Also cited in Lawton and Merrill, *Freer,* 187; Gunter, *Collector's Journey,* 134. It is possible that Freer developed this idea through his close friendship with philosopher and orientalist Ernest F. Fenollosa (1853–1908), who likewise avowed similar principles. Cf. Ernest F. Fenollosa, "The Collection of Mr. Charles L. Freer," *Pacific Era* 1/2 (1907): 57–66, esp. 59; more generally, idem, *Epochs of Chinese and Japanese Art: An Outline History of East Asiatic Art* (new and rev. ed.; 2 vols.; New York: Dover, 1963 [1913]); and Pyne, "Portrait of a Collector," 91–93.

an officer in the major company that built cars for America's railroads in the 1880s and 1890s. Thus, the "pure gaze" differentiated Freer from the stereotypical "captain of industry"—the powerful and aggressive American male who was also boorish and philistine. Freer's selectivity, his knowledge, and his discriminating gaze contrasted markedly with the collecting-as-power practices of the typical capitalist, J. P. Morgan [1837–1913], for example, who amassed a huge collection of artifacts, but did so indiscriminately, either by buying up whole lots of objects or by employing cognoscenti to choose for him. More profoundly, however, it was Pater's notion of the aesthetic moment as a mystical experience of a world beyond that stood at the base of Freer's compulsion to collect and that determined the types of art to which he was attracted.[13]

Although Freer began his art collecting with the purchase of inexpensive prints and etchings, over a period of four decades he carefully and painstakingly assembled a growing inventory of items, including Chinese and Japanese art, Syrian and Persian ceramics, late-nineteenth-century American paintings, and ancient Egyptian art and monuments.[14] With their economic circumstances rising substantially in the late 1880s, Freer and Hecker purchased adjacent building lots within a new Detroit suburb in close proximity to their Peninsular Car Company plant in 1887. Whereas Hecker immediately began construction of an opulent limestone mansion to house his large family and even larger dinner parties, Freer waited until 1890 to commission the architect Wilson Eyre Jr. (1858–1944) to design a dignified but modest limestone and shingle-style dwelling befitting his more private lifestyle and lifelong bachelorhood.[15] Freer's new home on 33 Ferry

---

13. Pyne, "Portrait of a Collector," 76. Cf. Lawton and Merrill, *Freer,* 19.

14. Lawton and Merrill (*Freer,* 18) speculate that "Freer's quickly forged reputation as a print collector may have assisted his election to the Detroit Club, which had been founded in 1882 primarily by the prominent Detroit citizens who had helped establish the art museum. In 1888, Freer became chairman of the art committee, responsible for organizing the first three of the club's annual exhibitions of American paintings. With that duty, he was compelled to consider the best methods of displaying works of art, which would become a lifelong concern. His position also led to acquaintances with several leading American painters of the day, including Gari Melchers [1860–1932], Dwight William Tryon [1849–1925], Charles A. Platt [1861–1933], and Frederick Stuart Church [1842–1924]."

15. The reasons for Freer's lifelong bachelorhood have been speculated upon by all his biographers. Suggestions range from the likely fanciful account of an early lover dying of a broken heart due to Freer's refusal to marry in the light of his impoverished status; his fear of passing on a family history of congenital syphilis to someone he might truly love; or the failure of any women to adequately meet his patrician sensibilities and Victorian expectations. See here the assessment of one of Freer's close confidants (and an apparent "unfeasible infatuation"), Agnes E. Meyer, *Charles Lang Freer and His Gallery* (Washington, D.C.: Freer Gallery of Art, 1970), 18; idem, "The Charles Lang Freer Collection," *Arts* 12/2 (1927): 40–42. Cf. Lawton and Merrill, *Freer,* 20; Pyne, "Portrait of a Collector," 86–87 (although on this point Pyne's feminist approach may be a little overinterpretive in what constitutes an otherwise excellent article).

Avenue was completed in 1892 and ultimately became his most beloved sanctuary; however, as his collection grew, so too did his personal residence. Eyre was commissioned a second time by Freer to draw up plans for the addition to his Ferry Avenue home of a new picture gallery—with leaded-glass skylight—which was completed in 1901, thus allowing him more space to display his new acquisitions. A second picture gallery, once again designed by Eyre and once again with leaded-glass skylight, was completed in 1911.

Likely influenced by the idea of "art as a route to social progress" espoused by his close friend Ernest Francisco Fenollosa (1853–1908) and the urging to present his collection to the Smithsonian Institution by the senatorial aide and later chairman of the National Commission of Fine Arts, Charles Moore (1855–1942), by 1902 Freer had begun to conceive of a plan to fund and construct a purpose-built public gallery to house his collection.[16] In December 1904 Freer wrote to the Smithsonian's Board of Regents and formally offered his collection as a gift with the stipulations that it remain in his possession during his lifetime, that upon his death it would become the property of the United States, that the collection be housed in a building constructed with funds from his bequest, that items in the collection never be displayed outside the building, that items not part of the collection never be displayed in the building, and that after his death nothing could be added to or taken away from the collection. In February 1905 the Smithsonian sent a delegation to view Freer's collection at his home in Detroit that included Secretary Langley, James B. Angell (1829–1916; president of the University of Michigan), former U.S. senator John B. Henderson (1826–1913), and Alexander Graham Bell (1847–1922; president of the National Geographic Society). Troubled with Freer's proviso prohibiting future acquisitions and by the fact that up until this time the Smithsonian had been primarily interested in matters of science, the Board of Regents deferred its acceptance of Freer's gift. However, at the strong urging of President Theodore Roosevelt (1858–1919), who invited Freer to the White House for dinner to discuss the donation, the Smithsonian Board of Regents formally accepted Freer's gift containing approximately two thousand items in January 1906.

In October 1912 Freer commissioned artist and architect Charles Adams Platt (1861–1933) to draw up plans for the building that would eventually house his growing collection—now containing over seven thousand items. Ground was

---

16. Pyne ("Portrait of a Collector," 91–93) shows clearly the growing influence upon Freer of Fenollosa's "gospel of art as a panacea for the wasteland that industrialism had made of the American environment." Lawton and Merrill (*Freer*, 183–84) link Freer's decision to present his collection to the Smithsonian Institute to the urgings of historian Charles Moore, assistant to Freer's friend Senator James McMillan (1838–1902), later chairman of the National Commission of Fine Arts (1910–1937), and Acting Chief of the Division of Manuscripts of the Library of Congress (1918–1927).

first broken for the building at a site on the National Mall in September 1916, but with the lack of building materials brought on largely by America's entrance into the First World War, construction came to a virtual halt until the November Armistice of 1918. Unfortunately, Freer had fallen seriously ill on Christmas Eve of that same year, and the small hope that he had of seeing his "Washington Building" completed was just short of realized when he passed away in September 1919. "Freer had not established a national gallery of art," write Lawton and Merrill of his truly philanthropic gift, "to fulfill a dream of personal glory."[17] When the Freer Gallery of Art opened in May 1923, one of Freer's early stated desires began to be fulfilled through his carefully and thoughtfully accumulated collection of approximately nine thousand items:

> The bonds you may sell to provide funds for my purchases, I care nothing about.... I can live happily, fortunately, without them. But the things I am getting are surely beyond price. Some day: many days after bonds or anything else can serve me, others will be served, well served, intelligently served by my slight efforts.[18]

Freer's Purchase of the Washington Manuscripts in Egypt

Freer's world travels, often conducted for the purpose of adding artifacts to his collection as well as meeting the artists of items he had already acquired, afforded him the opportunity to visit places that few of his contemporaries had ever been. Freer made three separate trips to Egypt, all part of larger Asian excursions.[19] On November 15, 1906, Freer and his close friend and personal physician, Dr.

---

17. Lawton and Merrill, *Freer,* 235. Cf. Freer to Langley, December 27, 1904. In general, Freer clearly disliked any type of notoriety, and while he appears not to have brooked any type of foolishness in his relationships or business dealings, he constantly evidenced a humble and charitable personality. These personality traits can be found, for example, all throughout his correspondence, as is the case in a letter to Francis W. Kelsey (1858–1927) seeking advice as to whether or not he should assist in funding the publication of a book written by a solicitous Reverend W. J. Heaton, who promised to dedicate the volume to Freer: "Of course, as regards the proposed dedication of his new book to me, that I cannot under any circumstance authorize. Notoriety of that sort is very disagreeable to me" (Charles Lang Freer to Francis W. Kelsey, July 7, 1913, CLFP).

18. Charles Lang Freer to Frank J. Hecker, July 12, 1903, CLFP. Also cited in Lawton and Merrill, *Freer,* 54. Freer's diary for Sunday, May 4, 1919, records that he included a codicil to his will. This codicil allowed for the continued acquisition of Asian, Egyptian, and Near Eastern art (but the exclusion of American art). See Charles Lang Freer Diary, Sunday, May 4, 1919, CLFP. Today the Freer Gallery of Art contains approximately twenty-seven thousand items.

19. Freer traveled on five separate occasions to Asia, September 1894–August 1895, November 1906–July 1907, April–September 1908, May–December 1909, and his fifth and final trip August 1910–April 1911.

Frederick Wharton Mann, set sail from New York aboard the SS *Hamburg*. After departing from Naples aboard the SS *Oceana* on December 6, he and Mann finally arrived in Alexandria two days later, thus beginning Freer's first Egyptian journey.[20] During the first two weeks of their six-week stay in Egypt, Freer and Mann resided at the famous Shepheard's Hotel in Cairo and from there visited ancient sites, museums, antiquarian shops, and private dealers. The following four weeks found them traveling up the Nile by both railway and boat, visiting many of the popular tourists destinations throughout Upper Egypt, including Luxor, Edfu, Aswan, Abu Simbel, Wadi Halfa, and the Second Cataract.[21] Perhaps Freer's most auspicious day in Egypt, however, came shortly after he and Mann first arrived in Cairo. On Wednesday, December 19, Freer inconspicuously records in his diary that he "Bought manuscripts in forenoon and paid for them in afternoon."[22] In contrast to his reserved diary entry, that same day Freer wrote a more colorful account to Frank Hecker, indicating that he had been completely swept off his feet by the manuscripts, had spent several days with two local Greek scholars studying them, and had fallen by the wayside in his excitement.[23]

Also recorded on blank sheets in his diary are two separate inventories outlining Freer's initial understanding of the content of these manuscripts, which he had purchased for £1,600 (or $7,750) from an Egyptian antiquities merchant named Ali Arabi, whose shop was located in Giza, near the pyramids. In what appears to be the earlier of the two lists, possibly recorded amid discussions of the manuscripts with Arabi (aided by translation by his "dragoman" Ibrahim Aly), Freer wrote in his own hand the following:

---

20. Remarkably complete itineraries of Freer's travels, and indeed for large portions of his life, can be found in the extensive twenty-nine-volume collection of his diaries dating 1889–1919 housed in the Freer Gallery of Art archives. For additional information pertaining to Freer's daily activities, see in the same archives the ledger December 1907–December 1910 kept by Joseph Stephens Warring (ca. 1863–1944), the caretaker of Freer's 33 Ferry Avenue residence. Freer's complete itinerary for the Egyptian portion of this, his second Asian journey is outlined in his diary entries of Saturday, December 8, 1906 (arrival in Alexandria) through to Tuesday, January 22, 1907 (Port Said departure to destinations beyond; CLFP).

21. In Freer's day, Egypt was traditionally divided by a horizontal boundary separating Lower Egypt (or the northernmost region inclusive of the Mediterranean Delta and environs around Cairo) and Upper Egypt (from Saqqara all the way south to Wadi Halfa and the Second Cataract, which now falls in the Sudan). While the British engineered construction of the "Great Dam" at Aswan in the late 1890s was undertaken to control the seasonal flooding of the Nile, the new Aswan High Dam constructed in the 1960s makes it impossible to see Upper Egypt as it was in Freer's day, since much of the Nile River basin between Aswan and Abu Simbel was flooded at that time, forcing many of the monuments to be re-erected elsewhere.

22. Charles Lang Freer Diary, Wednesday, December 19, 1906, CLFP.

23. Charles Lang Freer to Frank J. Hecker, December 19, 1906, CLFP. Cited as well in Lawton and Merrill, *Freer*, 66; Gunter, *Collector's Journey*, 93.

Deuteronomy inc. 5 parts Pentateuch also Joshua Greek-Complete 500 to 900
First period Greek writing-grand form
Songs of David in first period Greek Complete 500 to 900
Grand form, most artistic grand form
(Jesue (Jesus) son of Nabi [?] In first entry
Hebrew Bible—
Four Gospels of Matthew, John, Luke & Mark
in early primitive Greek small form
first period. 750 to 850
Fragment unknown in primitive Greek
Writing between grand & small form.
5th small samples of early Greek writing
of psalms very few sheets.[24]

The second more succinct itemization appears to be a later and more representative summary of the material actually purchased, perhaps recorded after Freer had the two local Greek scholars evaluate the manuscripts, and reads as follows:

4 Manuscripts
New Testament the four gospels of
Matthew, Mark, Luke & John—
The Psalms of David—
Part of the Old Bible
Book of instructions of Church
1800–1900[25]

---

24. Charles Lang Freer Diary, 1906, CLFP. The reference to "Jesue son of Nabi" is somewhat confusing. However, in Arabic (with a possible derivation from Syrian) the term "nabî" generally refers to one who is a "prophet" and is often used by Muslims to speak of Jesus ("Isa"), who is called "Nabî Isa." The Qu'ran, for example, refers clearly to Jesus in this prophetic sense (cf. Qur'an 19:30; 33:7; and more loosely 7:157). There is some controversy surrounding the full semantic range of the term "nabî," as it can also refer to the idea of an apostle or messenger; however, the term "rasûl" is more commonly used in this sense. It is not altogether unlikely that Freer simply misunderstood the Egyptian antiquities dealer's explanation of Jesus as a prophet or "Jesue Nabî."

25. Charles Lang Freer Diary, 1906, CLFP. Determining the order in which these two lists were produced by Freer aids our understanding of the historical process undertaken in the purchase of these manuscripts and helps to clarify the extent of the manuscripts originally offered to him. Regardless, the issue is ultimately incidental as manuscripts were indeed purchased, and arguments could bolster (in this case) the written priority of either list. Assuming the general maxim *lectio brevior lectio potior*, one could argue further that with the vagueness of the phrase "Part of the Old Bible," as well as the general (and incorrect) order of the four Gospels, this "less informed" and "more hastily recorded" account preceded the longer. However, despite the longer account's more detailed mention of Deuteronomy and Joshua, the quality of the Greek script, and the correct "Western order" of the Gospel books, one could still assert its priority by applying the dictum *lectio difficilior potior* to several of its more arcane readings, such as

Figure 1: Photograph taken in January 1907 by P. Dittrich in Cairo, during Freer's first trip to Egypt and as part of the first leg of his eight-month-long second Asian tour. The figures are, from left to right, Dr. Frederick W. Mann (Freer's close friend and personal physician), Freer himself, Ibrahim Aly (Freer's "dragonman," or translator and guide, whom Freer consistently employed on all his Egyptian trips), and Ali Arabi (the Cairo antiquities dealer from whom Freer purchased the Washington MSS in December 1906. Charles Lang Freer Papers, Freer Gallery of Art and Arthur M. Sackler Gallery Archives, Smithsonian Institution, Washington, D.C.: Gift of the Estate of Charles Lang Freer, Photographer: P. Dittrich. Used by permission.

It is often pointed out that, for the usually methodical and meticulous Freer, the biblical manuscripts marked for him an unexpected and uncharacteristically impulsive acquisition.[26] However, there seems to be good evidence suggesting that Freer had put considerable thought into his decision to purchase the biblical manuscripts.[27] He may have become acquainted with them as early as December 14, 1906, if not earlier, as his diary for that day records that he visited the pyramids and their surroundings, the antiquarians, and then lunched at the Hotel Mena (or Mena House Hotel)—the very same location of Arabi's antiquities shop.[28] For December 17, Freer's diary notes that he spent all day with an unnamed professor, while on December 18 he spent all forenoon and evening with Greek priests at the home of Arabi—most likely the same Greek scholars he spent several days with examining the manuscripts and whom he would write to Hecker about after making his purchase the following day.[29] Despite venturing outside of his usual collecting interests, Freer's keen intuition would be verified

---

"Jesue son of Nabi." This, taken in conjunction with its broader price ranges, brief mention of an unknown fragment, and the absence of any small Psalm fragments actually brought to light after purchase, may commend it as the earlier of the two accounts. The placement of the longer account upon blank pages preceding the shorter may again commend it as the earlier of the two; however, this assumption is made based on an examination of photocopies of Freer's diary and not the actual diary itself.

26. For statements to this effect, see Lawton and Merrill, *Freer,* 66; Gunter, *Collector's Journey,* 21. In support of this, Freer states in one of his many letters to Francis W. Kelsey, "You see I am at a great disadvantage! When Ali [Arabi] pulls from his cellar floor a MS in Coptic and calls it demotic or something else I am sitting in hot soup because I don't know the difference" (Charles Lang Freer to Francis W. Kelsey, August 1, 1909; contained in Francis W. Kelsey Records, Kelsey Museum Archives, Bentley Historical Library, University of Michigan, Ann Arbor; hereafter cited as FWKRecords).

27. In contrast to the above, Lawton and Merrill (*Freer,* 99) note the customary care Freer took in acquiring a work of art when they write, "A transaction between Freer and an art dealer involved more than a simple exchange of money. Unlike many other contemporary Western collectors of Asian art, Freer insisted on learning as much as possible about every Asian object that passed through his hands. He asked for, and usually received, details relating to the provenance of a particular artifact; he obtained translations of inscriptions and sought to understand the achievements of individual artists and particular schools. Wherever possible, Asian art dealers responded to Freer's requests and provided the information he wanted. When substantive details were lacking, less scrupulous dealers may have invented impressive pedigrees. But Freer's natural intelligence alerted him to such instances of benevolent guile and enabled him to move through the hazards of Asian connoisseurship with surprising success." See also Gunter, *Collector's Journey,* 21.

28. Charles Lang Freer Diary, Friday, December 14, 1906, CLFP.

29. See, respectively, Charles Lang Freer Diary, Monday, December 17, 1906, CLFP; and Charles Lang Freer Diary, Tuesday, December 18, 1906, CLFP. Cf. the earlier-cited letter from Freer to Hecker, December 19, 1906.

as the magnitude of his purchase made from the antiquities merchant he came to call "old Arabi" was soon recognized.[30]

In the autumn of 1907 Freer enlisted his close friend, Francis W. Kelsey (1858–1927), to oversee the preservation and publication of the manuscripts.[31] Kelsey, a professor of Latin literature at the University of Michigan, selflessly recommended several young faculty members to perform the actual work of producing the critical editions of the Greek texts.[32] Henry A. Sanders (1868–1956) was ultimately chosen for the task, and by December 1907 he had presented his initial findings to several academic bodies, including the Archaeological Institute of America and the American Philological Association.[33] The news of the

30. Freer, whose almost daily trips to Egyptian antiquarian shops fill the pages of his diaries, visited dealers such as Dikran Kelekian, Maurice Nahman, Tanios Girgis, Morgos Chanher, Alexander Dingli, Kalebjian Frères, Michael Casira, and Hajji Muhammad Mohassif. In the case of Ali Arabi, however, Freer developed a warm and mutually beneficial friendship through ongoing correspondence and subsequent visits in later years. "I am glad that you know my old friends [sic] Ali el-Arabi," wrote Freer to an acquaintance of the Egyptian dealer, "an amusing but still useful agent who has done me many kindnesses, notwithstanding, he has always made me pay well for them" (Charles Lang Freer to W. Max Muller, January 28, 1916, CLFP). If after their examination the manuscripts proved to be authentic, Freer promised to give Arabi's son a golden pocket watch like his own. The back pages of Freer's 1906 diary include a written memoir stating, "Send Mohamed Ali Abdulhi Antiquarian Ghizeh Cairo, Egypt a watch like mine." When Freer next returned to Egypt in 1908, he kept his word and a short while later even sent Arabi himself a gold watch. This seems to have become a custom for Freer, as he also presented a gold pocket watch to his Egyptian guide and translator Ibrahim Aly. See here Charles Lang Freer Diary, 1906, CLFP; Charles Lang Freer to Frank J. Hecker, May 16, 1908, CLFP; Charles Lange Freer to Francis W. Kelsey, May 23, 1908, CLFP; Charles Lang Freer to Ali Arabi, January 30, 1909, CLFP; and Charles Lang Freer to Ibrahim Aly, January 30, 1909, CLFP.

31. For Kelsey's formal acceptance of Freer's request to have him oversee the work, see Francis W. Kelsey to Charles Lang Freer, January 21, 1908, CLFP. A few days later Kelsey produced a document outlining an overall plan for the preservation and publication of the documents (Francis W. Kelsey, "The Freer Manuscripts: Handling and Publication: Plan and Specifications," January 25, 1908, CLFP).

32. For Kelsey's early recommendation to Freer of several young scholars to carry out the work, see Francis W. Kelsey to Charles Lang Freer, August 31, 1907, CLFP. Kelsey, a dedicated churchman and family man (with two daughters and a son), was remarkable in his own right. His humanitarianism often led him to assist younger scholars in the beginning of their careers through seeking on their behalf financial aid and academic opportunities. After the destruction of the First World War, he helped to secure funding that allowed German scholars to continue their work on the production of the great Latin Thesaurus; he was involved in the work of the Near East Relief Committee that sought to give aid after the Armenian Massacre of 1915–1923; and he served on the Belgium Relief Commission, whose goal was to provide food and clothing for Belgian children after the war. On Kelsey, see William H. Worrell, "Francis Willey Kelsey," in *Dictionary of American Biography* (ed. D. Malone; New York: Scribner, 1933), 313–14.

33. For Sanders's prepublication announcement of the manuscripts, see his program for the Chicago meeting of the Archaeological Institute of America dated December 30, 1907, CLFP. For

discovery of the manuscripts generated no small excitement in both the popular press and the scholarly world.[34] "Not since the discovery of the Codex Sinaiticus," wrote Kenyon in his archaeological report for the Egyptian Exploration Fund, "have Biblical students had such a windfall, and the publication of [Freer's] MSS. will be awaited with eagerness, but with a full recognition that the fortunate editor [Sanders] must not be unduly hurried."[35] By all accounts, Sanders went on to perform his academic duties with exceptional ability. Kelsey wrote of him:

> I do not think there is another American scholar who could have covered so much ground in the same time and have maintained so high a standard of completeness as I know Sanders has kept. Very few men can collate MSS *properly* anyway—you would be surprised to know how many errors are found in publications of scholars of standing in their field. The severest search by European scholars revealed no important error in Sanders's collation of the Deuteronomy and Joshua MS—and it will be the same with the gospels.[36]

The photography of the manuscripts (undertaken by George R. Swain, principal of the high school in Bay City, Michigan) and manufacture of the plates used

---

his early publications of the discovery, see Henry A. Sanders, "Proceedings of the Thirty-Ninth Annual Meeting of the American Philological Association Held at Chicago, Illinois, December, 1907," *Transactions and Proceedings of the American Philological Association* 38 (1907): xxii; idem, "New Manuscripts of the Bible from Egypt," *AJA* 12/1 (1908): 49–55; idem, "Four Newly Discovered Biblical Manuscripts," *The Biblical World* 31/2 (1908): 82, 138–42; idem, "Age and Ancient Home of Biblical Manuscripts in the Freer Collection," *AJA* 13/2 (1909): 130–41; and idem, "The Freer Psalter," *The Biblical World* 33/5 (1909): 290, 343–44.

34. Accounts in the popular media (many of which Freer retained and placed within scrapbooks now archived in the CLFP) ranged from temperate evaluations of the manuscripts to sensational stories asserting the discovery of new crucifixion narratives. For the latter, see Francis W. Kelsey to Charles Lang Freer, May 19, 1913, CLFP; and Freer's response in which he hopes to defer the media to Kelsey in Charles Lang Freer to Francis W. Kelsey, May 20, 1913, CLFP. The following day Freer wrote, "Every mail brings more or less correspondence concerning the facsimiles, much of which is ludicrous, but in the mass there are some inquiries and references of a commendable character" (Charles Lang Freer to Francis W. Kelsey, May 21, 1913, CLFP).

35. Frederic G. Kenyon, "B.—Graeco-Roman Egypt, 1907–8," *Archaeological Report: Egyptian Exploration Fund* (1907–1908): 48. For other early scholarly reactions to the announced discovery, see especially Edgar J. Goodspeed, "The Detroit Manuscripts of the Septuagint and New Testament," *The Biblical World* 31/3 (1908): 218–26; idem, "Notes on the Freer Gospels," *AJT* 13 (1909): 597–603; Caspar René Gregory, *Das Freer-Logion* (Leipzig: Hinrichs, 1908); idem, "Vier neue biblische Handschriften," *Theologisches Literaturblatt* 29/7 (1908): cols. 73–76; Adolf von Harnack, "Neues zum unechten Marcusschluß," *TLZ* 33/6 (1908): cols. 168–70; Carl Schmidt, "Die neuen griechischen Bibelhandschriften," *TLZ* 33/12 (1908): cols. 359–60; and Hermann F. von Soden, "Ein neues 'herrenwort,' aufbehalten als Einfügung in den Schluß des Markusevangeliums," *Die Christliche Welt* 22/20 (1908): cols. 482–86. Cf. B. H. Streeter, "The Washington MS. of the Gospels," *HTR* 19 (1926): 165–72.

36. Francis W. Kelsey to Charles Lang Freer, September 5, 1913, CLFP.

for reproducing the images (undertaken by W. C. Ramsay of the Heliotype Company in Boston, Massachusetts) resulted in the production of facsimile editions that were unsurpassed "in all of Europe" and soon became the standard for representing like material for some years to come.[37] In January 1914, as the first half of the scheduled work drew to a close and the accounts were balanced, Kelsey wrote warmly to Freer stating, "And I cannot close this letter without expressing warm appreciation of the vision and generosity with which you have so promptly, and in a form so approximating finality, made accessible to scholars the invaluable manuscripts in your possession. It is no exaggeration to say that no manuscripts of equal importance have ever before been given to the world in so satisfactory a form so soon after discovery."[38] The parchment codices of Deuteronomy and Joshua, the Psalms, the Gospels, and the Epistles of Paul constitute only four of the five Greek texts that would come to be called the Freer or Washington Manuscripts. In addition to his original cost to purchase the four manuscripts, Freer expended close to another $30,000 by the time their publication was complete.[39] There were, however, other ancient manuscripts yet to be purchased.

Freer began his third Asian journey by spending the last two weeks of May 1908 in Egypt. He departed from New York aboard the SS *Romanic* on the evening of Friday, April 24, spent several days in Naples, and then embarked upon the SS *Orient* on the evening of Sunday, May 10, finally arriving at Port Said in the mid-morning of Thursday, May 14.[40] On this (Freer's second) trip to Egypt, he purchased from Ali Arabi Coptic manuscripts of a Sahidic Psalter and a homily on the Virgin written by Theophilus, as well as fifty fragments from the Cairo

37. Francis W. Kelsey to Charles Lang Freer, October 17, 1908, CLFP. Note also Francis W. Kelsey to Charles Lang Freer, September 21, 1908, CLFP, wherein Kelsey states, "I had as guest yesterday our expert palaeographer. He told me that he had never seen—that there is not in existence—so perfect an example of reproduction of manuscript pages as is that of the Deuteronomy-Joshua manuscript. He could at a glance tell in the case of each page which was the hair side and which the flesh side of the original parchment—a test that will not hold of any other reproduction that I know of. But of course we had extraordinarily fine parchment to start with!" For further examples of Kelsey's high praise for the work of Swain and Ramsay, see Francis W. Kelsey to W.C. Ramsay, April 22, 1908, CLFP; and Francis W. Kelsey to Charles Lang Freer, August 29, 1908, CLFP. A comparison of the facsimile editions of the Washington Manuscripts—which still remain remarkable reproductions even in the current digital age—with any other contemporary facsimile edition of similar material quickly reveals the exceptional effort and ingenuity put into the successful accomplishment of this work.

38. Francis W. Kelsey to Charles Lang Freer, January 26, 1914, CLFP. For Freer's stoic response, see Charles Lang Freer to Francis W. Kelsey, January 28, 1914, CLFP.

39. This would equate to over $600,000 in today's currency, based on a conversion factor of 20.0303.

40. Cf. Freer's 1908 diary between the days of Thursday, May 14 (arrival in Alexandria), to Sunday, May 31 (his departure from Port Said to points beyond), for the itinerary of his second Egyptian trip (CLFP).

Genizah (a collection of medieval materials from the city's ancient Jewish community). Freer also acquired from the Cairo dealer and banker Maurice Nahman (1868–1948) additional fragmentary Greek and Coptic papyri.[41]

As part of his fourth Asian journey in 1909, Freer made his third and final trip to Egypt, staying there from late July to early August. After sailing from New York aboard the SS *Amerika* on Saturday, May 15, Freer spent the latter part of the month, all of June, and the first three weeks of July in Britain and Europe. On Saturday, July 24, he sailed from Naples on the SS *Schleswig* and arrived in Alexandria on the afternoon of Monday, July 26.[42] He purchased from Arabi and Nahman once again additional fragments of a Coptic Psalter and Byzantine paintings from an eleventh-century manuscript of the "Heavenly Ladder" (a popular Byzantine monastic composition).[43]

Freer occasionally made other purchases from Egypt *in absentia,* usually by employing various intermediaries. In 1909, Walter Dennison (1859–1917), a professor of Latin at the University of Michigan, was in Egypt and acquired from Nahman on behalf of Freer nine of the original thirty-six pieces of the

---

41. Shortly after his return from Asia, Freer had Kelsey look at some of the Egyptian material he had purchased. Kelsey writes, "The MS. and sheet which you were so kind as to let me take were of so great interest that I went to my study thinking to identify at least the MS. before going to bed. But it was not so simple a matter, for a more careful inspection showed that the language of the manuscript was not Greek at all but Coptic, of a very early date, written with many Greek words and in a character so like that of the Greek manuscripts that at a hasty glance anyone would think the MS. Greek! I was able only to identify the MS. as a Coptic version of the Psalms; then I called in a young but competent Coptic scholar which we have here, and who assisted in determining the amount of the MS. lost and what dialect of Coptic (Sahidic) used in the translation.... The sheet is not yet identified, but there appears to be magic symbols among the characters on the lower margin.... The discovery of this Coptic material is a matter of great importance for our study of the Greek manuscripts, and I am delighted that you secured it." See Kelsey to Freer, September 21, 1908.

42. See Freer's 1909 diary between the days of Monday, July 26 (arrival in Alexandria), to Thursday, August 5 (his departure from Port Said to points beyond), for the itinerary of his third Egyptian trip (CLFP).

43. On Arabi's acquisition of this material, and his holding it for Freer, see Francis W. Kelsey to Charles Lang Freer, July 8, 1909, CLFP. On the nature of the original deal Freer had with Arabi for the purchase of these 1909 acquisitions, he writes, "Referring to our conversation of this morning and your further talks with my dragoman Ibrahim Aly, I understand that you desire to have made about six photographs of specimens of the papyri manuscripts which you showed me recently. These photos you intend to send to me at Peking and I after their receipt will show them to my experts. If the experts deem the manuscripts important you are to send the two tin boxes of manuscripts which you recently showed me to my address at Detroit for full examination by experts and myself. After such examination I have the right to buy the entire collection from you for the sum of seven hundred pounds sterling, or to return them to you at your risk and expense" (Charles Lang Freer to Ali Arabi, August 3, 1909, CLFP).

now famous Byzantine Gold Treasure.[44] In 1912, Freer acquired nine additional Coptic fragments. During his own trip to Egypt in 1913, Sanders purchased from Nahman on behalf of Freer yet another fragment of a Coptic Psalter. And in 1916, Freer purchased another Greek manuscript from Nahman through the intermediary Dr. David L. Askren (b. 1875), who also purchased at the same time Coptic manuscripts for the Pierpont Morgan Library and would later purchase manuscripts for Yale. Askren, a medical missionary working in the Fayoum region of Egypt, became acquainted with Kelsey when the latter traveled to Italy in 1915 to settle the estate of Freer's close friend and attorney Thomas Spencer Jerome (1864–1914), a University of Michigan alumnus whose bequest went to the university.[45] Of his chance meeting with Askren, Kelsey wrote:

> In January, 1915 … I went to Capri in order to secure the manuscripts left by Thomas Spencer Jerome [his unpublished *magnum opus* on "Roman Morals"], divide his library [between the University of Michigan and the American Academy in Rome] in accordance with his will, and straighten out some complications that had arisen in the sale of Villa Castello. By pure accident on the way over I overheard a gentleman make reference to the Fayoum in such a way that I inferred that he knew the region in which the Freer Greek Manuscripts and the Morgan Coptic Manuscripts are said to have been discovered. This gentleman proved to be Dr. David L. Askren, a missionary, physician, and surgeon, living at the capital of the Fayoum, and I found that among his patients were the fellaheen who handled the Morgan Manuscripts.[46]

Following their meeting, Kelsey retained the services of Askren in the hope that his connections might be able to help disclose the origin of Freer's manuscripts and keep watch in case more were discovered. A short while later a deal was struck between Kelsey and Professor Eugene Henri Hyvernat (1858–1941), the scholar responsible for the publication of the Hamouli Monastery Coptic Library discovered in 1910 and purchased by J. Pierpont Morgan (1837–1917), wherein Askren would continue his search for manuscripts for both parties, with any Greek discoveries going to Freer and any Coptic to the Pierpont Morgan

---

44. The remaining pieces of the Byzantine Gold Treasure were purchased by J. Pierpont Morgan, Mrs. Walter Burns, and Friedrich von Gans, whose portions were respectively deposited in the Metropolitan Museum of Art, New York; the British Museum, London; and the Staatliche Museen zu Berlin. Freer's portion of the Byzantine Gold Treasure was, obviously, deposited in the Freer Gallery of Art, Washington, D.C.

45. Upon Freer's retirement in 1899, he and Spencer had purchased together a vacation villa on the island of Capri named the "Villa Castello."

46. Francis W. Kelsey to Frank J. Hecker, March 15, 1920, CLFP. Jerome's manuscript was edited and posthumously published by John G. Winter. See Thomas S. Jerome, *Aspects of the Study of Roman History* (ed. John G. Winter; New York: Putnam's, 1923).

Library.[47] In the fall of 1915 Nahman reported to Askren that he had on hand four more Coptic manuscripts found at Hamouli, a Hebrew medical book written on goatskin, a Coptic writing on papyrus containing songs and prayers, and part of the Old Testament in Greek written on papyri. After Askren sent several photographs of the Coptic texts to Kelsey, in May 1916 all parties agreed to Nahman's firm request of £1,000 (250 of which would be paid by Freer) for the purchase of the manuscripts. Upon receiving the full payment in October (a first payment being lost aboard a steamer that fell victim to a torpedo in the Mediterranean), Askren and Nahman deposited the manuscripts in a sealed tin box under the stamp of the United States Consul and placed it in a safety deposit vault at the National Bank of Egypt.[48] Kelsey had no idea that the sealed tin box held what would be a fifth Greek "Washington Manuscript" containing the text of the Minor Prophets. Indeed, due to the hazards of sea travel during the First World War, it was only when he was able to journey to Egypt in February 1920 and retrieved the contents of the sealed tin box that he discovered what it held. Writing from Cairo later in March, Kelsey relates the following:

> In preparation for the despatch to Rome I drew the manuscripts from the bank and brought them to the hotel in order to examine them carefully before taking them to the Museum in order to arrange for exportation. You cannot imagine my surprise to find that although the Greek papyrus is small and fragile, the writing is ancient and the amount of matter considerable. To state the fact in the fewest possible words, being afraid to disturb the pages, I took the tin box just as it was to Dr. Grenfell [1869–1926], who is the foremost living expert in the dating and deciphering of papyri. He opened up the leaves so far as was necessary to determine that the papyrus contains the Greek text of the Minor Prophets, nine of whom he identified; there is no reason to doubt that the other three are represented in large part in the fragments. The next day I took the box down to the Museum Library and compared a passage where Dr. Grenfell had opened the papyrus with the Greek text of Tischendorf. I found the text excellent. In the passage consulted it is nearer the Alexandrian manuscript in the British Museum than the other manuscripts covering the same passage. Without daring to disturb the fragile leaves further for extended collation, from what I saw I should say that the text will be fully as important as that of the

---

47. For the Hamouli Collection, see Henri Hyvernat, *A Checklist of Coptic Manuscripts in the Pierpont Morgan Library* (New York: privately printed, 1919); and Leo Depuydt and David A. Loggie, *Catalogue of Coptic Manuscripts in the Pierpont Morgan Library* (2 vols.; Corpus of Illuminated Manuscripts 4, 5; Oriental Series 1, 2; Leuven: Peeters, 1993).

48. For the full account of Askren's involvement in this matter, see David L. Askren to Francis W. Kelsey, October 22, 1915, CLFP; David L. Askren to Francis W. Kelsey, August 13, 1916, CLFP; Francis W. Kelsey to Charles Lang Freer, September 18, 1916, CLFP; and "Memoranda in Connection with the Publication of the Following University of Michigan (Humanistic Series) Publications, In Which Mr. Freer Has Aided Financially," May 11, 1918, CLFP.

Deuteronomy and Joshua already published. Dr. Grenfell dates the papyrus in the fourth century, and has already asked if he may announce the discovery of it in England later.[49]

In Cairo to help begin the University of Michigan's Near East Expedition of 1920, Kelsey immediately took all the manuscripts in the tin box to Rome, where the Coptic texts were delivered in person to Hyvernat for the Pierpont Morgan Library, and the Greek papyrus of the Minor Prophets was forwarded by the American Embassy to the Library of the University of Michigan.[50]

Often considered among the most important acquisitions of his collecting career, Freer's five Greek biblical manuscripts—consisting of Deuteronomy and Joshua, the Psalms, the four Gospels, the Epistles of Paul, and the Minor Prophets—were unanimously recognized by scholars as the most important collection of its kind outside of Europe.[51] Of the many thousands of items in the Freer Gallery of Art, it is perhaps the biblical manuscripts that have stimulated the most

---

49. Kelsey to Hecker, March 15, 1920.

50. Four years after the original decision to purchase the Greek papyri of the Minor Prophets, it finally arrived at the Library of the University of Michigan on May 14, 1920. "The manuscript appears to have reached us with very little damage," writes university librarian William W. Bishop to Kelsey, "There are evidences of a very slight break at one end, doubtless due to jarring in transit, but on the whole its condition appears to be as good as could have been expected after so long a journey, and the text is perfectly legible" (William W. Bishop to Francis W. Kelsey, May 14, 1920).

51. Both the Charles Lang Freer and Francis W. Kelsey Papers include letters expressing this very point from many of the day's outstanding scholars, including Sir Frederic G. Kenyon, Herman C. Hoskier (1864–1938), and Caspar R. Gregory (1846–1917). See, for example, Frederic G. Kenyon to Charles Lang Freer, February 12, 1908, CLFP, who writes regarding the first four Greek manuscripts in 1906, "The manuscripts are evidently of great interest and great importance, and I congratulate you and your country heartily on their acquisition." Interesting additions to this correspondence are numerous letters from Gregory in which he seeks to have Freer pay for the English translation of his *Das Freer-Logion*. Although Freer agreed to the request, Kelsey later put a stop to it, writing, "Professor Gregory sent on his manuscript some months ago when you were in the East; it did not reach our view of what the contribution should be and I mailed it back to him saying, in effect, that if he would rewrite it and bring some parts up to date that were behind the times we would be glad to go ahead with the publication on our original understanding. In strict confidence I may say that while Mr. Gregory's reply was most polite I do not think that he quite relished my criticism and the return of his manuscript for revision. However that may be, I have been always in the habit of judging matter by content and not by the distinguished name attached to it! I do not think we shall hear further from Mr. Gregory on the subject." See Francis W. Kelsey to Charles Lang Freer, July 8, 1914, CLFP. Kelsey then asked Freer if he might appropriate the funds set aside for Gregory's monograph in order to apply it to the proposed work of an English scholar named Rev. E. S. Buchanan. Again, Freer agreed, and again Kelsey reneged after receiving the work from Buchanan. See Francis W. Kelsey to Charles Lang Freer, September 11, 1915, CLFP.

sustained attention down through the decades. In referring specifically to the Egyptian artifacts contained in the gallery, curator Ann C. Gunter marks out the biblical manuscripts and the New Kingdom glass vessels as "world-class specimens."[52] In the following paragraphs I summarize scholarly views on particulars, drawing especially on the monumental analyses by Sanders and his colleagues involved in the original editions of these manuscripts.

The Washington Manuscript of Deuteronomy and Joshua (Washington MS I, Sanders Θ, Rahlfs WI, van Haelst 54) is dated to the fifth or sixth century (though occasionally the fourth century). One hundred and two leaves (ten quires of eight leaves, three of six leaves, and one of four leaves) are extant, but originally it almost certainly included Genesis through Numbers as well (i.e., well over five hundred pages in the lost portion). The manuscript appears to be written by a single scribe using dark brown ink (although the opening lines of each book are red) in a large, upright uncial hand. This double-columned parchment codex has pages about 26 x 30 cm, and thirty-one lines to each page. It was finely preserved at the time of its discovery and is noted for the exceptional quality of its text. Sanders completed both the facsimile reproduction and the critical edition of the Washington Manuscript of Deuteronomy and Joshua in 1910.[53]

The Washington Manuscript of the Four Gospels (Washington MS III, Gregory W, Gregory-Aland 032, van Haelst 331), which is commonly dated to the late fourth or early fifth century, is regarded as the third-oldest Greek parchment codex of the Gospels in the world. The first quire of John, however, is written in a later second hand and is evidently a replacement for a lost or damaged quire. Sanders published both the critical edition and facsimile volume of the Washington Manuscript of the Gospels in 1912.[54] This single-column manuscript contains

---

52. Gunter, *Collector's Journey,* 21, and, for similar statements, 18, 93. Gunter serves as Curator of Ancient Near Eastern Art at the Freer Gallery of Art and Arthur M. Sackler Gallery.

53. Henry A. Sanders, *The Old Testament Manuscripts in the Freer Collection, Part I: The Washington Manuscript of Deuteronomy and Joshua* (University of Michigan Studies, Humanistic Series 8/1; New York: Macmillan, 1910); idem, *Facsimile of the Washington Manuscript of Deuteronomy and Joshua in the Freer Collection* (Ann Arbor: University of Michigan, 1910). The cost to Freer to produce the Deuteronomy and Joshua monograph (992 copies) as well as the facsimile (265 copies) was $1,112.37 and $6,366.63, respectively ("Publications for Mr. Charles L. Freer: Statement of Accounts, January 26, 1914," CLFP; and William W. Bishop to H. B. Hutchins, May 13, 1918, CLFP). For standard summary descriptions, see Alfred Rahlfs and Detlef Fraenkel, *Verzeichnis der griechischen Handschriften des Alten Testaments* (rev. ed.; Stuttgart: Vandenhoeck & Ruprecht, 2004), 1:386–87; Joseph van Haelst, *Catalogue des papyrus littéraires juifs et chrétiens* (Paris: University of Paris-Sorbonne, 1976), 43–44 (catalogue no. 54).

54. Henry A. Sanders, *The New Testament Manuscripts in the Freer Collection, Part I: The Washington Manuscript of the Four Gospels* (University of Michigan Studies, Humanistic Series 9/1; New York: Macmillan, 1912); idem, *Facsimile of the Washington Manuscript of the Four Gospels in the Freer Collection* (Ann Arbor: University of Michigan, 1912). Freer's expense to produce both the Gospels monograph (994 copies) and facsimile (435 copies) was $3,204.02 and

thirty lines per page and measures about 14 x 21 cm. At some point it was evidently rebound and given well-preserved wooden covers with painted images of the four Evangelists, dated to the seventh/eighth century.[55] With the four Gospels in the "Western" order (Matthew, John, Luke, and Mark), this codex (containing 187 leaves) is written in a small, slightly sloping uncial hand. The text is generally regarded as uneven in quality (containing a large number of itacisms as well as metathesis, dittography, and slight omissions or insertions) and has curious shifts in textual affiliation from one part of the codex to another ("block mixture"), which may be indicative of a variegated exemplar or multiple exemplars. As well, the manuscript contains numerous notable variants, including an extracanonical saying of Jesus after Mark 16:14 (the famous "Freer Logion") and an interesting *subscriptio* possibly indicating ownership. Although the longer ending of Mark (16:9–20) as well as the doxology at the close of the Lord's Prayer in Matthew (6:13) are also present in the text, the *pericope adulterae* often found in manuscripts of John's Gospel (7:53–8:11) is absent.

The Washington Manuscript of the Psalms (Washington MS II, Rahlfs 1219, van Haelst 83) was badly decayed, worm-eaten, and bonded together upon discovery, and careful effort was required to separate the leaves. Scholars generally date it to the early fifth century. Almost a complete collection of the Psalms (107 leaves survive), with the addition of a psalm numbered 151 and *Odes Sol.* 1:1–6a, every page is now marred by deterioration. After Sanders painstakingly separated the leaves of this parchment codex, two separate scribal hands were revealed. The first and older hand, being written in large, rounded upright uncials, ends at Ps 142:8. The last seven leaves of the manuscript are written by a second and younger hand (possibly of the sixth century) in slightly larger, square sloping uncials. That these seven leaves were taken from another manuscript and added to the older and more valuable codex (rather than purposely written to complete the older manuscript) is indicated by the different size and shape of page, differences in text, and the repetition of verses 5–8 of Ps 142. The text is in a single column of thirty lines to a page, which originally measured approximately 25 x 35 cm. Written in dark brown ink that has occasionally peeled away (although red ink is used for numbers and titles), the manuscript preserves a remarkably clean and accurate text similar to the Psalms of Codex Vaticanus. Sanders published the critical edition of the Washington Manuscript of the Psalms in 1917; however, no facsimile of the text was ever produced.[56]

$13,029.75, respectively ("Publications for Mr. Charles L. Freer: Statement of Accounts, January 26, 1914," CLFP; and Bishop to Hutchins, May 13, 1918).

55. Charles R. Morey, "The Painted Covers of the Washington Manuscript of the Gospels," in *Studies in East Christian and Roman Art* (ed. Walter Dennison and Charles R. Morley; University of Michigan Studies, Humanistic Series 12/1; New York: Macmillan, 1918), 63–81.

56. Henry A. Sanders, *The Old Testament Manuscripts in the Freer Collection, Part II: The Washington Manuscript of the Psalms* (University of Michigan Studies, Humanistic Series 8/2;

The Washington Manuscript of the Epistles of Paul (Washington MS IV, Gregory I, Gregory-Aland 016, van Haelst 507) is dated to the fifth/sixth century and contains eighty-four fragmentary leaves representing parts of every Pauline letter in the New Testament except Romans (2 Thessalonians is followed by Hebrews). At one time the parchment codex likely also included Romans as well as Acts and most of the Catholic Epistles (on approximately twenty-six quires or about 210 leaves) but lacked Revelation. This single-column manuscript originally measured about 20 x 25 cm. It is written in a small uncial hand, originally had about thirty lines to a page, and was badly decayed and blackened upon discovery. Sanders referred to it as "a blackened, decayed lump of parchment as hard and brittle on the exterior as glue."[57] Despite the poor condition of this manuscript, the text is very accurate and free of interpolation. Sanders published the critical edition of the Washington Manuscript of the Epistles of Paul in 1918.[58]

The Washington Manuscript of the Minor Prophets (Washington MS V, Rahlfs W, Kenyon X, van Haelst 284), a fragmentary mid-third-century Greek papyrus codex, was considered at the time of its discovery to be the oldest existing witness containing a significant portion of the biblical text. Portions of thirty-three leaves survive of this single-column manuscript, which originally comprised probably forty-eight leaves. The largest extant portions contain 38–39 lines per page, but probably 46–49 lines per page originally, measuring about 15 x 35 cm. At the time of discovery, the top portion of the manuscript was likely

---

New York: Macmillan, 1917). See also idem, "The Freer Psalter," 290, 343–44. Freer's total cost to produce both the Deuteronomy-Joshua monograph as well as the Psalms monograph came to $4,036.32 ("Publications for Mr. Charles L. Freer: Statement of Accounts, January 26, 1914," CLFP; and Bishop to Hutchins, May 13, 1918). As to why no facsimile edition was ever produced of the Psalms manuscript, Kelsey writes to Freer stating, "If this were the only manuscript which you possess a much stronger argument could be made for reproduction in facsimile. The fact is, however, that the reproduction of the other two manuscripts in facsimile has made it possible for scholars to check up every page with the readings reported by Professor Sanders in the monographs which have been published; the results have been so favorable to the thoroughness and accuracy of the work of Professor Sanders, as you are already aware, that the readings reported in his monograph on the Psalms manuscript, which is now in preparation, will be accepted by all scholars without a question" (Francis W. Kelsey to Charles Lang Freer, August 7, 1914, CLFP). See as well similar but earlier assertions by Kelsey in Francis W. Kelsey to Charles Lang Freer, June 26, 1914, CLFP.

57. Henry A. Sanders, *The New Testament Manuscripts in the Freer Collection, Part II: The Washington Manuscript of the Epistles of Paul* (University of Michigan Studies, Humanistic Series 9/2; New York: Macmillan, 1918), 251.

58. Sanders, *Washington Manuscript of the Epistles of Paul.* The total cost to Freer to produce both the Four Gospels monograph as well as the Pauline Epistles monograph, which were bound together for distribution in 1918 (994 copies), came to $4,753.85 ("Publications for Mr. Charles L. Freer: Statement of Accounts, January 26, 1914," CLFP; and Bishop to Hutchins, May 13, 1918).

severed from the lower portion by an excavator's spade or some other digging implement, thus its fragmentary condition. The text is written in dark brown ink with a sloping uncial hand that leans toward an oval cursive. Although the writing is sometimes crowded and broad-columned, this is not likely indicative of the need for economy in the manuscript's production, as the original size of the papyrus sheets used for the double leaves was large and of higher quality. The text contains, as well as explanatory Coptic glosses, many corrections from both a contemporary as well as a later scribe. Reflecting a text most likely predating the Hexapla of Origen as well as the later editions, it is therefore important in revealing the text of the Minor Prophets prior to these.[59] In 1927, with money from the Freer Research and Publication Fund, Sanders published both a critical edition and a facsimile volume on the Minor Prophets manuscript, both of which incorporated Carl Schmidt's (1868–1938) work on the Berlin Fragment of Genesis (which the latter had purchased in 1906 from Akmim, Egypt).[60]

Between Arabi and Nahman, Freer had paid £1,850 for the five Greek manuscripts, but ever the philanthropist he also fully underwrote all the costs incurred in producing the critical editions and facsimile volumes of these texts—which upon completion he further insisted be freely distributed "to suitable institutions

---

59. See Kristin De Troyer's study of the text of the Freer Minor Prophets text of Jonah in this volume.

60. Henry A. Sanders and Carl Schmidt, *The Minor Prophets in the Freer Collection and the Berlin Fragment of Genesis* (University of Michigan Studies, Humanistic Series 21; New York: Macmillan, 1927); Henry A. Sanders, *Facsimile of the Washington Manuscript of the Minor Prophets in the Freer Collection and the Berlin Fragment of Genesis* (Ann Arbor: University of Michigan, 1927); and idem, "A Papyrus Manuscript of the Minor Prophets," *HTR* 14 (1921): 181–87. The publication of Schmidt's Genesis fragment was surrounded in controversy. In 1908 Schmidt had initially invited Alfred Rahlfs (1865–1935) to co-author a critical edition of the papyrus; however, Rahlfs refused after his own request to edit the text alone was declined by Schmidt. Awaiting the end of the First World War, Schmidt then enlisted the help of Sanders in 1922, after hearing of the latter's projected publication of the Minor Prophets. In 1924, after the first draft of the work was complete, Rahlfs had apparently requested photographs from Sanders of the Genesis fragment so that the text could be included in the Göttingen Septuagint apparatus of Genesis. Sanders had earlier been provided by Rahlfs with the entire Göttingen apparatus when beginning his work on the Minor Prophets. Thinking that he and Schmidt's work would be published much sooner than Rahlfs and that Rahlfs would in fairness await that time, Sanders sent the photographs ahead, neglecting to seek the prior approval of Schmidt. However, Rahlfs's Septuagint edition of Genesis appeared prior to the critical edition of Sanders and Schmidt and had without consent made use of Sanders's photographs in this prior publication. At the height of the controversy, Schmidt responded by pointing out the defects of Rahlfs's edition of the Genesis fragment and disclosed the latter's reproach that he "had entrusted to an American a publication, which should naturally have fallen to the Septuaginta-Unternehmen." See the section entitled "An Explanation" in Sanders and Schmidt, *Minor Prophets*, ix–x and 234–35.

and scholars" the world over.[61] In addition to these expenses, Freer also financed other University of Michigan Humanistic Series publications of his non-Greek materials acquired from Egypt. In 1914 Charles R. Morey (1877–1955) published a beautifully illustrated edition of the Byzantine Christian paintings Freer had purchased in Cairo in 1909, and this volume includes a study of the painted covers of the Gospels codex.[62] In 1916 William H. Worrell (1879–1952) produced a masterful critical edition of the fifth-century Coptic Psalter as well as the other Coptic materials in Freer's collection (including additional fragments of the Psalms, Job, and Matthew).[63] In 1923 Worrell also published the Coptic homily on the Virgin by Theophilus, together with a second homily by Celestinus owned by the British Museum (both originally forming part of the same manuscript).[64] Walter Dennison (1869–1917) was charged with the considerable task of producing a critical edition of, not just Freer's nine pieces of the valuable Byzantine Gold

61. For the formal agreement between Freer and Kelsey, see Charles Lang Freer to Francis W. Kelsey, March 19, 1908, CLFP: "It is understood that the University of Michigan … will perform all expert work incident to the proposed publications, and that you will personally direct and supervise the production…. I agree to pay all expenses connected with the publishing, such as charges for photographs, reproducing the photographs by Heliotype method, printing, binding, &c. &c. The money to be supplied promptly from time to time, on presentation of estimates bearing your [Kelsey's] approval…. The publications are to be distributed free to suitable institutions and scholars." A list of libraries formally sent the volumes is included as an appendix at the back of each of the Washington Manuscript publications. See Francis W. Kelsey to Charles Lang Freer, November 16, 1908, CLFP, for further particulars related to the gifting of the volumes to universities and the inscription to be printed on the inside cover of each.

62. Charles R. Morey, *East Christian Paintings in the Freer Collection* (Studies in East Christian and Roman Art 1; New York: Macmillan, 1914).

63. Worrell's work was very well received by other scholars, as Kelsey expresses to Freer after finding out that Worrell had humbly held back various letters of acclaim from individuals such as F. G. Kenyon, James H. Breasted (1865–1935), R. E. Brünnow (1858–1917), W. Max Müller (1862–1919), John P. Peters (1852–1921), James H. Ropes (1866–1933), and Charles C. Torrey (1863–1956). After requesting of Worrell to see the letters, Kelsey states, "He sent back the most remarkable group of acknowledgements which I have seen regarding any of our publications so soon after distribution; of these he had modestly said nothing before!" (Francis W. Kelsey to Charles Lang Freer, September 9, 1916, CLFP). As well, note the high commendation from the British Coptic scholar Walter E. Crum (1865–1944) in Walter E. Crum to William H. Worrell, July 18, 1916, CLFP.

64. William H. Worrell, *The Coptic Manuscripts in the Freer Collection, Part I: The Coptic Psalter* (University of Michigan Studies, Humanistic Series 9/1; New York: Macmillan, 1916); and idem, *The Coptic Manuscripts in the Freer Collection, Part II: A Homily on the Archangel Gabriel by Celestinus, Archbishop of Rome, and a Homily on the Virgin by Theophilus, Archbishop of Alexandria, from Manuscript Fragments in the Freer Collection and the British Museum* (University of Michigan Studies, Humanistic Series 10/2; New York: Macmillan, 1923). Worrell's publication of the homilies was bound together with the Coptic Psalter publication in 1923 and sold as a single volume.

Treasure, but all thirty-six pieces variously owned and located in America and Europe. Dennison's completed manuscript was published shortly after his premature death from pneumonia in 1917.[65] The Cairo Genizah fragments purchased by Freer in 1908 were eventually published by Worrell and Richard Gottheil (1862–1936) in 1927.[66] To each of these scholars Freer also extended extraordinary levels of hospitality, graciousness, and generosity—often opening his home to them, lending them the objects underlying their work, writing them letters of introduction, and even paying for their traveling expenses abroad if necessitated by the need for further study and research. With Freer's patronage, Kelsey's supervision, and the academic ability of Sanders, Morey, Worrell, Dennison, and Gottheil, the daunting task of producing this amount and quality of work was completed in a timely fashion and with admirable execution:

> It seems difficult to realize that this closes the account of the publication of your invaluable Greek Manuscripts, which have been a center of so deep interest, and the subject of so frequent correspondence, for thirteen years. To me it seems only yesterday that these precious parchments were opened in your gallery, remembering the utter amazement of Mr. Sanders and myself, who had never dreamed of seeing any manuscript—not to speak of four—of so great antiquity and value in the United States. Every conclusion which we transmitted to you regarding their value to scholarship has been more than confirmed by the judgment of European scholars in the publication of reviews, largely in foreign languages. I confess that it is a source of gratification to me that my original estimate of thirty thousand dollars ($30,000) as the approximate cost of the adequate publication of the four manuscripts [excluding the Minor Prophets] has not been exceeded.[67]

---

65. Walter Dennison, *Studies in East Christian and Roman Art, Part II: A Gold Treasure of the Late Roman Period From Egypt* (University of Michigan Studies, Humanistic Series 11/2; New York: Macmillan, 1918). Like Worrell's, Dennison's work was also well received, as Freer notes when writing a letter of condolence to Dennison's widow. Freer also adds, "My lack of physical strength during the period of my meetings with Professor Deninson [sic] in Detroit as well as elsewhere prevented an acquaintance such as I had hoped some day might have been established and enjoyed mutually; but our hurried meetings and brief conversations were to me ever a source of real pleasure, and I believe broadened some of my views of life. I regret not having been able to become better acquainted with the good Professor. You have suffered a very great loss, and I tender my keenest sympathy" (Charles Lang Freer to Anna Deninson [*sic*], June 17, 1918, CLFP).

66. Richard Gottheil and William H. Worrell, *Fragments from the Cairo Genizah in the Freer Collection* (University of Michigan Studies, Humanistic Series 13; New York: Macmillan, 1927).

67. Francis W. Kelsey to Charles Lang Freer, May 15, 1918, CLFP. In 1916 Kelsey similarly wrote, "This will close the work of Professor Sanders upon your Greek manuscripts, which was begun at the end of 1907. To have published the two great Facsimiles, and four monographs discussing the contents in so thorough a way as to meet the unanimous and unqualified approval of

THE ANCIENT ORIGINS OF THE WASHINGTON MANUSCRIPTS

One of the primary purposes of Freer's 1908 Egyptian excursion was to uncover as much as he could about both the ancient and more immediate origins of the manuscripts he had purchased in 1906, as well as to determine if more could be found. "Another question, which has been much considered," wrote Sanders in 1909, "concerns the place of origin of the MSS. To trace out and interpret all of the stories of Arab dealers is such a hopeless task that in despair I turned to the MSS. themselves."[68] In order to determine the ancient history of Freer's manuscripts, Sanders did just that, by noting the prayer for a certain individual named Timothy found in the subscription at the close of the Gospel of Mark. Written in three separate hands, with different shades of ink and multiple erasures, the original subscription was enclosed within labarum (or chi-rho) monograms and read Χριστὲ ἅγιε σὺ μετὰ τοῦ δούλο[υ]. This was immediately followed by the name of an early owner of the manuscript. A second and possibly successive hand, however, indicated by a similar shade of light brown ink as was used by the first hand, changed the owner's name and added an additional line followed by a single labarum that read καὶ πάντων τῶν αὐτοῦ. A slightly later third hand erased the second owner's name and rewrote in black ink υ σοῦ Τιμοθέου (see photographs on pages 43–44).[69] This same shade of black ink was also used to add a crude cursive lectionary notation within the Deuteronomy manuscript, which Sanders thought indicated scribal unfamiliarity with Greek and Greek biblical manuscripts in general.[70] Sanders distinguished the black ink of the later third hand from the brown shades of ink used by the earlier first and second hands of the Gospel subscription. The brown ink, which was used not only for the Gospel subscription but also to make other textual corrections, resembled the darker brown ink of the actual text of the manuscripts. These phenomena probably represented

---

the scholars of the world, is an achievement which might have well been spread over twenty years instead of ten. But the remarkable ability and extraordinary capacity for work which Professor Sanders contributed to this great undertaking would have had no chance to manifest themselves had it not been for your own vision and breadth of view in taking up the problem, and your generous support of the solution which was presented" (Francis W. Kelsey to Charles Lang Freer, September 12, 1916, CLFP). It should be noted that both of these affirmations of Freer by Kelsey were made *after* the purchase of the Washington Manuscript of the Minor Prophets but *prior* to any full knowledge of what the Greek manuscript actually contained as far as its content.

68. Sanders, "Age and Ancient Home," 137.

69. For discussion, see Sanders, "Age and Ancient Home," 138; idem, *Washington Manuscript of the Four Gospels,* 1–3; and, more briefly, idem, "Four Newly Discovered Biblical Manuscripts," 140. The final subscription can be translated as, "Holy Christ, be thou with your servant and all of his."

70. Sanders, *Washington Manuscript of the Four Gospels,* 3, 135; and idem, *Washington Manuscript of Deuteronomy and Joshua,* 11, 31–32. The Deuteronomy marginal or lexical notation is preceded by a labarum and reads as follows: ἐις την μνημην τω αγιω πτρω εἰς το λυχνηκο ("to the memory of the Holy Fathers for the evening time").

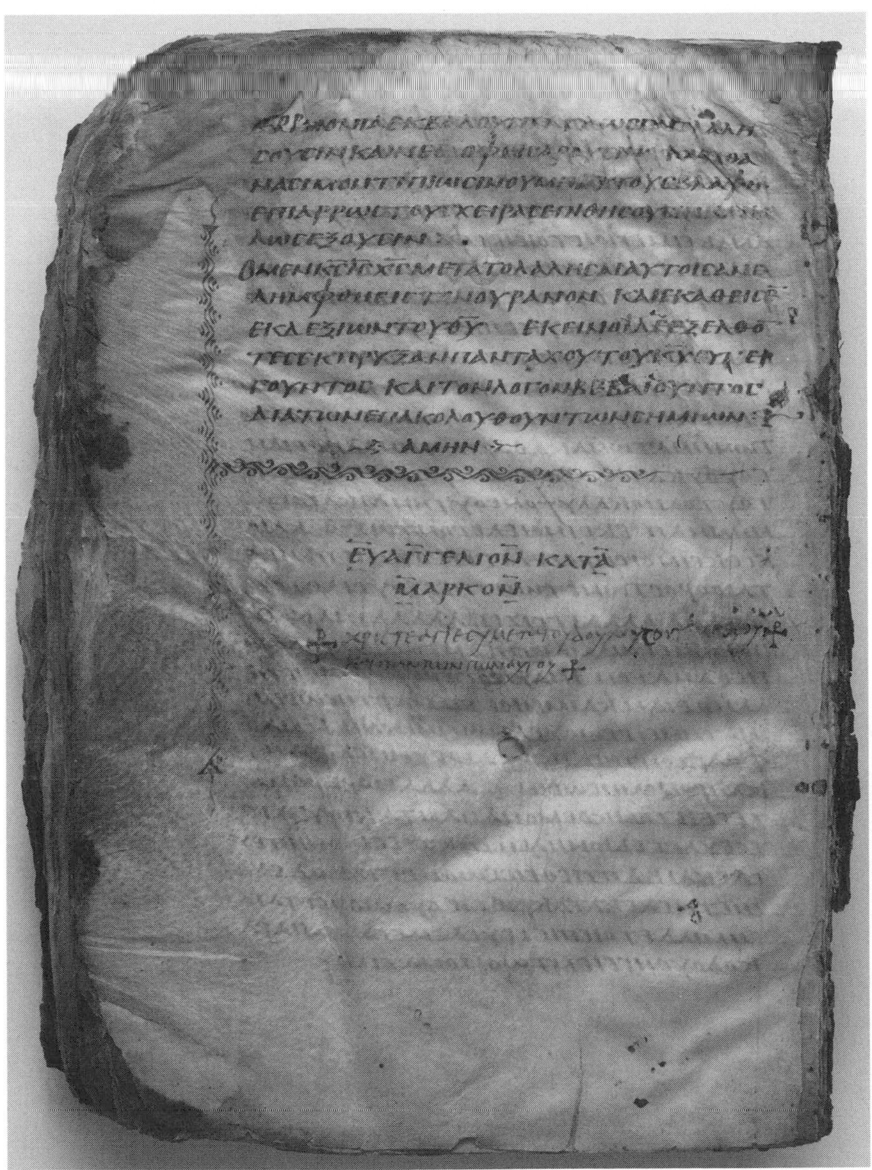

Figure 2: Freer Gospel manuscript of Mark 16:17–20. Freer Gallery of Art, Smithsonian Institution, Washington, D.C.: Gift of Charles Lang Freer, F1906.274 pg. 372. Used by permission.

Figure 3: Detail of Freer Gospel manuscript of Mark 16:17–20. Freer Gallery of Art, Smithsonian Institution, Washington, D.C.: Gift of Charles Lang Freer, F1906.274 pg. 372. Used by permission.

the work of several consecutive owners of the manuscript residing in the same Greek monastery, where *it was originally* produced in the fifth century. Since the black ink represented a cruder hand and was not used to make any corrections or additions to the actual text of the manuscripts, but was used only for extratextual elements, Sanders contended that it likely came from a sixth- or seventh-century monk in a Coptic monastery who, being less familiar with Greek, was therefore hesitant to alter the text.[71] Sanders explained the textual peculiarities, the absence of titles by first hand, and the uneven text in the manuscripts, and especially in the Gospels, as indicative of an exemplar that had originated in a time when biblical manuscripts came near to extinction, such as was the case when sacred books were ordered destroyed under Diocletian in 303 C.E.[72] Despite their differences in size, shape, and age, Sanders then concluded that the four manuscripts were brought together to form multiple volumes of a single but composite body of scriptural texts. "I am now inclined to believe that they once formed parts of a Bible in use in Upper Egypt. Either during or soon after the Moslem conquests in 636 a.d., this Bible ceased to be needed because of the withdrawal of the Greek Christians, and so was either buried or lost. The manuscripts are in consequence free from interpolations and corrections of later times."[73]

Sanders further posited from the Gospel subscription that the manuscripts were not in the possession of a private owner (contra Gregory and Goodspeed) but that the name of "Timothy" should be understood as St. Timothy and that "all his" indicated the worshipers in his church or the adherents of his monastery.[74] Citing the early thirteenth-century writings of the Armenian Abû Sâlih,

---

71. Sanders, *Washington Manuscript of Deuteronomy and Joshua*, 2.

72. Sanders, *Washington Manuscript of the Four Gospels*, 139.

73. Sanders, "New Manuscripts of the Bible," 55.

74. Sanders, "Age and Ancient Home," 138. For criticisms of Sanders's conclusions, see Gregory, *Das Freer-Logion*, 22; Goodspeed, "Notes on the Freer Gospels," 597–603. Goodspeed objected to a number of Sanders's conclusions based upon what he determined to be the likely

Sanders then argued that the only location in Egypt with a corresponding name was the church of Timothy (the namesake of which was a Roman soldier who had suffered martyrdom under Diocletian in 304 C.E.), located in the Monastery of the Vinedresser near the pyramids.[75] In the late fifth or early sixth century this Jacobite or Coptic monastery was partially [illegible] by the Melchites (Syrian, Palestinian, and Egyptian Christians who adhered to the Council of Chalcedon in 451 C.E. and rejected Monophysism). The final destruction of the Monastery of the Vinedresser seems to have taken place during the Muslim persecutions of the fourteenth century. However, Sanders maintained that it was possible that its ancient Bible was whisked away to the safety of a more remote monastery:

> The Monastery of the Vinedresser seems to have perished between 1208 and 1441, and from that date until 1906 we have no clue to the resting place of the MSS, though it is likely that they were preserved during a part of the remaining period in some more out of the way monastery. In such a ruined monastery or in some other hiding place of the desert the MSS were found, probably in 1906; for the desert sand still filled wrinkles and was incrusted on the exterior when I began work on them.... There are many doubtful points in this summary, but we may still hope that time will continue to bring additional evidence. Already I consider as certain the origin of the four MSS in Greek monasteries, their union in some Coptic monastery, such as that of the Vinedresser, and the continuance of their existence without separation from that time to the present.[76]

The Immediate Origins of the Washington Manuscripts

Although not unrelated, the question of the immediate origins of the Washington Manuscripts was considerably more litigious than the question of their ancient

---

frequency of monasteries ascribed to the name "Timothy"; the number of ancient monasteries whose names are now unknown, thus forcing Sanders to argue from silence; the absence of lectionary marks in these manuscripts, which possibly points to their not being used in monastic life; and the problematic bias expressed by Sanders in his distrust of the accounts given by Arabic dealers.

75. See Sanders, *Washington Manuscript of Deuteronomy and Joshua,* 3 n. 1, where he briefly counters Goodspeed on this issue by asserting, "A few lectionary marks are, however, found in the MS of Deuteronomy, and further I should not expect the Greek Bible to be much read in a Coptic monastery after the fifth century. Neither do Professor Goodspeed's statistics on the astounding number of early Egyptian monasteries seem to me in point. In this matter only those which survived until the eleventh or twelfth century, i.e. to the time of Abu Salîh, are of interest, for the MSS doubtless remained for a long time in the place where the last change was made in the subscription. While the MS of Abu Salîh is defective (notably on the Nitrian desert), it doubtless once contained all the monasteries and churches known to him."

76. Sanders, *Washington Manuscript of Deuteronomy and Joshua,* 3. Cf. Sanders, "Age and Ancient Home," 138–40; idem, *Washington Manuscript of the Four Gospels,* 1–3; and Abû Sâlih, *The Churches and Monasteries of Egypt and Some Neighboring Countries* (trans. B. T. A. Evetts and A. J. Butler; Oxford: Oxford University Press, 1895), 186–90.

origins. "Were Professor Sanders' theory established," wrote Goodspeed, "it would import but little, for it leaves untouched the main question of the *immediate* provenance of the manuscripts; whence they came in 1906?"[77] That this "main question" was often left "untouched" by individuals such as Freer, Kelsey, and Sanders was purposeful. Their successful efforts to veil the immediate provenance of the Washington Manuscripts extended directly from their certain conviction that there were additional manuscripts yet to be found that related to Freer's earlier 1906 purchases. Early in 1908 Kelsey wrote to Freer:

> The evidence is perfectly clear that these manuscripts formed part of a Bible and it is not improbable that other portions are still in existence. Have you any correspondent in Egypt who is sufficiently alert to be entrusted with the delicate task of so relating himself to collectors that the discovery of such manuscripts would be reported to him as soon as they might be found or come into the trade? If so, I am wondering whether you would not think it worth while to make an effort to get on track of further discoveries; for if you yourself should not feel like advancing the money to secure other manuscripts of the kind in case they should be discovered, there are other Americans who, in view of the great value which your manuscripts are now seen to possess, would be glad indeed to have the opportunity to purchase the supplementary folios; and if you could get the refusal of such manuscripts it would be possible to secure expert judgment in regard to them in a very brief time by the use of the telegraph.[78]

Sanders specifically noted the fresh appearance of the first page of the Deuteronomy and Joshua manuscript and from this concluded that it must have been divided at the time of discovery and that the first portion was probably still somewhere in Egypt.[79]

Upon Freer's purchase of the initial four Greek parchment manuscripts, Ali Arabi had told him they were discovered in Akmim (Akhmîm), also called the

---

77. Goodspeed, "Notes on the Freer Gospels," 600.

78. Francis W. Kelsey to Charles Lang Freer, January 10, 1908, CLFP. Cf. Francis W. Kelsey to Charles Lang Freer, January 15, 1908, CLFP, "I am much indebted to you for your kind letter of January 13. I thank you particularly for your effort to secure trace of the remaining parts of the Egyptian Bible."

79. Sanders, "New Manuscripts of the Bible," 50; idem, "Four Newly Discovered Biblical Manuscripts," 138. Even Goodspeed, who was often at odds with Sanders's other historical conjectures, believed there were further related manuscripts to be found and wrote, "Taken together, they [the Freer manuscripts] constitute the most important discovery of Greek biblical manuscripts made in many years. More than this, their sudden appearance, from an unknown source, combined with the excellent preservation of two of them, invites the hope that other parts of the larger codices from which these portions have come may even now be awaiting discovery in some remote convent, or in the hands of some dealer. Certainly in the case of the Septuagint manuscript of Deuteronomy-Joshua this seems likely" (Goodspeed, "Detroit Manuscripts," 218).

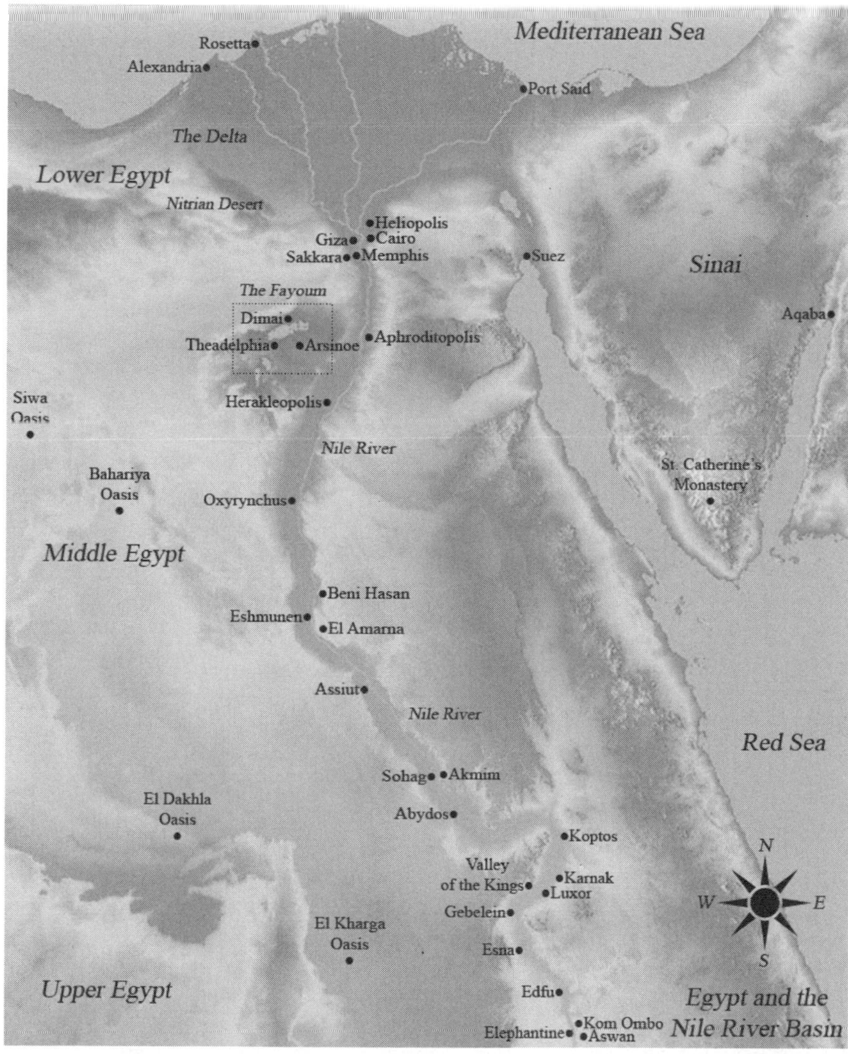

Figure 4: Egypt and its environs as related to the ancient and immediate origins of the Washington Manuscripts.

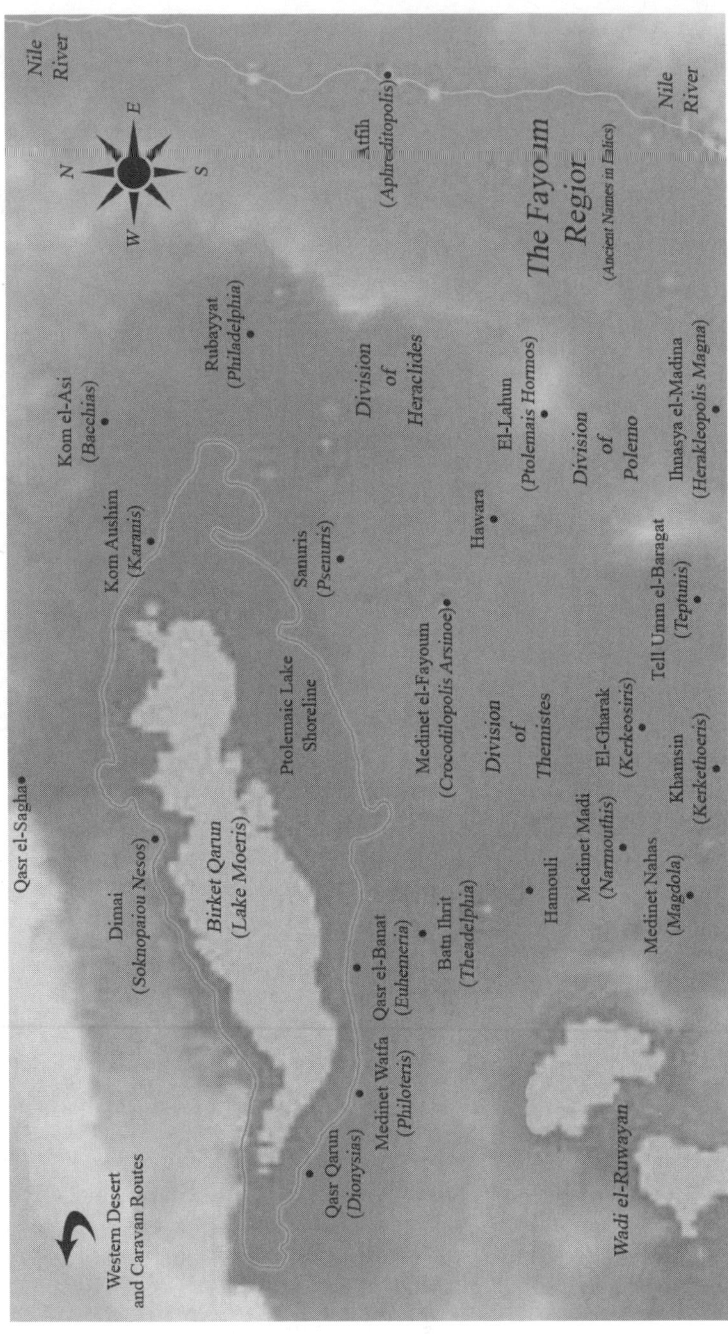

Figure 5: The Fayoum Region, ancient and modern, as it relates to the discovery of the Washington Manuscripts and other papyrus finds.

ancient Panopolis (see the maps on pages 47–48).[80] Initially this seems to have been little questioned, as in 1886 a small Greek manuscript containing the book of *Enoch*, the *Gospel of Peter*, and the *Apocalypse of Peter* was unearthed in an ancient cemetery at that location.[81] Scholars such as Kenyon and Sanders pointed out that the Akmim fragment of Enoch was written in an early sloping uncial hand that closely corresponded to the Washington Manuscript of the Gospels.[82] It was additionally noted that the last chapter of the Gospel of Mark corresponded to the *Gospel of Peter* in mentioning twelve rather than eleven remaining apostles. "This evidence is slight," wrote Kelsey to Freer, "but so far as it goes is confirmatory of the correctness of the statement in regard to the provenance of the manuscripts."[83] Further evidence was garnered to support the accuracy of Arabi's claim. In 1905 Schmidt had purchased three papyrus manuscripts containing a fourth/fifth-century Coptic epistle of *1 Clement,* a fourth/fifth century Coptic Proverbs, and an eighth-century Easter letter written in Greek. The provenance of these three manuscripts, which were all purchased together, was determined to be from a hidden library within the White Monastery near Sohag—just across the river from Akmim. The following year Schmidt purchased his Greek fragment of Genesis, which was also represented to be from the White Monastery. This bountiful and unprecedented cache of ancient texts found at the White Monastery led Schmidt to believe that the Washington Manuscripts were likely from the same location.[84] Only slightly less convinced was Goodspeed, who initially associated the Washington Manuscript of Deuteronomy with a British Museum palimpsest whose underwriting contained Homer, the Gospel of Luke, and Euclid (BL. Add. Ms. 17210–17211). Based upon what he regarded as resemblances in scribal hand and ruling a "little short of astonishing," Goodspeed speculated that Freer's manuscripts were of similar provenance to the Greek Homer, the latter found in the 1840s at the Syrian Convent of St. Mary Deipara in the Nitrian Desert west of Cairo.[85] In time, Goodspeed came generally to affirm Schmidt's belief that the

---

80. Sanders, "Proceedings," xxii; idem, "New Manuscripts of the Bible," 49; and idem, "Four Newly Discovered Biblical Manuscripts," 138.

81. For the *editio princeps,* see Urbain Bouriant, "Fragments du texte grec du livre d'Énoch et de quelques écrits attributés à saint Pierre," *Mémoires publiés par les members de la mission archéologique française au Caire* 9/1 (Paris, 1892): 93–147; J. A. Robinson and M. H. James, *The Gospel according to Peter and the Revelation of Peter* (2nd ed.; London: Clay & Sons, 1892); W. Schneemelcher and C. Maurer, "The Gospel of Peter," in Schneemelcher, *New Testament Apocrypha,* 1:216–27; and C. Detlef G. Müller, "Apocalypse of Peter," in Schneemelcher, *New Testament Apocrypha,* 2:620–38.

82. Kenyon, "Graeco-Roman Egypt," 47; Sanders, *Washington Manuscript of the Four Gospels,* 3, 138–139.

83. Kelsey to Freer, January 10, 1908.

84. Schmidt, "Die neuen griechischen Bibelhandschriften," 359–60.

85. Goodspeed, "Detroit Manuscripts," 218–20.

immediate provenance of the Washington Manuscripts was the White Monastery, although their ancient provenance was possibly one of the Nitrian Desert convents.[86] "The statement of the dealer that they came into his hands from Akhmîm is altogether likely," Goodspeed wrote, "since Akhmîm is not only a productive site for Christian antiquities, but serves as a gathering-point for antiques and curios from a wide district of Egypt."[87] Sanders likewise affirmed this:

> Considering that the manuscripts show unmistakable signs of having been long buried, I am inclined to accept the very general statement about their origin as indicating the place where they were found [in Akmim]. The four manuscripts contain portions of the Bible, in no case duplicating each other, and nothing of a different nature is contained in the collection.[88]

However, such notions began to change, at least among those immediately involved in the work on the Washington Manuscripts, following Freer's second trip to Egypt in 1908. Writing to Kelsey from the Shepheard's Hotel in Cairo on May 23, Freer began to weave a story regarding the provenance of his manuscripts purchased in 1906—a story somewhat akin to the famous travel logs written by the great explorers of the past.

> The plans made last winter in Detroit, beside a quiet hearth, seem to have worked well here, though I must say there is some difference in environment. Immediately after my arrival I met old Arabi, from whom I obtained the MSS. and found him awaiting my coming with deep interest. He was most friendly and I believe really glad to see me. The watch I brought from Detroit for his son pleased the old gentleman so much that he consented to having the son get it only after I had promised the father a better one next year! With the watch-

---

86. Goodspeed, "Notes on the Freer Gospels," 600–603. On page 602 Goodspeed writes, "[U]ntil a more probable immediate source (possibly in Nitria?) for the Freer manuscripts is proposed, most scholars will doubtless, with Schmidt, Gregory, Crum, and Hunt, refer them to the same rich deposit—the library of the White Monastery. As to their place of writing, for the Gospels codex at least there is not a little to suggest those Nitrian convents, which Jerome visited in 386, and where he may have encountered that curious reading [the Freer Logion] in Mark 16:15 which he and the Freer Gospels alone exhibit." Cf. Crum to Worrell, July 18, 1916, where the former expresses doubt in the possibility of Freer's manuscripts (and likely the Coptic ones) being discovered at the Monastery of the Vinedresser near Gizah, as it is "decidedly north of the provenance of hitherto found Sahidic texts."

87. Goodspeed, "Detroit Manuscripts," 218.

88. Sanders, "Four Newly Discovered Biblical Manuscripts," 138. Cf. idem, "New Manuscripts of the Bible," 55: "What I have thus far learned of the four manuscripts is not inconsistent with the statement that they came from Akhmîm." This is further confirmed in Francis W. Kelsey to Charles Lang Freer, January 28, 1908, CLFP, in which the former asks, "whether it would be worthwhile to have some competent scholar accustomed to such matters spend a month or six weeks at Akhmim and in the vicinity, establishing free and friendly relations with the natives; valuable information, and possible opportunities, might result."

> business amicably settled, I made immediate purchases, at liberal prices, from both father and son…. The grandson, too, was given a present and disposed of. The ladies of a Mohammedan family are never seen by strangers, so, the coast having been cleared, I went gently, but firmly, at my wily old friend for facts concerning the discovery of the MSS. He listened intently and patiently to my many questions but declined to make any promises that day, adding he must give a night of thought to the matter because another person, "the finder", must have consideration.[89]

Arabi then produced for Freer a badly deteriorated parchment manuscript, blackened and worm-eaten much like his fragment of the Pauline Epistles, written in ancient Greek and of a single column to each narrow page. Upon inquiring of Arabi where it had come from, Freer was told it had been dug up during his absence from the same place where the four earlier manuscripts were found. Freer immediately bought it and asked for more, hoping to acquire further portions of the Deuteronomy and Joshua or Gospels manuscripts.[90] After stating that he had no more manuscripts like those already purchased, Arabi promised to show Freer a few single sheets—one with a small portrait—and some early fragments of Greek pottery the following morning. They then returned together to Cairo, and after accompanying Arabi to a doctor's appointment, Freer "drank villainous coffee with old Arabi and my faithful dragoman [Ibrahim Aly] in a shocking café, until long past my usual bedtime."[91]

Returning the next day with his dragoman to the house of Arabi, Freer proceeded to purchase stone and pottery shards, a small stone stele of Isis, and several more badly deteriorated manuscripts consisting of a few single sheets and fragments of "biblical Greek writing" as well as one sheet of two leaves containing "Hellenic Greek."[92] Assuring Freer that he now owned everything that had been

---

89. Freer to Kelsey, May 23, 1908.

90. Freer has most certainly confused this "MS. on old parchment" and written in "ancient Greek" with what was really the Coptic Psalter. More curious in this regard is Freer's later statement that he took the manuscript to Professor D. P. Callimachos at the Greek College, who told him that the manuscript was "biblical and of an early period and that he believed it came from the place in which the others were found" (Freer to Kelsey, May 23, 1908). Though it seems improbable that someone from the Greek College would not be able to differentiate between Coptic and Greek, the manuscript's deteriorated and delicate state likely made it impossible to examine anything but the top leaves. Recall, as well, the difficulty Sanders initially had in identifying this same manuscript as Coptic (but "written with many Greek words," Kelsey to Freer, September 21, 1908).

91. Freer to Kelsey, May 23, 1908.

92. Once again, Freer's identification of these fragments is problematic. Professor Callimachos identified the one sheet of two leaves as an ode pertaining to one of the Grecian islands written in the style of the famous Greek poet Pindar (ca. 518–438 B.C.E.). The single sheets and fragments he determined to be in ancient Greek, but not from the same books. Some portion of this material also, however, almost certainly constituted the Coptic homily on the Virgin written

purchased from the original "digger," Arabi went on to disclose that the "digger" himself still had in his possession some small manuscript fragments as well as the original wooden table upon which the manuscripts originally sat. "This news lifted my hat," exclaimed Freer, who then proceeded to "beg" Arabi to take him to the digger wherever he might be. Arabi declined, explaining that he himself could not endure such a journey in the "blistering hot sun," even if it had to be made at night. Before parting that evening, Arabi introduced Freer to a "giant of an Arab" named Haggi, who lived near the pyramids. Haggi, who was also an antiquities dealer, knew the "digger" and promised to start out that evening for his house in order that he might bring back the wooden table and manuscript fragments for Freer's inspection. Stirred by the day's events, Freer wrote:

> When we parted late that night in town, Arabi took my right hand in his, pressed it warmly, made an earnest little speech in Arabic and then, after moving his right hand across his throat and after having pressed his fingers to his lips, he strode away. My dragoman then walked with me to my hotel and said that "everything, now, would end well"! Arabi had just pledged me in the presence of two Arab friends, that he would tell me only the truth about the MSS. and all that he knew with one exception—i.e. he would not divulge the name of the "digger."[93]

During Haggi's absence, Freer wrote of his meetings with Nahman and the latter's helpfulness in assisting with the difficult process of exporting antiquities out of the country despite the watchful eyes of the Egyptian Museum authorities.[94] Several days later Haggi returned to Cairo in possession of a little ebony

---

by Theophilus. Included within the Freer-Arabi correspondence (CLFP) are numerous pages of an undated itemization written on "Shepheard's Hotel & Ghezireh Palace Cairo" letterhead. Listed among all the items that Freer purchased on his second trip to Egypt in 1908 are his manuscript acquisitions. These included (as annotated by Freer) one fragment of a small parchment biblical book written in Greek; seven packages containing, in part, a portrait sheet and a sheet written in Hellenic Greek; a tin biscuit box filled with manuscripts and containing, in part, eight larger parchment sheets preserving a "chant" written in old Greek; forty-eight packages containing one manuscript each written variously in "Hebrew-Arabic" and Greek; one packaged roll containing one manuscript (modern); and one illuminated page of a Persian book.

93. Freer to Kelsey, May 23, 1908.

94. By the Egyptian laws governing the export of antiquities, individuals were required to clear their purchases through the director of the Egyptian Museum. Near the conclusion of his first trip to Egypt in 1906–1907, Freer recorded the great difficulty he had in gaining permission to export several of the items he had purchased. At that time, the museum director was a German Egyptologist named Émile Brugsch (1842–1930), whose guardianship over antiquities led to a heated argument between himself and Freer, prompting the latter to write to his office manager, "The red tape in this land surpasses that of all other countries. And as for getting antiquities out of Egypt, it's worse than getting oneself out of Hades" (Charles Lang Freer to J. M. Kennedy, January 22, 1907, CLFP). See also Gunter, *Collector's Journey,* 86, 98, 115.

table inlaid with ivory, a small wooden figure of Isis, and about fifty single sheets of "Hebrew Arabic" manuscript fragments—all found since Freer's last visit by the "digger" in the same location where the four biblical manuscripts were discovered. Although Freer expressed confidence in the stated discovery location of [illegible] script fragments, which turned out to be various letters and documents from the Cairo Genizah. Freer's letter to Kelsey exudes his excitement:

> Now, the place of digging is not Akhmim! but, according to Arabi and Haggi, at Medinet Dimay (Soonopaei Nesus) on the edge of the Libyan desert, in the mountains rising from Lake Karoun in the Fayoum district. One can reach the Fayoum in about two hours, by railroad, from Cairo, but from the railway station at Fayoum to Medinet Dimay takes three days, by camels, across the desert, as well as a boat trip across the lake; which in the present heat and low water is impossible for me. Another route, all land, is via the Gizeh pyramids, and from there, all desert, by camels, seven days. Haggi has volunteered to organize an expedition, as a shooting party, and start at once with myself as chief sportsman—save the term. My dragoman also volunteers, but warns me of the danger of the heat and the fact that the desert Arabs would know that this is not the hunting season and that they would follow us everywhere, and that even at night, we could not get to the "digging" without being seen.[95]

Arabi instead laid out a wiser plan, which would have Freer return to Egypt in November and under the authority of the Smithsonian Institution seek formal permission to conduct excavations at the site. Arabi then suggested that he and Haggi provide all the necessary funding up to £10,000 and join Freer as half partners. Arabi promised that the unnamed and unknown "digger" would direct them where to dig. "What a combination," Freer wrote in his letter to Kelsey, "The half I would receive could easily pass through the eye of a needle."[96] Nevertheless, the Egyptians expressed their willingness to take Freer hunting the following winter in the locality and at night to show him the very spot where the Washington Manuscripts were found. Freer closed his letter by writing:

> The earnestness of the party, together with the absolute acceptance of their story by my dragoman, convinces me that the MSS. now in Detroit and the little table recently bought were found in the old monastery at Medinet Dimay. I am told that only the "digger" has ever dug in this place, that only the lower walls of the monastery remain, that he has worked only in one corner of the large basement, and that the "digger" was jailed three years by Maspero, for similar misdeeds

95. Freer to Kelsey, May 23, 1908. To my knowledge, this letter constitutes the first instance in which the immediate provenance of the Washington Manuscripts is given as Dimai (ancient Soknopaiou Nesos) on the Northern shore of Birket Qarun in the Fayoum.

96. Freer to Kelsey, May 23, 1908.

> elsewhere, and that if caught at his present work, he will be sentenced to serve six years. The monastery is located in the centre of what was once a large walled city, now abandoned, but the city walls they say, are still partly standing.... Arabi is sure that there must be more at Medinet Dimay!!!!... Getting together these details, meeting the Arabs, the dealers and experts, and experiencing strange personal suggestions—both physical and mental—have made the ten days and nights rather eventful.... In working to get information, I deemed it unwise to refer to Arabi's statement of last year that the MSS were discovered at Akhmim. My dragoman warned me against facing an Arab with an untruth, fearing the majority of that class would enjoy telling another even worse. He should know, being himself Arab.[97]

In corroboration of this letter to Kelsey is an untitled and undated three-page document written in Freer's own hand. Likely recorded while Arabi related his account to Freer at his home, it adds a number of additional details pertaining to the Washington Manuscripts and their discovery, which I summarize here. Arabi and the "digger," for example, had been friends for many years. Arabi would advance him money to help cover the expenses of carrying on his clandestine work, and in return the "digger" would either bring all items found directly to Arabi alone or send them by the hand of Haggi Mahomedo. Arabi's refusal to disclose the name of the "digger" and to acquiesce to Freer's request to meet him was clearly occasioned by the man's genuine fear of serious reprisals should his unlawful "excavations" be discovered by the Egyptian authorities. The four biblical manuscripts that were purchased in December of 1906 were unearthed by the "digger" at night and only discovered a month or so before being shown to Freer. Prior to Freer's first examination of the manuscripts, Arabi showed them to only one other individual—an "Englishman"—who after finding out Freer had purchased them returned to Cairo and harshly scolded Arabi for selling what could have fetched £5,000 in England. Arabi apparently replied to the Englishman that he was satisfied with his sale to the "American."[98] The note goes on to

97. Freer to Kelsey, May 23, 1908. Cf. the earlier letter of Freer to Hecker, May 16, 1908. Freer's letter to Kelsey can be viewed alongside his diary entries beginning with Friday, May 15, 1908, and proceeding through to Tuesday, May 25, 1908. The reference to Maspero refers to Gaston Camille Charles Maspero (1846–1911), the French Egyptologist who was named the director of the first Egyptian Antiquities Museum located in Cairo. He served as the longtime director of the Egyptian Antiquities Service, which was the predecessor of the Supreme Council of Antiquities.

98. Sanders (*Washington Manuscript of Deuteronomy and Joshua,* 1) explains that just prior to Freer's acquisition of the manuscripts, Arabi had shown them to the distinguished British papyrologists Bernard P. Grenfell (1869–1926) and Arthur S. Hunt (1871–1934). Despite examining them in unfavorable light, they suggested to the archaeologist and Fellow of the Royal Geographic Society David G. Hogarth (1862–1927) that the manuscripts be recommended to the British Museum for purchase; however, nothing ever came of this. It seems likely that the "Englishman" Arabi refers to is Grenfell, Hunt, or Hogarth. A Professor Stern of the Royal

record further details regarding the geography and isolation of Dimai: the difficulty in traveling to the location, the fact that the "digger" was the first individual to "excavate" there, the discovery of the four biblical manuscripts on the "digger's" first attempt at that place, the spot within the temple or monastery at Dimai where Freer's manuscripts were found, and Freer's certainty that more manuscripts remained to be discovered there.[99]

Even more enthusiastic than Freer's letter to Kelsey is Kelsey's response to Freer dated June 18, 1908. "Your letter of May 23 (written on my birthday!) was the most absorbingly interesting communication that I ever received," wrote an exuberant Kelsey, adding, "It reads like those pages in Layard's Nineveh and in other books of exploration in lands under Turkish rule—no novel is compara-

---

Library in Berlin had also seen several poor-quality photographs of the manuscripts (though not the actual manuscripts themselves) but declined to purchase them at the determined price. In contrast to the statements of Arabi, see especially Henry A. Sanders to Charles Lang Freer, September 11, 1908, CLFP. Here Sanders outlines Schmidt's belief that the four manuscripts were first discovered at Akmim, that they initially appeared around 1895 rather than 1906, that they were first offered for sale at Eshmunen and Assiut rather than Cairo, and that Schmidt had apparently been shown the manuscripts at an unspecified time prior to their purchase by Freer. In addition, Sanders also states in this letter that Grenfell was offered the manuscripts prior to, rather than after, "the Germans" (i.e., Stern, but possibly Schmidt as well). There do not appear to be adequate explanations of Schmidt's specific assertions that the manuscripts first appeared around 1895 and that he had been shown them to others before Freer, but see below for further discussion of all these points.

99. Untitled and undated notes of Charles Lang Freer included in miscellaneous correspondence to Ali El Arabi, CLFP. It is important to note that the immediate provenance of the Washington Manuscript of the Minor Prophets, Freer's fifth Greek parchment codex purchased from Nahman through Askren later in 1916, may not be the same as the four Washington Manuscripts he purchased from Arabi in 1906. Arguing from the Coptic glosses in the manuscript, Sanders and Schmidt (*Minor Prophets*, 48) indicate only that "[T]he home of the MS was in Sahidic territory or in that of some closely allied dialect. Neither is the fact that both Greek and Coptic notes are found on the margins of W [Sanders's sigla for the Minor Prophets manuscript] a proof that the MS changed its home. Everything in the Greek text and Greek glosses of W tends to ally the MS with the Achmimic and Sahidic traditions. The monastery where it was preserved and for which it was probably written was either Coptic or affiliated with the Copts. With the waning of the Greek influence in the country districts during the fourth and fifth centuries Copts replaced the Greeks in some monasteries and in still more there ceased to be Greek speaking Copts. That is probably what happened in the ancient home of W." Askren stated (Askren to Kesley, August 13, 1916) that Nahman thought the Minor Prophets manuscript "came from Akmim" and was "a part of thc book that Mr. Freer bought some years ago." But cf. Francis W. Kelsey to Charles Lang Freer, October 7, 1916, CLFP, who stated that "Nahman is probably mistaken in asserting a direct connection between this Manuscript and the other Greek Manuscripts in your collection." However, see also Kelsey to Hecker, March 15, 1920, where Kelsey writes, "Mr. Grenfell, who has examined all this material with me, gives it as his opinion that the papyrus of the Minor Prophets has nothing whatever to do with the [Coptic] Hamouli manuscripts, and that very likely it came from the same place as the Freer parchments. It is totally unlike the Morgan material."

ble in interest, because you are dealing with actual persons and conditions, and instead of a fictitious plot there is a real and worthy underlying purpose to be carried out."[100] Kelsey then went on to extol their good fortune in light of the fact that the true provenance of the Washington Manuscripts had been further shrouded from inquirers by Carl Schmidt's recent but erroneous assertion in *Theologisches Literaturzeitung* that they were found in the White Monastery near Akmim:

> But the list of finds which were sold to [Schmidt] as from [the White Monastery] seems to me quite inconsistent with your finds. I will not stop to discuss the matter at length; your narrative seems to me to have the earmarks of actuality—I believe that you now have the ultimate facts, and will be able to make still further discoveries, provided not a breath is whispered in regard to the facts. So Mr. Sanders and I rejoice in Schmidt's cocksureness—which some day he will repent of! And meanwhile Mr. Sanders and I have agreed never to speak or write of the manuscripts to others unless asked about them, and in case of inquiries about the place of discovery, to refer the person to Schmidt's notice. This, you see, will throw everybody off the scent until you have had time to explore that monastic library (which I shall not refer to by name) and convince yourself that you have everything that it still conceals. It is best to let the whole matter sink out of public notice, so far as possible, until this has been done.[101]

This attempt to conceal the true origins of the Washington Manuscripts worked only in part, for after Freer's second trip to Egypt in 1908, and the information it garnered, all involved kept in strict confidence any mention of Dimai. However, they strongly disassociated these prized biblical treasures from Akmim. After receiving and responding to an offprint of Goodspeed's *Biblical World* article for March 1908, Kelsey shared with Freer, "In acknowledging it I felt obliged

---

100. Francis W. Kelsey to Charles Lang Freer, June 18, 1908, CLFP. For the reference to Layard, see among his numerous works on Nineveh, Sir Austen Henry Layard, *Nineveh and Its Remains: With an Account of a Visit to the Chaldæan Christians of Kurdistan and the Yezidis or Devil-Worshippers; and an Inquiry into the Manners and Arts of the Ancient Assyrians* (2 vols.; London: Murray, 1849); idem, *Discoveries in the Ruins of Nineveh and Babylon: With Travels in Armenia, Kurdistan and the Desert* (London: Murray, 1853).

101. Kelsey to Freer, June 18, 1908. See also Francis W. Kelsey to Charles Lang Freer, July 3, 1908, CLFP: "I am glad that you wrote as you did about keeping within the narrowest possible circle the information in regard to the place of discovery and any future plans. Mr. Sanders and I, in accordance with the understanding mentioned in our previous letter, are referring all to the communication in the *Theologisches Literaturzeitung,* which works like a charm, because the writer is so cock-sure! The success of future operations depends upon the care with which the truth is guarded. The site is so accessible that even a rogue hint would set excavators upon the hunt, and I suspect that very little digging would be necessary to uncover whatever may be left of similar sort to that already found." Cf. Schmidt, "Die neuen griechischen Bibelhandschriften," 359–60: "In Wahrheit stammen alle vier MSS. aus der berühmten Bibliothek des Schenute-Klosters von Atripe in der Nähe von Sohag (gegenüber Achmim gelegen)."

to say to him that the evidence seems to me to point to an altogether different source than the White Monastery."[102] In similar fashion, Sanders responded to Schmidt's article by stating that his Akmim manuscripts were all written on papyrus rather than parchment and showed absolutely no relationship to the Washington Manuscripts in their content or style of writing. Sanders asserted further that the decayed condition of the Washington Manuscripts, excluding the Gospels that had been protected by their wood covers, precluded their being discovered in so secure a place as the White Monastery.[103] Sanders concluded his response to Schmidt by contending:

> Professor Schmidt has probably been deceived by one of the numerous Arab stories; all are of equal value with the first one told, viz. that the MSS. came from Akhmim. To accept the White Monastery as the last home of the MSS. would imply that this first story was near the truth. Yet anyone acquainted with Arab stories would advise us to look in every other direction first, as toward the Nitrian Desert, or the Fayoum, or the region toward Sinai, if we wish to find the last resting place of this ancient Bible.[104]

Freer's affirmation, however, of the story relayed to him by Arabi and Haggi appears to have some warrant. Many of the details pertaining to both the general region and specific location where the Washington Manuscripts were supposedly discovered reveal close similarities to independent descriptions of Dimai and its environs. Grenfell, Hunt, and Hogarth, for example, discussed such features as the general location and remoteness of Dimai, its placement upon the summit of a slope located just north of the lake named Birket Qarun, the seasonal fluctuation of water levels in Birket Qarun, the stone causeway dividing the town site,

---

102. Francis W. Kelsey to Charles Lang Freer, March 16, 1909, CLFP. Cf. Goodspeed, "Detroit Manuscripts," 218–26.

103. Sanders, "Age and Ancient Home," 140–41.

104. Ibid., 141. Cf. Sanders, *Washington Manuscript of the Four Gospels*, 3–4: "The dealer long since acknowledged that his statement about buying the MSS in Akhmîm was made merely to mislead. Through him Mr. Freer has been able to get in touch with the supposed finders, and various other purchases have been made of articles which are said to have come from the same ruined monastery, and which are entirely consistent with such an explanation. Of these I may mention a diminutive Coptic Psalter of the fifth or sixth century; a badly decayed cluster of parchment leaves with Coptic writing, out of which two fragments of five or six different MSS, all diminutive, have been secured, notably a Psalter of the fourth (?) century; a single leaf of a Greek MS of an unknown church writer (Slavonic uncial of the eighth or ninth century); a small holder or seat having a curved top of wood inlaid with ivory, a fine piece of work, but badly decayed.... While I am not yet allowed to publish the exact spot where the MSS were found, the statements made by the finders fix it definitely and are consistent with the evidence gathered. The place would be a likely refuge for monks from the ruined Monastery of the Vinedresser, and diggers finding MSS there would naturally take them to Gizeh for sale." But cf. Goodspeed's response to Sanders in Goodspeed, "Notes on the Freer Gospels," 600–603.

the wall-encircled temples, the size and layout of the temples, and the remains of houses whose partly collapsed walls preserved objects underneath the rubble. All these aspects support, and at times remarkably so, the account of Arabi and Haggi.[105] Although the description of Dimai provided by Grenfell, Hunt, and Hogarth predates the discovery of the Washington Manuscripts by over half a decade, it is unlikely that the "digger," Arabi, or Haggi were influenced by this or any other written narrative. It seems equally unlikely that a more popular knowledge of the area served as a basis for the account furnished by Arabi and Haggi, especially given the region's isolation as well as the unambiguous details proffered. If the Washington Manuscripts were not actually discovered at this location, a great deal of thought and effort went into correctly describing Dimai and the surrounding area. If false, wherever the story related to Freer came from, it appears to have originated from an individual closely familiar with Dimai.[106]

The town of Dimai (Dime, Dimê, Dimei, Dimey, or Dimia) or Dimeh al-Siba ("Dimeh of the Lions") was likely established by Ptolemy II Philadelphus (309–246 B.C.E.), although excavations have shown habitation of the site as far back as the Neolithic period.[107] The town is situated about ninety kilometers southwest of Cairo on the northern shore of modern Birkat Qarun (ancient Lake Moeris and the Korah of Num 16:1), in the region of the Fayoum (Fayum, Fayûm, Faiyum,

---

105. Bernard P. Grenfell, Arthur S. Hunt, and David G. Hogarth, *Fayûm Towns and Their Papyri* (London: Egypt Exploration Fund, 1900), 6–7, 18–19, 22–25.

106. The discordant details in the account given by Arabi and Haggi include (1) the location of discovery of the manuscripts (Akmim or Dimai), (2) the number of people who were first shown the manuscripts (Grenfell alone or Schmidt as well), (3) the date the manuscripts initially appeared (1895 or 1906), (4) where the manuscripts were first shown (Eshmunen and Assiut or Cairo), and (5) the assertion that the "digger" was the first individual to "excavate" at Dimai. The first two discrepancies have already been discussed above. For discussion of the next two discrepancies, see below. With regard to the final discrepancy, Grenfell and Hunt remarked that the ruins of Dimai showed clear evidence of having been thoroughly ransacked by native diggers and even went on to refer to several excavations undertaken at the site between 1887 and 1894. Following this period they mention a specific Copt who, after receiving permission to dig at Dimai, destroyed many of the papyri that had been left there, as he was only interested in statuettes. Grenfell and Hunt also noted, most interestingly, that Dimai constituted one of the richest sites for papyri in Egypt, that it had papyri spread evenly over it, and that none of the many finds there dated later than the third century. They noted further that they themselves purchased a "find" that came from the Dimai temple and contained nearly one hundred well-preserved Demotic and Greek rolls concerning the priests and dating to the second century B.C.E. (the Greek texts now constitute part of the Amherst Papyri Collection). See Grenfell, Hunt, and Hogarth, *Fayûm Towns*, 7, 10, 15–16, 18–20, 22.

107. For contemporary accounts of this region, see John Baines and Jaromír Málek, *Atlas of Ancient Egypt* (New York: Facts on File Publications, 1984), 53, 121, 131; and the famous *Baedeker's Egypt* (4th ed.; Upper Saddle River, N.J.: Prentice Hall, 1990), 184–89.

or Fayyum from Coptic Peiom or Phiom meaning "the Lake").[108] The ancient Ptolemaic town site served as a port where goods were brought from Medinet el Fayoum (ancient Crocodilopolis Arsinoe) across the lake by boat to stock the caravans departing into the Western Desert and beyond to the Mediterranean [illegible] (Σοκνοπαίου Νῆσος), meaning "Island of the crocodile god," and may indicate that it once lay as an isle in the midst of Lake Moeris, although more recent geological and topographical studies indicate it was more likely a peninsula.[110] Ptolemy II continued the earlier process of land reclamation in the region, and the level of the lake was significantly lowered through a series of canals and locks, thus providing irrigation and fertile land for retired Greco-Macedonian soldiers and settlers.[111] A Roman cemetery located on a prominent hill to the southwest of Dimai indicates that soldiers were once stationed here. The site probably served as an isolated frontier post protecting against desert marauders, while other sites such as Karanis and Philadelpha, with more cultivated and therefore hospitable land, became more thoroughly populated by the Romans. Dimai flourished until approximately 336 C.E. and, due in large part to its remoteness, was one of the earliest Fayoum cities to be abandoned.

Today Dimai stands sixty-five feet above and two and a half kilometers from the greenish and slightly brackish waters of Birkat Qarun. The widely spread ruins of the town consist of well-preserved multilevel houses, underground storage chambers, and two mudbrick temples encircled by walls measuring in some places 10 m in height by 5 m in depth. The larger of the two temples, or the northern temple, was built from stone and was likely dedicated to the god Soknopaios (a form of the Egyptian crocodile god Sobek-en-Pai, later known as Suchos). The

108. Based upon his travels to Egypt, the famous Greek historian Herodotus (ca. 485–424 B.C.E.) described the dimensions of the "astonishing" Lake Moeris as being 3,600 *stades* or sixty *schoeni* in circumference (about 445 miles) and equal to the length of the entire Egyptian coastline, its greatest depth being fifty fathoms (*Hist.* 2.149–150). Cf. Pliny the Elder (23–79 C.E.), who portrayed the lake as even larger (Pliny, *Natural History* [trans. J. Bostock and H. T. Rily; 6 vols.; London: Bell, 1898], 1:49).

109. An early account of ancient Crocodilopolis Arsinoe (Medinet el Fayoum), one of the largest ancient sites in Egypt, is given by the Greek historian and geographer Strabo (ca. 63 B.C.E.–24 C.E.; *Geogr.* 17.1.35).

110. Herodotus (*Hist.* 2.71) writes of the adoration of the Lake Moeris crocodiles.

111. Strabo (*Geogr.* 17.1.37) writes, "The lake Moeris, by its magnitude and depth, is able to sustain the superabundance of water which flows into it at the time of the rise of the river, without overflowing the inhabited and cultivated parts of the country. On the decrease of the water of the river, it distributes the excess by the same canal at each of the mouths; and both the lake and the canal preserve a remainder, which is used for irrigation. These are the natural and independent properties of the lake [*contra* Herodotus above], but in addition, on both mouths of the canal are placed locks, by which engineers store up and distribute the water which enters or issues from the canal."

smaller temple, or the southern temple, was built from stone and brick and may date back to the early Christian period. The town is divided in half by an ancient Roman road 370 meters long, which was at one time flanked by sculpted crouching lions and was therefore known as the "Avenue of the Lions." This wide road begins at the entrance to the temples and runs down to the water's edge, where it ends at several stepped limestone piers where an ancient quay was once located. Just eight kilometers north of Dimai, the German botanist and explorer Georg August Schweinfurth (1836–1925) discovered the Old Kingdom temple of Qasr el Sagha in 1884, which legend says was built by a young pharaoh who, being chased by wild dogs to the edge of the lake, was rescued by a crocodile and, thus, the young pharaoh erected the temple in its honor.

Despite the certainty expressed by individuals such as Freer, Kelsey, and Sanders regarding the veracity of Dimai as the long-time resting place of the Washington Manuscripts, it is interesting to note that at every opportunity verification of this "fact" was sought. In 1908 Sanders traveled to Europe in order to compare the Washington Manuscripts with other ancient manuscript collections, hoping to see if he could draw out affinities that would be indicative of provenance. Having already been fully apprised of Freer's dealings with Arabi and Haggi earlier in May, Sanders traveled to Berlin on two separate occasions for the purpose of personally interviewing Schmidt. Writing to Freer in September regarding the content of these meetings, Sanders described Schmidt's mistaken but sincere belief that Freer's manuscripts were from the White Monastery, that Schmidt's own three manuscripts were discovered in a grave in Akmim and purchased shortly after his 1895 trip, that Freer's manuscripts appeared about this time, that Arabi had shown the Washington Manuscripts to Schmidt prior to their purchase by Freer, and that they were first shown in Eshmunen and Assiut.[112]

Just prior to Dennison's departure to take part in the Archeological Congress in Cairo in 1909, Kelsey wrote to him on behalf of Freer requesting that "when

---

112. Sanders to Freer, September 11, 1908. Although primarily recording what Sanders believed to be Schmidt's erroneous understanding of the history of the Washington Manuscripts, this letter adds other important "possibilities" to the scenario, such as the purchase of these manuscripts by Arabi from another dealer (perhaps the "digger" or Haggi) for £500, Arabi's initial inability to sell the manuscripts and his attempt to return them to the dealer, the possession of the ebony and ivory reading table by Arabi as early as March 1907, and Schmidt's belief that Freer had paid £1,500 for the manuscripts. The letter also records details surrounding the purchase of manuscripts by Schmidt following his 1895 trip to Egypt, including false accusations leveled at him by the Egyptian authorities asserting he had bribed the monks of the White Monastery in order to coerce them into selling him manuscripts illegally. For unexplained contradictory statements regarding the date Schmidt purchased his three manuscripts containing *1 Clement* in Coptic, a Coptic Proverbs, and an Easter letter in Greek, compare Sanders's letter to Schmidt (wherein 1895 is the given date) with Sanders, "Age and Ancient Home," 140 (wherein 1905 is the given date).

in Cairo you might avail yourself of such opportunities as might be presented for gaining any additional information in regard to the place of discovery of the Greek manuscripts, besides learning whether any additional manuscripts have come to light within the past year."[113] Kelsey then went on to list for Dennison [illegible] Akmim, the White Monastery, Eshmunen, Assiut, the Fayoum, Dimai, the Nitrian Desert, and the Monastery of the Vinedresser near the pyramids.[114] Kelsey later wrote to Freer, who had already embarked upon his fourth Asian journey and last trip to Egypt, telling of Dennison's meeting with Arabi:

> The gist of the matter is that before leaving Cairo Mr. Dennison procured the services of the dragoman whom you recommended and had a final conference with Ali Arabi. This astute Arab made to Mr. Dennison substantially the same statement which he made to you a year ago, but reported that the man who then acted as a go-between [possibly Haggi] was now dead, his place being taken by another; that greater caution than ever was necessary in bringing the finds to Cairo; that some manuscript material, of the value of which he was not informed, had been discovered and it would be some time yet before it could safely be brought to Cairo. It seemed to me extremely probable that the manuscript material to which Ali Arabi referred was already in Cairo, but that he, not unnaturally, desired to reserve it for your eyes alone. I sincerely hope that when you do see it you will find it of like value with the manuscripts which you have already bought.[115]

After actually visiting and photographing the site of Dimai with Worrell in 1913, the conviction Sanders held that this served as the location of the imme-

---

113. Francis W. Kelsey to Walter Dennison, March 19, 1909, CLFP.

114. Regarding the dismissal of an early rumor that the Washington Manuscripts were discovered at Eshmunen or Assiut, or at least first shown there by a dealer, see Sanders, "Age and Ancient Home," 141, "I further learned from Professor Schmidt, that the Freer MSS. were first heard of in the hands of a dealer of Eshmunên, who showed them at the Mission School in Assiut, and then sold them to Ali Arabi. On inquiry, however, I learned from Dr. Grant of the school, and from the Rev. Dr. Kyle of the United Presbyterian's Missions, that the MSS. were never shown at the school." See also Sanders, *Washington Manuscript of Deuteronomy and Joshua,* 2, where he states further, "The story that they were shown in Assiut has been proved false, and no reliance can be placed on the first statements of the dealer and others that they were bought in Akhmim or Eshmunên, especially as both statements have since been denied. This denial also takes away support from Professor Schmidt's statement (*Theolog. Literaturzeit.*), that these four MSS came from the White Monastery near Sohag, opposite Akhmim, whence were derived four MSS (two Coptic and two Greek) bought by him. Schmidt's assertion is still more discredited by the failure thus far of any of the MSS to show that close text relationship to the Coptic versions of the Bible which he anticipated" (Sanders to Freer, September 11, 1908).

115. Kelsey to Freer, July 8, 1909. The "manuscript material" mentioned here most certainly comprised at least part of the content of Freer's purchases upon his arrival in Egypt in late July.

diate provenance of the Washington Manuscripts was slightly shaken. Failing to find what he expected would be clear evidence of a Christian presence at Dimai, he expressed in a letter to Freer that he was "much disappointed at not finding definite proofs of Christian occupation of Dime, but I had to confess that such was the case. Dr. Worrell, to be sure, thought that certain signs looked 'somewhat Christian' and the walls must have been capable of defense even 500 years ago." Sanders concluded the issue by affirming that "Christian occupation of Dime very doubtful and in any case temporary."[116] Although these results were clearly disappointing for Sanders, he became only a little less resolute that the ruins of Dimai had concealed the Washington manuscripts up until 1906. "As Professor Sanders points out," wrote Kelsey to Freer after reading Sanders's initial report, "nothing decisive can be learned until the ruins of Dime have been so fully excavated that any remains of occupation in the Christian period will have come to light."[117] Sanders felt confident enough in his now long-held convictions that he recommended broad-ranging excavations of Dimai. Even Kelsey remarked further that it was incredible to think that a company of monks large enough to have had the manuscripts in their charge could have sojourned on the site long enough to select a place for their hiding without leaving some trace of their presence.[118] As late as 1917, in the critical edition of the Washington Manuscript of the Psalms, Sanders commented that he had nothing to add to the story of the purchase and immediate provenance of the manuscripts, as he had personally visited "the supposed place of discovery and find it not inconsistent with the story told."[119]

---

116. Henry A. Sanders to Charles Lang Freer, June 26, 1913, CLFP.

117. Francis W. Kelsey to Charles Lang Freer, April 9, 1913, CLFP.

118. Kelsey to Freer, April 9, 1913.

119. Sanders, *The Washington Manuscript of the Psalms*, 107. The following reconstruction provides an outline of the contradictory statements surrounding the purchase of the Washington Manuscripts. In the summer of 1895 Schmidt hears of his three manuscripts. Schmidt later tells Sanders that they were bought a short time after this on his recommendation (but Sanders later contradicts this by stating Schmidt's three manuscripts were purchased together in 1905). The Freer manuscripts are said to have appeared about this time (i.e., 1895; but Arabi claims they were discovered one month before Freer purchased them in 1906). Schmidt asserts they were discovered at Akmim (but Sanders later rejects this based on Arabi's admission that this statement was meant to mislead and on evidence pointing to their Dimai provenance). Schmidt asserts they were first shown by a dealer at Eshmunen and then Assiut (but Sanders rejects this after Schmidt's statements are denied by authorities in Assiut). Arabi then buys the manuscripts for £500 from the Eshmunen dealer (but Arabi tells Freer he acquired them directly from the digger just prior to their purchase by Freer). Arabi takes several photos of the manuscripts and uses these in an attempt to sell them to "the Germans" (Stern sees the photos, but it is uncertain if these photos also occasion Schmidt's claim that he too was shown the Washington manuscripts prior to their purchase by Freer). The manuscripts are shown by Arabi to Grenfell (either before or after "the Germans" have seen the photos). Freer later purchases the manuscripts in December of 1906. Schmidt returns to Egypt in search of the manuscripts in

The ongoing commissioning of Askren (whose medical work with the fellaheen in the Fayoum kept him appraised of any happenings in and around the area) to ferret out any further information or discoveries pertaining to the Washington Manuscripts attests further to the ongoing importance of Dimai in the ruminations of Freer, Kelsey, and Sanders. Kelsey wrote to Freer (regarding the librarian, agent, and adviser to J. Pierpont Morgan), "I have never felt at liberty to tell [Bella da Costa Greene] the reason why we hope, through Dr. Askren, to obtain information in regard to the place of origin of your Greek Manuscripts, and possibly get on track of other material in the same Monastery collection of which your Manuscripts formed a part."[120] Askren apparently had fellaheen contacts in the area of Dimai who were involved in the "harvesting" of fertilizer. The decomposition of organic material in many of the rubbish heaps throughout Egypt provided a nitrogen-rich growing medium that was especially sought after by agriculturalists. When excavating these mounds to procure this material, artifacts, including papyri, were often unearthed as well. The Egyptian Antiquities Service established "caretakers" to oversee such work and ensure that any valuable artifacts went to the proper authorities. However, the laborers involved in digging for the fertilizer would often conceal these treasures and later sell them to local dealers. "Regarding the excavating for fertilizer at Dimé," Askren wrote to Kelsey, "my friend gave the job up as it was costing him too much for labor and transportation so there is nothing being done there. I am going over to Dimé sometime soon now on a little holiday and if I find any others digging fertilizer I will arrange with them to bring me in any thing they may find."[121]

As part of Kelsey's preparations for the University of Michigan's Near East Expedition of 1920, he wrote what would be one of his last letters to Freer. After noting Freer's generous funding of the trip that Sanders and Worrell had made to "the desolate and inaccessible site designated by old Ali with so much secrecy as the place of discovery," he requests further modest financing to conduct a careful excavation of the monastery that would be neither difficult nor costly. "That would settle the matter," he wrote, "and if Ali told the truth, other manuscripts ought to appear; no monastery would have merely those that he sold to you, without others also—and you remember that the last leaf of the manuscript of

1907 but is told by Arabi that they have been sold and are now in America. Again, compare here Sanders, Washington *Manuscript of Deuteronomy and Joshua,* 1–2; idem, "Age and Ancient Home," 140–41; Freer to Kelsey, May 23, 1908; and Sanders to Freer, September 11, 1908.

120. Francis W. Kelsey to Charles Lang Freer, October 12, 1916, CLFP.

121. David L. Askren to Francis W. Kelsey, July 27, 1915, CLFP. Cf. Kelsey to Hecker, March 15, 1920, wherein Kelsey writes that Askren "had acquaintance also among fellaheen who were proposing to excavate for fertilizer on the site of ancient Dimay, where the Freer Manuscripts were said by Ali Arabi, with solemn assurances to Mr. Freer, to have been found. He said he would most gladly do anything possible to assist in solving the problem of the place of discovery of these manuscripts, and would keep close watch for us in case more were discovered."

Deuteronomy and Joshua was fresh, showing that it had been torn off."[122] Freer accepted Kelsey's proposal and provided the requested funds, as is indicated by his annotation directly upon Kelsey's letter, "Appropriate $1500." For Kelsey, however, the "matter" would ultimately remain unresolved. After personally visiting Dimai in February of 1920, Kelsey wrote to the paleontologist and secretary of the Smithsonian Institute Charles D. Walcott (1850–1927):

> When I wrote you on February 11, I thought it would be worth while to conduct a trial excavation on the site of Dimay, to see if evidence could be found regarding the probable discovery of the Freer Manuscripts on that site. After visiting the site, I concluded that under present conditions it would not be best to undertake such an excavation, not at least until fuller study has been given to the problem. In the most precise and emphatic terms Mr. Freer was assured by Ali Arabi that the manuscripts were found at Dimay; on the other hand, after I wrote you, I found that another dealer in Cairo who had relations with Mr. Freer, Maurice Nahman, was equally positive in asserting that the Freer manuscripts were found at Batn-Harit [Kharabet Ihrit or ancient Theadelphia].[123]

Despite Kelsey's own hesitation to go ahead with excavations, the site of Dimai has been successively explored since the first modern account of the area was given by Giovanni Battista Belzoni in 1819. Following Belzoni would be E. W. Lane (1825–1828), K. R. Lepsius (1843), Grenfell and Hunt (1900–1901), F. Zucker (1909–1910), Ahmed Bey Kamal (1916), and G. Caton-Thompson and E. W. Gardner (1925–1926).[124] The first scientific excavation of the site took place in

---

122. Francis W. Kelsey to Charles Lang Freer, July 12, 1918, CLFP. Cf. again Sanders, "New Manuscripts of the Bible," 50, where it is noted that the "first page of Deuteronomy" was unmarred. Kelsey goes on to write, "The site designated by Ali is of such a character that in order to excavate it would be necessary to create a special organization for both living and work while the excavations should be going on. I do not believe, however, that it would take more than twenty five days for a staff of thirty workmen or thereabouts, to clear the site and determine the truth of the whole matter. I do not know what the wages of workmen are in Egypt now, nor what it would cost to organize the excavation as I have suggested, but an allowance of $1200, or $1500 at the outside, ought to cover everything."

123. Francis W. Kelsey to Charles D. Walcott, October 6, 1920, CLFP. Significantly, the 1920 Near East Expedition of the University of Michigan—a joint effort that also included the Freer Research and Publication Fund, the Pierpont Morgan Library, and the University of Wisconsin—managed to retrieve from various sources in the winter and spring of that year over six hundred individual papyri.

124. In general, see G. B. Belzoni, *Belzoni's Travels: Narrative of the Operations and Recent Discoveries in Egypt and Nubia* (ed. A. Siliotti; London: British Museum Press, 2001); E. W. Lane, *Description of Egypt: Notes and Views in Egypt and Nubia* (ed. J. Thompson; Cairo: The American University in Cairo Press, 2000); K. R. Lepsius, *Denkmäler aus Aegypten und Aethiopien* (6 vols.; Berlin: Nicolai, 1849–1856); Grenfell, Hunt, and Hogarth, *Fayûm Towns;* and G. Caton-Thompson and E. W. Gardner, *The Desert Fayum* (London: Anthropological Institute

1931–1932 under the auspices of the Archaeological Mission of the University of Michigan, directed by Enoch E. Peterson. Undertaken as part of the university's ongoing excavations at Karanis between 1924 and 1935, the Dimai excavations were halted because of difficulties posed by the site's isolation and the failure to turn up anything of significance.[125] Perhaps the most sustained excavations to be undertaken at Dimai have been recently conducted by the Joint Archaeological Mission from the Universities of Lecce and Bologna. Having now run for multiple seasons, the first one taking place from February to March of 2003, these excavations have proved formative in experimenting with how an ancient site is both mapped and photographed. During the second season, which ran from November to December of 2004, a total of forty-seven Greek papyri, seventeen Demotic papyri, and sixty-one ostraca were discovered. Although well preserved, most of the Greek papyri are fragmentary and incomplete, containing nondistinct texts, and date from between the first and second centuries C.E.[126]

Conclusion

Much of Charles Lang Freer's life was spent enduring sickness, including a serious and debilitating stroke in May 1911 (just a month after his return from what would be his final trip to Asia) that left him favoring his right leg for the rest of his life. On Christmas Eve of 1918, Freer again became seriously ill. Traveling in early February to New York to receive medical treatment, he stayed temporarily in a local clinic. Freer's close friend Katharine Nash Rhoades (1885–1965) wrote to Kelsey,

> Mr. Freer was taken sick in Detroit, about Christmas time, and as he wrote you, was restricted greatly in his activities, for three weeks. Since his last letter to

---

of Great Britain and Ireland, 1934). Note that the latter three explorations by Zucker, Kamal, and Caton-Thompson and Gardner took place in close proximity to Freer, Kelsey, and Sanders's speculations of and even visits to Dimai. Remarkably, these three never, to my knowledge, mention these explorations.

125. See here Arthur E. R. Boak, "Dimê," *AJA* 36 (1932): 522–23; idem, *Soknopaiou Nesos: The University of Michigan Excavations of Dimé in 1931–32* (Ann Arbor: University of Michigan Press, 1935).

126. Paola Davoli, "Excavations at Soknopaiou Nesos (Dime) El-Fayyum," *Egyptian Archaeology* 25 (2004): 34–36; idem, "New Excavation at Soknopaiou Nesos: The 2003 Season," in *Tebtynis und Soknopaiu Nesos: Leben im römerzeitlichen Fajum* (ed. S. L. Lippert and M. Schentuleit; Wiesbaden: Harrasowitz, 2005), 29–39; M. Capasso and Paola Davoli, eds., *New Researches on the Fayyum: Proceedings of the International Meeting of Ehyptology and Papyrology, Lecce, June 8–10, 2005* (forthcoming). I can also report from recent correspondence with Professor Paola Davoli (who has served as one of the directors of the Bolgna-Lecce excavations at Dimai) that to this point his excavations have revealed no further Christian texts, nor even Christian occupation at Dimai.

> you he improved in strength and came on here to New York at the advice of his medical advisers here, to advise with them and to have the benefit of their examination. Unfortunately, since his arrival in New York, he has been sick again, and is at present resting, under his doctor's care, at a small sanatarium [sic] here in the city. He is improving each day, and we hope that ere long he will be entirely recovered again.[127]

Moving from the clinic, Freer later took rooms in the Pennsylvania Hotel and then more permanently in the Gotham Hotel, where his doctors, nurses, and such close friends as Rhoades, Agnes Meyer (1887–1970), and Louisine Havemeyer (1855–1929) oversaw his care. Freer's diary for the year 1919 records the extent of his illness and provides one with a remarkable window into the closing days of his life. Although seriously ill, Freer continued to meet and entertain friends and associates, conduct his affairs as best he could, and even venture out on occasional excursions such as going "motoring" with Hecker or Rhodes.[128] The entries in his diary vividly outline the ebb and flow of Freer's health. Some days he recorded a full and busy itinerary; on other days he noted only briefly that he was "ill indoors all day" or simply "ill." In one entry Freer recorded that he was "ill with many illusions" and that during the night he had a "great fire illusion."[129] As summer faded and autumn approached, more and more pages in his diary were left blank. Freer's diary, which he faithfully kept from 1889, falls eerily quiet after his last brief entry of Friday, September 12. "You have undoubtedly, ere this, heard the sad news," Rhoades wrote to Kelsey, "of Mr. Freer's death, which occurred on September 25th, at the Gotham Hotel in New York." Rhoades (who attended Freer on the day of his death) continued, "Not knowing your foreign address I was unable to cable you at the time. Since Mr. Freer's death I have been attending to his correspondence at the request of the executors, and I wish to acknowledge receipt of your letter, and to also advise you that the negatives of the Psalms MSS. were safely delivered to 33 Ferry Avenue, some little time ago."[130] Colonel Hecker later wrote to Kelsey, noting, "While the death of Mr. Freer was a great loss not only to his personal friends but as well to the art lovers and students of America, indeed of much of the world, his condition during the latter months of his life was such that it was a relief when the call to the Long Journey came."[131] Shortly after his death, Freer was buried in his birthplace of Kingston, New York. As affirmation of Hecker's assertion that Freer's death was an inter-

---

127. Katharine N. Rhoades to Francis W. Kelsey, February 11, 1919, CLFP.

128. Cf. Charles Lang Freer Diary, Wednesday, January 15, 1919, to Saturday, January 18, 1919, CLFP.

129. Charles Lang Freer Diary, Monday, April 28, 1919, CLFP.

130. Katharine N. Rhoades to Francis W. Kelsey, October 20, 1919, CLFP.

131. Frank J. Hecker to Francis W. Kelsey, April 15th, 1920, CLFP.

national loss, in 1930 a special memorial service for Freer was held at Kōetsu Temple in Kyoto, Japan.

To overcome the many periods of physical illness and emotional depression during his lifetime, Freer immersed himself in the beauty of art, culture, and nature:

> You will, I trust, forgive the delay in answering your letters of May 25th and 27th. My departure from Detroit and visits in Boston and New York drew so heavily upon my impaired strength that I deemed it wise to postpone correspondence until after I could get settled here. In the quiet of my present surroundings, life indeed seems much saner—and I trust during my present stay here to leisurely review the work of the recent past, and plan that for the near future. The collections in my care, along with the completion of the building for their housing in Washington, their future installation and preservation provide interesting occupation, both physical and mental, so I am never quite as idle as my medical advisors demand; but without some activity both for body and mind existence would simply end in annihilation of service and identity.... Should you visit the Atlantic coast during the war season and thirst for a sniff of the pines, do come to me in the Berkshires; the Inn is simple but refreshingly clean, and I will provide a bed for any date if you will send me advance notice. In these war times my own little bungalow grows but slowly—next year the latch string will, I hope, hang outside and reach to you. With every good wish for you and yours.[132]

In some sense Freer's offer to his friend Kelsey is equally extended to us. Through Freer's legacy of that other "little bungalow" known as the Freer Gallery of Art, he has left a "latch string" hanging outside and in reach of us all. "Last week in Washington I saw your noble building, and was shown through it," Kelsey wrote to Freer, "It is a glorious memorial, as substantial in construction as it is dignified and appropriate in its design. I congratulate you warmly on the early completion of this splendid architectural work."[133] A "memorial" indeed! And like most memorials, built for an individual who would never have the pleasure of seeing it. It is appropriate that we celebrate the centenary of the Smithsonian Institution's formal acceptance of Freer's collection and his plan to construct a building to house it. However, a building is at least partly measured by the contents within it, and in that light we particularly celebrate the centenary of the 1906 acquisition of Freer's manuscripts. "I cannot close this letter without expressing my deep appreciation of the vision, breadth of view and generosity which you have manifested in dealing with these most important matters," wrote Kelsey to Freer shortly before the completion of the work on the first four Washington Manuscripts. He then went on to link Freer's manuscripts and his

132. Charles Lang Freer to Francis W. Kelsey, June 8, 1918, CLFP.
133. Francis W. Kelsey to Charles Lang Freer, June 28, 1919, CLFP.

building: "You have rendered a very great service to the advancement of learning; and your contributions in this field will be counted in future ages worthy to be placed beside your contributions to art in the founding of your glorious building."[134] One may appropriately be reminded of Freer's words quoted earlier: "Some day, many days after bonds or anything else can serve me, others will be served, well served, intelligently served by my slight efforts."[135] The Freer biblical manuscripts, however, are much more than ancient artifacts to be academically studied, although, in light of his provision of a formal context and the materials wherein that very task could be accomplished, Freer would be immensely pleased with the academic interest in them reflected in this volume. One of Freer's great desires was to provide for those who would come after him the opportunity to experience through his collection the same sense of consoling beauty that it inspired in him. "Your project is full of splendid daring, of superb altruism! You are like the knight-errant of old, setting forth upon a heroic quest," Kelsey extolled Freer, "only you have a definite aim—to add something to the world's resources of the beautiful, while the knight-errant too often went for the adventure merely. All your friends will follow your course with eagerness matched only by good wishes for the fullest possible attainment of your purpose."[136] The Freer biblical manuscripts embody this finer sense of beauty that Freer so diligently sought and recognized through his collection. For if we allow them to do so, these ancient texts can set to race our imagination with stories of amazing discoveries buried in far-off sands. They can tell us something of the past—a past we might decide to claim as our own. The story of the acquisition and publication of these manuscripts can remind us of the generosity, graciousness, and foresight of a single individual who began in meager circumstances and sought to share with others the benefits of his success.

Appendix: A Select Chronology of Freer's Life and Travels

1854 February 25: Charles Lang Freer born in Kingston, New York

1873 Freer appointed by Colonel Frank J. Hecker (1846–1927) as accountant and paymaster of New York, Kingston, and Syracuse Railroad

1876 Freer relocates to Logansport, Indiana, to work for the Detroit and Eel River and Illinois Railroad with Hecker

1880 Freer moves to Detroit and with Hecker participates in the formation of the Peninsular Car Works, with a capital stock of $300,000

1883 Freer appointed vice president and secretary when Peninsular Car Works is succeeded by Peninsular Car Company; Freer also begins collecting European prints

134. Francis W. Kelsey to Charles Lang Freer, August 5, 1919, CLFP.

135. Freer to Hecker, July 12, 1903.

136. Francis W. Kelsey to Charles Lang Freer, August 9, 1910, CLFP.

1884	Peninsular Car Company builds plant at Ferry and Russell streets in Detroit
1887	Freer begins collecting the work of American-born artist James McNeill Whistler (1834–1903)
[illegible]	Freer and Hecker purchase building lots on Ferry Avenue
1888	Due to ill health, Hecker is forced to retire from business
1889	Freer meets painters Frederick Stuart Church (1826–1900) and Dwight William Tryon (1849–1938) in New York
1890	March: Freer makes his first trip to London and gains an audience with Whistler, thus beginning a close association and friendship
1892	Freer moves into his newly constructed home, designed by Wilson Eyre (1858–1944) and decorated by Tryon and Thomas Wilmer Dewing (1851–1938), on Ferry Avenue in Detroit
1892	The Michigan-Peninsular Car Company, employing 5,000 individuals and valued at $8 million, is formed in September by the consolidation of Hecker and Freer's Peninsular Car Company, the Michigan Car Company, the Detroit Car Wheel Company, the Detroit Pipe and Foundry Company, the Michigan Forge and Iron Company, and the Baugh Steam Forge
1893	Freer lends several American paintings to the World's Columbian Exposition in Chicago
1894–1895	September 1894–August 1895: Freer's first Asian tour, traveling extensively in India, China, and Japan
1897	The first public exhibition of portions of Freer's collection at Hillyer Art Gallery at Smith College in Northampton, Massachusetts, and later at Williams College in Williamstown, Massachusetts
1899	March: the Michigan-Peninsular Car Company becomes one of thirteen other independent railway car manufacturers consolidated into the American Car and Foundry Company; after taking part in this merger, Freer retires from active business and begins to pursue his passion for collecting works of art
1900	Freer attends the Exposition Internationale Universelle in Paris
1900	Freer and attorney Thomas S. Jerome (1864–1914) purchase Villa Castello in Capri
1901	Freer meets Siegfried Bing (1838–1905) and Ernest Fenollosa (1853–1908)
1902	The idea to present his collection to the Smithsonian Institution first forms in Freer's mind, at the urging of his friend and historian Charles H. Moore (1840–1930)
1902	Freer spends summer in Britain building collection of Whistler paintings
1902	Freer meets fellow collector Dikran Kelekian (1868–1951)
1903	July 17: Whistler dies in London

1904 Freer proposes to donate his collection and the funds necessary to build a housing museum for them to the Smithsonian Institute

1904 Freer purchases Whistler's Peacock Room

1905 Smithsonian Committee, consisting of the Smithsonian Institution secretary, astronomer, and aeronautic engineer Samuel P. Langley (1834–1906), University of Michigan president James B. Angell (1829–1916), the former U.S. senator John B. Henderson (1826–1913), and the inventor Alexander Graham Bell (1847–1922), visits Freer in Detroit

1906 January 24: the Smithsonian Institution accepts Freer's donation at the urging of President Theodore Roosevelt (1858–1919), to be formally received on Freer's death

1906–1907 November 1906–July 1907: Freer's second Asian tour

1906 November 15: Freer and close friend Dr. Frederick Wharton Mann (1854–1926) set sail from New York on the SS *Hamburg,* traveling to Cairo, Egypt, via Naples, thus beginning Freer's first Egyptian journey

1906 Wednesday, December 5: Freer and Mann sail from Naples on the SS *Oceana,* arriving in Alexandria on Saturday, December 8

1906 Sunday, December 9: Freer and Mann depart for and arrive in Cairo by train, spending their first three days in Cairo visiting primarily Coptic, Fatimid, Ayyubid, and Mamluk monuments and other tourist destinations

1906 Friday, December 14: Freer and Mann visit the pyramids and surroundings at Giza as well as antiquarian shops

1906 Sunday, December 16: Freer meets the private collector and Egyptologist Dr. Daniel Marie Fouquet (1850–1914)

1906 Wednesday, December 19: Freer makes what is often considered the most important acquisition of his collecting career by purchasing from Ali Arabi four Greek parchment manuscripts containing Deuteronomy and Joshua, the Psalms, the Gospels, and the Epistles of Paul, dating variously from the fourth to the sixth centuries

1906 Friday, December 21: Freer and Mann visit the southern Delta site of Tell al-Yahudiya, or the "Mound of the Jews"

1906 Sunday, December 25: Freer and Mann spend their last full day in Cairo, visiting sites just south of the city, including Helwan, Memphis, and Saqqara

1906 Sunday, December 23: Freer and Mann leave Cairo for Luxor by train, arriving in Luxor the next morning and spending most of Christmas week there visiting the Luxor and Karnak temples and environs

1906 Sunday, December 30: Freer and Mann journey from Luxor to Aswan aboard the new Hamburg and Anglo-American Nile Steamer Company's *Mayflower,* visiting en route Edfu and Kom Ombo

1907 January 1: Freer and Mann arrive in Aswan, departing the same day on an eight-day maiden voyage up the Nile aboard the *Hamburg* and Anglo-American Nile Steamer Company's SS *Nubia,* visiting many temple sites on the way, including Ramesses II's spectacular rock-cut temple at Abu Simbel

1907 January 4: Freer meets the American watercolor painter Henry Roderick Newman (1833–1918) in Abu Simbel

1907 January 6: Freer and Mann begin return journey from Abu Simbel to Aswan, stopping en route at Wadi al-Sebua, or the "Valley of the Lionesses," containing the avenue of carved sphinxes, Kalabsha, and Philae

1907 January 7: Freer and Mann arrive back in Aswan aboard the SS *Nubai* and later board the *Mayflower* in order to return to Luxor, where they remain a further six nights visiting antiquarian shops and dealers

1907 Monday, January 14: Freer and Mann depart Luxor by train to Baliyana, stopping en route in Qena to tour the temple of Hathor at Dendera

1907 Tuesday, January 15: Freer and Mann depart from Baliyana via train, stopping at the temples of Ramesses II and Sety I and traveling by donkey to the traditional cultic center of Osiris in Abydos

1907 Wednesday, January 16: Freer and Mann arrive back in Cairo

1907 Thursday, January 17: Freer meets with the U.S. consul general and diplomatic agent Lewis M. Iddings (d. 1921) to obtain the latter's signature on custom papers allowing him to export his newly acquired antiquities and books home to Detroit

1907 Sunday, January 20: Freer meets with the German Egyptologist Émile Brugsch (1842–1930) of the Egyptian Museum, who is initially unwilling to grant permission to export several of Freer's purchased antiquities

1907 Monday, January 21: Freer and Mann leave Cairo, reaching Port Said four hours later, where Mann boards a steamer for Italy

1907 Tuesday, January 22: Freer sails on the North German Lloyd liner the *Princess Alice* through the Suez Canal and the Gulf of Aden, en route to Ceylon for the remainder of his second Asian journey

1907 July: Freer arrives home from his world travels

1908 May–September: Freer's third Asian tour, traveling extensively in West Asia and the Middle East

1908 Thursday, May 14: Freer arrives via Naples in Port Said aboard the SS *Orient,* thus beginning his second trip to Egypt, one of the primary reasons of which being the determination of the source of the biblical manuscripts he acquired in December 1906; on this 1908 trip, which later has Freer traveling a third time to Asia as well, he also purchases from Ali Arabi Coptic manuscripts of the Psalter and the homily on

	the Virgin, as well as fifty fragments from the Cairo Genizah (a collection of medieval materials written by the city's Jewish community); and from the Cairo dealer Maurice Nahman (1868–1948) additional fragmentary Greek and Coptic papyri
1908	September 21: Freer's close friend Fenollosa dies of a sudden heart attack in London
1909	Freer travels throughout Europe visiting various art museums
1909	May–December: Freer's fourth Asian tour, upon which he attends Fenollosa's memorial service in Miidera, Japan
1909	Monday, July 26: Freer lands in Alexandria aboard the SS *Schleswig*, thus beginning his third and final journey to Egypt, during which he would purchase, once again from Arabi and Nahman, additional fragments of a Coptic Psalter and Byzantine paintings from an eleventh-century manuscript of the Heavenly Ladder, a popular Byzantine monastic composition
1910	Freer loans portions of his collection to the University of Michigan, Ann Arbor, for an exhibition marking the opening of the University's Alumni Memorial Hall, dedicated to alumni killed in the Spanish-American War
1910–1911	August 1910–April 1911: Freer's fifth and last Asian tour, upon which he visits the Longmen Buddhist Caves in China
1911	May: Freer suffers a stroke that affects the right side of his body
1912	April 15–June 15: The Smithsonian Institution Exhibition marks one of the largest public showings of Freer's collection during his lifetime
1912	Freer purchases nine additional Coptic fragments
1913	Freer commissions Charles Adam Platt to design the museum building in Washington
1913	Freer meets Eugene (1875–1957) and Agnes E. (1887–1970) Meyer
1914	Freer meets Katharine Nash Rhoades (1885–1965) in Detroit
1914	As honorary vice president of the Japan Society, Freer participates in an exhibition of Chinese, Korean, and Japanese ceramics held by that society at the Knoedler Galleries, marking the first exhibition of its kind in New York
1916	The Department of Far Eastern Art at the Metropolitan Museum of Art in New York organizes an exhibition on Chinese pottery, sculpture, and bronzes, to which Freer lends pieces from his collection
1916	Freer purchases a fifth Greek biblical manuscript, containing the Minor Prophets, from Nahman through the intermediary Dr. David L. Askren, the latter also purchasing Coptic manuscripts for the Pierpont Morgan Library
1916	September: ground for the Freer Gallery broken on the National Mall in Washington

1917 November 15–December 8: the Art Institute of Chicago holds an exhibition, to which Freer lends Chinese Jades, paintings, and ceramics

1918 Christmas Eve: Freer falls seriously ill at home in Detroit

1918 Work on the Freer Gallery is delayed by the First World War

1919 February: Freer is well enough to travel to New York for a week of extensive medical testing, after which he takes a suite in the Gotham Hotel, where he receives ongoing medical treatment and many visits from friends and colleagues

1919 Freer adds codicil to his will allowing for the purchase of select acquisitions of Asian, Egyptian, and Near Eastern art

1919 Thursday, September 25: Freer passes away in his suite at the Gotham Hotel and is buried in his birthplace of Kingston, New York

1919 Freer Gallery of Art completed

1920 John E. Lodge (1876–1942) appointed director of the Freer Gallery of Art

1923 May 9: Freer Gallery of Art opens to the public

1930 Special memorial service for Freer is held at Kōetsu Temple, Kyoto

The Freer Twelve Minor Prophets Codex—A Case Study: The Old Greek Text of Jonah, Its Revisions, and Its Corrections

Kristin De Troyer

Previous Scholarship

According to Henry A. Sanders, the editor of the Freer Minor Prophets Codex (Rahlfs W; hereafter FMP), there are "cases where the manuscript inclines toward the Hebrew in opposition to many of the Septuagint manuscripts, [and] the type of text is almost never in accord with that reported for the Hexapla of Origen."[1] Sanders then points to the fact that in many of these cases there is no evidence available from Aquila, Symmachus, or Theodotion. Moreover, in the instances where we do have the readings of Aquila, Symmachus, or Theodotion, these do not overlap with the readings from the Freer Codex. In total, Sanders has identified thirty-three such cases. Sanders discussed some of these readings where, however, there is a "semblance of support found in Aquila, Symmachus, or Theodotion," namely, Hab 3:1 (Symmachus or Quinta); Zeph 3:10 (Aquila or direct influence from the Hebrew text); Nah 3:18. He also noted the readings

1. Henry A. Sanders and Carl Schmidt, *The Minor Prophets in the Freer Collection and the Berlin Fragment of Genesis* (University of Michigan Studies, Humanistic Series, 21; New York: Macmillan, 1927), 25 (hereafter cited as Sanders, *Minor Prophets in the Freer Collection*). Note also Henry A. Sanders, *Facsimile of the Washington Manuscript of the Minor Prophets in the Freer Collection and the Berlin Fragment of Genesis* (Ann Arbor: University of Michigan, 1927). For brief standard descriptions of the codex, see Alfred Rahlfs and Detlef Fraenkel, *Verzeichnis der griechischen Handschriften des Alten Testaments* (Stuttgart: Vandenhoeck & Ruprecht, 2004), 387–89; Sidney Jellicoe, *The Septuagint and Modern Study* (Oxford: Clarendon, 1968), 233–34; Joseph van Haelst, *Catalogue des papyrus littéraires juif et chrétiens* (Paris: University of Paris-Sorbonne, 1976), 106 (for the Minor Prophets text, van Haelst catalogue number 284), 226–27 (for the Coptic marginalia, van Haelst 636, discussed by Malcolm Choat in the present volume); and Kurt Aland, *Biblische Papyri: Altes Testament, Neues Testament, Varia, Apokryphen* (vol. 1 of *Repertorium der griechischen christlichen Papyri;* PTS 18; Berlin: de Gruyter, 1976), 26–27 (Aland 08).

that have "a little direct testimony on the relationship to the other translations in passages where the Greek forms vary from each other rather than from the Hebrew original," namely, Amos 4:4 (Symmachus); Hab 2:9 (Symmachus); Jonah 4:1 (Symmachus); Amos 8:3 (Aquila); Obad 1:19 (Aquila); Mic 1:16 (Theodotion or direct from Hebrew text), Zech 14:17 (Symmachus); Joel 3:4 (Aquila, Theodotion, or direct from Hebrew text); and Zech 3:5 (no conclusion). Many of these readings are found in some sort of combination with the Septuagintal text, which seems to imply that "some of these direct or indirect accommodations to the Hebrew were glosses in the parent manuscript."[2] In some cases (e.g., Zeph 3:10), the newer reading was written on top of the older one. In other cases a second corrector deleted one of the readings (e.g., Nah 3:18) or erased one reading and replaced it with another (e.g., Mic 1:16).[3] The second hand is that of the "Diorthotes" (discussion of his identity continues).[4] The fact that a second hand corrected the readings of the first scribe is in itself a remarkable phenomenon. Maybe the Diorthotes realized that the Greek text in front of him or her did not represent the known Hebrew text, or perhaps the Diorthotes had (a) different Greek text(s) with which to make comparisons. The corrections might also shed light on the first scribe. Maybe the first scribe had multiple (Greek) texts in front of him or her or perhaps had (as Sanders stated it) a "parental" text with some glosses and corrections.[5]

What the Freer Minor Prophets Codex offers us is a peek at the actual writing and rewriting of the Old Greek (OG) text. Indeed, we have here a manuscript that offers a Greek biblical text, revisions and corrections all from the first scribe, plus revisions and corrections made by a second scribe, and, finally, those of a third scribe. It has been known for a long time that revisions were made from the moment the OG came into being. There were, as there still are, two ways of revising a translation. The first option was to revise the *language* of the translation, for instance, making the Greek better Greek. A second possibility was to correct the translation *toward its source text.*

The phenomena that one can witness in the FMP are also of importance to the scholar interested in the reconstruction of the history of the Greek text and also the final stages of the Hebrew text before it was entirely standardized by the Masoretes. In the reconstruction of these textual histories, the pre-Hexaplaric

---

2. Sanders, *Minor Prophets in the Freer Collection,* 27–28.

3. Sanders (ibid., 28) also discusses the case of Zech 3:5 and points to a possible doublet in the text. Due, however, to the very fragmentary state of the manuscript, he could not come to a final conclusion regarding this case.

4. See, e.g., Malcolm Choat, "The Unidentified Text in Freer Minor Prophets Codex," in this volume.

5. See Sanders, *Minor Prophets in the Freer Collection,* 44, who also thought that the "corrector is following a similar type of text to that used by the first hand."

stage of the Greek Bible is of utmost importance. What did the OG text look like before Origen adapted it toward the Hebrew text of his days? Can we find traces of adaptation to a Hebrew text older than the one that Origen used? Past research on different books and witnesses of the Septuagint has shown us that there is indeed such a thing as pre-Hexaplaric corrections. The question before us now is this: What sort of early revisions can one observe in FMP?

In order to complicate things just a tiny bit more, there is also evidence of a third hand in the codex. This third scribe simply added "many glosses written between the lines, usually with careless deletion of the original text."[6] Sanders could not identify any of these readings with a known recension, so he concluded "that some ancient reader knew Hebrew and corrected certain portions to the text of the Hebrew form known to him."[7] Sanders does, however, seem to acknowledge that there is some resemblance between a dozen of these readings of the third corrector and the Vulgate as well as another nine cases where the third corrector agrees with the Achmimic version.[8]

In the introduction to his critical edition of the Minor Prophets, Joseph Ziegler agrees with most of Sanders's remarks concerning FMP.[9] Ziegler also points to two more witnesses, however, with readings that resemble the Hebrew text: the Achmimic (although this version was acknowledged by Sanders); and the text reflected in biblical citations by Justin Martyr. Ziegler follows Grossouw, who aptly stated his opinion as follows:

> It is perhaps best expressed by stating that the numerous "Hebrew corrections" in Ach-Sa [Achmimic and Sahidic versions], unlike those of the Greek MSS, in which they are derived (in substance) from Theodotion via the Hexapla, were mainly taken from the translations of Aquila and Symmachus and from one or more other translations of which we have hardly any knowledge (quinta, sexta, septima?); similar cases are found in the closely allied Egyptian papyrus W [FMP]. Direct dependence from the Hebrew remains very unlikely.[10]

The question of where the pre-Hexaplaric corrections come from is very interesting. Grossouw was correct in pointing to other Jewish translations as the possible source for many of the readings in the Freer codex. Ziegler also reminds readers that already in 1921 Rahlfs had identified the citation of Mic 4:1 in Justin

6. Ibid., 28.

7. Ibid.

8. Ibid., 44.

9. Joseph Ziegler, *Duodecim Prophetae* (3rd ed.; Septuaginta: Vetus Testamentum graecum 13; Göttingen: Vandenhoeck & Ruprecht, 1984), 33.

10. Ziegler (ibid., 34), quoting Willem Grossouw, *The Coptic Versions of the Minor Prophets: A Contribution to the Study of the Septuagint* (Monumenta biblica et ecclesiastica 3; Rome: Pontifical Biblical Institute, 1938), 113.

as dependent on Aquila.[11] Since the publication of the FMP and the Ziegler critical edition of the Minor Prophets, other texts have come to light that may shed a different light on the topic.

A Further Look

I have two aims in this essay. First, I compare the text of the Freer Minor Prophets codex, especially its variant readings, with the readings of the Minor Prophets Scroll of Nahal Hever. The text preserved in this scroll has been labeled by Barthelémy and Tov as the καιγε (*kaige*) text.[12] This *kaige*-text manuscript (first century B.C.E.) proves that there were revisers at work long before the appearance of Aquila in the early second century C.E. The Nahal Hever Minor Prophets Scroll was not yet available, however, when the critical edition of the Göttingen Septuaginta Minor Prophets volume was published in 1943.[13] As the first fascicle of the Biblia Qumranica on the Minor Prophets was published in 2004, it will also be easy to trace all possible existing Hebrew texts along the way.[14]

Taking a closer look at the readings that seem to reflect a (different?) Hebrew text is the second goal of this essay. The latter task involves studying some of the thirty-three cases where Sanders noted the influence of the Hebrew text. As a test case, FMP readings in the book of Jonah will be analyzed here.

For this, I verified the text of the edition of the Freer codex published by Sanders by using new color photos of the Freer biblical manuscripts.[15] For the Old Greek text, I used the text as established in the Ziegler critical edition.[16] I also consulted the *Kollationshefte* of the *Septuaginta Unternehmen* in Göttingen.[17]

---

11. Ziegler, *Duodecim Prophetae,* 34, referring to Alfred Rahlfs, "Über Theodotion-Lesarten im Neuen Testament und Aquila-Lesarten bei Justin," *ZNW* 20 (1921): 182–199.

12. The full photographic facsimile is by Emanuel Tov with the collaboration of R. A. Kraft and a contribution by P. J. Parsons, *The Greek Minor Prophets Scroll from Naḥal Ḥever (8ḤevXIIgr) (The Seiyâl Collection, 1)* (2nd ed.; DJD 8; Oxford: Clarendon, 1995). The key earlier study was Dominique Barthélemey, *Les devanciérs d'Aquila: Première publication intégrale du texte des fragments du Dodécaprophéton trouvés dans le désert de Juda* (VTSup 10; Leiden: Brill, 1963).

13. Ziegler, *Duodecim Prophetae.* The collection of texts used was put together in 1952–1954.

14. Beate Ego, Armin Lange, Hermann Lichtenberger, and Kristin De Troyer, *Minor Prophets* (Biblia Qumranica 3B; Leiden: Brill, 2004).

15. These photos were produced with the agreement of the Freer/Sackler Galleries, with arrangements made by the Society of Biblical Literature, the actual photography done by staff of the Institute for the Study and Preservation of Ancient Religious Texts (Brigham young University). I would like to thank especially Patrick Durusau (then at the Society of Biblical Literature) for providing me with a copy of these splendid new images.

16. Ziegler, *Duodecim Prophetae.*

17. I would like to express my thanks to Dr. Bernhard Neuschäfer for providing me with the *Kollationshefte.*

I noted the variants between the OG and the FMP as reported in the *apparati* of Sanders and Ziegler, as well as the variants between the OG and the old Jewish recensions identified in the notes provided by Sanders and in second apparatus of Ziegler, and I paid special attention to the indications by Sanders of "more Hebrew" readings. Also, I carefully studied the notes made by Sanders indicating changes by especially the second hand.[18] Finally, I compared all the variants with the relevant evidence from manuscripts of the Judean Desert.

The following analysis of readings in the book of Jonah uses these abbreviations: FMP for the text of the Freer Minor Prophets Codex; NH for the Minor Prophets Scroll of Nahal Hever; OG for the Old Greek Text; and MT for the Masoretic Text. In each case I cite first the reading in FMP, then make observations about its relationship to the other textual evidence.

1. Jonah 1:1: ιωνα. Sanders noted that the reading is in agreement with the Boharic version. The second hand adds a final *sigma*.[19] Ziegler points to the Masoretic Text, and, indeed, the reading without the final *sigma* is tuned more toward the Hebrew than toward the OG, which reads ιωνας. The shorter form is also found in Aquila and the Syrohexapla.[20] There are no data from NH regarding this verse. The name "Jonah," however, appears on other occasions. In 3:3, for instance, the name of Jonah appears, but, unfortunately, the NH text has only the *omega* present and visible.[21] In 4:1 of the NH text, the following characters of the name have been preserved: ωνα,[22] followed by a noun. Hence, the name of Jonah here was spelled in the form characteristic of the *kaige* recension, without the final *sigma*. The reading of the Freer codex is thus, likewise, the reading of the *kaige* text, and Aquila later also took over this reading. There is no need to point to a direct Hebrew influence on the FMP.

2. Jonah 1:8: τινος ενεκεν η κακια αυτη. According to Sanders, this reading stems from the Hebrew. The reading as it stands, however, is the OG text. There are no extant data from NH with regard to this verse. There is, however, the use of τα κακα α in Jonah 3:10 in FMP. The OG and *kaige* texts read τη κακια η here, however, not τα κακα α.[23] The FMP thus uses two expressions in these two verses for the same Hebrew word רעה. There is no sign of correction in the Freer codex. This is not strange, for the OG also uses these two Greek expressions (compare readings at Jonah 1:2, 7, 8; 3:10; 4:2 with 4:6). The reading τινος ενεκεν η κακια αυτη, however, is followed in the OG by εστιν εν ημιν, which is absent in FMP. This phrase can be seen as a translation from the Hebrew text לנו. According to

18. I focus here on the second hand, not on the third hand.
19. Sanders, *Minor Prophets in the Freer Collection*, 90.
20. Ziegler, *Duodecim Prophetae*, 244.
21. Tov, *Greek Minor Prophets Scroll*, 30–31.
22. Ibid.
23. Ibid.

Sanders, the entire phrase τινος ενεκεν η κακια αυτη εστιν εν ημιν could easily have been omitted through *homoioteleuton,*[24] but this does not explain why only a part of the sentence is missing in the Freer codex. The full reading is a repetition of the sentence in Jonah 1:7, in which the sailors say to one another, "Come, let us cast lots so that we may know on whose account this calamity has come upon us." FMP agrees in 1:7 with the OG and thus has the entire clause: τινος ενεκεν η κακια αυτη εστιν εν ημιν. In my opinion, in 1:8 FMP simply did not repeat the entire clause;[25] there is no need to resort to a suggestion of direct influence from the Hebrew.

3. Jonah 1:11: ποιησομεν. The second hand changes the second *omicron* into an *omega.*[26]

4. Jonah 1:12: The second hand adds the article before μεγας, as in the OG.[27]

5. Jonah 1:13: The second hand changes επορευετο into επωρυετο.[28]

6. Jonah 2:5: FMP reads the article in front of ναον, with OG,[29] unlike *kaige.*[30]

7. Jonah 2:6: FMP reads υδωρ μοι, with OG, though transposed, and unlike the reading in *kaige:* με υδατα. The latter reading could be considered closer to the Hebrew.[31]

8. Jonah 2:7: In FMP εις σε εκ φθορας την ζωην is added by the second hand. No data are extant from NH. The FMP reading is not found in the OG.[32] According to Ziegler,[33] Aquila has εκ διαφθορας, whereas Symmachus and Theodotion

---

24. Sanders, *Minor Prophets in the Freer Collection,* 184.

25. There is one other instance in Jonah where parts of earlier sentences are repeated and omitted by the first scribe of FMP. In 3:4 and 4:2, FMP omits και ειπεν. In 4:2, however, the phrase does occur a bit later in the verse. The first hand of FMP must have noticed the error and added it in between the lines, without deleting the transposed section. The second hand then deletes this και ειπεν (Sanders, *Minor Prophets in the Freer Collection,* 94). Strangely, Sanders states that "the *diorthotes* did not notice the error, so probably similar trouble in the parent MS" (187).

26. Ibid., 91. The correction was undone by the third hand.

27. Ibid.

28. Ibid. For the additional witnesses, see Ziegler, *Duodecim Prophetae,* 246.

29. For the list of witnesses, see Ziegler, *Duodecim Prophetae,* 248.

30. Sanders, *Minor Prophets in the Freer Collection,* 185; Tov, *Greek Minor Prophets Scroll,* 28–29. Tov notes that "R [= the recension that is known as the *kaige* text] retains the article of the LXX before combinations of nouns with pronominal suffixes…, while it even adds the article against the LXX.… In 9 instances, however, R omits the article under these conditions" (117). One of these exceptions is in Jonah 2:5.

31. Sanders, *Minor Prophets in the Freer Collection,* 185; Tov, Greek Minor Prophets Scroll, 28–29 and see also 135.

32. Sanders, *Minor Prophets in the Freer Collection,* 92, 185; Ziegler, *Duodecim Prophetae,* 248. Note, however, the resemblance with Ps 102 (103):4.

33. Ziegler, *Duodecim Prophetae,* 248.

read εκ φθορας (see Syh; this reading is also found in S^c, Λ, Q, V, rell; not, however, in B and S*) followed by η ζωη μου. The latter words are different from the reading of the second hand of FMP, who, however, has correct Greek. The FMP reading is also found in the Sahidic.[34] The first part of the FMP variant, εις φθ, is nowhere else attested.

9. Jonah 3:1: The second hand of FMP corrected δετου into δευτεου,[35] probably intending on correcting to δευτερου. In comparison with Ziegler's established Greek text of the Minor Prophets, FMP, cursive manuscript 26, and the Ethiopic text have transposed phrasing: εκ δευτερου προς Ιωναν.[36] No data are extant from NH.

10. Jonah 3:3: FMP reads καθως ελαλησεν with OG, against the *kaige*, which has καθα το ρημα.[37] The reading καθως seems to have been selected by Ziegler on the basis of FMP, for many witnesses read καθα.[38]

11. Jonah 3:3: The second hand of FMP corrects $\overline{\theta\omega}$ into $\overline{\kappa\omega}$,[39] a variant that is also attested in the Achmimic and Sahidic texts.[40] This curious correction—Why did the word "God" need to be replaced by an alternative?—in my opinion shows that the reading Κυριος became over time, although not initially, what one might call the "majority alternative" for the divine Name and related epithets.[41]

12. Jonah 3:4: FMP reads εισελθειν with OG, against *kaige* πορευεσθαι.[42] Similarly, FMP has here τρεις with OG, against the *kaige* text's τεσσερακοντα.[43] Both variants in the *kaige* text reflect the Hebrew text. The more significant reading of "forty days" instead of "three days" is well attested. According to Ziegler, "forty" appears in all the early Jewish revisions.[44] As it is also found in the *kaige* text, it must be a correction in the Hebrew text that was made rather early.[45] The passage first states that Nineveh is a large city and that it takes three days to cross it by foot (Jonah 3:3 MT). In the OG, the inhabitants have only three days

---

34. Ibid.

35. Sanders, *Minor Prophets in the Freer Collection*, 92, 186.

36. Ibid., 186; Ziegler, *Duodecim Prophetae*, 249.

37. Sanders, *Minor Prophets in the Freer Collection*, 186; Tov, *Greek Minor Prophets Scroll*, 30–31. The second hand also corrects $\overline{\theta\omega}$ to $\overline{\kappa\omega}$. See Sanders, *Minor Prophets in the Freer Collection*, 92.

38. Ziegler, *Duodecim Prophetae*, 249.

39. Sanders, *Minor Prophets in the Freer Collection*, 92 and 186.

40. Ziegler, *Duodecim Prophetae*, 249.

41. See Kristin De Troyer, "The Pronunciation of the Names of God, with Some Notes Regarding *nomina sacra*," in *Der Name Gottes* (ed. I. U. Dalferth, Konrad Schmid, and Philip Stoellger; Religion in Philosophy and Theology; Tübingen: Mohr Siebeck, forthcoming).

42. Sanders, *Minor Prophets in the Freer Collection*, 93 and 186.

43. Ibid.

44. Ziegler, *Duodecim Prophetae*, 249–50.

45. Tov, *Greek Minor Prophets Scroll*, 30–31.

to change their mind, whereas in the MT they are given a symbolic forty days, similar to the length of time that the flood remained on earth or the time Israel spent in the wilderness.[46] That in the FMP neither the first nor the second hand changed "three" into "forty" indicates that the latter reading was more characteristic of the identifiably Jewish Greek texts of Jonah.[47]

13. Jonah 3:5: The second hand of the FMP corrects the reading ενεπιστευσαν, which is preferred in the OG,[48] to the reading επιστευσαν, which is also found in *kaige*.[49] It is difficult to say which verb is closer to the Hebrew text. As both verbs, the *simplex* and the *compositum*, appear only here in Jonah, a study of the translation technique is not very helpful. I note, however, that the *kaige* text has a preference for *simplex* verbs,[50] and thus the corrected reading in FMP here certainly resembles the *kaige* tendency.

14 Jonah 3:5: The second hand also deletes the *epsilon* from μεικρου.[51]

15. Jonah 3:7: The FMP has transposed the following reading: και ερρεθη και εκηρυχθη. Sanders writes, "Doubtless the parent of W [FMP] originally omitted και ερρεθη, but it was added between the lines and so read by our scribe in wrong order."[52] No data are extant from NH.

16. Jonah 3:7: The second or first hand adds deletion points on the first three characters of μηδεν.[53] According to the *Kollationsheft*, it was the second hand that added the deletion points. The reading without the deletion points certainly reflects the MT.

17. Jonah 3:8: FMP has the reading απεστρεψαν, in common with the OG and against *kaige*, which reads επεστρεψεν. The reading favored here by FMP, however, is closer to the Hebrew[54]

18. Jonah 3:10: FMP reads εκαστος preceding απο, unlike the OG and the *kaige*.[55] This addition of εκαστος is found in other manuscripts, too, but according to Ziegler does not represent the OG. In the Syro-Hexapla, the word was

---

46. Marvin A. Sweeney, *The Twelve Prophets* (2 vols.; Collegeville, Minn.: Liturgical Press, 2000), 1:325.

47. More research could be done on the change from three days to forty. Since, however, the FMP simply follows the OG here, I will not elaborate on this issue in this discussion.

48. For the additional witnesses, see Ziegler, *Duodecim Prophetae*, 249.

49. Sanders, *Minor Prophets in the Freer Collection*, 93 and 186. According to Tov (*Greek Minor Prophets Scroll*, 127), the *kaige* text often uses a *simplex* for a *compositum* in LXX.

50. Tov, *Greek Minor Prophets Scroll*, 127–28.

51. Sanders, *Minor Prophets in the Freer Collection*, 93.

52. Sanders, *Minor Prophets in the Freer Collection*, 186–87.

53. Ibid., 93. According to Ziegler (*Duodecim Prophetae*, 250), the points were added by the second hand.

54. Sanders, *Minor Prophets in the Freer Collection*, 187; Tov, *Greek Minor Prophets Scroll*, 30–31. Tov (127) mentions this change as an example of where the *kaige* text changes the preverb. He also notes that here the OG, and not the *kaige*, reflects the MT (see 151).

55. Ziegler lists the other witnesses in favor of the addition.

marked with an obelus, but, as Ziegler indicates in his apparatus, there is a note in the margin of the manuscript stating “hic obelus non erat in hexaplis.”[56] The same reading, και απεστρεψαν εκαστος απο, appears, however, just a bit earlier in 3:8. So it seems that in 3:10 the FMP reading precisely repeats the words from 3:8.[57] A bit further along in 3:10 FMP also reads τα κακα (α) instead of τη κακια, which is favored by the OG and *kaige*.[58] Ziegler points to the reading of Symmachus here in the apparatus: επι τη κακωσει.[59] In both of the FMP readings noted here, there is no need to point to direct influence of the Hebrew text.

19. Jonah 4:1:[60] συνεθυμησεν. According to Sanders, there is no other Greek support for this reading. The second hand corrected the reading to ηθυμησεν by putting dots on top of συν and also under the letters συνε and by rewriting on top of the ε and η, thus creating the reading ηθμησεν. [61] Sanders judged that this is “probably from Symmachus (Syro-Hex),”[62] and it is attested in the Vetus Latina (MS W). The correction is, however, also found in NH and thus stems from the predecessor of Aquila, the leader of the *kaige* recension ([Ur-]Theodotion). Moreover, Ziegler notes that this reading is supported indirectly by Justin Martyr (Dial. 107.3).[63]

20. Jonah 4:2: With the OG, FMP reads ω preceding κυριε, unlike *kaige*, which does not have the *omega*. *Kaige* does, however, add a *paragraphos* sign here.[64] For the omission of και ειπεν in 4:2 by the second hand in FMP, see note 25.

21. Jonah 4:4: The second hand adds a final *nu* on top of the last letter of the name of Jonah.

22. Jonah 4:5: The second hand corrects π into φ in αφιδη.[65]

23. Jonah 4:6: The second hand adds an *iota adscriptum* to κολοκυνθη.

24. Jonah 4:9: The second hand adds a final *nu* to the name of Jonah.[66]

---

56. Ziegler, *Duodecim Prophetae*, 250.

57. The *kaige* text here does not repeat the ανηρ (a word typical of the *kaige*) but renders the rest of the sentence consistenly. See Tov, *Greek Minor Prophets Scroll*, 30–31.

58. Sanders, *Minor Prophets in the Freer Collection*, 187; Tov, *Greek Minor Prophets Scroll*, 30–31.

59. Ziegler, *Duodecim Prophetae*, 250.

60. Note again the addition of final *sigma* to the name of Jonah by the second hand (Sanders, *Minor Prophets in the Freer Collection*, 93).

61 Ibid., 93.

62. Ibid., 187.

63. Ziegler, *Duodecim Prophetae*, 251.

64. Sanders, *Minor Prophets in the Freer Collection*, 187; Tov, *Greek Minor Prophets Scroll*, 30–31.

65. Ibid.

66. Sanders, *Minor Prophets in the Freer Collection*, 94.

Summary

The following is a survey of the twenty-four cases studied above.

	1, the first hand		2, the second hand		(3, the third hand)[67]	
	OG	MT	OG	MT	(OG	MT)
1:1		x = *kaige* = α'	x			
1:8	x[68]					
1:11			x (corr. of Greek)			
1:12			x			
1:13			x (corr. of Greek)			
2:5	x (>< *kaige*)					
2:6	x (appr.[69]; >< *kaige*)					
2:7			(x)[70]	(x)[71]		
3:1			x (appr.[72])			
3:3	x (>< *kaige*)					
3:3			(x)			
3:4	x (>< *kaige*)					
3:4	x (>< *kaige*)					
3:5				x (= *kaige*)		
3:5			x (corr. of Greek)			
3:7	x (appr.[73])					
3:7			?			
3:8	x (>< *kaige* and MT)					
3:10	x[74]					
4:1				x (= *kaige;* Symm?)		
4:2	x (>< *kaige*[75])					

67. I will study the third hand in another discussion.
68. I admit that FMP does offer its own (shorter) version of the OG here.
69. FMP transposes the OG text.
70. Only part of the reading is a correction of OG.
71. Only part of the reading is also found in Symmachus and Theodotion.
72. FMP transposes the OG reading.
73. FMP has the reading transposed.
74. FMP has its own leveled version of the OG here.
75. *Kaige,* however, does have a *paragraphos* sign here.

4:4	x
4:5	x (corr. of Greek)
4:6	x (corr. of Greek)
4:9	x

From this analysis of the twenty-four variants in the book of Jonah, we can come to the following conclusions.

1. The text of the first scribe truly stands in the tradition of the OG.
2. The text of the first scribe has one reading in common with the early Jewish revisionists, especially with *kaige* in 1:1, where the main character, Jonah, is called by his Jewish name, "Jonah," not by his Greek name, "Jonas."
3. The text of the first scribe, however, has many readings that are non-*kaige* (2:5; 2:6; 3:3; 3:4; 3:4; 3:8; 4:2), and thus this text cannot be identified with *kaige*.
4. In two cases, the first scribe offers his or her own version of the OG (1:8; 3:10).
5. The second hand made corrections whenever there was an easy way to enter corrections.
6. The text of the second hand also stands in the tradition of the OG.
7. Two corrections from the second hand are identical with the text of *kaige*, 3:5 and 4:1, the latter also being the variant offered by the later Symmachus. The 2:7 correction is also, but only partially, found in Symmachus and Theodotion.
8. Most of the corrections by the second scribe, however, are toward the OG text (1:1; 1:12; 3:1; 4:4; 4:9) or simply corrections of the Greek language itself (1:11; 1:13; 3:5; 4:5; 4:6).

In sum, the text of the book of Jonah copied by the first scribe of the Freer Minor Prophets Codex firmly stands in the tradition of the Old Greek. The second hand also stands in the same Old Greek tradition. Several of his or her corrections could be seen as reflecting a text closer to the Hebrew text. These corrections, however, do not reflect a systematic revising of the Old Greek text in the direction of MT.

The Unidentified Text in the Freer Minor Prophets Codex*

Malcolm Choat

The codex of the Minor Prophets, MS V in the Freer Gallery of Art,[1] contains one of the earliest (almost complete) texts of the *Dodekapropheton*. In its text, and the

* This essay, in particular the edition of the unidentified text, is the result of autopsy of the manuscript in The Freer Gallery of Art in Washington, D.C., on three separate occasions: March 2001, November 2003, and November 2005. The productivity of these visits was substantially enhanced by the hospitality and assistance of the Freer Gallery staff, among whom I am particularly indebted to Tim Kirk, Susan Kitsoulis, and Christina Popenfus of Collections Storage and Martha Smith (Paper Conservator, Department of Conservation and Scientific Research) for her advice and expertise in reassembling the papyrus. My thanks to the Freer Gallery for permission to publish the text and image of the unidentified text on pp. 79–80 of the codex, to Cory Grace for facilitating this, and to Neil Greentree for arranging for new images to be made of the last page of the codex. The first trip to Washington, D.C., was funded by a traveling fellowship awarded by the Australian Academy for the Humanities, to whom I am grateful for the support that allowed this project to begin.

1. The codex is commonly known as "Washington MS V" or "Freer MS V"; the Freer Gallery inventory number is F1916.768. Below I refer to it simply as MS V. It was edited by Henry A. Sanders in Henry A. Sanders and Carl Schmidt, *The Minor Prophets in the Freer Collection and the Berlin Fragment of Genesis* (University of Michigan Studies, Humanistic Series 21; New York: Macmillan, 1927). Although the edition was to some extent cooperative, because Sanders was responsible for the edition of the Minor Prophets I refer to this edition under his name alone below. A photographic facsimile appeared in Henry A. Sanders, *Facsimile of the Washington Manuscript of the Minor Prophets in the Freer Collection and the Berlin Fragment of Genesis* (Ann Arbor: University of Michigan, 1927). The first (very preliminary) report on the manuscript appeared in Henry A. Sanders, "A Papyrus Manuscript of the Minor Prophets," HTR 14 (1921): 181–87. The manuscript is W in the Rahlfs list (Alfred Rahlfs and Detlef Fraenkel, *Verzeichnis der griechischen Handschriften des Alten Testament* [Göttingen: Vandenhoeck & Ruprecht, 2004], 1:387–89) and the Göttingen edition of Joseph Ziegler, *Duodecim prophetae* (2nd ed.; Göttingen: Vandenhoek & Ruprecht, 1967) (see p. 8). It is no. 284 in Joseph van Haelst, *Catalogue des papyrus littéraires juifs et chrétiens* (Paris: Sorbonne, 1976); no. 08 in Kurt Aland, *Biblische Papyri: Altes Testament, Neues Testament, Varia, Apokryphen* (vol. 1 of *Repertorium der griechischen christlichen Papyri;* PTS 18; Berlin: de Gruyter, 1976); and no. 3124 in the Leuven Database of Ancient Books (http://ldab.arts.kuleuven.be/).

numerous and various corrections made to it, we have an important early witness to, and insights into the transmission and textual history of, the Minor Prophets. But the codex itself also reflects the circumstances of its production and how it came to be used. Many aspects of this story remain untold, however, for despite the long-recognized importance of the text, only rarely has the codex itself been investigated in any detail. In this essay, as well as drawing together what is known about the codex, I give attention to the nature and language of marginal glosses and a first edition of the acephalous and unidentified text that follows the Minor Prophets. These matters provide the basis for new observations about the ancient life of the manuscript.

Acquisition and Provenance

The most recent stages in the history of MS V are the easiest to reconstruct. As is the case with so many manuscripts from Egypt purchased in the early decades of the twentieth century, it came via the Cairo antiquities dealer Maurice Nahman. David Askren,[2] an American missionary living in Medinet el-Fayoum in the Fayum, had acquired the codex in 1916, along with a large consignment of Coptic papyri, which came in the first instance to Nahman and his Cairo antiquities dealership.[3] In 1915, Askren had discussed with Francis Kelsey the possibility of the latter purchasing such papyri as Askren could acquire in Egypt. Perhaps because no formal arrangement had been made, and probably because Kelsey's fundraising efforts on behalf of the University of Michigan (later to result in the largest North American papyrus collection) had not yet begun, Kelsey persuaded J. P. Morgan Jr.[4] and Charles Freer to collaborate in purchasing the papyri. So, in 1916 they purchased, apparently sight-unseen,[5] the lot of papyri, under an agreement

2. Askren later also acquired the University of Michigan Papyrus Collection's portion of $\mathfrak{P}^{46}$ = P.Mich. inv. 6238, the Epistles of Paul. See Arthur E. R. Boak, "The Building of the University of Michigan Papyrus Collection," *Michigan Alumnus Quarterly Review* 66/10 (1959): 35–42 (esp. 41).

3. Sanders, *Minor Prophets in the Freer Collection,* 1; Boak, "University of Michigan Papyrus Collection," 36–37; Leo Depuydt, *Catalogue of Coptic Manuscripts in the Pierpont Morgan Library* (Leuven: Peeters, 1993), lxxiv–lxxv. Depuydt makes use of the unpublished catalogues (not seen by me) of the Coptic manuscripts in the Pierpont Morgan Library by Henri Hyvernat (1935) and T. C. Petersen (1948), which bear considerably on these questions. [Ed. note: See also the discussion of Askren and the acquisition of these materials by Kent Clarke in this volume.]

4. The son of the founder of the New York Library that bears his name, J. Pierpont Morgan, who had already acquired the large Coptic library of the monastery of Hamouli and the former collection of Lord Amherst before his death in 1913. See Depuydt, *Catalogue of Coptic Manuscripts,* lvi–lxxiv.

5. "By correspondence," according to Boak ("University of Michigan Papyrus Collection," 36). It is not clear if either millionaire collector had a representative in Egypt at the time.

whereby Morgan would take Coptic texts and Freer Greek ones.[6] Duly divided, once received by Kelsey in 1920, the lot proved to contain only a single Greek item (MS V) alongside Coptic manuscripts of various ultimate provenances. Sanders stated in his edition of MS V that the Coptic sections of the purchase "belonged with the important collection acquired by J. Pierpont Morgan in 1911,"[7] thereby reporting the assertion[8] that these manuscripts likewise came from the library of the monastery of St. Michael at Hamouli in the Fayum, the bulk of whose library Pierpont Morgan Sr. had acquired in December 1911.[9] But those who have worked with the Coptic items have doubted this.[10] They are mixed in character; some come from a religious institution in the Fayum but not the monastery of Hamouli.[11]

Little more can be said, then, on the provenance of the Minor Prophets manuscript. Not even the purchase history is totally clear. On the best testimony, Askren acquired the manuscripts "in the Fayum" and then sold them on through Nahman, although the various accounts present slightly different details.[12] The provenance of MS V is routinely given as the Fayum,[13] resting largely (or perhaps totally?) on the testimony that Askren acquired them (or that they were acquired from Nahman?) "in the Fayum."[14] Sanders states that the manuscripts were purchased from Cairo; that is, their immediate home before being sold was Nahman's antiquities dealership, which makes sense, but one would want to be certain that the codex did not come from elsewhere and formed part of the "lot" only when combined by Nahman with the Coptic manuscripts acquired by Askren, to be

---

6. Depuydt, *Catalogue of Coptic Manuscripts,* lxxiv.

7. Sanders, *Minor Prophets in the Freer Collection,* 1

8. Of unknown ultimate origin but presumably from Askren (and from whomever he bought the manuscripts) or Nahman.

9. See Depuydt, *Catalogue of Coptic Manuscripts,* lvi–lxix.

10. See esp. the doubts of Henri Hyvernat cited in ibid., lxxv.

11. Two British Library codices almost certainly from the same source as and roughly contemporaneous with the five Coptic codices in this Morgan purchase were donated to a shrine at Ihrit, in the Fayum north of Hamouli; see ibid., lxxvi.

12. Boak ("University of Michigan Papyrus Collection," 36–37): "Freer … purchased by correspondence, from Maurice Nahman … a papyrus codex or book of the Minor prophets, acquired by Dr. Askren in the Fayum"; Sanders (*Minor Prophets in the Freer Collection,* 1): "bought in Cairo in 1916 from Maurice Nahman. It formed part of a purchase of manuscripts … made by Dr. David L. Askren; Depuydt (*Catalogue of Coptic Manuscripts,* lxxiv with n. 109), reporting T. C. Petersen describing one of the Coptic codices: "part of a find … purchased in 1916 in the Fauym, from a Cairo dealer."

13. E.g., Aland, *Biblische Papyri,* 27 (on I, 08); more cautious remarks by van Haelst, *Catalogue des papyrus littéraires,* no. 284 ("très probablement le Fayoum") and Kurt Aland and Hans-Udo Rosenbaum, *Kirchenväter-Papyri, Teil 1: Beschreibungen* (vol. 2 of *Repertorium der griechischen christlichen Papyri;* Berlin: de Gruyter, 1995), 39 (on 09): "vermutlich Faijum."

14. Sanders, *Minor Prophets in the Freer Collection,* 1.

assured that such was also its find-spot. Such certainty not forthcoming, there is little to impugn the traditional provenance. Dealers' reports cannot always be believed: that the provenance of texts can be falsified to enhance the interest of the buyer is shown in the same purchase, with the false claim that the Coptic leaves proceeded from the monastery at Hamouli. However, it is less clear what would be gained in the case of MS V by deliberately falsifying such information.

The dialect of the Coptic glosses that line many pages suggests no association with the Fayum. Their dialect is the main Sahidic, named (via Arabic *Sa'id*) for Upper Egypt. Dialect need not necessarily indicate geography, as Sahidic was both the primary literary vehicle and quotidian vehicular dialect throughout Upper Egypt[15] and commonly used in both capacities throughout the country. As these are glosses, a more private production than a full literary text, we may reasonably suppose that the scribe used the dialect with which he was most comfortable. Note, for instance, the Middle Egyptian ("Mesokemic") dialect used in the glossary to Hosea and Amos from a similar date to the Minor Prophets codex.[16] Were the glosser a native of the Fayum, one might have expected the Fayumic dialect (itself an extremely productive literary dialect in the period) to have been used.[17] As already noted, however, to say that Sahidic was the scribe's usual dialect scarcely delimits the geographical possibilities, except to point it away from Lower Egypt and the Fayum. Affinities in the Minor Prophets text in MS V with the text preserved in the Achmimic dialect should be less relied upon in this regard. Groups of biblical manuscripts are commonly given geographical associations, but the impulse should be suppressed when the name comes from Coptic dialects, which mostly have only the most general association with the town or district from which they derive their name. Such a case is that of Akhmim (Panopolis) and Achmimic, which suggest an Upper Egyptian provenance but little

---

15. Roughly Hermopolis and farther south. Sahidic's currency as a documentary *koine* extended much farther, but not seemingly into the Fayum, where the local dialect was used for documents centuries after most other less enchoretic dialects had ceased being used thus.

16. H. I. Bell and H. Thompson, "A Greek-Coptic Glossary to Hosea and Amos," *JEA* 11 (1925): 241–46, plates XXXI–XXXIV. Greek and Coptic are written in the same hand, a crude, documentary, semicursive resembling more Greek hands than contemporary Coptic styles. Bell and Thompson compared the hand to the colophon of BL Or. MS 7594 (dated to the first half of the fourth century), but the glossary hand is earlier. As glossary (on the verso side of the papyrus) is not likely to be more than a century after the recto text (a [property?] register dated to the mid-second century C.E. [ca. 200 C.E. according to Hunt, cited by Bell and Thompson, 241–42]), Bell and Thompson suggested the late third century for the verso. "Environ 300," van Haelst, *Catalogue des papyrus littéraires*, no. 286; third/fourth century C.E., M. Hasitzka, *Neue Texte und Dokumentation zum Koptisch-Unterricht* (Vienna: Hollinek, 1990), no. 257a.

17. Compare the glosses in an archaic form of Fayumic alongside the Greek text of Isaiah in P.Beatty VII. See Frederic G. Kenyon, ed., *Isaiah, Jeremiah, Ecclesiasticus* (vol. 6 of *Chester Beatty Biblical Papyri;* London: Emery Walker, 1937).

more. This was evidently the conclusion drawn by Sanders, for whom "the home of the MS was in Sahidic territory, or in that of some closely related dialect."[18]

Thus there are factors pointing away from the Fayum, and nothing except [illegible] or third hand, and at times contradictory reports of its purchase history to suggest that provenance. These indications by no means rule out that the codex found a home in the Fayum close to or after its death as a living book, but it might be more prudent to list its provenance (as with so many early biblical manuscripts) as "unknown."[19]

Physical Description, Hand, and Date

The codex gives the appearance of having been a "well-loved book." Marginal annotations were made for at least a century, and possibly more, after its production. Nor was the book buried early in its life in a fully preserved state but, instead, was passed through generations until it lost pages that are no longer found with it. Such suggests that over time it became neglected, but it testifies to a long life.

As reconstructed by Sanders when received in Michigan in 1920,[20] the codex was formed in a single quire,[21] from thin, fine-quality papyrus. In all probability, it originally consisted of twenty-four sheets of papyrus, making forty-eight leaves and a total of ninety-six single pages,[22] each measuring 14 cm wide by 32 cm high.[23]

The first six leaves, and probably the last eight,[24] were lost, likely in antiquity. No system of page numeration was used. The Minor Prophets stood on the

---

18. Sanders, *Minor Prophets in the Freer Collection*, 48.

19. At the very least, a question mark should follow "Fayum."

20. Sanders's presence in Michigan was, of course, the reason for the codex's first destination; see Sanders, *Minor Prophets in the Freer Collection*, 1–10. Kelsey had obtained the manuscript in Egypt (Boak, "University of Michigan Papyrus Collection," 37). [Ed. note: See also Kent Clarke's discussion of the details of the acquisition of the manuscript in his essay in this volume.]

21. See, e.g., Eric G. Turner, *The Typology of the Early Codex* (Philadelphia: University of Pennsylvania Press, 1977), 181 (no. OT 187).

22. Throughout this essay I use "codex page" to refer to pages in the *original* codex as reconstructed, and I refer to the codex page-numeration as assigned by Sanders in his edition of the text of the manuscript and also in the facsimile volume as Text/Facs followed by his page number(s).

23. The largest that survives is 14 cm (W) x 29.5 (H). For varying reconstructed measurements, see Turner, *Typology of the Early Codex* ([32] x 14, followed here); van Haelst, *Catalogue des papyrus littéraires*, no. 284, (35 x 15); Sanders (*Minor Prophets in the Freer Collection*, 10, who had posited a measurement for a double leaf of the codex as 34.4 x 30 cm); Aland, *Biblische Papyri* (no. 08) (34.4 x 14.6 cm).

24. "Six-seven," according to Sanders (*Minor Prophets in the Freer Collection*, 9), but it may not have been so few.

first thirty-nine leaves; the majority of Hosea is lost, although fragments remain; Amos, Micah, Joel, Obadiah, Jonah, Nahum, Habakkuk, Zephaniah, Haggai, Zechariah, and Malachi are substantially preserved, to the last words of Malachi on page 78 of the original codex (= Facsimile 68). Following the Minor Prophets, and perhaps some time later, an unidentified work was copied onto one or more of the blank pages at the end of the codex. This latter text is edited below.

The text of the Minor Prophets is laid out professionally. Generous margins flank a "textual footprint" approximately 26.3 cm high and 10.8 cm wide, allowing forty-six to forty-nine lines per page.[25] The hand is a literary adaptation by a scribe more accustomed to using a cursive, to which he sometimes tends. On the basis of documentary parallels, Sanders dated the hand to the second half of the third century,[26] and subsequent commentators have largely concurred;[27] only Turner suggested a date in the fourth century.[28]

Sanders's palaeographical comparisons are not invalid, but a further piece of evidence on which he relied cannot stand. In some fragmentary lines at the close of the Minor Prophets,[29] Sanders thought he read:

προφ/ κ . . . . . ει[

$\overline{\varepsilon}$ ολοκ^{ο}

While admitting defeat with the first line of this "subscription," he interpreted the second line as "5 *holokottinoi*," referring to the charge for copying the work or the price of the text itself. Taking *holokottinoi* to represent silver denarii, he thus argued that the copying must have been completed prior to around 270 C.E., which agreed with his dating both of the Minor Prophets and of the note.[30] Turner, however, read the second line of the annotation more naturally as ἐ[ξ] ὁλοκλ(ήρου), "complete," a common phrase in such circumstances at the end a work. He also judged that the hand of this subscription was "in any case very definitely later than that of the main scribe of the manuscript."[31]

---

25. See ibid., 9–10, with full marginal measurements.

26. Sanders (ibid., 11–12): "between the middle and the end of the third century."

27. Late third century, van Haelst (*Catalogue des papyrus littéraires*, no. 284); III/IV (i.e., late third/early fourth century), Leuven Database of Ancient Books, no. 3124; later third century, Colin H. Roberts (*Manuscript, Society and Belief in Early Christian Egypt* [London: Oxford University Press, 1979], 16, n. [h]); third century, Aland, *Biblische Papyri* (no. 08).

28. Turner, *Typology of the Early Codex*, 181 (OT 187); cf. 59 (n. *).

29. At the foot of *Text/Facs*, 68. For what follows, see Sanders, *Minor Prophets in the Freer Collection*, 19–24.

30. Sanders, *Minor Prophets in the Freer Collection*, 19: "in a larger hand with blacker ink is a second note of approximately the same date."

31. *Typology of the Early Codex*, 59 (n. *).

The form of the codex, constructed in a single quire, is characteristic of many early (second–third century) codices, and the format was superseded in favor of codices of multiple gatherings of papyrus as codicological technology progressively developed. But the more primitive book-making technique remained in use into the fourth century, and it will not form a guarantee of a pre-Constantinian date in this instance.

An estimate of the date must thus rely largely on palaeography, and here Sanders's comparisons are reasonable; despite the fact that codex was used into the fourth century, from which period the majority of the additions to its margins and final pages likely come, it still seems preferable to locate its original production in the second half of the third century C.E., perhaps toward the close of the century.

Glosses and Marginalia

After the completion of the manuscript, the text continued to be adjusted. Some annotations correct infelicities in the first scribe's words; others store data about the text of the Minor Prophets: another translation, an interpretation, or a clarification. Others gloss the text in another language, in single words or short phrases.

The orthography was subject to revision, and many corrections, both in spelling and grammar, were made. Glosses that had crept into the main text were excised or signaled, and variants were at many points substituted. Other variants were noted in the margins, and in some places a better form of a verse was written at the foot of the page.[32]

This work proceeded with painstaking deliberation,[33] resulting in a far better text (in terms both of orthography and text-character) than that bequeathed by the scribe. Sanders repeatedly referred to the second hand (i.e., the first corrector) as the *diorthotes,* the "corrector," whom Sanders took to have been attached to a scriptorium. Following the work of Kim Haines-Eitzen and others, however, we now recognize that the scribe who gave the manuscript its first thorough set of corrections is more likely to have been the codex's first owner than an employee of a scriptorium. The 274 corrections[34] are the result, not of the methodical checking by one paid for his services, but of the erudition, and tastes, of the person in whose library the text found its first home.

---

32. See Sanders, *Minor Prophets in the Freer Collection,* 25–45.

33. See ibid., 18: "the manuscript was written with care, and corrected with exceptional care."

34. By Sanders's count of those which "appear[ed] to be contemporary" (ibid., 43).

If Sanders's interpretation of the early emendations of the manuscript is correct,[35] then this first owner used the parent manuscript itself as the guide for his corrections; more specifically, the owner used the annotations and glosses on the text, which the original scribe as a rule had ignored.[36] Although the standard explanation for this would posit the work of a scriptorium, we may instead have the sort of private textual transmission one finds mentioned in literary sources.[37] The owner may have had his own scribe, or a professionally trained fellow-Christian, copy the manuscript before correcting it himself to his satisfaction; he then presumably returned the parent manuscript to its owner. Other scenarios, requiring both manuscripts to have remained permanently in the possession of one person or institution, seem to me less likely.

Over time, other hands began to feature in the margins. The ink of these is in the main darker, and most look to have been made some time later.[38] A second corrector (i.e., a "third hand"[39]), operating probably in the fourth century,[40] added elements that seemed to Sanders to have been derived from the corrector's own knowledge of Hebrew rather than from any known translation.[41] Later hands continued to add some few notes on the text in Greek.[42]

Whether or not some of those who emended the text may have had a facility with Hebrew, a certain bilingual environment is attested to by the appearance of a number of short Coptic glosses in the left, right, and bottom margins at *Text/Facs,* pp. 14, 16, 18, 20, 22, 24, 28, 32, 34, 39, 42, 46, 48, 50.[43] Virtually none are complete, although Sanders's readings can at times be improved. At p. 39, in the left margin opposite ἐξέλιπον ἀπὸ βρώσεως πρόβατα (Hab 3:17), where Sanders gives ⲁϥⲛⲟ|ⲭϥ | ⲉⲃⲟⲗ, read rather ⲁⲩⲛⲟ|ⲭϥ | ⲉⲃⲟⲗ. This could be read as an active verb, "they cast him out," and would thus retain the rare plural form found

35. Ibid., 44.

36. Although some were erroneously incorporated into the text; see ibid., 44.

37. Kim Haines-Eitzen, *Guardians of Letters: Literacy, Power, and the Transmitters of Early Christian Literature* (Oxford: Oxford University Press, 2000), esp. 19–40.

38. Sanders, *Minor Prophets in the Freer Collection,* 10; cf. 43–45.

39. In so far as the hands can be differentiated; see ibid., 44.

40. "At least a century later than the first scribe," in Sanders's opinion (ibid., 44).

41. Ibid., 28, 44–45. Sanders's position was refined somewhat by Ziegler in his Göttingen edition (*Duodecim prophetae,* 32–34). A similar tendency toward independence from the known Greek versions (especially the LXX) has been detected among the early Coptic versions; see Willem Grossouw, *The Coptic Versions of the Minor Prophets: A Contribution to the Study of the Septuagint* (Rome: Pontifical Biblical Institute, 1938), 112–19, who takes as his starting point, however, that a lost Greek version (or lost sections of known versions) is the intermediary between the Hebrew and the Coptic. Cf. the contribution of Kristin De Troyer to this volume.

42. E.g., at *Text/Facs,* 30, where another more cursive hand ("fourth?") writes a gloss in the left margin (not the right, as stated by Sanders, *Minor Prophets in the Freer Collection,* 46), perhaps a lost variant (?) or interpretation of the text of Jonah 2:6 opposite.

43. Sanders, *Minor Prophets in the Freer Collection,* 46–48.

here in MS V. However, comparison with the Achmimic version[44] indicates that the passive was intended: “it was cast forth,” that is, the flock. Here, however, the verb differs. Where the Achmimic uses ⲧⲉⲕ⸗,[45] the scribe glosses the text with [illegible];[46] the reading of the Sahidic version, lost at this point,[47] may be preserved here. Above, opposite Hab 3:11, Sanders read ⲕⲛⲁ. This occurs nearby in the Achmimic version at Hab 3:12,[48] where in MS V the first corrector has added a final sigma to ολιγωσει to form a second-person verb (as is ⲕⲛⲁ). But if this was the intended referent, it is not clear why the gloss would have been added opposite Hab 3:11; the word looks in fact more like ⲕⲃ̣ⲁ (“to be cool/coolness”?[49]), but any relationship with the nearby Greek is no more obvious. In the bottom margin of p. 16 (Mic 2:10–3:9), read ⲛⲁⲩ ⲉⲣⲟϥ (“see/behold him/it”) or the palaeographically superior but less readily explicable ⲛⲁϥ ⲉⲣⲟϥ,[50] instead of ⲛϣ ⲉⲣⲟϥ. On p. 50, opposite Zech 3:8–9, something like]ϩ̣ⲓ̣ⲏ̣ϥ |]ϣⲁ (or ϣⲛ̣)? looks preferable to Sanders’s]ⲉⲣⲟϥ |]ϣⲁ, despite the appropriateness of the restoration suggested to him by Schmidt.[51] Further conjectural readings could be listed,[52] but detailed textual analysis is not likely in the short term to reveal any more relations with

---

44. ⲟⲩϣϩⲉ ⲛⲉⲥⲁⲩ ⲁⲩⲧⲉⲕϥ ⲁⲃⲁⲗ ϩⲛ̄ ⲧⲉϥϣⲉⲉⲓⲣⲉ: “a flock of sheep is cast out if its fold”; see Walter Till, *Die Achmîmische Version der zwölf kleinen Propheten* (Hauniae: Gyldendalske Baghande-Nordisk, 1927), 67.

45. From ⲧϣⲕ; see Walter Ewing Crum, *A Coptic Dictionary* (Oxford: Oxford University Press, 1939), 404a.

46. From ⲛⲟⲩϫⲉ; see ibid., 248a.

47. See Grossouw, *Coptic Versions of the Minor Prophets,* 5; cf. the fragments edited at C. Wessely, *Griechische und Koptische Texte theologischen Inhalts* (Leipzig, 1914; repr., Amsterdam: Hakkert, 1967), 4:168, which just fail to preserve the relevant words.

48. ϩⲙ̄ ⲡⲕϭϣⲛ̣ⲧ ⲕⲛⲁ ϩⲓ ⲡⲕⲁϩ, for which Till (*Die Achmîmische Version,* 66 n. e) suggested “du kommst auf die Erde?”

49. See Crum, *Coptic Dictionary,* 100a.

50. As a lacuna stands to the left, a verb with direct and indirect objects may be imagined.

51. Sanders, *Minor Prophets in the Freer Collection,* 48.

52. E.g., in the left margin near the foot of *Text/Facs,* p. 20, read]ϣⲧⲛ̄ for]ϣⲡⲟ̄ opposite Mic 7:5; cf. ⲁⲛⲉⲧϩⲓϫϣⲧⲛⲉ in the Achmimic (Till, *Die Achmîmische Version,* 48), which would be Sahidic ⲉⲛⲉⲧϩⲓϫϣⲧⲛ̄, where W has επι ηγουμενοις σου. At the bottom of the same page ⲉ̣ⲧⲛⲁϥⲙ̣ⲁⲣⲟⲥ̣ (Sanders: ⲉⲧⲛⲁϥⲙⲁⲣⲟ..) is likely. It is difficult to see a letter before the *tau,* but one seems required for a complete word; nor does the reconstructed word (“he who will bind it”?) obviously relate to anything in the text of Micah above. At *Text/Facs,* p. 32 (in left margin opposite Nah 1:2), read] ⲕ̣ⲃ̣ⲁ for]ⲕ̣ⲛⲁ: cf. again the Achmimic: ⲟⲩⲛⲟⲩⲧⲉ ⲛ̄ⲣⲉϥⲕϣϩ ⲡⲉ ⲡϫⲁⲉⲓⲥ ⲉϩⲁⲣⲉϥϫⲓⲕⲃⲁ at Nah 1:2; it is likely that all the many words down this margin gloss words from the opening verses of this book, but the rest are too common for precise identification or not sufficiently legible. At p. 22, in the left margin]ϣⲗ̄ⲧ may be an abbreviation for ϣⲉⲗⲉⲉⲧ, as νυμφην stands opposite in the Greek at Joel 1:9, and ϣⲉⲗⲉⲉⲧ is used to translate this Greek word here in the Achmimic and elsewhere in the other Coptic versions of the Minor Prophets (Crum, *Coptic Dictionary,* 560b).

the attendant Greek text than those few deduced by Sanders where the Coptic provides a version or interpretation of the nearby text.[53]

As indicated earlier, the dialect of the text is Sahidic, as far as can be gauged. Note in particular the consistent o-vocalization in ⲉⲃⲟⲗ, ⲉⲣⲟϥ, and so forth, which shows little affinity with the dialect of the Fayum,[54] where the codex was allegedly purchased.

The date of the Coptic glosses is not easy to estimate. The hand is less cursive and does not look as early as the glossary to Hosea and Amos,[55] which is roughly contemporary with the production of the codex itself.[56] However, the semicursive hand used compares well with other fourth-century hands,[57] and there is no necessity to assign it to a later date than that.

As judged by Sanders (not uncommonly among scholars when faced with these types of texts), the Coptic writer did "not know Greek very well" and had used the glosses as a preaching aid.[58] These are logically independent assertions, but neither need necessarily be the case. That the scribe was able to gloss the text speaks against the assertion that he had a poor knowledge of Greek, for unless he was copying from another glossary, the translations and interpretations would have been his own. If the glosses were to serve as a preaching aid, on Sanders's interpretation they would have been used "to interpret the text orally, probably in a sermon after he had read it," that is, the Greek text.[59] Actually, however, the

---

53. Viz. at *Text/Facs,* pp. 14, 39, 46, and perhaps 50 (but see above); see the discussion at Sanders, *Minor Prophets in the Freer Collection,* 47–48. Identified in the glass plates as pp. 1–2, and appearing thus in the facsimile edition, are fragments that Sanders thought may have come from Hosea or the binding on the codex (Sanders, *Minor Prophets in the Freer Collection,* 228; but see below). That some of these fragments bear hieroglyphics shows decisively that the box of manuscripts was not a homogenous entity, but such contamination could easily have taken place, e.g., in the papyrus dealer's store. Among the fragments are two, labeled d and e, that bear Coptic words, the words of one giving the distinct appearance of being marginal glosses to a Greek text (with script, as far as can be judged, not dissimilar to that of the Minor Prophets), which survives only to one letter's width on one side. These may be further fragments of Coptic marginal glosses from any one of the numerous pages where the margins are missing, but as their nature is not obvious, examination of them (along with more detailed consideration of the marginal glosses on the manuscript itself) must await a future opportunity.

54. Specifically, there are none of the vocalizations and lambdacisms characteristic of that dialect.

55. See above, at n. 16.

56. In the opinion of the editors. But Hunt, again, felt it could be later (Bell and Thompson, "Greek-Coptic Glossary," 241: "if not fourth").

57. Note examples especially among those found in the Kellis papyri. See Iain Gardner, ed., *Kellis Literary Texts* (Oxford: Oxbow, 1996); and Iain Gardner, Anthony Alcock, and Wolf-Peter Funk, eds., *Coptic Documentary Texts from Kellis* (Oxford: Oxbow, 1999).

58. Sanders, *Minor Prophets in the Freer Collection,* 48.

59. Ibid., 48; cf. Bell and Thompson, "Greek-Coptic Glossary," 243 (although doubting the explanation in that case).

writer's sound knowledge of Greek is again suggested in this proposal. The Coptic glosses are likely to have been made in the fourth century at the latest, centuries before common knowledge of Greek faded. Nor need they be preaching aids: Coptic writers at times made their own "on-the-spot" translations of scripture from Greek when quoting, and the manuscripts they used must have come to resemble one such as this, with felicitous expressions or reminders written in the margins.

Ancient Acquisition History

As far as we are able to trace it, the ownership of the codex begins with Askren and/or Nahman in 1916. As to the context of production and use in antiquity, where and by whom the codex was made and used, we have next to no direct testimony and must rely on inferences.

As noted already, Sanders's discussion explicitly assumed that both the production and the first, thoroughgoing correction took place in a scriptorium. At one stage Sanders even asserts matter of factly that this was a "pagan scriptorium."[60] This, too, is not an uncommon assumption, but there is to my knowledge little evidence for such "cross-religion" copying.[61] Nor, indeed, is there much evidence for Christian scriptoria in the period prior to Eusebius's lifetime, when our manuscript was most likely produced.[62] "Private scribal networks," formed of people who could both read and afford books, largely transmitted literature of all types, including Christian texts, throughout Egypt.[63] Allowance must be made by the third century, however, for the bishop, as (in the majority of cases) a relatively prominent and comfortable (if not rich) member of Christian communities, to have attached his own node of his "scribal network" to a church, in effect creating an embryonic "scriptorium" (even if such consisted of one scribe). We are a long way from the monastic scriptoria of the later fourth century and still further from the medieval scriptoria sometimes incautiously used as the model for how things "must" have been, but that the production of the codex took place within

60. Sanders, *Minor Prophets in the Freer Collection,* 22: "*the* pagan scriptorium" (emphasis added).

61. Note that I do not rule out the likelihood of some form of cooperation in the copying of Greek versions of the Hebrew Bible. The place to start a (still necessary) search for a broader context, it seems to me, would be the so-called "magical papyri," among whose syncretic texts can be found the *nomina sacra* compendiums first used by Christians, for both pagan deities and "the gods."

62. See Haines-Eitzen, *Guardians of Letters,* 83–91. But cf. also Harry Y. Gamble, *Books and Readers in the Early Church: A History of Early Christian Texts* (New Haven: Yale University Press, 1995), 82–143.

63. The phrase is that of Haines-Eitzen; see *Guardians of Letters,* 77–104.

the confines of such "churches" as existed in the second half of the third century[64] should remain a possibility.

According to Sanders, the "MS probably arose in a Coptic community."[65] He based this opinion, not only on textual alliances with the Achmimic version,[66] but also on the presence and dialect of the Coptic glosses. Moreover, he regarded the community as a monastery:

> The monastery in which it was preserved and for which it was probably written was either Coptic or affiliated with the Copts. With the waning of Greek influence in the country districts during the fourth and fifth centuries Copts replaced the Greeks in some monasteries and in still more there ceased to be Greek speaking Copts. This is probably what happened in the ancient home of W [Minor Prophets codex].[67]

Sanders wrote these words in the 1920s, but it is still frustratingly common that monasteries, which only began appearing in the fourth century, are invoked as the producers or intended destinations of manuscripts written in the *third* century. Either the manuscript is misdated, or this is simply not possible. Even if the codex was produced first in the fourth century, there is quite simply no necessity whatsoever for a monastery to have been involved. A Christian book culture had developed long before monasticism, and such continued even when monasteries began to have their own scriptoria in the fourth century. Nor does the presence of Coptic in the margins prove the involvement of a monastery, as the use of Coptic by Christians also arose before monasteries and continued outside a monastic context for centuries.[68] The textual relationship with the Achmimic version is notable and significant, but this does not mean that an actual Coptic version of the Minor Prophets was extant in the second half of the third century. In actual fact, however, there is no inherent implausibility in that, since translations of the LXX/Old Greek versions predate copies of the New Testament in the

---

64. Evidence is slim, and archaeologically nonexistent in Egypt, although the excavators of the Dakhleh Oasis village of Ismant el-Kharab (Roman Kellis) believe the small church, which they take for a "house church," dates to the latter part of the third century; see Gillian E. Bowen, "The Small Church at Ismant el-Kharab, Ancient Kellis," *Bulletin of the Australian Centre for Egyptology* 11 (2000): 29–34; idem, "The Fourth-Century Churches at Ismant el-Kharab," in *The Dakhleh Oasis Project: Preliminary Reports on the 1994–1995 to 1998–1999 Field Seasons* (ed. C. A. Hope and G. E. Bowen; Oxford: Oxbow, 2002), 65–85.

65. Sanders, *Minor Prophets in the Freer Collection,* 21

66. Ibid., 25–45. The surviving Achmimic text was clearly a rendering of a previous Sahidic version; see Grossouw, *Coptic Versions of the Minor Prophets,* 121.

67. Sanders, *Minor Prophets in the Freer Collection,* 48.

68. Indeed, as time went on and the use of Greek faded, Coptic became more commonly used outside monasteries (e.g., for everyday documentation by the late Byzantine and early Arab period); only with the supersession of Coptic by Arabic as a quotidian language in the second millennium did the former retreat behind the walls of the monasteries.

Coptic manuscript record.[69] But the textual tradition represented by MS V could just as easily be interacting with the Greek ancestor of the Achmimic version, with no necessity for it to be done in a "Coptic community."

In the end, we have next to no information on where and for whom the codex was produced and by whom it was used. The subscription at the end of the text of the Minor Prophets was not associated with the original copying and does not refer to it. It may, indeed, have been added after the unknown work that follows Malachi,[70] perhaps to signal that the Minor Prophets ended at that point. Notwithstanding the similarity with a text now largely witnessed to by Coptic manuscripts, the codex was produced in Greek and emended in Greek. It has been suggested that one or more of the subsequent commentators annotated the manuscript, at times perhaps on the basis of their own knowledge of Hebrew. If such was not the case, however, and these variants can be explained by our lacunose knowledge of the versions (or, indeed, by lost versions), then the manuscript still found its home in a community where more than one version of scripture was known. This is supported by the unidentified Greek text in the manuscript, which cites Ezekiel in the version of Symmachus. At some stage in the fourth century, the manuscript was annotated by someone who wrote and/or preached in Coptic. If we assume one ancient home, then it must have contained the following elements: a good library, the presence of those with above-average knowledge of the text (i.e., "scholars"), and a multilingual character. These data can be used to imagine the early life of the manuscript, but they will not allow us to pronounce definitively.

The Unidentified Text

In addition to the numerous corrections and glosses made in at least four hands, the codex was used, probably less than a century after the completion of the Minor Prophets, to accommodate another text. Such, at least, is the natural conclusion from the fragments of a text in another hand (that were found in both boxes), but on similar papyrus.

69. See, e.g., the Coptic Glosses to *P. Beatty* VII; the glossary published in Bell and Thompson, "Greek-Coptic Glossary"; Bernd Diebner and Rodolphe Kasser, eds., *Hamburger Papyrus bil. 1: Die alttestamentlichen Texte des Papyrus bilinguis 1 der Staats- und Universitätsbibliothek Hamburg* (Geneva: Cramer, 1989); Rodolphe Kasser, *Livre des Proverbes* (Papyrus Bodmer 6: Leuven: Secrétariat du CorpusSCO, 1960); Walter Ewing Crum, "Un psaume en dialect d'Akhmim," in *Orient grec, romain et byzantin* (vol. 2 of *Mélanges Maspero;* Cairo: Institut français d'Archéologie orientale, 1934), 73–76.

70. See Turner, *Typology of the Early Codex*, 59 (n. *).

Sanders allowed the possibility that, despite being found in the same two boxes in which the manuscript was delivered,[71] these fragments did not actually derive from the Minor Prophets codex.[72] It is true that fragments that manifestly did not come from the manuscript were contained in the two boxes, notably, three pieces bearing hieroglyphs.[73] These most probably entered the boxes in the papyrus dealer's store or were found with the papyrus.[74] However, the papyrus of the fragments that interest us here compares in its quality and production with that of the Minor Prophets,[75] and it is easiest to believe (as assumed in Sanders's subsequent discussion) that the work reflected in these fragments stood on some or all of the pages left blank at the end of the codex when the Prophets had been completed.

As conserved at the close of Sanders's work, and illustrated thus in the facsimile edition, forty fragments of the unidentified text were placed together in the glass plates as pp. 69/70 of the manuscript. The largest measured at its farthest extent 5.3 cm wide by 8.4 cm high. In visits I made to the Freer between 2001 and 2005, further joins were made, so that a contiguous group of fragments measuring at its farthest extent 15.7 cm high by 9 cm wide were assembled, with another

---

71. Fragments of the text are clearly visible in plates II and III in Sanders, *Minor Prophets in the Freer Collection,* which show these fragments in the bottom of both boxes after the manuscript had been removed.

72. Sanders, *Minor Prophets in the Freer Collection,* 9: "These leaves [the nine spare at the end of the codex] may have been used somewhat later for another work, as fragments in a slightly different hand, but of the same general date, were found in both boxes of fragments." See also the introduction to Sanders, *Facsimile of the Washington Manuscript of the Minor Prophets,* viii: "a number of very dim fragments, which seems to come from a different manuscript and to have been written by a different hand."

73. See plates 1–2 in Sanders, *Facsimile of the Washington Manuscript of the Minor Prophets.* The largest fragment can be seen in the photo of the "second box of fragments" (Sanders, *Minor Prophets in the Freer Collection,* plate 3). Sanders believed that "certain small fragments [on plates 1–2] … seem to have come from the binding" of the codex (*Minor Prophets in the Freer Collection,* 228), but it seems likely that the outside six leaves of the codex were lost before its modern purchase history began, perhaps long before, as some rearrangement of loose leaves appears to have happened in antiquity (*Minor Prophets in the Freer Collection,* 4, 9). In these circumstances, it is not likely that many (any?) fragments from the cartonage would be found with the manuscript in this manner, as the finders seem to have taken care to preserve everything they could locate from the manuscript. Sanders had hypothesized in his first report that there was never any binding ("A Papyrus Manuscript of the Minor Prophets," 182) but revised this in light of his full examination (Sanders, *Minor Prophets in the Freer Collection,* 3–4, 7–8).

74. Nahman's store might be thought more likely, but note that Sanders assumed that the boxes in which the manuscript and other fragments arrived represented the state in which they were packed *by the finders* (Sanders, *Minor Prophets in the Freer Collection,* 3).

75. Sanders's assessment (ibid., 9: "the papyrus is also similar, but it too decayed to venture the assertion that it is the same") is confirmed by inspection, and there are no differences sufficient to justify the opposite view.

block of fragments measuring 6.2 cm high by 5.3 cm wide sitting just below it (although not quite joining the other assemblage of fragments).[76] It is the text of these two bodies of assembled fragments that is edited here. Before we look at the proposed transcription, it is necessary to consider some technical matters about [illegible]

Of the opening of the codex, where Hosea once stood, only fragments remain, and it is likely that the book suffered a commensurate damage in its final leaves. Also, it is likely that the fragments of the unidentified text all (or nearly all) come from the one page at the end of the manuscript.[77] On the most probable reconstruction of the codex, the leaf on which stood the unidentified text is pp. 69/70 in the facsimile (pp. 79–80 of the original codex). The conjugate leaf (i.e., the other half of the folded sheet of papyrus) is represented as pp. 7/8 of the facsimile (pp. 17/18 of the original codex), containing Amos 4:1–5:15.

Sanders gave a transcription of the text of the largest fragment of what he regarded as pp. 69/70 of the codex and identified the recto and verso sides of the fragment (i.e., the sides with papyrus fibers running, respectively, horizontal or vertical relative to the writing).[78] He judged the recto to be the side on which Ezekiel is quoted (Ἐζεκιῆλ βοᾷ καὶ λέγει). However, as Sanders himself admitted,[79] it is sometimes difficult to tell which side of the papyrus is written along the fibers and which across them. Let us look more carefully at the matter.

The codex is formed of a single quire (or "gathering"), and the sheets of papyrus from which the book was constructed were laid one on another with the side with horizontal fibers facing up. Consequently, the verso side of each leaf precedes the recto to the center of the codex, from which point on the order is

---

76. Some initial joins were made during May 2001 by Martha Smith (the Freer's Paper Conservator) and me, but as the papyrus is extremely fragile, further work has proceeded largely on the basis of high-quality digital images provided by the Gallery. Some of the fragment placements made here remain provisional, therefore, although they are in my view certain.

77. It is quite possible that further fragments lie among those put between glass sheets and listed as "Unplaced Fragments." Indeed, I believe I can see tiny fragments with similar handwriting among these, but it has not seemed worth extracting them.

78. Sanders, *Facsimile of the Washington Manuscript of the Minor Prophets*, 228–29. [Ed. note: In the study of parchment codices, however, the terms "recto" and "verso" designate respectively the right and left pages of an open book. Note Eric G. Turner's admonition to avoid the terms in papyrological discussion and instead to refer to sides on which papyrus fibers run vertically or horizontally relative to the writing, or, as a shorthand device, to use ↓ for the former and → for the latter (*Greek Papyri: An Introduction* [Oxford: Clarendon, 1980], 14–15). This is the convention adopted now in volumes of the Oxyrhynchus Papyri, but "recto" and "verso" also remain in widespread use among papyrologists, as in this essay, and outside of papyrological circles as well. Hence, Choat uses the terms here with respect for the wider circle of readers for whom this volume is intended.]

79. Sanders, *Minor Prophets in the Freer Collection*, 7, noting the very thin and compressed nature of the papyrus.

reversed. Thus, at the point where the unidentified text stood, toward the end of the codex, the recto side comes first. And here we have a problem.

There are distinct similarities between p. 69 and p. 7 of the codex in the facsimile, the latter page identified as a verso (by the order of the chapters of Amos).[80] Yet, as noted, Sanders considered his p. 69 a recto page. If this is correct, then it was an odd-numbered, right-hand facing page, and the following page (his p. 70) was the "outside" leaf, which, in Sanders's reconstruction, would be conjugate with codex p. 7, a verso. But although the fiber patterns cannot be precisely matched (difficult given the fragmentary nature of preservation in both sheets), the similarities between p. 7 (verso) and p. 69, on the one hand, and p. 8 (recto) and p. 70, on the other hand, are such that pp. 69 and 70 must be considered the verso and recto, respectively, rather than vice versa. In short, what Sanders took to be the "verso" portion of the text (his p. 70 in the facsimile) should be considered rather as the *recto* and thus should have been p. 69 of the codex in the facsimile edition (or what would have been p. 79 of the full codex). The side shown in the facsimile edition as p. 70 is actually the *recto* and *preceded* what is p. 69 of the facsimile edition.[81]

To turn to another matter, in only one place does a portion of a margin survive in the fragments of the leaf in question. The writing finishes before the right-hand edge of the first eleven lines of the verso often enough to make it almost certain that we have here part of the right-hand margin extant. Following the codicology that I have suggested above (the recto side preceding the verso on this leaf), this is the inside margin of this page (verso). On the recto (the other side of this leaf), however, the copyist clearly began closer to the *inside* (left) margin of this page. Indeed, the writing appears to be up to three letters longer at the start of each line of lines 1–11 (and proportionally more in other fragments). The (right-handed?) scribe apparently could not copy as far as he approached the right edge (inside) of the verso, so there is a wider right-edge margin than the left-edge (inside) margin of the recto. Of the outside margins nothing survives, nor do we have the top or bottom margins.

As the text stands, with some twenty-four smaller fragments still unplaced, parts of forty-six lines of the text have been preserved, ranging from thirty-one characters per line to places where only a few characters remain of each line. There was also at least one line above the first that I have been able to transcribe on each side of the leaf, and the lowest fragment of the reconstructed leaf gives no

---

80. Note in particular the darker strips that run down both pages; a similar phenomenon on *Text/Facs* p. 5, the preceding verso page. It seems to have been a feature of the manufacture of the papyrus.

81. From this point on "recto" and "verso" will be used as I have assigned them here; i.e., the opposite to Sanders, for whom the "recto" = the text on p. 70 of the facsimile and the "verso" = the text on his p. 69 of the codex.

indication of containing the last line on the page. However, we probably have not lost much of the original height of the page, as the Minor Prophets have forty-six to forty-nine lines per page in the fully intact ones.

Based on the section where Isaiah is quoted on the recto side of the reconstructed page, and in a version sufficiently faithful to the LXX to allow calculations, the scribe seems to have used a line length of between forty-four and forty-eight characters per line. If we adopt the median, forty-six, it is clear that the majority of the text is lost in most lines. Only a vertical strip of text from the leaf remains of the work; even at the widest extant part, in lines 25–26, at least sixteen letters are lost per line.[82]

The text is written in a well-executed informal literary hand, inclined to the right; ligaturing is largely restricted to obvious combinations such as *iota* following *alpha* or *epsilon*, and the copying is clearly that of a practiced scribe. Sanders dated the hand "somewhat later" than the second half of the third century, the period he assigned to the main text.[83] He did not, however, provide an explicit date for the text either in his introduction or where he gives a provisional text of one of the fragments.[84] Among the standard catalogues, van Haelst gives the date as the "third century," [85]as does Aland.[86] The latter cites the treatments of Thackeray (on which, see below), but Thackeray refers (179) only to the third-century date of the Minor Prophets itself. At the end of his treatment, however (190), he implicitly accepts that the subscription is contemporary with the unidentified text and that both therefore date to "III^{2}" (latter half of the third century). However, Turner's reinterpretation of the subscription rules this out, and he dates the patristic text "IV?" (fourth century), the same date (without the question mark) to which he assigned the Minor Prophets. Although Sanders's date for the Minor Prophets, roughly 250–300, is likely to be right, this seems too early for the unidentified text. Given the textual history of the codex, it seems safer to assign this text to the fourth century, although it may have been written early within it.

If the hand is later than that of the Minor Prophets itself, it is probably not too far removed from other subsequent additions to the original text. At the foot

---

82. The scribe of the Minor Prophets, with its considerably more generous margins, uses only ca. thirty letters per line.

83. Sanders, *Minor Prophets in the Freer Collection,* 9. For the date of the codex, see 10–12; cf. Sanders, *Facsimile of the Washington Manuscript of the Minor Prophets,* vii: "about the middle of the third century."

84. See Sanders, *Minor Prophets in the Freer Collection,* 9, 228–29.

85. Van Haelst, *Catalogue des papyrus littéraires,* no. 636. At no. 284, however, the date for the Minor Prophets itself is given as "late third century."

86. Aland and Rosenbaum, *Kirchenväter-Papyri, Teil 1,* 9. See also Roger A. Pack, *The Greek and Latin Literary Texts from Greco-Roman Egypt* (Ann Arbor: University of Michigan Press, 1965), appendix, no. 10.; Orsolina Montevecchi, *La papirologia* (Milan: Vita e Pensiero, 1988), 325.

of what is p. 45 of the manuscript in the facsimile, the first corrector of the manuscript wrote an apparent doublet of two lines of the text;[87] a similar substantial lower-margin insertion, which restores the "correct" text for a deleted passage on the page, is made in the same hand on p. 16 of the facsimile.[88] Although the hand is not identical to that of the unidentified text, letter formation and character spacing follow sufficiently similar principles to suggest that they are not far apart in time.

The scribe of the unidentified text attempts to use *iota* adscript consistently (recto 9, 23, 37; verso 7, 15, 28), but adherence to the rule is not total, as demonstrated by βοᾷ (verso 24) and perhaps προφήτῃ (verso 42) and αὐτῷ (verso 25). Such inclinations, but a similar lack of total control, were also shown by both the scribe of the Minor Prophets and the first annotator.[89] There are no accents or breathings. A dieresis is used five times; all except καθῗδρυται (verso 21) and Ησαϊ̣[ου (less certainly read at recto 8) are over an initial *iota* or *upsilon* (recto 3; verso 7, 26). The following *nomina sacra* are used: ιλημ (verso 5), ουνου (verso 6), χς (verso 42), κς, and θς (both in recto 27). The words ανθρωπος (verso 19) and πατρος (recto 21) are uncontracted.

On pp. 228–29 of his facsimile edition of the Minor Prophets, Sanders gave an unaccented text of the largest fragment of the unidentified text, "in order that scholars may have a chance to help in identifying them" (228). His tone held out little hope that he thought this possible, yet within two years H. St.-J. Thackeray claimed to have accomplished just that, in the course of publishing a reedition of the large fragment based on the plates published in both the facsimile volume and the edition of the Minor Prophets.[90]

Lexical suggestions within the text led Thackeray to identify the fragments as a lost treatise on prophecy by Clement of Alexandria, either the work *Concerning Prophecy* (Περὶ Προφητείας) that Clement mentioned in *Stromata* 4.13.93 and 5.13.88 or some other lost work by Clement. In any event, Thackeray had "little doubt [that the text] comes from a lost work of Clement" (189). Primary among the verbal elements adduced by Thackeray were the phrase βοᾷ καὶ λέγει to introduce a biblical quotation (verso 24), σκ(ε)ι[γραφία] (verso 16), and οἰκο]δόμου ἔργῳ πο[λλῷ (recto 15), as well as other words that occur commonly throughout ancient Christian authors but for which Thackeray, following his hypothesis, gave Clementine references. As will be seen from the text below, however, a number

87. Noted and ascribed to "man 2" in Sanders, *Minor Prophets in the Freer Collection*, 116 n. 9. The text as preserved is identical to the main text, but a variant may have been lost in the lacuna in the annotation.

88. Ibid., 71 (n. 6); see also 167.

89. Ibid., 18.

90. Henry St.-J. Thackeray, "A Papyrus Scrap of Patristic Writing," *JTS* 30 (1929): 179–90, plate opposite 184.

of these readings were not able to be confirmed by autopsy of the original. Where Sanders read προφ/ κ̣η̣ρ̣υ̣κ̣ε̣ι̣[α] at the close of the Minor Prophets, taking the words for a designation of what preceded, Thackeray[91] restored προφ(ητικὴ) κηρυκεία, "A Prophetic Proclamation," as the title of the work that followed.[92] However, this reading of the "title" could not withstand the treatment of Turner; the latter's rereading of the subscription—in which he both showed that "it is finished" stood *below* the "title" and failed to confirm to his own satisfaction Sanders's interpretation of the second word[93]—ruled out Thackeray's suggestion. If there was a title to this work, it is lost at the top of page (codex page) 79.

Thackeray's proposal is not wholly without merit, for among the pre-Constantinian Christian writers Clement is by far the one most characteristically concerned with "sophists" (see recto 13) and maintaining a healthy interest in prophecy. However, much of the "distinctive" Clementine vocabulary in the unidentified text is so only "if our fragment is coeval with or only slightly later than the third-century text of the Minor Prophets,"[94] that is, only if the text belongs in the pre-Constantinian period. But the text could easily have been written in the early fourth century, when Eusebius uses the phrase βοᾷ καὶ λέγει to introduce a biblical quotation.[95] By the end of the century, it was relatively commonplace, and John Chrysostom frequently introduces biblical citations in this manner.[96] So, it may be a text of Clement, but nothing demands this, and it would preferable if it were not listed as a "possible work of Clement." In most lines, only two or three words survive, and the syntax is often impossible to deduce with any certainty. A translation scarcely seems justified, but a summary of the content will still be instructive.

The text opens with a quotation of LXX Isa 54:12–15. In view of the interest that the writer goes on to show in Isa 54:11, the quotation probably began with 54:11, which would have required three lines above the first extant line. This quotation is attributed to "the blessed Isaiah" (recto 8). Then, in recto 9, there is a reference to the "new covenant" (perhaps "in the new covenant," *vel sim.*, as the words are in the dative). In the next line, "For the Apocalypse" signals a second focal point of the text. In so far as the text is preserved here, it seems to quote this important section of Isaiah's prophecy before introducing the theme of how

---

91. Ibid., 189–90.

92. This is something Sanders considered less likely (*Minor Prophets in the Freer Collection*, 21).

93. Turner could make nothing of the word following προφ/ and suggested that it was "the note … of a subsequent scribe (or perhaps of the librarian of the monastery) 'Prophets [and]…'" (*Typology of the Early Codex*, 59, n. *).

94. Thackeray, "A Papyrus Scrap of Patristic Writing," 181–82.

95. *Hist. eccl.* 10.4.7. This is distinct from using the phrase to introduce speech by a mob or in some similar manner, as, e.g., in *Passio Perpetuae* 21.

96. See esp. the *Commentaries on Genesis*, among others of his works.

this is fulfilled or developed in the New Testament, much of the imagery and the vocabulary notably found in Rev 21.

Where we can grasp some sense again, in recto 13, "sophists" are mentioned, and preaching by or about them *may* be at issue. In the next line, the writer mentions the church, and perhaps something concerning the church is related, explained, or interpreted (διηγεῖτο). The partially preserved "...]δομου" in recto 15 suggests οἰκοδόμου, "of the builder." "The now by many [?]" in the next line has lost the adjacent words that would have provided context, and "of the words, and others'" in recto 17 does not clarify anything.

In recto 18 there is renewed attention to the text of Isa 54:11 and following verses: "[the/a] garnet stone [carbuncle], I prepare" (ἑτοιμάζω). The next line mentions a character of the λίθος ἄνθραξ, "the fiery (substance)" (τὸ πυρῶδες). In recto 20 Isa 54:11 is again quoted: "[he says] 'Behold I shall prepare (for you) the/a garnet [stone]....'" But the quote is not continued in the next line, the extant portion of which begins "by the father," before again beginning a reprise of the biblical verse, "(I?) prepare [for you]...." In recto 22 there begins more detailed exegesis, starting with the "in the last/latter [days?]" and proceeding with "revealed in glory" in recto 23, as the writer warms to the theme. As appropriate, in the next line a judge makes an appearance: "of those being the judge..." (?). Developing the point further, at recto 25 the writer introduces "another witness worthy of mention" on the matter, but who that witness is remains obscure. It is tempting to restore [προφ]ή̣της at the start of recto 26, but in the next words the writer introduces more evidence, perhaps contesting an interpretation of the "witness" whom he has cited: "Was he not then making some expression..." (οὐκ ἄρα ἦν τινα φράσιν ποιούμεν[ος). Thereafter, the text becomes even less continuous: "the Lord my God" (written as *nomina sacra*) in recto 27 likely enough quotes a LXX passage where these words stand, but the possibilities are numerous. Little else can be prised from the text by way of translation in this section of the page, although a number of words are clear.

Farther down the page, however, the writer returns to the theme of revelation in glory (recto 37); in the lower section (recto 39–45), a number of words are clear, but the sense remains frustratingly obscure (mostly because many words are difficult to confirm): "upon you and (?) ... to the king/kingdom (?)" (recto 41); "you suffered justly and" (recto 42); and "to reveal and witness" (recto 43). But little more can be said except that the writer maintains the theme he has developed thus far.

The other side (verso) of the sheet opens with a reference to the "unspoken (?) mysteries" (or something "of the mysteries"?) in verso 2. Then comes another citation of a "witness" (verso 3). As the lines that follow clearly refer to Jerusalem (and probably the new Jerusalem), heaven, and a jasper stone, it is fair to speculate that this "witness'" is John, author of the Apocalypse (see here esp. Rev 21). The first line of the small fragment that stands to the left of the main text at this point cannot be read, but perhaps it was not a long quote, as "for thus (it written?)

also" in verso 4 probably signals a further quote. As already noted, in verso 7–10 a succession of words makes it clear that the writer deals here with Rev 21: the "new (?) Jerusalem," which descends from (?) "heaven" and shines "like the jasper stone" "clear as crystal."

The writer then turns to explicating the picture of the new heaven and earth: "therefore in truth it is…" (13); in 15, "lest anyone believe/regard the city…" might give a clue as to the position the author of the text took, perhaps, on the issue of whether the city in question was real or allegorical. Artists and art (τεχνίται, τέχνη) are mentioned in verso 17–18, before mention of the "awakening" (raising, resurrection? [ἔγερσις]) and discussion of something "around the church" (verso 20). Then (verso 21) comes a contrast. Something has been "established" (καθΐδρυται); then follows "but the will/purpose…" (βούλη[σις]). In this line, if]ịρεσεị[could be resolved as a form of the word ἅιρεσις, an attack on someone who established "false opinions" may be in train.

After some fragmentary lines in which a reference to "your walls" (τειχη σου) is notable, a second biblical text is introduced (verso 24): Ezek 40:2ff., where the prophet sees and describes the temple. This passage is quoted at length (verso 24–33) and in a form that resembles the Symmachus text of Ezekiel here.

Little can be deduced from the fragmentary lines farther down the page, save that Christ is introduced into the discussion (verso 42) for the first time in the extant fragments and prophets remain of interest to the writer.

Ultimately, we have neither identified the text nor elucidated it to the point where its content can defined conclusively. However, some of the language, not to mention the extended quotation of Isa 54:11–15, suggests that millenarian issues concerned the composer. The Isaiah passage was a proof text, and the imagery recurs. The last days, revelation in glory, and a judge clearly cast attention forward to the end of days. The verso lines seem to take up the New Testament echoes of the Isaiah passage in Rev 21, and, before more detailed discussion, these themes are apparently developed. Whether the Ezekiel quotation introduced a new theme or was part of the same discussion is difficult to say, as the text is fragmentary below where the quotation is cited.

Given that the text begins with a verbatim quotation of Isa 54:11–15 and proceeds to exegete the passage, it may have been written as notes on the passage, perhaps as a commentary or for a sermon. If the Ezekiel quotation formed the start of a separate discussion of that passage, we may have a series of comments on verses important to the writer. Throughout the writer was conscious of gathering "witnesses"; again and again the direct testimony of texts is brought to bear and cited (even if we have largely lost many of the citations and have only the introductory clauses). This, likewise, may suggest a commentary or similar more developed work. In its more assembled state (as I offer it here), the text looks much less like a work "on prophecy" such as Thackeray supposed. Prophecy is attendant in the passages cited, but the new Jerusalem and its implications are closer to the writer's heart.

In the final analysis, I must repeat the plea of Sanders. I offer here an improved edition of this text "as an assistance towards identifying the work" (229). Those better versed in ancient Christian texts such as this, and with the texts our writer draws upon, may be able to elucidate further the contents of this text. In any case, however, now this task can proceed on a surer footing.

Of our scribe himself we can ultimately say little. The handwriting betrays someone confident with writing, and the use of *iota* adscript and vocabulary suggests an advanced education. The composer of the text, if not the same person who copied our text, had an impressive library (or memory; but, if so, the standard of quotation is striking). Quotes are drawn from both the Septuagint and the version of Symmachus. This text may be a lost work of Clement or Origen, but we may do the composer a disservice by necessarily assuming such. Below these Alexandrian luminaries in Roman Egypt stretches a theologically vibrant Christian community capable of producing many who could compose a text such as this. That their names are lost to us does not mean that all their works should be ascribed to their better-known compatriots.

Recto

— — — — —

[.....].[..]....[λιθ-]
[ους]κρ̣υσ̣ταλλου κ̣[αι τον περιβολον σου λιθους ελεκτους και]
[παν]τας τους υϊου[ς σου διδακτους θ̅υ̅]και εν̣ π̣[ολληι ειρηνηι]
[τα]τεκνα σου κα[ι εν δικαιοσυνηι οικοδο]μηθη̣[σηι απεχου]
[απ]ο̣ αδικο̣υ κ̣α̣ι̣ ο̣υ̣[φοβηθησηι και τρομος] ουκ ε[γγιει σοι ιδου]
[προσ]η̣λ̣υτοι δι εμου[και παροικησουσιν σοι και επι σε κατα-]
[φευ]ξ̣ονται ταυτ.[
[του]μακαριου Ησαΐ̣[ου
[τηι]καινηι διαθη[κηι
[απο]καλυψις γαρ α̣[
[...]ων ει δε μ.[
[........].[...]..... ν̣α̣υ̣ [
[........]σοφιστων κ̣ε̣κ̣ηρυ[
[........]εκκλησιας δ[ι]ηγειτο ..[
[.... οικο]δομου ο̣υ̣ν η.[.]κ̣α̣ι̣ εν υ.[

[........]. ν την νυν υπο πολλη̣[ς
[........] . ν λογων και ε̣τ̣ε̣ροι τ[
[........][illegible] . [
[........]το πυρωδες κ̣α̣ι̣[.]ε̣[.]ηριος. [
[..... ειπ]εν ιδου εγω ετοιμαζω̣ ανθρ̣α̣[κα
[.........υ]π̣ο του πατρος ε̣τ̣οι̣[μ]αζο̣μ̣. [
[..........]το εν υστεροις.. [..].... [
[.........]εν δοξηι αποκαλ[υφθη]σ̣.... [....]ο̣σ̣[
[........]των μεν κριτης γενομεν[ος..]υ̣ν αε[
[........]υ̣λ̣η̣ν̣ και ετερος μαρτυς̣ αξιολογος .. [.......]
[........]ητης ουκ αρα ην τινα̣ φ̣ρασι̣ν ποιουμεν. [........]
]π̣ο̣τ̣[ε κ]α̣ι̣ κ̅ς̅ ο θ̅ς̅ μου̣[ca.?]ιας. [
]... [.]. ι̣α̣ ηι ο̣υ̣κ εστ̣η[ ]σ̣ει. [
— — — —]και η̣...... [ ].. γι. [
[...]....... [ ]. εσ̣τ̣. [ca.?]. οσ ε[
[...]. α̣σ̣τ̣η̣ τη. [— — — — — — —
[...]υ αυτου ει[
[....]. ε̣σ̣ται κα̣[
[.......]... [
— — — — — — — —
]....... [
(b)].... εθνο̣ς. [
]εν δοξηι απ̣ο̣[
]. θενη̣μ̣ε̣.. [
— — — — — — — — — — — — —
(c)]κ̣εινη . ε[
]... [...]. σ̣αν την[
]και επι σε̣ κ̣α̣[.]̅.̅ ̅ς̅ εις βασιλε[

]. δικαιως πασ̣χ̣ε̣ι̣ς̣ και τ .[
απο]καλυπτε̣ι̣ν δ̣ε̣ μαρτυρ[
]ω̣σ̣τος εν .... [
]σ̣αι α̣πο̣ρρ̣ . υ̣σ[
]κ̣α̣σ̣ο̣ν̣ σ̣υ̣ ο̣ . . . . .[
]... αυτ̣ο̣ι̣ ν̣[

— — — — — —

(d)].. α̣η̣υ̣[
] ω̣φω̣ [
].. π̣ρ̣. [

— — — —

13 τ̣ο̣υ̣των α̣ S (=Sanders); σοφιστων T (=Thackeray) 15 μου̣ συνπ S; [οικο]δομου εργω πο[λλω] T. 16 ι̣ν την νυν υπ[αρχουσαν] T. 17.. ι̣δ̣ου ε̣ι̣μι ... S; χ̣η̣δονι̣α̣ν κα̣λ̣[ουμενην T. 20 ιδου εγω ειπ̣ S; [ειπ]ε̣ν̣ ιδου εγω ετοι̣[μαζω T. 21 τ̣ο του πατρος S. 22 ενυστερον S; το εν υστερον T. 23 ... β̣η̣ι̣ν̣ηκ̣αλ̣ S; ε̣ν δοξηι αποκαλ[T. 26 .... ο̣υ καρυ̣ιτων̣ S; η̣της ουκ αρα̣ ην τινι η̣ T, revised in proof (p. 190) to δις]η τρις.

Verso

		— — — — — —
		].. [
		]ητων μυστη
— — — — —		]ς μαρτυρ̣ε̣ι̣ ο
[..........].. ατ .. λ̣[		]. γαρ ουτως κ̣αι
[......... δ]ευρο δε̣. [	ca. 18	]. αν ι̅λ̅η̅μ̅ τ̣η̣ν̣
[..........]...... [		]ου ο̅υ̅ν̅ο̅υ̅ κ̣α̣[ι]
— — — — —		]ω̣ς λιθωι ϊασπι-
[δι		].. υ̣κ̣ αλλος ι̣ν.
		]. ν ορα. δια το

]κρυσταλλιζων̣
]κατα τ̣αυτον
]υ̣[..]ο̣ι̣ δια..[
]οντως ουν εστιν.[
]. ας π̣αλ̣ι̣ν μαρτυρου[
]μ̣η τις νο̣μ̣ισηι την πολ[
]σ̣ω̣ κ̣α̣λ̣ο̣υ̣μενην ε̣κε̣ι[
]και δια̣ τ̣[ο] των τεχνιτω̣[ν
]ε̣λουν τη̣ν̣ τεχνην το[
].τ. οτυρ. ε̣γ̣ερσιν ανθρωπο[
]κ̣. το δ[ε] π̣ερ̣ι̣ τ̣ην εκκλησια̣ν̣ α̣[
]ιρεσει [κ]α̣θϊδρυται αλ̣λ̣ η βουλ̣[
]ν̣ατου[....]η του παθ̣η̣μ̣ατο̣[
]..[ ]. μελης[... τα]τειχη σο̣υ τα υπ[
]ο̣λ̣[ca. 6].. ι̣ εζεκιηλ βοα και λεγει και̣[ανεπαυσε]
[με επ ορους]υ̣ψ̣η̣λ̣ο̣υ̣ σ̣φοδρα και επ αυτω̣ ω̣ς οικοδο̣[μη πολε-]
[ως απο ν]ω̣του και α̣νηγ̣α̣γ̣ε̣ν̣ μ̣ε εκει και ϊδου α̣[νηρ]
[κ]α̣ι η[ορασις α]υτου ω̣ς ορ̣α̣[σις] χ̣α̣λ̣κ̣ο̣υ σ̣τ̣ι̣λ̣[β̣οντος και ην σπα-]
[θ]ιον[οικοδομων εν]τηι̣ χειρι αυτου̣ καλ̣[αμος μετρου και αυτος]
[ει]στη[κει επι της]π\υ̣/λης και ε̣ι̣π̣[ε προς με ο ανηρ Εορακας υιε]
[ανο]υ ιδε[εν τοις οφθαλμοις σ]ου κα[ι ακουε εν τοις ωσι σου και]
[ταχον εις την καρδιαν σου παν]τ̣α̣[οσα εγω δεικνυω σοι]ενεκεν γα[ρ]
[του δειχθηναι σοι εισηχθης ωδε και δειχεις παντα]οσα συ ορα[ς]
[τω οικωι $\overline{\text{ιηλ}}$]]ος α̣λ̣λ̣α.[
]λ̣ου.[

— — — — — —

]..ος μεν τις[
(b)].τιον του γα[

]. . . . υ̣ποσ̣. [

——————————

]. . . . . [. . .] . . . . . [. .] . [

(c)] . αναπ̣ει̣[. . . .]ηντ[. .]υ̣[

]ουν ον ορα[. .]. ημεν̣ην ε̣[

]χων την . τ̣α̣ο̣υ̣ . ε̣[.]κο̣σι̣[

]προφητη̣ $\overline{\text{χ̣ς}}$ ο̣ πα̣λ̣αι̣ . [

]. . . κ̣. . ο̣. δ̣ες της και[

]. . . α̣π. . . μ̣εν δια̣ τ̣[

]. . . σ̣ω̣υ̣. ρ̣ο̣ρ̣. [

]. . . . τ̣ου[

———————

(d)]. . . . [

] . ηαν . [

]. . ζαι . [

——————

13 [Ιησου]ς ουν εστιν? T. 15 ισηι (so S); . ησαί or μσαί T. 16 . . . θελην σ̣κε̣ι̣[S. 19 τ̣ερσιν S; [ε]γερσιν T. 21 α̣υται ανηβ̣οτ S; υ ηι ανεβο T. 22 παθ . . λ̣ετε S; παθη̣ $\overline{\text{χ̣υ̣}}$? T. 25 επ αυτω . . σ̣οι κ̣αλο S; και μ̣α̣ρτ[υρε]ς οι καλο[υμενοι δωδεκα(?) T. 26 λ̣οε̣ ε̣κει ϊδου S; τ̣α̣δε λ̣εγ̣ε̣ι̣ $\overline{\text{κς}}$ ϊδου T.

Commentary

Recto

1–7 A quotation of LXX Isa 54:12–15 begins what remains of the text here; more is probably lost above these lines. The position of the surviving edge of the fragment here relative to the original left margin is unknown but is likely to be close. The Minor Prophets text features inner margins of ca. 1.6 cm and outer of 2.5 cm. Here we are close to the inside edge (as the verso shows), but the recto (inner) margin is less than on the verso, with two to three letters lost at the start of each line. I have broken λιθους in lines 1–2 because the whole word will not fit at the start of line 2. What is preserved in the fragment follows the standard LXX text remarkably closely until lines 6–7. See Joseph Ziegler, ed., *Isaias* (5th ed.; Göttingen: Vandenhoeck & Ruprect, 1983).

6] . [illegible] could also be considered but does not occur in any known LXX manuscript, and the reading printed here is palaeographically preferable in any case. In the citation of Isa 54:15 here, there is no support among LXX manuscripts for the omission of προσελεύσονται, which follows προσήλυτοι, although some manuscripts omit the σοι. However, the verb cannot be read at the start of this line. It may have been omitted by error, unless it was transposed to after δι' ἐμοῦ or before the noun (in which case there are line spacing issues to consider). If the verb προσελεύσονται did not follow δι' ἐμοῦ, a reconstruction such as that printed in the lacuna will be required to fill the space to the end of the quote in the following line; that given here has some manuscript support (see the *app. crit.* on Isa 54:15 in Ziegler, *Isaias,* 326).

7 The second word is probably ταῦτα. As the word follows καταφεύξονται in no manuscript of Isaiah, the text proper probably begins here: i.e., "these" [are the things we read in the prophecy] "of the blessed Isaiah" *vel. sim.*?

11 εἰ δὲ μή[(?) The trace of the last letter should belong to an *eta* rather than *epsilon.*

12–26 The number of missing letters to the left of the extant text is a rough guide only.

13 The reading of the last word is difficult, and this is the only sense I can make of the traces to give a real reading. Restore perhaps [τὸν διὰ τῶν] σοφιστῶν κ̣ε̣κ̣ηρυ[γμένον] *vel sim.*?

14 The fit between the fragments is here not exact, and there is sufficient room for [ι] in what may be διηγειτο. δὴ γείτοσ̣ι̣ might be considered, but then τοῖς would be expected. The last two letters are illegible but might be ερ or σι.

15 [οἰκο]δόμου (Thackeray) is difficult to resist in context; ἕβδομου would normally take a pronoun or noun following. ο̣υ̣ν (οὖν) here could be σ̣υ̣ν, but I incline to the former. Both Sanders and Thackeray read the following letter as π, but I judge η to be more likely; otherwise, *alpha* is most likely. But neither these readings nor the divisions in the text above are secure (e.g., one could read ο̣ ε̣ν for ο̣υ̣ν or divide ου νη . , and the formation of α̣ι̣ later in the line is unusual). In the final analysis, the last letter in the line might be a *sigma.*

16 The illegible first letter in the line could be *iota* or *epsilon,* presumably part of a noun or pronoun (e.g., αὐτήν), with what follows describing it

("the…," "the one now…," "by many"?). Alternately, the end of an infinitive begins the line.

18 ἑτοιμάζω would usually make λίθος ἄνθραξ its object in citations of this type, but the nominative ending of λιθος suggests that a new clause may start with the verb. The final letter (*omega?*) is doubtfully read on the adjoining fragment, but the *zeta* will still indicate an active voice, and ετοιμασ̣- to allow a middle or passive looks unlikely.

19 Two letters may be lost on either side of the doubtfully read *episilon.*

22 Cf. 1 Tim 4:1, ἐν ὑστέροις καιροῖς, and patristic citations of the verse. But although the next letter may be a *kappa,* those that follow are illegible.

23 The traces after the lacuna fail to confirm the ending of the verb, but as Thackeray remarks ("A Papyrus Scrap of Patristic Writing," 187), "there can be no mistake about the verb."

24 At the beginning, τῶν or ζώντων, "being the judge of the living." Following γενόμεν[ος], the lacuna looks to be sufficient for, e.g., [γο]υν but too wide for only one letter (e.g., [σ]υν or [ο]υν). Read perhaps [γο]ῦν ἀε[ί?

25 The first four letters are indistinct, in particular υ̣ and η̣.

26 [προφ]ητης is tempting as the first word. οὐκ ἄρα will mark the start of a new clause.

27 As the initial words,]π̣ο̣υ̣[λέγ]ε̣ι is a less preferable reading.

28 At the end, ἐστι̣ν̣[could also be read.

31 The first four restored letters are uncertain; the next two are clear. The last letter could be an *iota* or a *nu.*

36 The line may begin] . α̣ρ̣α̣ι̣

37 Probably a repeat of the phrase from line 23.

38 A participial form of ἐχουθενέω?

39 [ἐ]κείνη[ς] . ? The tail of an *iota* (for the dative) is not apparent, and a small *sigma* may have been lost.

40 The trace at the start of what is legible suggests another *sigma,* perhaps θάλασσαν or γλῶσσαν.

41 In the middle of the line, the κ̣α̣ and ς look secure, yet a lacuna with barely enough space for κ̣α̣[ι is followed by a supralinear stroke, seemingly that of a *nomen sacrum.* The space looks too tight for κ̣α̣[ι] κ̣̅ς̅, but κ̣α̣[ι] ̅.̅ι̅ς̅ may just fit.

42 πάσ̣χε̣ι̣ς̣ is a not entirely satisfactory reading, especially the *chi.*

44 The start of the line recalls Ps 75.2.1: Γνωστὸς ἐν τῇ Ἰουδαίᾳ ὁ θεός, but I am reluctant to restore it; after εν, ι is likely, but after that, the traces are too faint to confirm, e.g., Ιουδαιαι.

45 A range of verb forms built on απορρ- may be imagined here.

46–47 The readings here are divined rather than seen clearly.

Verso

1 There are traces above the fully first preserved words. The second trace has a descender reminiscent of an *upsilon.*

2 τῶν ἀπορ]ήτων μυστη[ρίων] suggests itself naturally. Alternatively, divide the letters as η τῶν μυστηρίων.

3 Although various supplements could be imagined, in the context of repetitive citing of scriptural witnesses, ὡ]ς μαρτυρ̣ε̣ῖ̣ ὁ [προφήτης λέγων (*vel sim.*) gives the best sense. There are, of course, various possibilities for the restored noun and participle. This should lead to a scriptural quotation, but it cannot now be identified.

4 The letters in the left-hand fragment may be] ̣ αηατ ̣ ̣ λ[. Γὰρ οὕτως often introduces a scriptural quotation in early Christian writers (e.g., Clement of Rome, Barnabas, Origin; less so in Clement of Alexandria). Although this is not exclusively the case, in the present context we may reasonably restore a verb of writing or saying, and the trace at the left edge of the fragment is a vertical stroke that might belong to λέγει or γέγραπται. Biblical verses beginning with καί (if this is not something that is "also" said or written) are not difficult to find. In the present context, Revelation (esp. Rev 21) is not unlikely to be the source.

5]ευρο δε ̣ [. The concentration of allusions to Rev 21 further on makes δεῦρο δείξω (Rev 21:9) likely, but this leaves only ca. eighteen letters before the next legible words, which do not themselves as closely follow δεῦρο δείξω either in Rev 21:9 or 17:1. As the next letter after δε does not closely resemble the remains of an *iota,* perhaps δεῦρο δὲ should be read. The αν before Ἰερουσαλήμ invites resolution as ἁγ]ί̣αν, but the traces resemble most strongly a *sigma.* Οὖσαν, therefore, could be considered (see, e.g., Didymus the Blind, *Comm. in Zac.* 1.166.1; 5.122.4; *Frag. in Psalmos* 1194.13). But the broken letter could also be the remains of an *epsilon,* and a reference to the "new Jerusalem," ν]έ̣αν Ἰερουσαλήμ, would certainly suit the context. In Rev 21:2 the author talks of Ἰερουσαλὴμ

καινήν, but νέας is used of the holy city by (among others) Hippolytus, Eusebius, Gregory Nazianzus, Socrates Scholasticus, and John Chrysostom.

6 At the end, κ̣α̣[ί] is not a perfect reading but seems the most likely. τ]οῦ οὐ(ρα)νοῦ κ̣α̣[ὶ τῆς γῆς] comes to mind, but possibilities are numerous, and a reference (although not a direct quotation) of Rev 21:2 or 21:10 is most likely.

7 Rev 21:11, ὡς λίθῳ ἰάσπιδι κρυσταλλίζοντι, could be quoted here.

8 The traces before υ̣ are virtually unreadable, but ο̣υ̣ is likely and consistent with what little survives. I have divided the words on the assumption that the phrase is οὐκ ἄλλος, but ου κάλλος would also be possible. At the end, ἵνα̣ gives better sense than ινο, but the *iota* is not totally secure.

9 ὅρα? ορᾱ̣? The character following this resembles a large oblique *zeta,* which is not formed thus elsewhere. As this is the end of a word, possibilities are limited; e.g., λλ, which this somewhat resembles, does not help either. It is perhaps a lectional sign.

10 The theme of Rev 21:11 is again invoked.

12 In Christian authors, the combination δι δια is frequently found in phrases such as τῇ Ἑβραΐδι/Ἑλληνίδι διαλέκτῳ. The trace earlier in the line might be the tail of a *rho,* but this seems too far from δι to read [Ἑβ]ρ̣[αΐ]δι. The tail could also be that of an *upsilon,* and there are many other possible supplements.

13 ὄντως, "really," "verily," or the end of δεόντως or of an adverb.

14 π̣αλ̣ι̣ν is read with difficulty, and components (esp. π and λ) could be challenged, but I have failed to find another acceptable reading.

15 πόλ[ιν is likely, probably as part of an accusative-infinitive construction.

16 καλουμένην is clear enough, although the first letters are indistinct. Preceding and following letters are difficult. Thackeray took the next letters as σ̣κε̣ι̣[, as read by Sanders, for the start of σκ(ε)ιγραφία, "outline," "adumbration," which in Clement is a positive term for old and treasured writings (see Thackeray, "A Papyrus Scrap of Patristic Writing," 182). But we should not assume iotacism from a scribe who is careful elsewhere, and the phrase would have to be κ̣α̣λ̣ο̣υ̣μένην σκ{ε}ι[γραφίαν "so-called sketches," with the force of the participle seemingly negative, which would not fit the attitudes of Clement noted by Thackeray. In any case, the first letter of the word is more likely to be an *epsilon,* forming a reference to what something is called "there" (ἐκεῖ) or acting as a demonstrative (i.e., part of ἐκεῖνος). The thing "so-called" can also precede the participle in

such constructions. The *omega* of σ̣ω̣ is wide and unusually formed and could be read as σ̣α̣μ̣, perhaps the end of a Hebrew place or personal name.

17 τεχνιτων. The plural indicates the reference is to one of the many meanings the word can have for humans rather than the divine referents (see Lampe, *PGL*, s.v.)

18 συντελοῦν (*vel sim.*) might be considered at the start. το[ῦ is likely at the end.

19 Before ἔγ̣ερσιν the letters are unclear.

20 τὸ δὲ is more likely than τόδε, but what is "about the church" is lost.

21 There is probably sufficient space for]ιρεσει[ς κ]α̣θΐδρυται, allowing αἱρέσεις or διαιρέσεις. For internal dieresis in this context, cf. καθϊδ . [at *P.Kell.* VI (= I. Gardner, *Kellis Literary Texts II* [Oxford: Oxbow, forthcoming]) Gr. 97 B I r.16. αλλ̣ η βουλ̣[ ] is scarcely a perfect reading, and βοτ̣ . [ ] might also be possible at the end, but ἀλλ' ἡ βουλ̣[ήσις offers a better solution.

22 θα]ν̣ατου is probable in context. Before the following η, a raised vertical stroke makes ψ or φ likely. After παθ, πάθους would be an attractive reading, but the traces do not resemble ους. I read what is printed in the text with no great confidence, but the traces are not discordant with it. ἡ του παθηματο[ς ἡμέρα will not be correct if the letter before η is a consonant.

23 "your … walls." The writer has discursed here, and the phrase need not be a direct scriptural quotation. The walls in Isa 60:10 or 60:18 may have been in mind. Cf. Deut. 28:52, τὰ τείχη σου τὰ ὑψηλά, and the reference to the walls of Jerusalem in Tob 13:17.

24 The letter before εζεκιηλ may have been an *iota,* so the form used could have been Ἰεζεκιήλ, but the spacing suggests that the form without initial *iota* (also preferred by Clement and Origen) was used here. Note that βοᾷ is not written βοαι, showing that the scribe's control over the use of use *iota* adscript is not complete. With the name of the prophet there begins a quotation of Ezek 40:2 and following. The reconstruction given in the text reflects an assumption of an average line length of ca. forty-six characters derived from the Isaiah quotation on the recto, and that the quotation begins with καί. Problems remain with the relative line lengths, largely caused by the positioning of the small fragments to the left and right of the main fragment, both of which clearly formed part of the quotation. Even though gaps remain, the scribe clearly quotes the version of Symmachus here; we are well served in regard to the version at this point. See F. Field, *Origenis Hexaplorum quae supersunt* (Hildesheim: Olms, 1964),

2:873–75; Joseph Ziegler, ed., *Ezechiel* (2nd ed.; Göttingen: Vandenhoeck & Ruprect, 1977). But the gaps in the papyrus remain difficult to fill with certainty.

24 At the end of the line one expects ἀνέπαυσε with Symmachus, although the LXX ἔθηκε(ν) would arguably fit the space better. Perhaps ανεπαυ|σε?

25 ὡς for ὡσεί (so also in line 27) has solid LXX manuscript support. The scribe's model read ἐπ' αὐτῷ̣ with B, but other witness prefer ἐπ' αὐτοῦ. Note that the text here is very faint and that αυτο̣υ̣ is not completely excluded; note also that if επ αυτω̣ is correct, the scribe again omits *iota* adscript.

26 ἀπὸ νότου is found only in Symmachus, and it is also better reflective of the Hebrew (even if the Hebrew phrase itself is probably a later interpolation into Ezek 40:2). Εἰσήγαγεν, found (as far as is known) in all the versions (and all manuscripts apparently, see Ziegler, *Ezechiel, app. crit.* [p. 282]), cannot be read in line 26, although ἀ̣ν̣ήγ̣α̣γ̣ε̣ν̣ can be; δ̣ι̣ηγα̣γ̣ε̣ν̣ is less likely.

27 Near the left margin stands a fragment that does not join but clearly belongs here. On into the line, the traces do not confirm σ̣τ̣ί̣λ̣[βοντος], but neither are they incompatible with the beginning of the word.

27–28 ἦν σπαθ]ίον [οἰκοδόμων ἐν]τῆι̣ χειρὶ αὐτοῦ. The inversion is commonly found in LXX manuscripts. The words are difficult to divide between the lines, and it is possible an unknown textual variant or idiosyncratic rendering is lost in the lacunae.

29]π\ύ̣/λης καὶ ε̣ἶ̣π̣[ε. Neither the first or last word are satisfactorily read, and I cannot account for the mark over καὶ (visible in the facsimile).

30 For the transposition of ἴδε and ἄκουε, see Ziegler, *Ezechiel, app. crit.* (282). No stroke for a *nomen sacrum* is evident over the surviving *upsilon* of ανου at the beginning of the line, but such is not decisive, and the compendium seems necessary to preserve line length. Such "profane" use of *nomina sacra* forms is of course common among Christian scribes.

31]ἕνεκεν γά̣[ρ fixes the stray fragment's vertical alignment, and the discolored section on its right fixes the horizontal alignment by reference to the similarly discolored section on lines 1–11. This should leave ca. sixteen letters back from these traces (which cannot be read with any certainty; I restore thus here merely *exemplum gratia*). There is room for ca. twenty more letters to the start of the line, prior to the partially preserved τα. My restoration (twenty-four letters long) seems, thus, slightly too long, and it may be that the author cites here one of the shorter readings of Ezek 40:4 found in some LXX manuscripts.

33 The text is damaged here and not clearly read. Though ἀνδ]ρ̣ὸς κ̣ά̣λ̣αμ̣[ος might be possible, far too much text needs to come between the end of 32 and here to complete Symmachus Ezek 40:5 (longer than the LXX version, itself already too long for here). So,] . ος ἀλλά . [, supposing the analysis of the quotation to have begun here, may be preferable.

35 The second letter may be a χ.

36 ἐνα]ν̣τίον τοῦ is plausible, but the noun is not immediately deducible.

37 τ̣η̣ν̣ *may* be possible before υ̣ποσ, but τ̣ὴ̣ν̣ ὑ̣πόστ̣[ασιν is extremely conjectural.

39 While αν αιτει might also be possible, the frequency of words on the stem ἀναπει- encountered in texts of a similar genre inclines one to the reading given in the text.

41 –την ο̣ν̣τα ους̣? Following that, perhaps ε̣ι̣κ̣ο̣σι̣, although the sense is not clear.

42 προφητη̣ seems the best reading, as there is little space between the *tau* and the *chi* that follows. Comparing βοα for βοᾷ elsewhere, the η in this word may signal the dative here, but προφητε̣ι̣ would just be possible. The lacuna renders the case of the *nomen sacrum* obscure. Ink traces above and to the left and right of the lacuna are difficult to account for with a single letter, and, although *omega* would account for those at the left and right (e.g., χ[ριστ]ω), only a compendium such as χρς would account for all the traces, and not perfectly at that. Following that, ο παλαι is preferable to απαλαι; the final letter has a tail and is *upsilon, tau,* or *iota.* Another quotation from a "prophet" may follow (e.g., [ἐν τῷ]προφήτῃ), but if so, its source is not obvious.

43 Several readings could be proposed for the start of the line:] . π̣ε̣ικο̣,] . τ̣ι̣σι, or] . γ̣ι̣σι could all be considered. Later in the line, δες could be λες, and one might equally divide δε στης.

41–46 The readings here are so difficult that it might have been better not to print anything. Except for the second half of line 41, I have no particular confidence in what is printed here and hold out no great hope of elucidating the text further. In line 46, read perhaps θων . του[.

47–49 Fragment (d) again does not join exactly to what comes above and is placed horizontally but not vertically.

Figure 1: Freer MS V, unidentified work, recto (=F1916.768, p.70), digitally modified. Copyright Freer Gallery of Art and Arthur M. Sackler Gallery Archives, Smithsonian Institution, Washington, D.C. Used by permission. Note: these images are included primarily to show the positioning of the fragments edited above and are not intended to constitute a definitive photographic reproduction of the leaf.

Figure 2: Freer MS V, unidentified work, verso (=F1916.768, p.69), digitally modified. Copyright Freer Gallery of Art and Arthur M. Sackler Gallery Archives, Smithsonian Institution, Washington, D.C. Used by permission.

The Text of Matthew in the Freer Gospels: A Quantitative and Qualitative Appraisal

Jean-François Racine

In 1912, Henry Sanders published a volume giving a detailed study of the paleographical features of the Freer Gospels Codex (Codex W, Gregory-Aland 032, Washington MS III).[1] Sanders also addressed matters such as the various corrections made to the text of the manuscript and the relationships of the text of each of the four Gospels both to other manuscripts and to some early church writers. He also provided a full collation of the text of each Gospel against the Textus Receptus. The work was done carefully, and most of his observations are still relevant. Yet 323 pages are actually not enough to make a complete study of the four Gospels found in Codex Washingtonianus. Standing on the shoulders of Sanders to look further, the present study will offer a second, and more restricted, analysis of the relationship of the text of Matthew in W/032 with other manuscripts, through a quantitative analysis. In addition, I will make some remarks on that text from a qualitative point of view, using insights from applied linguistics.

Codex W in Matthew in Relation to Other Manuscripts.

We may begin with Sanders's effort to identify the text-type of Matthew found in W. At that time, the most recent theory had been formulated by von Soden, who classified manuscripts into three categories, each corresponding to a major recension. There was the K (= Κοινή) text, which was deemed to have originated from Lucian of Antioch at the beginning of the fourth century, the H (=Ἡσύχιος) text, connected with Hesychius of Egypt, and the I (=Ἱεροσόλυμα, Jerusalem) text.[2]

1. Henry A. Sanders, *The New Testament Manuscripts in the Freer Collection, Part I: The Washington Manuscript of the Four Gospels* (University of Michigan Studies, Humanistic Series 9/1; New York: Macmillan, 1912); idem, *Facsimile of the Washington Manuscript of the Four Gospels in the Freer Collection* (Ann Arbor: University of Michigan, 1912).

2. Hermann von Soden, *Die Schriften des Neuen Testaments in ihrer ältesten erreichbaren Textgestalt* (vol. 1.1; Göttingen: Vandenhoeck & Ruprecht, 1913).

Following that nomenclature, Sanders determined that the text of Matthew in W should be classified as the most ancient witness of the *K1* text, that is, the oldest and best form of the Κοινή text-type of which other major witnesses are Ω, S, and V.[3]

Even though some of von Soden's classification scheme is problematic, particularly his *I* group, several of the subgroups he suggested for the *K* group appear to have some validity.[4] Nevertheless, von Soden's explanations concerning the manner in which he had achieved these groupings were often so brief that the groupings have mostly remained difficult to use. Much work remains to be done in that regard, and in the present study I do not intend to embark on such a task.

In this essay, rather, I aim to provide a statistical comparison of the text of Matthew in Codex W with twenty other manuscripts that represent the main textual trends listed according to the most common textual groups.[5]

Primary Alexandrian:	א, B
Secondary Alexandrian:	C, L, f^1, 33[6]
Caesarean:[7]	Θ, f^{13}
Byzantine:	E, Δ, Π, Σ, Ω, 565, 700
Western:	D, a, b, e, k[8]

For the purpose of this study, I discarded scribal errors that involve nonsense readings, unless they are widespread. Similarly, scribal tendencies due to stylistic

3. Sanders, *New Testament Manuscripts in the Freer Collection,* 42, 48.

4. David O. Voss, "Is von Soden's Kmd K^r a Distinct Type of Text?" *JBL* 57 (1938): 311–18. Voss limited his investigation, however, to Mark.

5 I use here the quantitative approach taken in Jean-François Racine, *The Text of Matthew in the Writings of Basil of Caesarea* (SBLNTGF 5; Atlanta: Society of Biblical Literature; Leiden: Brill, 2004), laid out more fully in 239–43.

6. The group of "minuscule" (cursive writing) manuscripts designated "family 1" (f^1 in my tables) has sometimes been linked with the "Caesarean" text-type, especially in Mark. My previous research indicated, however, that in Matthew this group belongs to the secondary Alexandrian category rather than to the Caesarean one (Racine, *Text of Matthew,* 252–54).

7. The validity of the "Caesarean" text-type in Matthew is somewhat problematic, as its specific textual character is far from being well described. Among the witnesses used here, at most it would include only two: Θ and f^{13}, the latter a group of minuscule manuscripts actually displaying statistically strong ties to manuscripts assigned to the Byzantine text-type. I, therefore, retain reference to the so-called Caesarean text-type, even though it only has one strong witness here, Θ.

8. I included four Latin manuscripts—a, b, e, and k—in order to give some consistency to the so-called Western group, which otherwise would include only D. Working with versional evidence has limitations, however, because of the differences between Latin and Greek. For instance, Latin does not have a definite article or a middle voice, which makes the testimony of these manuscripts useless when a variant reading involves that type of variation.

preferences (e.g., *nu*-movable, itacisms, and abbreviations) were excluded from the apparatus.[9]

The data used for this study were mostly gathered for my previous study concerning the text of Matthew in the works of Basil of Caesarea.[10] They are the product not of a full collation of these manuscripts against W but from a collation done at random.[11] One could wish to have at one's disposal full collations of all these manuscripts, but these would take an enormous amount of time to gather. Nonetheless, a collation at random that includes a large number of variation units allows one to estimate fairly accurately the relationship among manuscripts, especially if the tables derived from it indicate error correction, a figure which has mostly been absent from such collations so far. As a rule of thumb, the greater the sample, the smaller the error correction.

Still, one may question the validity of statistically putting on the same level all sorts of variant readings, if, e.g., a difference in the spelling of a name is considered to be equivalent to a large omission.[12] One may concede that these variant readings are of very different types, and may involve a larger number of words. But anyone who has attempted to make a collation is aware that many variation-units are of mixed types. A variation-unit may include addition/omission of an article, word order, substitution of preposition, case ending, singular/plural, or other sorts of variants. Creating single categories for each type of variant reading would therefore be an endless process. Furthermore, calculating agreements among manuscripts for each of these types of variant readings would fraction the data so much that the results would become meaningless. Finally, one should not request from such quantitative analysis what it cannot provide. We cannot obtain, for example, an exact estimation of the proximity of a given manuscript to an established group of manuscripts such as a text-type, either on the basis of sharing a reasonable quantity of specific variant readings, or an estimation of the stylistic and theological tendencies of a manuscript. The comprehensive profile method developed by Bart Ehrman allows one to answer the first question, and qualitative analysis allows one to answer the second ques-

---

9. William L. Richards, *The Classification of the Greek Manuscripts of the Johannine Epistles* (SBLDS 35; Missoula, Mont.: Scholars Press, 1977), has demonstrated that the latter type of variants are of no use in establishing relationships among manuscripts. This does not mean, however, that they have no value as one studies the other features of a manuscript.

10. Racine, *Text of Matthew*.

11 More specifically, the variation units are those that appear in the many passages of Matthew cited by Basil. In this essay, I have checked what variants are supported in each of these passages. In this sense, therefore, the counts are of "random" passages of Matthew.

12. This is a remark made by Dirk Jongkind in his review of my *Text of Matthew*, published in *Review of Biblical Literature* (http://www.bookreviews.org/pdf/4142_4036.pdf), consulted on 27 January 2006.

tion.[13] The results of the quantitative analysis presented below simply give a general sense of the proximity and/or distance of Codex W to some manuscripts representative of various textual proclivities, in order to locate it on that map.

I will present the data in seven tables presenting the percentage of agreements among manuscripts in small sections of Matthew in order to detect possible "block mixture."[14] One should keep in mind that the precision of the results is limited by the small size of the sample of variation-units.[15] That small size makes useless the mention of error correction.

TABLE 1. AGREEMENTS OF CODEX W/032 IN MATTHEW 1–4

Manuscripts	Agreements	Total Variants	Agreements
ℵ	36	60	60.0%
B	37	61	60.7%
C	42	61	68.9%
D	16	41	39.0%
E	46	61	75.4%
L	43	60	71.7%
Δ	50	61	82.0%
Θ	11	16	68.8%
Π	49	61	80.3%
Σ	49	61	80.3%
Ω	46	61	75.4%
f^1	46	61	75.4%
f^{13}	43	61	70.5%
33	41	53	77.4%
565	47	61	77.0%
700	51	61	83.6%
a	10	45	22.2%
b	13	48	27.1%

13. For a description of the method, see Bart D. Ehrman, "Methodological Developments in the Analysis and Classification of New Testament Documentary Evidence," *NovT* 29 (1987) 22–45.

14 The term "block mixture" refers to the observable shifts in the textual affiliation of some manuscript withins a given writing, which are commonly thought to have been caused by a copyist using different exemplars for different parts of the writing. E.g., the text of Mark in W is widely seen as having a significant agreement with "Western" witnesses up to some point in Mark 5, but thereafter shifts markedly.

15 In the following tables, the differences in the number of variation-units in the third column (from the left) arises from lacunae in some manuscripts at certain points, and other factors. The percentages of agreement, however, allow for comparison of the relative strength of agreement of W with the various witnesses.

e	0	0	0%
k	11	36	30.6%

Table 2. Agreements of Codex W/032 in Matthew 5–8

Manuscripts	Agreements	Total Variants	Agreements
ℵ	83	131	63.4%
B	87	131	66.4%
C	28	41	68.3%
D	36	74	48.6%
E	106	131	80.9%
L	88	119	73.9%
Δ	102	131	77.9%
Θ	93	131	71.0%
Π	105	131	80.2%
Σ	104	129	80.6%
Ω	105	131	80.2%
f^{1}	87	131	66.4%
f^{13}	91	131	69.5%
33	82	120	68.3%
565	102	131	77.9%
700	102	131	77.9%
a	29	111	26.1%
b	28	110	25.5%
e	0	0	0%
k	34	108	31.5%

Table 3. Agreements of Codex W/032 in Matthew 9–12

Manuscripts	Agreements	Total Variants	Agreements
ℵ	94	129	72.9%
B	94	129	72.9%
C	95	129	73.6%
D	53	128	41.4%
E	110	130	84.6%
L	84	130	64.6%
Δ	102	130	78.5%
Θ	107	130	82.3%
Π	113	130	86.9%
Σ	105	130	80.8%
Ω	110	130	84.6%
f^{1}	100	130	76.9%

f^{13}	100	130	76.9%
33	90	125	72.0%
565	102	130	78.5%
700	99	130	76.2%
a	32	103	31.1%
b	30	106	28.3%
e	1	40	25.0%
k	43	106	40.6%

Table 4. Agreements of Codex W/032 in Matthew 13–16

Manuscripts	Agreements	Total Variants	Agreements
א	54	85	63.5%
B	54	86	62.8%
C	69	86	80.2%
D	40	84	47.6%
E	76	86	88.4%
L	75	86	87.2%
Δ	73	86	84.9%
Θ	53	86	61.6%
Π	76	76	88.4%
Σ	63	86	73.3%
Ω	74	86	86.0%
f^{1}	55	86	64.0%
f^{13}	52	86	60.5%
33	77	77	76.6%
565	69	84	82.1%
700	61	85	71.8%
a	18	69	26.1%
b	22	61	36.1%
e	23	70	32.9%
k	17	45	37.8%

Table 5. Agreements of Codex W/032 in Matthew 17–20

Manuscripts	Agreements	Total Variants	Agreements
א	34	59	57.6%
B	28	57	49.1%
C	22	29	75.9%
D	29	59	49.2%
E	47	59	79.7%

L	38	59	64.4%
Δ	48	59	81.4%
Θ	34	59	57.6%
Π	50	59	84.7%
Σ	44	59	74.[illegible]%
Ω	48	56	85.7%
f^1	44	59	74.6%
f^{13}	41	59	69.5%
33	42	58	72.4%
565	44	57	77.2%
700	39	59	66.1%
a	18	46	39.1%
b	18	47	38.3%
e	19	46	41.3%
k	0	0	0%

Table 6. Agreements of Codex W/032 in Matthew 21–24

Manuscripts	Agreements	Total Variants	Agreements
א	34	63	54.0%
B	36	63	57.1%
C	29	37	78.4%
D	30	63	47.6%
E	53	63	84.1%
L	33	63	52.4%
Δ	50	63	79.4%
Θ	34	63	54.0%
Π	54	62	87.1%
Σ	51	62	82.3%
Ω	55	63	87.3%
f^1	37	63	58.7%
f^{13}	46	63	73.0%
33	36	60	60.0%
565	49	62	79.0%
700	44	63	69.8%
a	21	50	42.0%
b	14	44	31.8%
e	17	51	33.3%
k	1	1	100.0%

Table 7. Agreements of Codex W/032 in Matthew 25–28

Manuscripts	Agreements	Total Variants	Agreements
ℵ	57	112	50.9%
B	62	112	55.4%
C	57	91	62.6%
D	54	112	48.2%
E	92	112	82.1%
L	65	109	59.6%
Δ	96	112	85.7%
Θ	63	112	56.3%
Π	100	112	89.3%
Σ	90	112	80.4%
Ω	92	112	82.1%
f^{1}	78	112	69.6%
f^{13}	89	112	79.5%
33	70	107	65.4%
565	95	112	84.8%
700	69	112	61.6%
a	18	70	25.7%
b	27	96	28.1%
e	1	2	50.0%
k	0	0	0%

Looking at the various tables, one notices that table 3, which shows the rates of agreements in Matt 9–12, indicates a significantly higher rate of agreement of W here with several witnesses (i.e.,), B, Θ, f1, and f13), whereas W shows different rates of agreement with these same witnesses in other parts of Matthew. To explain this phenomenon, one could suggest block mixture. However, if there were block mixture, a higher rate of agreement with these manuscripts should be matched with a lower rate of agreements with other manuscripts, such as E, Δ, Π, Σ, Ω, and 565, which is not the case here. That is, in Matthew, W does not seem to shift from a closer affiliation with one group of manuscripts to a closer affiliation with another. A more plausible explanation for the high agreement of W and certain witnesses solely in Matt 9–12 is the nature of the sample, which counts a higher number of variant readings where most manuscripts align together against a smaller number, typically, in the Gospels, against D, a, b, e, and k (witnesses of the so-called Western text). A larger sample for these chapters could provide different results.

Looking at all seven tables, the varying rates of agreement of L with W are also surprising, as they vary from a high of 87.2 percent (table 4) down to 52.4 percent (table 6). In this case, one may indeed suspect the presence of block mixture, but probably in L. As noted, however, since W does not as a whole show a correspondingly dramatic change of alignment with the other manuscripts listed, one may dismiss the possibility of block mixture as a significant factor in W.

The two tables below display the overall (in Matthew) quantitative relationship of W with these twenty manuscripts. Table 8, which includes error correction, ranks the manuscripts according to their percentage of agreement with W, whereas table 9 displays the rate of agreement of W with the other witnesses, grouped according to their alleged text-type.

TABLE 8. WITNESSES RANKED ACCORDING TO PROPORTIONAL AGREEMENT WITH W IN MATTHEW (LEVEL OF CONFIDENCE = 95%)[16]

Rank	MSS	Agreements	Total Variants	Agreement	Error Correction
1	Π	547	641	85.3%	2.7%
2	Ω	530	639	82.9%	2.9%
3	E	530	642	82.6%	2.9%
4	Δ	521	642	81.2%	3.0%
5	565	508	637	79.7%	3.1%
6	Σ	506	639	79.2%	3.2%
7	700	465	641	72.5%	3.5%
8	C	342	474	72.2%	4.0%
9	f^{13}	462	642	72.0%	3.5%
10	33	420	600	70.0%	3.7%
11	f^{1}	447	642	69.6%	3.6%
12	L	426	626	68.1%	3.7%
13	Θ	395	597	66.2%	3.8%
14	B	398	639	62.3%	3.8%
15	א	392	639	61.3%	3.8%
16	D	258	561	46.0%	4.1%
17	e	61	173	35.3%	7.1%
18	k	106	296	35.8%	5.5%
19	a	146	494	29.6%	4.0%
20	b	152	512	29.7%	4.0%

16. These ranks should not be taken as absolute, as one may realize by considering the error correction. Manuscripts Ω, E, and Δ are so close to each other that they practically may be seen as *ex aequo* in regard to the error correction.

TABLE 9. PROPORTIONAL RELATIONSHIPS OF WITNESSES WITH W032, ARRANGED BY TEXTUAL GROUP IN MATTHEW

Primary Alexandrian

MSS	Agreements	Variants	Agreement	Error Correction
ℵ	392	639	61.3%	3.8%
B	398	639	62.3%	3.8%
Total	**790**	**1278**	**61.8%**	

Secondary Alexandrian

MSS	Agreements	Variants	Agreement	Error Correction
C	342	474	72.2%	4.0%
L	426	626	68.1%	3.7%
f^1	447	642	69.6%	3.6%
33	420	600	70.0%	3.7%
Total	**1635**	**2342**	**69.8%**	

"Caesarean"

MSS	Agreements	Variants	Agreement	Error Correction
Θ	395	597	66.2%	3.8%
f^{13}	462	642	72.0%	3.5%
Total	**857**	**1239**	**69.1%**	

Byzantine

MSS	Agreements	Variants	Agreements	Error Correction
E	530	642	82.6%	2.9%
Δ	521	642	81.2%	3.0%
Π	547	641	85.3%	2.7%
Σ	506	639	79.2%	3.2%
Ω	530	639	82.9%	2.9%
565	508	637	79.7%	3.1%
700	465	641	72.5%	3.5%
Total	**3607**	**4481**	**80.5%**	

"Western"

MSS	Agreements	Variants	Agreements	Error Correction
D	258	561	46.0%	4.1%
a	146	494	29.6%	4.0%
b	152	512	29.7%	4.0%
e	61	173	35.3%	7.1%
k	106	296	35.8%	5.5%
Total	**723**	**2036**	**35.5%**	

It is obvious that in Matthew W has a significantly higher rate of agreement with the Byzantine textual group than with any other, which indicates that W belongs more naturally to that group. A comprehensive profile analysis would allow one to qualify further its affinities with the Byzantine group by seeing the proportion of readings that are exclusive to that group, distinctive of it, and/or primarily found in manuscripts associated with that group. For that purpose, an increase of the sample size would be desirable as well as the addition of a few other manuscripts deemed to belong to the Byzantine textual group. I chose to take another direction in the study of the text of Matthew in W by looking more closely at its texture in comparison with another manuscript.

Elements of Comparison between W032 and B03 in Matthew

The second part of this study concentrates on some stylistic features of the text of Matthew in W. The analysis is prompted by the following question: What is the difference between reading the Gospel according to Matthew from W and reading it from another manuscript? This is basically a question that may more readily reflect our own setting, however, than the ancient settings in which W or other Gospels manuscripts were read. We do not know much about the particular geographical, social, religious, and practical settings of the use of the Freer Gospels. If this manuscript was copied sometime in the late fourth or fifth century and used in a context where Greek was understood, likely in Egypt, we still do not know for how long it was used or in what kinds of settings, such as liturgical, semiprivate, or private. Moreover, we have no knowledge about the way the text of the Freer Gospels would have been appreciated by its ancient readers or even if these readers would have been familiar with the text of other manuscripts. Given the lack of information concerning the early reception of the text of W, any question concerning its reception and the appreciation of its text remains difficult to answer with confidence. Furthermore, it is also an elitist question, for only a handful of people are interested in such an experience and equipped to appreciate it. Not only does one need to know Greek and have access to a reproduction of the manuscript, but one must also perceive that some profit may be gained by attempting to read a manuscript of the Gospels rather than the text printed in a modern edition of the Greek New Testament.

The limited scope of this essay does not allow me to explore all the aspects of the experience of reading Matthew in W. Thus, I will limit myself to a comparison of the cohesion of the text of Matthew in W and in Codex Vaticanus (B; Gregory-Aland 03). I selected Vaticanus as a point of comparison for three reasons. First, the results of the quantitative analysis displayed above show that W and B are fairly different from each other in Matthew. Second, B can be considered to be the backbone of the most common editions of the Greek New Testament, such as UBS^4 and NA^{27}. As readers, we therefore have some familiarity with the sort of text represented by B, which has come to represent something of the "standard" text of New Testament writings, including Matthew. Third, studies by Eldon Epp and Jenny Read-Heimerdinger on the text of Acts of the Apostles in Codex Bezae (D; Gregory-Aland 05) also used Codex B as a point of comparison.[17] Although their studies were focused on another New Testament writing and on another manuscript, it will be useful to draw some comparisons with their work, as I wish to place mine in that current of study that explores the "personality" of a manuscript by comparing it with another manuscript.

Epp's study of D is also important for opening new horizons for the study of New Testament manuscripts, as it takes seriously Hort's often quoted recommendation that "knowledge of documents should precede final judgment upon readings."[18] Thus, Epp concentrated on the anti-Judaic tendencies of Codex Bezae in Acts and demonstrated that the accumulation of divergences between D and B creates a different reading experience as regards the representation of the relationships between the Jews and various characters such as Jesus, the Gentiles, the early Christians, and the apostles.

More recently, Read-Heimerdinger has opened a new avenue for exploring the texture of a specific manuscript by using insights from discourse analysis, a branch of applied linguistics. Discourse analysis had already generated numerous studies on New Testament texts, taking as a basis the "standard" text printed in UBS and Nestle-Aland editions.[19] The originality of Read-Heimerdinger's work is to apply this method to a particular manuscript.

To define discourse analysis broadly, one could say that it is the study of language use beyond the sentence and the clause level. It is also focused on the purposes and functions for which the language is produced and its effectiveness on the hearers or the readers of texts. Additionally, it involves attention to the social context within which a given discourse is produced.[20] In that regard, dis-

---

17. Eldon J. Epp, *The Theological Tendency of Codex Bezae Cantabrigiensis in Acts* (SNTSMS 3; Cambridge: Cambridge University Press, 1966); Jenny Read-Heimerdinger, *The Bezan Text of Acts: A Contribution of Discourse Analysis to Textual Criticism* (JSNTSup 236; London: Sheffield Academic Press, 2002).

18. B. F. Westcott and F. J. A. Hort, *Introduction to the New Testament in the Original Greek* (London: Macmillan, 1882; repr., Peabody, Mass: Hendrickson, 1988), 31.

19. See, e.g., A. H. Snyman, "Discourse Analysis: A Semantic Discourse Analysis of the Letter to Philemon," in *Text and Interpretation: New Approaches in the Criticism of the New Testament* (ed. Patrick J. Hartin and Jacobus H. Petzer; NTTS 15; Leiden: Brill, 1991), 83–99; David A. Black, ed., *Linguistics and New Testament Interpretation: Essays on Discourse Analysis* (Nashville: Broadman, 1992); Stanley E. Porter and D. A. Carson, eds., *Discourse Analysis and Other Topics in Biblical Greek* (JSNTSup 113; Sheffield: Sheffield Academic Press, 1995); Jeffrey T. Reed and Stanley E. Porter, eds., *Discourse Analysis and the New Testament: Approaches and Results* (Sheffield: Sheffield Academic Press, 1999).

20. Textbooks and handbooks on the topic provide various definitions on the method. One can consult with profit David Nunan, *Introducing Discourse Analysis* (Penguin English Applied Linguistics; London: Penguin English, 1993), 20; Barbara Johnstone, *Discourse Analysis*

course analysis shares aspects of the agendas of rhetorical criticism, ideological criticism, and reader-response criticism. Several schools of discourse analysis applied to the study of the New Testament have appeared since the 1970s.[21] These have concentrated mostly on the study of language itself and its rhetorical features. Read-Heimerdinger's study is no exception, as she pays attention to matters such as cohesion, word order, the absence/presence of the article, and the use of proper names in Codex Bezae. She suggests that in Acts Codex Bezae shows a textual cohesion superior to that of Codex Vaticanus and a more nuanced picture of the apostles, especially Peter and Paul.[22]

Focusing on the textual cohesion of manuscripts is particularly appropriate for making comparisons between W and B. Anyone familiar with methods such as source criticism, form criticism, and redaction criticism as applied to the study of the text of the Gospels has some experience of textual cohesion, as these methods pay attention to transitions between pericopes. Anyone who has graded student papers, especially when dealing with plagiarism, also has practical experience of this notion. "Textual cohesion" can be described as the set of resources available to a writer for constructing relations in discourse that transcend grammatical structure.[23] Roughly said, it is what makes the difference between a coherent text and a juxtaposition of unrelated sentences. As one considers "text" as a "textile" or "fabric," that is, as the weaving together of clauses in order to develop and convey ideas, cohesion may be considered as the quality, or even the tightness, of that textile/fabric. A text also has a thematic structure; that is, some elements must stand in prominence to indicate what is its topic, otherwise the discourse would be about everything and nothing in particular. The basis for the study of cohesion in texts has been laid out by Halliday and Hasan.[24] They identify five aspects of cohesion.

1. *Reference* is defined as the resources used for referring to a participant or circumstantial element whose identity is recoverable. In English, this role is fulfilled by elements such as demonstratives, definite articles, pronouns, comparatives, and phoric adverbs such as *here, there, now,* and *then.*

(Introducing Linguistics; Malden, Mass.: Blackwell, 2002); and Adam Jaworski and Nikolas Coupland, *The Discourse Reader* (London: Routledge, 1999), 1–3. The last item provides no less than ten definitions of discourse analysis drawn from various sources and illustrating the different tendencies of the method, leaning mostly toward linguistics in some cases and toward social sciences in others.

21. For a survey of these various schools, see Stanley E. Porter, "Discourse Analysis and New Testament Studies: An Introductory Survey," in Porter and Carson, *Discourse Analysis and Other Topic,* 14–35.

22. Read-Heimerdinger, *Bezan Text of Acts,* 350–55.

23. I borrow this definition from J. R. Martin, "Cohesion and Texture," in *The Handbook of Discourse Analysis* (ed. Deborah Schiffrin et al.; Malden, Mass.: Blackwell, 2001), 35.

24. M. A. K. Halliday and Ruqaiya Hasan, *Cohesion in English* (London: Longman, 1976).

2. *Ellipsis* can be defined as the resources for omitting a clause, or some part of a clause or group, in contexts where it can be assumed.

3. *Substitution* designates the resources that serve as place holders. In English, these are adverbs such as *so* and *not* for clauses, *do* for verbal groups, *one* for nominal groups, and pronouns.

4. *Conjunction* is defined as the connectors that link clauses into discourses. Halliday and Hasan include links that connect sentences but exclude conjunctions of subordination considered to be structural. Gutwinski, another cohesion theoretician, suggests including these, however, as they also play a grammatical role.[25]

5. *Lexical cohesion* is the repetition of lexical terms, synonymy, or near synonymy.

These five aspects of cohesion in English apply also to Koine Greek. Still, there are some differences worth mentioning between Koine Greek and English. For instance, Greek has the genitive-absolute construction in addition to conjunctions of coordination and of subordination.[26] Also, in contrast to English, Koine Greek does not require the use of a personal pronoun as subject of the verb; use of a pronoun is, rather, a choice to express emphasis. This feature gives additional weight to the personal pronoun before the verb as a means of reference. Finally, although Koine Greek has pronouns used for generic substitution (e.g., εἷς), it does not have a verbal equivalent of the English verb "to do" or the adverbs "not" (e.g., "isn't it?") and "so" (e.g., "so do I").

Based on the aforementioned aspects of cohesion, I suggest as a premise that discourses in Koine Greek that make frequent use of reference, conjunctions, and lexical cohesion prove to have an overall textual cohesion superior to an equivalent discourse that uses these means of cohesion more sparingly. If the reader accepts the validity of this premise, I will attempt to demonstrate that Codex W gives a general impression of greater cohesion than Codex B in Matthew because of its greater usage of reference, conjunctions, and lexical cohesion. Let us now consider the evidence by focusing on the use of proper names, pronouns, and conjunctions in W and B.

The following detailed comparison of W and B rests upon a full collation of these two manuscripts in Matthew. The first thing I wish to note is that W has a significantly higher number of proper names than B in the same passages. In fact, one notices that in twenty instances a proper name found in W is absent from

---

25. See Waldemar Gutwinski, *Cohesion in Literary Texts. A Study of Some Grammatical and Lexical Features of English Discourse* (Janua Linguarum Series Minor 204; The Hague: Mouton, 1976).

26. This is suggested by Jeffrey T. Reed, "The Cohesiveness of Discourse: Toward a Model of Linguistic Criteria for Analyzing New Testament Discourse," in Reed and Porter, *Discourse Analysis and the New Testament*, 36.

B[27] and that the opposite occurs only in two instances.[28] Assuming that Jesus is the main character of the narrative in Matthew, one may not be surprised that his name occurs about 150 times, corresponding to the aspect of lexical cohesion in the five field categories suggested by Halliday and Hasan. According to the same principle, one may not be surprised to encounter the term κύριος, to refer to him about twenty-two times in Matthew. Of the twenty instances where W has a proper noun absent from B, fifteen refer to the name "Jesus" and three to the title κύριος/ὁ κύριος.[29] In other words, in its more frequent use of the name "Jesus" and the term κύριος in comparison to the usage in Codex B, W shows a stronger lexical cohesion by making more explicit references to the main theme of the discourse.

While B uses fewer proper names, it is interesting to note that it proportionally uses them more often in an anarthrous way. There is, however, no unanimity among scholars about the value of anarthrous proper names versus articular ones. Blass and Debrunner consider the anarthrous proper name the default use in classical and New Testament Greek. Hence, the articular proper name would be anaphoric, that is, referring to a previous anarthrous proper name. Still, they warn about taking the rule too strictly, considering the numerous exceptions encountered in the New Testament.[30] Read-Heimerdinger confirms that rule but suggests that in the book of Acts Codex Bezae tends to use anarthrous proper names in order to draw attention to them, a claim that she supports by looking at all instances of proper names in Acts.[31] Wallace comments that Read-Heimerdinger's suggestion has real merit but needs to be checked with a larger corpus in order to reach any conclusion for the whole New Testament.[32] Unfor-

---

27. Proper names in W but not in B: ο ιησους (4:12, 23; 8:3, 7; 11:20; 12:25; 13:36; 14:14; 18:2); ιησους (8:29; 15:16; 16:20; 17:20; 22:37; 24:1); ο κυριος (28:6); κυριος (13:51; 28:6); ιωαννης (3:14); ο πετρος (17:26).

28. Proper nouns in B but not in W: $\overline{\chi\upsilon}$ in $\overline{\chi\upsilon\ \iota\upsilon}$ (1:18); ο θεος in ο θεος ο πατηρ (6:8).

29. ο ιησους (4:12, 23; 8:3, 7; 11:20; 12:25; 13:36; 14:14; 18:2); ιησους (8:29; 15:16; 16:20; 17:20; 22:37; 24:1); ο κυριος (28:6); κυριος (13:51; 28:6).

30. F. Blass and A. Debrunner, *A Greek Grammar of the New Testament and Other Early Christian Literature* (trans. and ed. Robert W. Funk; Chicago: University of Chicago Press, 1961), §260.

31. Read-Heimerdinger, *Bezan Text of Acts*, 116–44, esp. 117. In that discussion Read-Heimerdinger builds on the foundation laid out in Jenny Read-Heimerdinger and Stephen H. Levinsohn, "The Use of the Definite Article before Names of People in the Greek Text of Acts with Particular Reference to Codex Bezae," *FiloNT* 5 (1992): 15–44. Ironically, Porter seems to suggest the opposite principle for the New Testament: "It is difficult to regularize all usage: but several reasons for use of the article with names seem prevalent: (a) emphasis, i.e., calling attention to the name; (b) designation of case, especially for names that are indeclinable; (c) designation of title (ὁ κύριος, ὁ χριστός), and (d) anaphora." See Stanley E. Porter, *Idioms of the Greek New Testament* (2nd ed.; Sheffield: JSOT Press, 1994), 107.

32. Daniel B. Wallace, *Greek Grammar beyond the Basics: An Exegetical Syntax of the New Testament* (Grand Rapids: Zondervan, 1996), 246 n. 76.

tunately, as long as further study, including other books of the New Testament in various manuscripts, remains undone, it will be difficult to interpret the significance of the differences between B and W on the use of the article with proper names.[33]

Let us now turn to the use of pronouns in both manuscripts. Our collation shows that in ninety-two instances W has a pronoun where B has none. In contrast, one can identify twenty-four cases where a pronoun found in B is absent from W.[34] In other words, W has sixty-eight more pronouns than B in Matthew. That could also indicate that W has a tendency to add pronouns rather than to delete them. The function of pronouns is essentially anaphoric. That is, they help to show the relationship between the new clause or sentence and a previous one. Thus, they increase the tightness of the text, envisioned as a piece of fabric. The tendency of W to have more pronouns, therefore, creates stronger cohesion in its text of Matthew by making it easier to relate new information to previous information.

Conjunctions also play an important role in the cohesion of a text, not only by linking elements of discourse to each other, but also by giving some idea of the type of link that exists between them. Thus, conjunctions of coordination (e.g., καὶ, δὲ, γὰρ, ἀλλά, ουν, ἤ, οὔτε, εἴτε) indicate items standing on the same level (parataxis), while conjunctions of subordination (e.g., ὅτι, εἰ, καθώς, ώς, γάρ, ὅτε, ἵνα, ὅταν, ἐάν, ὅπως, ἕως, μή, μὴποτε) indicate the hierarchy of items in a sentence (hypotaxis) and help to reveal relationships of cause and effect among the various elements of the discourse. Finally, Reed points out that conjunctions, including genitive absolutes, also serve as boundary markers that help to organize the text into sections and paragraphs.[35]

I note, thus, that W also reveals a propensity to have more conjunctions than B. As one compares the two manuscripts, one finds that in fifty-four instances W has a conjunction where B does not. In comparison, only twenty times does B have a conjunction where W does not. Table 10 lists these conjunctions along with the references where variation occurs in the two manuscripts.

33. Gordon Fee had initiated such work in "The Use of the Definite Article with Personal Names in the Gospel of John," *NTS* 17 (1970–71): 168–83.

34. The bulk of these are personal pronouns. In a few cases B omits demonstrative pronouns (13:22, 40; 15:15; 18:27; 19:11; 20:23), relative pronouns (1:25; 13:46; 18:30, 34; 20:15), and indefinite pronouns (9:14; 13:44, 54; 18:29; 24:6) otherwise found in W. The pronouns found in B but absent from W are similarly mostly personal pronouns. Among these twenty-four cases, one finds only two demonstrative pronouns (10:22; 24:13), one relative pronoun (11:16), and one indefinite pronoun (25:29).

35. Reed, "Cohesiveness of Discourse," 36.

Table 10. Variation between W and B concerning the Use of Conjunctions

Conjunctions in W and Absent from B	Conjunctions in B and Absent from W
και (23 instances): 3:2, 16; 4:24; 5:13; 6:21; 8:7; 12:40; 13:4; 13:41; 15:6, 36; 16:19; 18:15; 20:23; 24:27, 37, 39; 25:35; 26:26, 33, 49, 60, 71	και (7 instances): 10:2; 13:26; 14:29; 15:36; 18:12; 26:26; 27:41
δε (11 instances): 7:15; 12:46; 13:1, 20; 14:9; 20:14; 22:39; 25:16, 21, 22; 26:35 (emphatic δε και)	δε (6 instances): 5:33; 13:46; 17:26; 18:1; 20:21; 28:5
οτι (11 instances): 5:31; 6:5, 16; 8:17; 10:7; 19:9; 20:12; 21:43; 23:36; 26:29; 26:65	οτι (2 instances): 6:29; 24:3; οτι δε (2 instances): 7:14; 16:28
γαρ (4 instances): 1:18; 11:10; 15:27; 24:28	γαρ (3 instances): 25:3,14; 26:45
εαν (3 instances): 5:32; 7:9; 12:36	
αν: 6:5	
ει: 27:42	
	ωσει: 14:21
	ως: 15:38

Looking at this chart, one notices that only common conjunctions are involved. In addition, W and B proportionally exhibit the same preferences for conjunctions such as καὶ, δὲ, and γάρ. The only difference can be seen in the use of the conjunction ὅτι, which proportionally seems to be more common in W. Yet the small quantity of data should prevent us from suggesting a stylistic preference for ὅτι in W. We can, nevertheless, observe that the larger quantity of conjunctions found in W may result in a stronger textual cohesion, as it allows the reader to grasp better the type of relationships (paratactic and/or hypotactic) among the elements of the discourse.[36]

The discrepancy between W and B concerning the quantity of proper names, pronouns, and conjunctions may give the impression that W's superiority in terms of textual cohesion can be perceived at first glance. However, one should realize that we are looking at a collection of evidence from a large body of text,

36. Interestingly, in cases involving a substitution of conjunction, one finds no clear instance of the replacement of a conjunction marking parataxis (e.g., και) with a conjunction conveying hypotaxis (e.g., οτι), and vice versa.

the twenty-eight chapters of the First Gospel. In reality, the difference of cohesion between the two manuscripts is very subtle and becomes evident only as one pays close attention to it. To illustrate that subtlety, I reproduce below Matt 8, by laying in parallel columns the text of W and of B. The differences between the two manuscripts are italicized. Among these italicized words, I put in boldface those that have some impact on cohesion.

Matthew 8 in Codex W	Matthew 8 in Codex B
[1] Καταβαντος δε αυτου απο του	[1] Καταβαντος δε αυτου απο του
ορους ηκολουθησαν αυτω οχλοι	ορους ηκολουθησαν αυτω οχλοι
πολλοι [2] και ιδου λεπρος *ελθων*	πολλοι [2] και ιδου λεπρος *προσελθων*
προσεκυνει αυτω λεγων κε εαν	προσεκυνει αυτω λεγων κε εαν
θελης δυνασαι με καθαρισαι [3] και	θελης δυνασαι με καθαρισαι [3] και
εκτινας την χειρα ηψατο αυτου ***ο ις***	εκτεινας την χειρα ηψατο αυτου
λεγων θελω καθαρισθητι και ευθεως	λεγων θελω καθαρισθητι και ευθεως
εκαθαρισθη αυτου η λεπρα· [4] και	εκαθαρισθη αυτου η λεπρα· [4] και
λεγει αυτω ο ις ορα μηδενι ειπης	λεγει αυτω ο ις ορα μηδενι ειπης
αλλα υπαγε σεαυτον διξον τω	αλλα υπαγε σεαυτον δειξον τω
ιερει και *προσενεγκε* το δωρον ὸ	ιερει και *προσενεγκον* το δωρον ο
προσεταξεν Μωυσης εις μαρτυριον	προσεταξεν Μωυσης εις μαρτυριον
αυτοις [5] *εισελθοντι δε αυτω* εις	αυτοις [5] *εισελθοντος δε αυτου* εις
καπερναουμ προσηλθεν αυτω	*καφαρναουμ* προσηλθεν αυτω
εκατονταρχης παρακαλων αυτον	*εκατονταρχος* παρακαλων αυτον
[6] και λεγων κε ο παις μου βεβληται	[6] και λεγων κε ο παις μου βεβληται
εν τη οικεια παραλυτικος δινως	εν τη οικια παραλυτικος δεινως
βασανιζομενος [7] ***και*** λεγει αυτω ***ο ις***	βασανιζομενος [7] *λεγει* αυτω
εγω ελθων θεραπευσω αυτον [8] *και*	εγω ελθων θεραπευσω αυτον [8]
αποκριθεις ο εκατονταρχος εφη	*αποκριθεις δε* ο εκατονταρχος εφη
κε ουκ ιμει ϊκανος ϊνα μου υπο την	κε ουκ ειμι ϊκανος ινα μου υπο την
στεγην εισελθης αλλα μονον ειπε	στεγην εισελθης αλλα μονον ειπε
λογω και ϊαθησεται ο παις μου· [9] και	λογω και ιαθησεται ο παις μου [9] και
γαρ εγω ανοσ ειμει υπο	γαρ εγω ανθρωπος ειμι υπο
εξουσιαν εχων υπ	εξουσιαν *τασσομενος* εχων υπ
εμαυτον στρατιωτας και λεγω τουτω	εμαυτον στρατιωτας και λεγω τουτω
πορευθητι και πορευεται και αλλω	πορευθητι και πορευεται και αλλω
ερχου και ερχεται και τω δουλω μου	ερχου και ερχεται και τω δουλω μου
ποιησον τουτο και ποιει [10] ακουσας	ποιησον τουτο και ποιει [10] ακουσας
δε ο ις εθαυμασεν και ειπεν τοις	δε ο ις εθαυμασεν και ειπεν τοις
ακολουθουσιν αμην λεγω υμιν	ακολουθουσιν αμην λεγω υμιν
παρ ουδενι τοσαυτην πιστιν εν τω	παρ ουδενι τοσαυτην πιστιν εν τω
ϊσραηλ ευρον· [11] λεγω δε υμιν οτι	ισραηλ ευρον [11] λεγω δε υμιν οτι
πολλοι απο ανατολων και δυσμων	πολλοι απο ανατολων και δυσμων

ηξουσιν και ανακλειθησονται μετα	ηξουσιν και ανακλειθησονται μετα
αβρααμ’ και ϊσαακ’ και ϊακωβ’ εν τη	αβρααμ και ισαακ και ιακωβ εν τη
βασιλεια των ουρανων [12] οι δε	βασιλεια των ουρανων [12] οι δε
υιοι της βασιλειας εκβληθησονται	υιοι της βασιλειας εκβληθησονται
εις το σκοτος το εξωτερον εκει	εις το σκοτος το εξωτερον εκει
εσται ο κλαυθμος και ο βρυγμος	εσται ο κλαυθμος και ο βρυγμος
των οδοντων [13] και ειπεν ο ις τω	των οδοντων [13] και ειπεν ο ις τω
εκατονταρχη ϋπαγε ως επιστευσας	εκατονταρχη υπαγε ως επιστευσας
γενηθητω σοι και ϊαθη ο παις *αυτου*	γενηθητω σοι και ιαθη ο παις
εν τη *ἡμερα* εκεινη· [14] και ελθων ο	εν τη *ωρα* εκεινη [14] και ελθων ο
ις εις την οικιαν πετρου ειδεν την	ις εις την οικιαν πετρου ειδεν την
πενθεραν αυτου βεβλημενην και	πενθεραν αυτου βεβλημενην και
πυρεσσουσαν [15] και ηψατο της	πυρεσσουσαν [15] και ηψατο της
χειρος αυτης και αφηκεν αυτην ο	χειρος αυτης και αφηκεν αυτην ο
πυρετος και ηγερθη και διηκονι	πυρετος και ηγερθη και διηκονει
αυτω· [16] οψειας δε γονομενης	αυτω [16] οψιας δε γονομενης
προσηνεγκαν αυτω δαιμονιζομενους	προσηνεγκαν αυτω δαιμονιζομενους
πολλους· και εξεβαλεν τα πντα	πολλους και εξεβαλεν τα πνευματα
λογω και παντας τους κακως	λογω και παντας τους κακως
εχοντας εθεραπευσεν [17] οπως	εχοντας εθεραπευσεν [17] οπως
πληρωθη το ρηθεν δια ησαϊου του	πληρωθη το ρηθεν δια ησαιου του
προφητου λεγοντος ***οτι*** αυτος τας	προφητου λεγοντος αυτος τας
ασθενειας ημων ελαβεν και τας	ασθενειας ημων ελαβεν και τας
νοσους εβαστασεν· [18] ιδων δε ο ις	νοσους εβαστασεν [18] ιδων δε ο ις
οχλον *πολυν* περι αυτον εκελευσεν	οχλον περι αυτον εκελευσεν
απελθειν εις το περαν [19] και	απελθειν εις το περαν [19] και
προσελθων εις γραμματευς ειπεν	προσελθων εις γραμματευς ειπεν
αυτω διδασκαλε ακολουθησω σοι	αυτω διδασκαλε ακολουθησω σοι
οπου αν απερχη [20] και λεγει	οπου εαν απερχη [20] και λεγει
αυτω ο ις αι αλωπεκες φωλαιους	αυτω ο ις αι αλωπεκες φωλεους
εχουσιν και τα πετινα του ουρανου	εχουσιν και τα πετεινα του ουρανου
κατασκηνωσεις ο δε ϋΐος του	κατασκηνωσεις ο δε υιος του
ανθρωπου ουκ εχει που την κεφαλην	ανθρωπου ουκ εχει που την κεφαλην
κλεινη· [21] ετερος δε των μαθητων	κλεινη [21] ετερος δε των μαθητων
αυτου ειπεν αυτω κε επιτρεψον μοι	ειπεν αυτω κε επιτρεψον μοι
πρωτον απελθειν και θαψαι τον	πρωτον απελθειν και θαψαι τον
πρα μου [22] ο δε ις *ειπεν* αυτω	πατερα μου [22] ο δε ις λεγει αυτω
ακολουθει μοι και αφες τους	ακολουθει μοι και αφες τους
νεκρους θαψαι τους εαυτων νεκρους	νεκρους θαψαι τους εαυτων νεκρους
[23] και εμβαντι αυτω εις *το* πλοιον	[23] και εμβαντι αυτω εις πλοιον
ηκολουθησαν αυτω οι μαθηται	ηκολουθησαν αυτω οι μαθηται
αυτου [24] και ϊδου σισμος μεγας	αυτου [24] και ιδου σεισμος μεγας

εγενετο εν τη θαλασση ωστε το	εγενετο εν τη θαλασση ωστε το
πλοιον καλυπτεσθαι	πλοιον καλυπτεσθαι
υπο των κυματων αυτος δε	υπο των κυματων αυτος δε
εκαθευδεν [25] και προσελθοντες	εκαθευδεν [25] και προσελθοντες
οι μαθηται αυτου ηγειραν αυτον	ηγειραν αυτον
λεγοντες κε σωσον ***ημας***	λεγοντες κε *σωσον*
απολλυμεθα· [26] και λεγει αυτοις	απολλυμεθα [26] και λεγει αυτοις
τι δειλοι εσται ολιγοπιστοι τοτε	τι δειλοι εστε ολιγοπιστοι· τοτε
εγερθεις επετιμησεν τοις ανεμοις	εγερθεις επετειμησεν τοις ανεμοις
και τη θαλασση και εγενετο	και τη θαλασση και εγενετο
γαληνη μεγαλη [27] οι δε ανθρωποι	γαληνη μεγαλη [27] οι δε ανθρωποι
εθαυμασαν λεγοντες ποταπος εστιν	εθαυμασαν λεγοντες ποταπος εστιν
ουτος ***ο ανος*** οτι και οι ανεμοι και η	ουτος οτι και οι ανεμοι και η
θαλασσα αυτω υπακουουσιν· [28] και	θαλασσα αυτω υπακουουσιν [28] και
ελθοντι αυτω εις το *περαν* των	*ελθοντος αυτου* εις το περαν *εις την*
γεργεσηνων υπηντησαν	*χωραν* των *γαδαρηνων* υπηντησαν
αυτω δυο δαιμονιζομενοι εκ των	αυτω δυο δαιμονιζομενοι εκ των
μνημιων εξερχομενοι χαλεποι λιαν	μνημιων εξερχομενοι χαλεποι λειαν
ωστε μη ϊσχυειν τινα παρελθειν δια	ωστε μη ισχυειν τινα παρελθειν δια
της οδου εκεινης [29] και ϊδου *εκραζον*	της οδου εκεινης [29] και ιδου *εκραξαν*
λεγοντες τι ημιν και σοι ***ιυ*** υϊε του θυ	λεγοντες τι ημιν και σοι υϊε του θυ
ηλθες ωδε *απολεσαι ημας και προ*	ηλθες ωδε *προ*
καιρου βασανισαι [30] ην δε	*καιρου βασανισαι ημας* [30] ην δε
μακραν απ αυτων αγελη χοιρων	μακραν απ αυτων αγελη χοιρων
πολλων *βοσκομενων* [31] οι δε	πολλων *βοσκομενη* [31] οι δε
δαιμονες παρεκαλουν αυτον	δαιμονες παρεκαλουν αυτον
λεγοντες ει εκβαλλεις ημας	λεγοντες ει εκβαλλεις ημας
επιτρεψον ημιν απελθειν εις την	*αποστειλον ημας* εις την
αγελην των χοιρων [32] και ειπεν	αγελην των χοιρων [32] και ειπεν
αυτοις υ*παγεται οι δε εξελθοντες	αυτοις υπαγετε οι δε εξελθοντες
απηλθον εις ***την αγελην των χοιρων***	απηλθον εις *τους χοιρους*
και ϊδου ωρμησεν πασα η αγελη	και ιδου ωρμησεν πασα η αγελη
κατα του κρημνου εις την θαλασσαν	κατα του κρημνου εις την θαλασσαν
και απεθανον εν τοις ϋδασιν [33] οι δε	και απεθανον εν τοις ϋδασιν [33] οι δε
βοσκοντες εφυγον και απελθοντες	βοσκοντες εφυγον και απελθοντες
εις την πολιν απηγγειλον παντα	εις την πολιν απηγγειλαν παντα
και τα των δαιμονιζομενων· [34] και	και τα των δαιμονιζομενων [34] και
ιδου πασα η πολις εξηλθεν εις	ιδου πασα η πολις εξηλθεν εις
συναντησιν τω ιυ και ϊδοντες αυτον	*υπαντησιν* τω ιυ και ιδοντες αυτον
παρεκαλεσαν ϊνα μεταβη απο των	παρεκαλεσαν ινα μεταβη απο των
οριων αυτων	οριων αυτων

In looking at this sample, one notices that the concentration of relevant phrases (i.e., boldface fonts) is very low in W. Thus, the impression of the overall superior cohesion of W over B appears through the accumulation of more subtle differences. For instance, on lines 4, 10, and 87 W has the proper name (ο) ις̅, which contributes to increased lexical cohesion by mentioning more frequently the main character of the discourse. Also, on line 18 the conjunction και links more explicitly the new clause to what precedes. On line 56 the conjunction οτι helps to set the boundary of the Isaiah quotation. One of the most interesting features of lexical cohesion is found on line 81: the noun phrase οι μαθηται αυτου is redundant with the previous mention of the same phrase on lines 75–76, the text of W thereby reinforcing lexical cohesion.[37] Line 82 has the pronoun ημας, making anaphoric reference to οι μαθηται αυτου found on the previous line. On line 89 B simply has ουτος, whereas W has the noun phrase ουτος ο α̅ν̅ο̅ς̅, which reinforces the reference to Jesus by the use of a near synonym and also promotes lexical cohesion with οι δε ανθρωποι (line 87) by the repetition of that lexical term.[38] Finally, on line 107 W has opted for a stronger lexical cohesion by repeating the noun phrase την αγελην των χοιρων found on line 100, whereas B has opted for ellipsis by having τους χοιρους.

But one should not assume that the overall stronger cohesion of Codex W is the result of some thoughtful editorial strategy systematically applied through the whole Gospel according to Matthew. There are in fact many cases where B has a proper name, a pronoun, or a conjunction where W has none. If a consistent editorial strategy had been applied through Matthew in W, the discrepancy between W and B concerning the quantity of proper names, pronouns, and conjunctions would be even greater. I suggest, therefore, that in the present case the superior textual cohesion exhibited by W is not the result of a conscious project but rather the result of sporadic modifications of the text. As Epp remarks: "The copying and editing of manuscripts necessarily involve a certain considerable degree of respect for the text; these procedures represent, after all, a basically conservative endeavor."[39] We should therefore not be surprised with the inconsistency of the editorial work, and we should resist the temptation of seeing in

---

37. W has the noun phrase οι μαθηται αυτου in 14:22; 17:10; 26:8, 36, 45, but it is absent from the corresponding passages in B.

38. At the end of an article on the *nomina sacra,* Larry Hurtado suggests that "the *nomina sacra* can be thought of as 'hybrid' phenomena that combine textual and iconographic features and functions, with particular sacred words presented in a special written form that was intended to mark them off from the surrounding text and express special reverence for them as visual signs." One may wonder how much the abbreviated form of ανθρωπος, i.e., α̅ν̅ο̅ς̅, contributes to reinforce the reference to Jesus, whose name W typically writes in a *nomina sacra* form, i.e., ι̅ς̅. See Larry W. Hurtado, "The Origin of the Nomina Sacra: A Proposal," *JBL* 117 (1998): 672–73.

39. Epp, *Theological Tendency of Codex Bezae,* 38.

each variant the mind of a scribe carrying out a thoughtful editorial plan that the text critic should try to unveil. Ancient scribes are not here any longer to tell us what their intentions were and/or to confirm that they were fully conscious of modifying the text. There is thus no way to validate our educated guesses concerning their intentions.[40]

Our incapacity to map scribal intentions behind each type of textual variation does not make void the overall task of textual criticism, however, which consists in recovering the most ancient text possible and of tracing the history of the transmission of that text. Instead, we should be more aware of our own particular aesthetic preferences when the time comes to establish a text and make choices among variants.

During the last twenty-five years biblical scholarship has become more aware of the reader's role in biblical interpretation, that is, how the location and biases of exegetes influence the manner in which they apply the various methods of interpretation to the text and interpret the results drawn from these methods. Curiously, such awareness seems to have bypassed New Testament textual criticism and its practitioners, perhaps because the discipline still perceives itself as an act occurring before interpretation.[41] Is it not the role of textual criticism to establish the text prior to its interpretation, that is, before the application of the various methods of interpretation? From that point of view, one could pretend that no interpretation takes place when establishing the text; textual criticism simply levels the ground on which interpretation will take place. Any practitioner of textual criticism should, nonetheless, be aware that the act of establishing the text is interpretive.

Not only does the critic approach the text with a set of theological and social presuppositions,[42] but there are also a set of aesthetic presuppositions spelled out in rules such as *lectio difficilior lectio potior* (the more difficult reading is the more probable reading) and *lectio brevior lectio potior* (the shorter reading is the more

---

40. For an exposition of the problem of scribal intention, see Bart D. Ehrman, "Intentional Fallacies: Scribal Motivations and the Rhetoric of Critical Discourse" (paper presented at the SBL Annual Meeting, Atlanta, 2003.

41. Comfort's recent article pays attention to the reader's input in establishing the text but identifies the reader solely with the ancient scribe without raising the possibility that the contemporary critic is also a reader whose decisions about establishing the text are influenced by social and theological contexts. Philip Comfort, "Scribes as Readers: Looking at New Testament Textual Variants according to Reader Reception Analysis," *Neot* 38 (2004): 28–53.

42. Epp's article on the Junia/Junias variant in Rom 16:7 gives a good idea of the way such presuppositions may come into play in establishing the text. Eldon J. Epp, "Text-Critical, Exegetical, and Social-Cultural Factors Affecting the Junia/Junias Variation in Romans 16,7," in *New Testament Textual Criticism and Exegesis: Festschrift J. Delobel* (ed. Adelbert Denaux; BETL 161; Leuven: Leuven University Press/Peeters, 2002), 227–91.

probable reading).[43] Although these describe likely developments of the tradition, they also create aesthetic expectations. Hence, for example, the critic may attempt to reconstruct a text by choosing rougher and shorter readings. Ironically, such aesthetic criteria are different from those we would have for evaluating most texts. Assuming that most of my implied readership has some experience in grading student papers, one generally tends to enjoy more reading papers whose style is smooth, clear, and explains things at length when necessary. Difficulty and obscurity are rarely regarded as virtues in the world of editing, and brevity may be considered a two-edged sword.

As one compares the sample printed above, which sets in parallel columns the text of W and B in Matt 8, one realizes that the difference of lengths between them is barely perceptible. Besides, none of the italicized readings of B, for which W has an alternate reading, presents difficulty or obscurity. In other words, the critic is presented with two basically equivalent texts whose major differences are a slightly different length and a slightly different cohesion resulting in a small difference in aesthetic effect.

Just as critics have become more cautious recently concerning the validity of the principle of the shorter reading to determine the most ancient text,[44] they should also be careful about using cohesion to determine which manuscripts display the most ancient text. Thus, Read-Heimerdinger partly bases her claim that Codex Bezae reproduces a more ancient text than Codex Vaticanus in Acts on the basis that Bezae exhibits a superior level of cohesion to Vaticanus. Her premise is that redaction would disturb an original cohesion rather than improve it.[45] Still, if it is possible to disturb cohesion by reworking a text, it is also possible to improve it. Cohesion, as an aesthetic quality, should thus not be brought as an argument for priority or posteriority of one textual witness in relation to another one. Textual cohesion should be located at a synchronic level as an effect of the discourse

---

43. These two rules are listed as such, or rendered in equivalent terms, in works such as Kurt Aland and Barbara Aland, *The Text of the New Testament* (2nd ed.; trans. Errol F. Rhodes; Grand Rapids: Eerdmans, 1989), 280–81; J. Harold Greenlee, *Introduction to New Testament Textual Criticism* (2nd ed.; Peabody, Mass.: Hendrickson, 1995), 112; Bruce M. Metzger and Bart D. Ehrman, *The Text of the New Testament: Its Transmission, Corruption, and Restoration* (5th ed.; New York: Oxford University Press, 2005), 302–3.

44. See the caveat made by Aland and Vaganay (Aland and Aland, *Text of the New Testament,* 282; Léon Vaganay and Christian-Bernard Amphoux, *Initiation à la critique textuelle du Nouveau Testament* [2nd ed.; Études Annexes de la Bible de Jérusalem; Paris: Cerf, 1986], 122–23). Taking Matt 6:33 as a test case, Hendriks suggests that the rule retains a certain value. See Wim Hendriks, "Brevior lectio praeferenda est verbosiori," *RB* 112 (2005): 567–95.

45. See Read-Heimerdinger (*Bezan Text of Acts,* 39), "The more cohesive a discourse is, the more it is likely to be the result of deliberate composition and correspondingly less of sporadic modification, haphazard correcting or unintentional mistakes."

upon the reader. Even though it may be part of the authorial or editorial intent, it is effective only when recognized as such by the listener/reader.[46]

Conclusion

Our quantitative study has demonstrated that W has closer relationships to manuscripts such as Π Ω, E, Δ, 565, Σ, and 700, which are considered to be representative of the Byzantine textual tradition in Matthew, than to representatives of the other main text-types. It has little relationship to manuscripts considered to represent the "Western" textual tradition in Matthew, such as D, a, b, e, and k. In addition, no block mixture has been detected through the quantitative analysis. The qualitative study concentrated on textual cohesion by comparing the text of W in Matt 8 with the parallel text in B. It showed that, through its usage of proper names, pronouns, and conjunctions, W may exhibit a greater cohesion in Matthew than does B. Nevertheless, this greater cohesion has no implication for estimating whether W reproduces a text chronologically anterior to the one found in Vaticanus. This study is, however, limited to the indications of cohesion of the text of Matthew in W. Further study could be undertaken concentrating on other features of discourse analysis such as boundary markers, word order, and the use of the article. In addition, variant readings unique to W in Matthew could be studied to see more fully the specificity of this manuscript.

46. Thus Reed ("Cohesiveness of Discourse," 36): "It must be repeated that cohesiveness is both a product of the speaker's use of the linguistic code and a result of the listener's interpretation of the discourse. There is no guaranteed one-to-one correspondence between the authorial intent of cohesiveness and the reader's response to it."

The Use and Nonuse of *Nomina Sacra* in the Freer Gospel of Matthew

J. Bruce Prior

The Concept of *Nomina Sacra*

The expression "*nomina sacra*" was coined and introduced among scholars as a theoretical construct in a 1907 monograph by Ludwig Traube, Professor of Philology at the University of Munich, just after Charles Freer purchased four important biblical manuscripts in Egypt, including the Freer Gospels, but shortly before these manuscripts became known to the scholarly world.[1] Traube identified fifteen Greek words and their inflection forms, which ancient scribes typically rendered as abbreviated *nomima sacra*.[2] Typically, the abbreviated forms involve "contraction," the first and last letters of the inflected form of the word. Less regularly, but still relatively often, the contraction includes one or more of the medial letters as well. In some instances, notably in some early instances of forms of Ιησους, the scheme of abbreviation is by "suspension," involving the first two letters. A horizontal stroke placed over the abbreviation is a regular and distinctive feature of *nomina sacra* forms, whatever the type of abbreviation.

Patterns of use and nonuse of *nomina sacra* changed over the history of the early Christian church. Based on the work of Paap,[3] Roberts,[4] Hurtado,[5]

1. Ludwig Traube, *Nomina Sacra: Versuch einer Geschichte der christlichen Kürzung* (Munich: Beck, 1907).

2. See Traube's detailed tabulation and discussion of inflected forms (ibid., 56–121).

3. A. H. R. E. Paap, *Nomina Sacra in the Greek Papyri of the First Five Centuries A.D.: The Sources and Some Deductions* (Leiden: Brill, 1959).

4. Colin H. Roberts, *Manuscript, Society and Belief in Early Christian Egypt* (The Schweich Lectures 1977; London: Oxford University Press, 1979).

5. Larry W. Hurtado, "The Origin of the Nomina Sacra: A Proposal," *JBL* 117 (1998): 655–73; idem, *Lord Jesus Christ: Devotion to Jesus in Earliest Christianity* (Grand Rapids: Eerdmans, 2003), 625–27.

Parker,[6] Comfort,[7] Charlesworth,[8] and others, it is evident that the use of *nomina sacra* was emblematic of early Christian scribal practice. Hurtado wrote: "The *nomina sacra* were intended to register religious devotion visually. They are textual phenomena with an iconographic function. And, at the earliest stage of this early Christian scribal convention, Jesus figures centrally in the religious devotion that prompted it."[9]

The current state of scholarly discussion on the *nomina sacra* is summarized in Hurtado's 1998 article[10] and the chapter in Comfort's 2005 book.[11] Hurtado continued to treat the same fifteen words and their inflections identified by Traube[12] that are commonly rendered in nomen sacrum form, but he organized them into three groups:[13]

Primary group:	ιησους, χριστος, κυριος, θεος
Secondary group:	πνευμα, ανθρωπος, σταυρος
Tertiary group:	πατηρ, υιος, σωτηρ, μητηρ, ουρανος, ισραηλ, δαυειδ, ιερουσαλημ

In the case of the Freer Gospels, Henry A. Sanders described the topic in some detail,[14] but not exhaustively. Since Sanders completed his work, scholarly

6. David C. Parker, *Codex Bezae: An Early Christian Manuscript and Its Text* (Cambridge: Cambridge University Press, 1992), ch. 6: "The Nomina Sacra."

7. Philip Wesley Comfort, *Encountering the Manuscripts: An Introduction to New Testament Paleography and Textual Criticism* (Nashville: Broadman & Holman, 2005), ch. 4: "The Nomina Sacra in New Testament Manuscripts."

8. Scott D. Charlesworth, "*Nomina sacra* as Windows on Textual Authority and Comparative Transmission of Canonical and Non-canonical Gospels in the Second Century." Paper presented at the Society of Biblical Literature Annual Meeting, Philadelphia, Penn., 18–22 November 2005.

9. Hurtado, *Lord Jesus Christ*, 627. [Ed. note: The meaning of the *nomina sacra* is, however, a disputed matter. See C. M. Tuckett, "'Nomina Sacra': Yes and No?" in *The Biblical Canons* (ed. J.-M. Auwers and H. J. De Jonge; BETL 98; Leuven: Peeters, 2003), 431–58; and Larry W. Hurtado, *The Earliest Christian Artifacts: Manuscripts and Christian Origins* (Grand Rapids: Eerdmans, 2006), ch. 3: "The *Nomina Sacra*."]

10. Hurtado, "Origin of the *Nomina Sacra*."

11. Comfort, *Encountering the Manuscripts.*

12. Traube (*Nomina Sacra*, 36) grouped the fifteen words into seven categories (Reihen) and argued for a Jewish origin of the *nomina sacra:* (1) θεος, κυριος; (2) πνευμα, πατηρ; (3) ουρανος, ανθρωπος; (4) Δαυειδ, Ισραηλ, Ιερουσαλεμ; (5) Ιησους, Χριστος; (6) υιος, σωτηρ, σταυρος; and (7) μητηρ.

13. Hurtado's tripartite classification is derived from Roberts, *Manuscript, Society and Belief*, 27.

14. Henry A. Sanders, *The New Testament Manuscripts in the Freer Collection, Part I: The Washington Manuscript of the Four Gospels* (New York: Macmillan, 1912), 8, 10–12. Sanders did not use the expression *nomina sacra.* In the Gospels volume and earlier in *The Old Testament*

attention to the Freer Gospels has been scarce.[15] Sanders outlined the ways in which the Freer texts fit into the New Testament textual tradition. Hurtado and the editors of the Text und Textwert series[16] have carried through that analysis in more detail.

In this essay I discuss the use and nonuse of *nomina sacra* forms in the Freer Gospels (Codex Washingtonianus, W, 032) text of Matthew, with occasional reference to *nomina sacra* in the rest of the Freer Gospels. My discussion of *nomina sacra* is organized according to Hurtado's three groups, beginning with the third ("tertiary") group. For each word, I give a table offering four possible combinations of sacral and nonsacral *nomina sacra* and sacral and nonsacral full spelling of the words. References to the anomalous nonsacral use of *nomina sacra* forms and the anomalous sacral full words are printed in bold. Diacritical marks in the manuscript are not reproduced in these tables but are recorded fully in the Prior and Brown transcription.[17]

Tertiary *Nomina Sacra*

Hurtado wrote that these eight third-rank terms "are abbreviated less consistently and appear to have joined the list of sacred terms latest."[18]

Manuscripts in the Freer Collection, Part I: The Washington Manuscript of Deuteronomy and Joshua (New York: Macmillan, 1910), he called them simply "abbreviations." In *The Old Testament Manuscripts in the Freer Collection, Part II: The Washington Manuscript of the Psalms* (New York: Macmillan, 1917), he referred to them as "[t]he usual church abbreviations." In his volume on the Pauline codex, *The New Testament Manuscripts in the Freer Collection, Part II: The Washington Manuscript of the Epistles of Paul* (New York: Macmillan, 1918), he called them, "[t]he regular abbreviations of early Christian MSS." Even twenty years after Traube's monograph was published, in their edition of the Minor Prophets codex, Sanders and Carl Schmidt wrote of "[t]he regular church abbreviations" rather than "*nomina sacra*" (*The Minor Prophets in the Freer Collection and the Berlin Fragment of Genesis* [New York: Macmillan, 1927]).

15. Two exceptions are Eugen Helzle, "Der Schluß des Markusevangeliums (Mk 16, 9–20) und das Freer-Logion (Mk. 16, 14 w), ihr Tendenzen und ihr gegenseitiges Verhältnis: Eine wortexegetische Untersuchung," (Ph.D. diss., Tübingen University, 1959), and the 1973 Case Western Reserve University dissertation by Larry Weir Hurtado, "Codex Washingtonianus in the Gospel of Mark: Its Textual Relationships and Scribal Characteristics." A revised version of Hurtado's dissertation was subsequently published as *Text-Critical Methodology and the Pre-Caesarean Text: Codex W in the Gospel of Mark* (Grand Rapids: Eerdmans, 1981).

16. Kurt Aland, Barbara Aland, Klaus Wachtel, with Klaus Witte, *Text und Textwert der griechishchen Handschriften des Neuen Testaments* (Berlin: de Gruyter, 1998, 1999).

17. J. Bruce Prior and T. A. E. Brown, *The Freer Gospels: Transcription of Washington Manuscript III* (forthcoming).

18. Hurtado, "Origin of the *Nomina Sacra*," 656.

πατηρ

Sacral *nomen sacrum*	Nonsacral *nomen sacrum*	Sacral Full Word	Nonsacral Full Word	Verses in Freer Gospels Matthew
			πατρος	2:22
			πατερα	3:9[19]
			πατερων	23:30; 23:32
		πατερ		**6:9**[20]**; 11:25; 26:39**[21]**; 26:42**
$\overline{\pi\eta\rho}$				5:48; 6:4; 6:6; 6:8; 6:14; 6:15; 6:18; 6:26; 6:32; 7:11; 11:26; 11:27; 15:13; 16:17; 18:35; 23:9; 24:36
$\overline{\pi\rho\varsigma}$				5:45; 7:21; 10:20; 10:33; 11:27; 12:50; 13:43; 16:27; 18:10; 18:14; 18:19; 20:23; 25:34; 26:29; 28:19
$\overline{\pi\rho\iota}$				6:1; 6:6; 6:18
$\overline{\pi\rho\alpha}$				5:16; 11:27; 26:53
	$\overline{\pi\eta\rho}$			**10:21**
	$\overline{\pi\rho\varsigma}$			**10:35; 21:31**
	$\overline{\pi\rho\iota}$			**15:5**
	$\overline{\pi\rho\alpha}$			**8:21; 10:37; 15:4** (twice); **15:6; 19:5; 19:19; 23:9**

The scribe of W (032) wrote inflections of πατήρ as unabbreviated words only eight times in Matthew, four of those being vocative πάτερ in the sacral sense. The use of πάτερ in John and Luke is mixed in W. In John, the principal

19. Since πατερα in Matt 3:9 refers to Abraham, it could be considered a sacral usage.

20. The use of the full vocative form, πάτερ, in the Lord's Prayer in W is most anomalous.

21. In Matt 26:39, and again in 26:42, the vocative πάτερ in Jesus' wrenching prayer in the Garden of Gethsemane is written as unabbreviated.

scribe wrote it in full four times[22] and as $\overline{\pi\varepsilon\rho}$ four times.[23] In Luke, the same scribe wrote πάτερ in full four times[24] and used $\overline{\pi\varepsilon\rho}$ six times.[25] Πάτερ does not occur in the extant text of Mark.

On the other hand, the scribe used *nomina sacra* for the πατήρ word family eleven times in Matthew where there is no reference to the deity. It appears that *nomina sacra* forms for the πατήρ family were, on balance, overused by the scribe of W or used inconsistently, if the purpose was to highlight words of sacred significance for Christian readers.

υἱός

Sacral Full Word	Nonsacral Full Word	Verses in Freer Gospels Matthew
	υιος	1:20; 7:9
	υιω	22:2
	υιον	10:37; 17:15; 21:5; 21:37 (twice); 21:38; 23:15
	υιοι	5:9; 5:45; 8:12; 9:15; 12:27; 13:38 (twice); 20:21; 23:31
	υιων	17:25; 20:20 (twice); 27:9; 27:56
	υιους	26:37
υιος		**3:17; 4:3**[26]**; 4:6; 8:20; 9:6; 9:27; 11:19; 11:27** (twice); **12:8; 12:23; 12:40; 13:37; 13:41; 13:55**[27]**; 14:33; 15:22; 16:16; 16:27; 17:5; 17:9; 17:12; 17:22; 18:11; 19:28; 20:18; 20:28; 20:30; 20:31; 22:42; 22:45; 24:44; 25:31; 26:2; 26:24** (twice); **26:45; 26:63; 27:40; 27:43; 27:54**

22. All occurrences—John 11:41; 17:11, 24, 25—are in sacral contexts.

23. John 12:27, 28; 17:1, 5. John 17:21 has an instance of $\overline{\pi\eta\rho}$.

24. The referents of the word in Luke 10:21; 11:2; and 22:42 are sacral. Luke 15:12 has a nonsacral use.

25. Luke 15:18, 21; 16:24, 27, 30; 23:46. Jesus' famous cry of forgiveness in Luke 23:34a, where πάτερ occurs in some manuscripts, is absent from the text of W.

26. υἱός in Matt 4:3, 6 refers to Jesus, but since it is spoken by the devil, its sacral sense may have seemed to the scribe to be tarnished.

27. Since the expression οὐχ οὗτος ἔστιν ὁ τοῦ τέκτονος υἱός is used derisively of Jesus in Matt 13:55, this could also be considered a nonsacral situation.

υιου		1:1 (twice); 12:32; 24:27; 24:37; 24:39; 28:19
υιω		21:9; 21:15
υιον		1:21; 1:23; 1:25; 2:15; 11:27; 16:13; 16:28; 24:30; 26:64
υιε		8:29

The scribe of W used no *nomina sacra* forms for the υἱός family in the Gospel of Matthew, although $\overline{\text{υς}}$ for υἱός appears six times in the Gospel of Mark, the last in the codex, and $\overline{\text{υις}}$ is also used for υἱός in Mark 10:45 and $\overline{\text{υν}}$ for υἱόν in Mark 14:62.

σωτήρ

There are no occurrences of σωτήρ and its inflections in the Freer Gospels of Matthew or Mark. The full word σωτηρι appears in Luke 1:48, and σωτηρ is used in Luke 2:11. The scribe of the first quire of John uses $\overline{\text{σηρ}}$ in 4:42.

μήτηρ

Sacral *nomen sacrum*	Nonsacral *nomen sacrum*	Sacral Full Word	Nonsacral Full Word	Verses in Freer Gospels Matthew
			μητρος	10:35; 14:8; 19:12
			μητρι	14:11; 15:5
			μητερα	10:37; 15:4; 15:6
		μητρος		**1:18; 2:11**
		μητερα		**2:13; 2:14; 2:20; 2:21**
$\overline{\text{μηρ}}$				12:46; 12:47; 12:48; 12:49; 12:50[28]; 13:55
	$\overline{\text{μηρ}}$			**20:20; 27:56** (twice)
	$\overline{\text{μρα}}$			**15:4; 19:5; 19:19; 19:29**

28. Jesus is speaking allegorically in Matt 12:50 of μου … μήτηρ, so the *nomen sacrum* $\overline{\text{μηρ}}$ could also be interpreted as nonsacral.

The pattern of *nomen sacrum* use and nonuse for forms of μήτηρ by the scribe of W in Matthew is mixed. There are fourteen expected uses and thirteen anomalous uses.

οὐρανός

Sacral Full Word	Nonsacral Full Word	Verses in Freer Gospels Matthew
	ουρανου	6:26; 8:20; 13:32
	ουρανων	24:29
ουρανος		**5:18; 16:3; 24:35**
ουρανου		**3:17; 11:23; 11:25; 16:1; 16:3; 21:25** (twice); **24:29; 24:30; 26:64; 28:2**
ουρανω		**5:34; 6:10; 6:20; 18:18** (twice); **19:21; 22:30; 23:22; 24:30; 28:18**
ουρανων		**3:2; 4:17; 5:3; 5:10; 5:19**[29]**; 5:20; 7:21** (twice); **8:11; 10:7; 11:11; 11:12; 13:11; 13:24; 13:31; 13:33; 13:44; 13:45; 13:47; 13:52; 16:19; 18:1; 18:3; 18:4; 18:23; 19:12; 19:14; 19:23; 20:1; 22:2; 23:13; 24:31; 24:36; 25:1**
ουρανοις		**5:12; 5:16; 5:45; 6:1; 6:9; 6:14; 6:26; 6:32; 7:21; 10:32; 10:33; 12:50; 16:17; 16:19** (twice); **18:10** (twice); **18:14; 18:19; 23:9**

Although the οὐρανός family is overwhelmingly used in the sacral sense of "heaven" or "heavens," and only four times in the physical sense of "sky" or "skies" in the Gospel of Matthew, *nomina sacra* forms are never used by the principal scribe of W. However, the scribe of the supplemental first quire of John uses ουρου in sacral contexts in John 1:32; 3:13, 27, 31 and ουρον sacrally in John 1:51 and 3:13.

29. ουρα[νων] in Matt 5:19 is obscured by parchment damage.

Ισραήλ

Sacral *nomen sacrum*	Sacral Full Word	Verses in Freer Gospels Matthew
	ισραηλ	**2:6; 2:20; 2:21; 8:10; 9:33; 10:6; 10:23; 15:24; 15:31; 19:28**[30]**; 27:9**
ισρλ		27:42

All uses of Ἰσραήλ in the New Testament treat the nation with reverence. The scribe of Matthew in W, however, rendered the term in *nomen sacrum* form only once, in 27:42, the mocking reference to Jesus as βασιλευς ισραηλ by religious authorities. The scribe of the supplemental first quire of John uses ιηλ in John 1:31, 49 and 3:10.

Δαυεὶδ

Sacral *nomen sacrum*	Sacral Full Word	Verses in Freer Gospels Matthew
	δαυειδ	**1:1;**[31] **1:6** (twice); **1:17** (twice); **1:20; 9:27; 12:3; 15:22; 20:30; 20:31; 21:9; 21:15; 22:42; 22:43; 22:45**
δαδ		12:23

The *nomen sacrum* form δαδ is not completely unknown to the principal scribe of W, since it appears in Matt 12:23, where crowds ask whether Jesus could be a son of David, and twice more in John 7:42 regarding the prophecy about the Messiah's coming from David's village of Bethlehem. The full word δαυειδ is used in Luke 1:32.

Ἰερουσαλήμ

Sacral Full Word	Verses in Freer Gospels Matthew
ιερουσαλημ	**23:37** (twice)

30. The W spelling in Matt 19:28 is ιστραηλ in this instance.

31. The Prior and Brown transcription records δα[υε]ιδ, as the first page of the Freer Gospels has suffered parchment damage.

ιεροσολυμ	**2:1**
ιεροσολυμα	**2:3; 3:5; 5:35; 16:21; 20:17; 20:18; 21:1; 21:10**
[illegible]	[illegible]

The principal scribes of the Freer Gospels, including the scribe of the first quire of John, always use full words for the Ἰερουσαλήμ family. We have no evidence, therefore, that they knew of any *nomina sacra* forms for these words.

Secondary *Nomina Sacra*

Hurtado wrote that these three second-rank forms "appear to be slightly later and less uniformly treated" than the primary four.[32]

πνεῦμα

Sacral *nomen sacrum*	Nonsacral *nomen sacrum*	Nonsacral Full Word	Verses in Freer Gospels Matthew
		πνευματων	10:1
$\overline{\text{πνα}}$			3:16; 10:20; 12:18; 26:41; 27:50
$\overline{\text{πνς}}$			1:18; 1:20; 4:1; 12:31; 12:32; 28:19
$\overline{\text{πνι}}$			3:11; 5:3; 12:28; 22:43
	$\overline{\text{πνα}}$		**12:43**
	$\overline{\text{πντα}}$		**8:16**[33]**; 12:45**

The scribe of W used *nomina sacra* for the πνεῦμα family fairly consistently. In sixteen cases they were used or not used consistently with whether the uses were sacral or nonsacral. The scribe used *nomina sacra* three times, however, where the context was nonsacral. The same scribe used two unusual *nomina sacra* in the Freer Logion following Mark 16:14: $\overline{\text{πνατων}}$ is used for πνευμάτων

32. Hurtado, "Origin of the *Nomina Sacra*," 655.

33. The original scribe started to write $\overline{\text{πνα}}$ in Matt 8:16 for πνευμα, as in M, Ω, and 778, according to Reuben J. Swanson, *New Testament Greek Manuscripts: Variant Readings Arranged in Horizontal Lines against Codex Vaticanus, Matthew* (Sheffield: Sheffield Academic Press, 1995), 64 n. B. The scribe then immediately corrected it to read $\overline{\text{πντα}}$ for πνευματα.

in a nonsacral reference, and πνικην is a *nomen sacrum* form for the adjectival πνευματικὴν in a sacral sense. Comfort argued that the sacral *nomina sacra* uses of this word family should be ranked very high and early.[34] The data from the Matthew text W 032 is entirely consistent with Comfort's high standing applied to "Spirit" in the divine sense.

ἄνθρωπος

Sacral *nomen sacrum*	Nonsacral *nomen sacrum*	Sacral Full Word	Nonsacral Full Word	Verses in Freer Gospels Matthew
			ανθρωπος	4:4; 12:11; 13:31; 13:44; 16:26; 25:14; 25:24; 26:24
			ανθρωπου	12:43; 21:26
			ανθρωπω	13:24; 13:52
			ανθρωπον	10:35; 15:20
			ανθρωποι	8:27; 12:36
			ανθρωπων	4:19; 6:1; 6:2; 15:9; 16:23; 22:16; 23:7
			ανθρωποις	6:5; 6:14; 6:15; 6:16; 6:18; 12:31; 23:5; 23:28
			ανθρωπους	5:19
		ανθρωπου		**8:20; 12:40; 13:37; 13:41; 18:11; 20:28; 24:27; 24:39; 25:31**

34. Comfort wrote: "If one reads the literature on *nomina sacra*, it is clear that most scholars think that the four divine titles discussed above ('Lord,' 'Jesus,' 'Christ,' and 'God') were the primary titles to be written as *nomina sacra* and that all other titles were developed later. But the evidence of the extant manuscripts strongly suggests that the 'Spirit' was also written as a nomen sacrum very early in the transmission of the text, if not from the beginning. If *pneuma* was not among the earliest *nomina sacra*, then scribes, beginning in the early second century, began to make exegetical decisions as to whether it should be written as a nomen sacrum, representing the divine Spirit, or written out in full (in *plene*), so as to designate another aspect of the *pneuma*, such as the human spirit, evil spirit, or a spiritual condition" (*Encountering the Manuscripts*, 231).

		ανθρωπω		**18:23**
		ανθρωπον		**26:72**
ανος				8:27
ανου				9:6; 10:23; 11:19; 12:8; 12:32; 16:13; 16:27; 16:28; 17:9; 17:12; 17:22; 19:28; 20:18; 24:30; 24:37; 24:39; 24:44; 26:2; 26:24 (twice); 26:45; 26:64
ανον				26:74
	ανος			**7:9; 8:9; 11:19; 12:10; 12:12; 12:35** (twice); **13:28; 16:26; 17:14; 19:5; 19:6; 21:28; 21:33; 25:26; 27:57**
	ανου			**10:36; 12:45; 19:10**
	ανω			**12:13; 13:45; 18:7; 18:12; 19:3; 20:1; 22:2; 26:24**
	ανον			**9:9; 9:32; 11:8; 15:11** (twice); **15:20; 22:11; 27:32**
	ανοι			**7:12**
	ανων			**5:13; 5:16; 10:17; 10:32; 10:33; 17:22; 19:12; 21:25; 23:4; 23:13**
	ανοις			**9:8; 12:31; 19:26**
	ανους			**13:25**

The scribe of W used *nomina sacra* and full words for the ἄνθρωπος word family inconsistently, perhaps even arbitrarily. Only when the word referred directly to Jesus, or when it is included in various form of υἱός τοῦ ἀνθρώπου, does a *nomen sacrum* form make any sense, at least according to our current understanding about the function of *nomina sacra.*

It is possible to try to measure the randomness of "expected" and "anomalous" uses and nonuses of the ἄνθρωπος word family, using the nonparametric Runs Test, which quantifies the relative randomness of the order of a binary series, such as "expected" versus "anomalous."[35] To do this, the verse references where the abbreviated and nonabbreviated forms of ἄνθρωπος are used are listed in their order of occurrence. In the following list of references, I indicate "expected/regular" uses in ordinary font and "anomalous" instances in boldface.[36]

4:4 4:19 **5:13 5:16** 5:19 6:1 6:2 6:5 6:14 6:15 6:16 6:18 **7:9 7:12 8:9 8:20** 8:27a 8:27b 9:6 **9:8 9:9 9:32 10:17 10:32** 10:23 **10:33** 10:35 10:**36 11:8** 11:19a **11:19b** 12:8 **12:10** 12:11 **12:12 12:13** 12:31 12:32 **12:35a 12:35b** 12:36 **12:40** 12:43 **12:45** 13:24 **13:25 13:28** 13:31 13:44 **13:37 13:41 13:45** 13:52 15:9 **15:11a 15:11b** 15:20a **15:20b** 16:13 16:23 **16:26a** 16:26b 16:27 16:28 17:9 17:12 **17:14** 17:22a **17:22b 18:7 18:11 18:12 18:23 19:3 19:5 19:6 19:10 19:12 19:26** 19:28 **20:1** 20:18 **20:28 21:25** 21:26 **21:28 21:33 22:2 22:11** 22:16 **23:4** 23:5 23:7 **23:13** 23:28 **24:27** 24:30 24:37 **24:39** 24:44 25:14 25:24 **25:26 25:31** 26:2 26:24a **26:24b** 26:24c 26:24d 26:45 26:64 **26:72** 26:74 **27:32 27:57**

There are fifty-five expected uses of the ἄνθρωπος word-family in the text of Matthew in W, whereas sixty uses are anomalous. There are fifty-eight "runs," or sequences of expected verses anomalous uses. The possible range of runs is from two to 110, applying the Runs Test, z = -0.073. Mathematically, the pattern could not exhibit a more random pattern than with fifty-eight runs.[37] We must conclude that the pattern of use and nonuse of *nomina sacra* forms of ἄνθρωπος by the scribe of W could not possibly be more random than it is. In the terms of Hurtado's description of his list of secondary *nomina sacra,* the ἄνθρωπος word family in the Matthew text in W could not be "less uniformly treated."[38]

35. The One-Sample Runs Test of Randomness is described in Sidney Siegel and H. John Sastellan Jr., *Nonparametric Statistics for the Behavioral Sciences* (2nd ed.; New York: McGraw-Hill, 1988), 58–64 and 331 (table G), and 319 (with reference to table A).

36. In cases where there are two or more uses of the word in the same verse, the verse numbers are repeated.

37. The situation is analogous to a collection of 115 marbles, 55 of which are yellow and 60 of which are purple. After being thoroughly mixed and then distributed one at a time, the chance of their coming out all yellow in a row and all purple in a row (two runs) is extremely remote. Similarly, the chance that they would be so perfectly mixed to produce 110 runs would also be a remarkable coincidence. Thus, as the number of runs approaches either of those extremes, their randomness is increasingly unlikely. Similarly, as the number of runs approaches the center of the distribution ($z \approx 0$), their randomness is increasingly likely. In this case, the mathematical center of the distribution is between 58 ($z = -0.0734$) and 59 ($z = 0.1142$). Since -0.0734 is actually closer to 0 than 0.1142, 58 runs is the most random number of runs possible.

38. Hurtado, "Origin of the *Nomina Sacra,*" 655.

σταυρός

Sacral Full Word	Verses in Freer Gospels Matthew
σταυρου	**27:40**
σταυρον	**10:38; 16:24; 27:32**
σταυρωσαι	**20:19**
σταυρωθηναι	**26:2**
σταυρωσεται	**23:34**
σταυρωθητω	**27:22; 27:23**
σταυρωθη	**27:26**
εσταυρωμενον	**28:5**

The Freer Gospels contain no *nomina sacra* for the σταυρός word family.

Primary *Nomina Sacra*

Hurtado wrote that the primary *nomina sacra* group were "the four earliest attested and most consistently rendered words."[39]

Ἰησοῦς

Sacral *nomen sacrum*	Verses in Freer Gospels Matthew
$\overline{\text{ις}}$	1:16; 3:13; 3:15; 3:16; 4:1; 4:7; 4:10; 4:12; 4:17; 4:23; 7:28; 8:3; 8:4; 8:7; 8:10; 8:13; 8:14; 8:18; 8:20; 8:22; 9:2; 9:4; 9:9; 9:12; 9:15; 9:19; 9:22; 9:23; 9:28; 9:30; 9:35; 10:5; 11:1; 11:4; 11:7; 11:20; 11:25; 12:1; 12:15; 12:25; 13:1; 13:34; 13:36; 13:51; 13:53; 13:57; 14:13; 14:14; 14:16; 14:27; 14:31; 15:16; 15:21; 15:28; 15:29; 15:32; 15:34; 16:6; 16:8; 16:13; 16:17; 16:20; 16:21; 16:24; 17:1; 17:7; 17:9; 17:17; 17:18; 17:20; 17:22; 17:25 (twice)[40]; 17:26; 18:2; 18:22; 19:1; 19:14; 19:18; 19:21; 19:23; 19:26; 19:28; 20:17; 20:22; 20:25; 20:30; 20:32;

39. Ibid.
40. The first $\overline{\text{ις}}$ in Matt 17:25 is marked by a scribe for deletion.

$\overline{\iota\varsigma}$ (*cont.*)	20:34; 21:1; 21:6; 21:11; 21:12; 21:16; 21:21; 21:24; 21:31; 21:42; 22:1; 22:18; 22:29; 22:37; 22:41; 23:1; 24:1; 24:2; 24:4; 26:1; 26:10; 26:19; 26:26; 26:31; 26:34; 26:36; 26:50; 26:52; 26:55; 26:63; 26:64; 27:11 (twice); 27:37; 27:46; 27:50; 28:9; 28:10; 28:16; 28:18
$\overline{\iota\upsilon}$	1:1; 1:18; 2:1; 8:29; 8:34; 9:10; 9:27; 14:1; 14:12; 15:1; 15:30; 17:4; 17:19; 18:1; 21:27; 26:6; 26:17; 26:49; 26:51; 26:59; 26:69; 26:71; 26:75; 27:1; 27:55; 27:57; 27:58
$\overline{\iota\nu}$	1:21; 1:25; 14:29; 17:8; 26:4; 26:50; 26:57; 27:17; 27:20; 27:22; 27:26; 27:27; 27:54; 28:5

Since the Ἰησοῦν Βαραββᾶν variant in Matt 27:16 does not appear in W, there are no instances in any of the Freer texts where forms of Ἰησοῦς occur with a nonsacral reference. The scribes of W render all occurrences of the name consistently in *nomina sacra* form throughout the Freer Gospels. The Ἰησοῦς word family is therefore appropriately assigned to the first-rank *nomina sacra* group for the Freer Gospels.

Χριστός

Sacral *nomen sacrum*	Verses in Freer Gospels Matthew
$\overline{\chi\varsigma}$	1:16; 2:4; 16:16; 16:20; 23:10; 24:5; 24:23; 26:63
$\overline{\chi\upsilon}$	1:1; 1:17; 11:2; 22:42
$\overline{\chi\nu}$	27:17; 27:22
$\overline{\chi\varepsilon}$	26:68

Similarly, the principal scribe of W in all instances wrote forms of Χριστός as *nomina sacra* throughout the codex.[41] Here again this word must therefore be assigned to the Freer Gospels' first-rank *nomina sacra* group.

41. On the last page of Codex Washingtonianus, at the end of the Gospel of Mark, a later scribe wrote: Χριστε αγιε συ μετα του δουλου σου τιμοθεου και παντων των αυτου.

κύριος

Sacral *nomen sacrum*	Nonsacral Full Word	Verses in Freer Gospels Matthew
	κυριος	10:25; 18:32
	κυριοις	6:24
κ̅ς̅		12:8; 18:25; 18:27; 18:34; 20:8; 21:3; 21:40; 22:44; 24:42; 24:45; 24:46; 24:48; 24:50; 25:19; 25:21; 25:23; 25:26; 27:10; 28:6
κ̅υ̅		1:20; 1:22; 1:24; 2:13; 2:15; 2:19; 9:38; 21:9; 21:42; 23:39; 25:18; 25:21; 25:23; 28:2
κ̅ω̅		5:33; 18:31; 22:44
κ̅ν̅		4:7; 4:10; 10:24; 22:37; 22:43; 22:45
κ̅ε̅		7:21 (twice); 7:22 (twice); 8:2; 8:6; 8:8; 8:21; 8:25; 9:28; 11:25; 13:27; 13:51; 14:28; 14:30; 15:22; 15:25; 15:27; 16:22; 17:4; 17:15; 18:21; 18:26; 20:30; 20:31; 20:33; 21:30; 25:11 (twice); 25:20; 25:22; 25:24; 25:37; 25:44; 26:22; 27:63

The deployment of abbreviated and nonabbreviated forms of κυριος by the scribe of W in Matthew is entirely as expected. All renderings are *nomina sacra* forms, except in three nonsacral cases, where the full words are written. Thus the κυριος word family also belongs properly to the first category of *nomina sacra,* that is, those most regularly and consistently used.

Θεός

Sacral *nomen sacrum*	Sacral Full Word	Verses in Freer Gospels Matthew
	θεε	**27:46**
	θεε	**27:46**
θ̅ς̅		1:23; 3:9; 6:30; 15:4; 19:6; 19:17; 22:32 (four times)

θ̅υ̅		3:16; 4:3; 4:4; 4:6; 5:9; 5:34; 6:33; 8:29; 12:4; 12:28 (twice); 14:33; 15:3; 15:6; 16:16; 16:23; 19:24; 21:12; 21:31; 21:43; 22:16; 22:21; 22:29; 22:30; 22:31; 23:22; 26:61; 26:63 (twice); 27:40; 27:43; 27:54
θ̅ω̅		6:24; 19:26; 22:21
θ̅ν̅		4:7; 4:10; 5:8; 9:8; 15:31; 22:37; 27:43

With the important exception of the vocative form, θεέ, discussed in detail below, the inflections of θεός are all written as *nomina sacra* throughout the Freer Gospels codex. The θεός word family can still be assigned to the first category of *nomina sacra* but should be ranked fourth in that group, as to consistency of scribal practice, because of the instances of θεέ written out fully. I now turn to an expanded discussion of this matter.

The Vocative θεέ in Matthew 27:46

The vocative form θεέ occurs only twice in the New Testament, both times in Matt 27:46. The Freer Gospels text reads:

περι δε την ενατην ωραν εβοησεν ο ι̅ς̅
φωνη μεγαλη λεγων   ηλι ηλι μα σαβα—
χθανει   τουτ εστιν θε$^{\varepsilon}$ μου θεε μου
ῑνατι με ενκατελειπες

In the Freer Gospels here, the first vocative was written θε, unmarked by a *nomen sacrum* supraline and then corrected by the principal scribe to θε$^{\varepsilon}$. The second vocative in the same line is written out fully as θεε (see fig. 1).

In his discussion of abbreviations in Matthew, Henry A. Sanders neglected to mention this θεε as an exceptional case.[42] Sanders identified the inserted *epsilon* in Matt 27:46 as the work of the principal scribe, but in his collation in the same volume he marked the correction as the work of another scribe.[43] Goodspeed was ambivalent as to whether the superscript *epsilon* had been inserted by the original scribe or by a second hand.[44] The *epsilon* was most likely inserted immediately by the principal scribe, however, because of the absence of a supralinear stroke over the initially written θε.

---

42. Sanders, *Washington Manuscript of the Four Gospels,* 8.

43. Ibid., 28, 164.

44. Edgar J. Goodspeed, *The Freer Gospels* (Chicago: University of Chicago Press, 1914), 20.

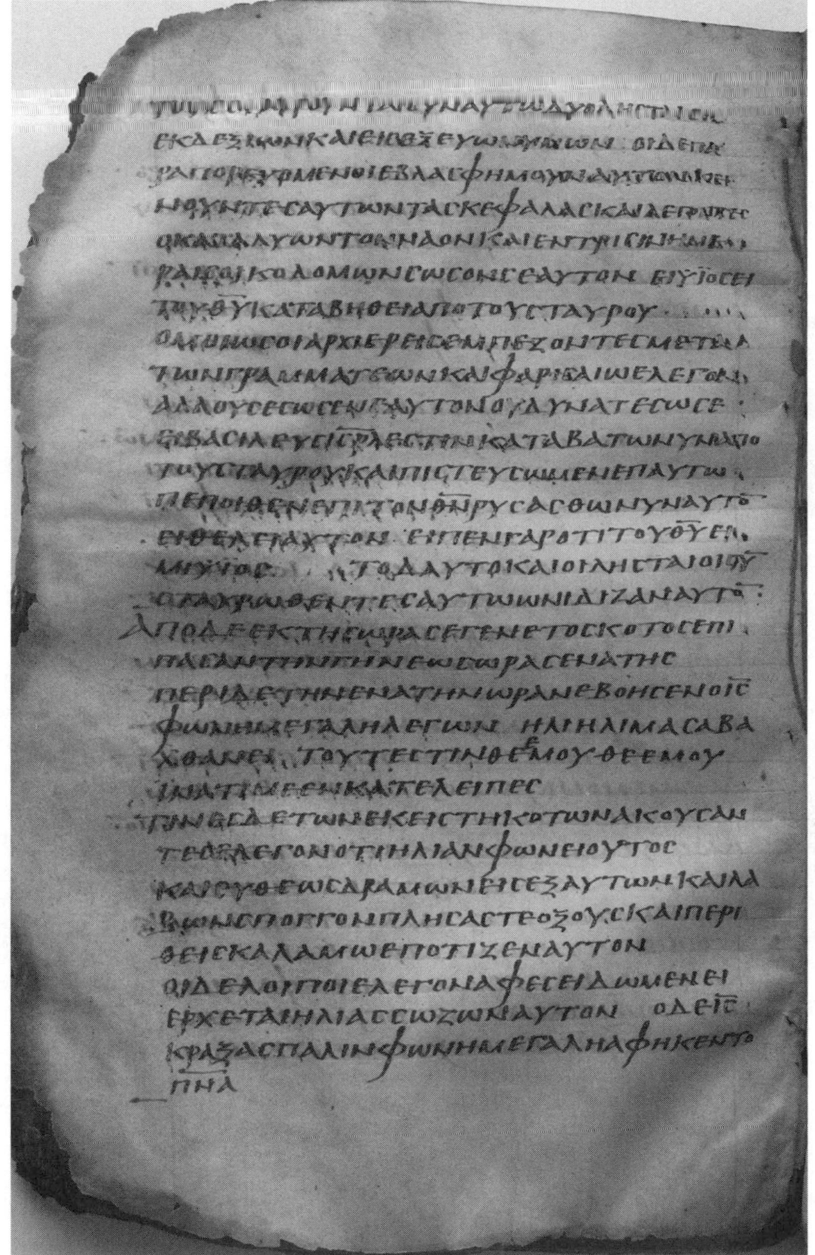

Figure 1: Freer manuscript of Matthew 27:38–50. Freer Gallery of Art, Smithsonian Institution, Washington, D.C.: Gift of Charles Lang Freer, F1906.274 pg. 108. Used by permission.

The overwhelming majority of New Testament manuscripts do not use a *nomen sacrum* form for θεέ here. According to Swanson, only ℵ, A, D, L, Δ, and 69 use the *nomen sacrum* $\overline{\theta\varepsilon}$ in both instances of the vocative form in Matt 27:46.[45] Majuscule manuscripts F and G use $\overline{\theta\varepsilon}$ in the second occurrence in this verse. The corresponding O θεος μου ο θεος μου passage in Mark 15:34 is part of a missing leaf in W. But in all other manuscripts in which the words of Mark 15:34 are extant, the nominative form is used with a vocative sense, and it is always written in *nomen sacrum* form as $\overline{\theta\varsigma}$.

Traube spoke of the θεε in Matt 27:46 as one of a few peculiarities ("einzelne Eigenheiten") meriting some discussion.[46] As he noted, when θεε is written in *nomen sacrum* form, it not clear whether the resulting $\overline{\theta\varepsilon}$ is a contraction or a suspended form from θεε.[47] Paap wrote,

> Comparatively large is the number of instances in which the vocative singular [θεε], which is only used in the sacral meaning, is written in full: 7 (6 sources) out of 13 (11 sources). A striking example in this connection is 254 (4th.-beg. 5th. c. A.D.): [Paap is referring here to W, 032] although in all the other 274 instances where the singular of θεός occurs, the word has been contracted, the only 2 vocatives have been written in full. This may well indicate a consciousness of the difference in meaning between suspension and contraction, and of the special connotation of the latter.[48]

Parker's discussion of the *nomina sacra* in his study of Codex Bezae makes no mention of $\overline{\theta\varepsilon}$ in this codex, one of the few manuscripts that use a *nomen sacrum* form for the Greek vocative θεέ.[49] Codex Bezae (D, 05) also uses $\overline{\text{ds}}$ for the Latin vocative sense of $\overline{\text{deus}}$.[50] In his seminal 1998 article on the *nomina sacra,* Hurtado is silent about θεε and $\overline{\theta\varepsilon}$. Hurtado's doctoral dissertation was a detailed technical analysis of the text of the Washingtonianus text of Mark, but, as noted above, the parallel Mark 15:34 passage appeared on a now-missing leaf of the manuscript. Similarly, Comfort's otherwise thorough and very well-written *nomina sacra* chapter makes no mention of θεέ and $\overline{\theta\varepsilon}$.[51] This vocative form of

45. Swanson, *New Testament Greek Manuscripts,* 286 n. B.

46. Traube, *Nomina Sacra,* 89.

47. To give familiar examples in English-language usage, "Rd." is a contraction from "Road," whereas "Ave." is a suspended form of "Avenue."

48. Paap, *Nomina Sacra in the Greek Papyri,* 100

49. Parker, *Codex Bezae,* ch. 6.

50. See Frederick H. Scrivener, *Bezae Codex Cantabrigiensis, Being an Exact Copy, in Ordinary Type, of the Celebrated Uncial Graeco-Latin Manuscript of the Four Gospels and Acts of the Apostles, Written Early in the Sixth Century, and Presented to the University of Cambridge by Theodore Beza, A.D. 1581* (Cambridge: Deighton, Bell, 1864; repr., Eugene, Ore.: Wipf & Stock, 1996), 92.

51. Comfort exhibits one minor oversight when he writes, "In not one canonical New Testament manuscript is 'King' (βασιλεύς) ever written as a nomen sacrum" (*Encountering the*

θεός is also not discussed in Roberts' 1977 British Academy lecture on *nomina sacra*.[52] Much of Comfort's and Roberts' scholarly attention regarding *nomina sacra* has focused on papyrus manuscripts, and as this volume goes to press, I have found no early papyrus manuscript that includes Matt 27:46. I have, therefore, no evidence from the New Testament papyri of how θεέ was treated by those earliest Christian scribes.

Thus far, therefore, scholars have incomplete knowledge about the treatment of θεε by ancient Christian scribes. A useful next step would be a careful examination of manuscripts of patristic texts, to see whether there is a paucity of the $\overline{\theta\varepsilon}$ form in that tradition paralleling the pattern in the biblical manuscripts.

In any case, we do not have a cogent explanation for why $\overline{\theta\varepsilon}$ was so rarely employed in biblical manuscripts. The fact that the two occurrences of the vocative form of θεος in the New Testament appear in a single verse may be a factor. Also, the correction of the abbreviated vocative form in Matt 27:46 by the principal scribe of W may point to the lack of a firm convention among skilled scribes in how to write this form. Another complication is that θεέ is already a very short word. On the other hand, the tragic, anguished prayer of Jesus on the cross epitomizes a sacred moment, a poignant case where the *nomen sacrum* $\overline{\theta\varepsilon}$ would seem to be the only appropriate choice for ancient Christian scribes.

Conclusion: Ranking the *Nomina Sacra* Word-Families

Hurtado's groupings of the *nomina sacra* provides a starting point for understanding the use and nonuse of these scribal devices by generations of early Christian scribes. We now have information that we can use to begin to recast Hurtado's proposed groups of word families into a ranking based on empirical study of instances, recognizing that the data on which this ranking rests come from a single sample: the Gospel of Matthew in W.

Rank[53]	Word Family	Remarks
2	Ἰησοῦς	The consistency is perfect.
2	Χριστός	The consistency is perfect.

Manuscripts, 205). The supplemental first quire of John in the Freer Gospels includes two such *nomina sacra:* $\overline{\beta\lambda\varepsilon\upsilon\varsigma}$ in John 1:51 and $\overline{\beta\lambda\varepsilon\iota\alpha\nu}$ in John 3:3.

52. Roberts, *Manuscript, Society and Belief,* 26–48.

53. The ranking is in the algebraic style, whereby tied ranks are assigned the mean of those ranks that are tied. [Ed. note: From another standpoint, however, Ιησους, Χριστος, and Κυριος tie for first place in consistent use of *nomina sacra* forms with "sacral" referrents, and Θεος runs a close second.]

2	Κύριος	The consistency is perfect.
4	Θεός	The use and nonuse is quite consistent (96%), with the important exceptions of vocative $\theta\varepsilon^{\varepsilon}$ and θεε.
5	πνεῦμα	The use and nonuse is 84% expected.
6	πατήρ	The use and nonuse is 72% expected. Vocative sacral πάτερ is an important nonuse.
7	μήτηρ	The use and nonuse is 52% expected.
8	ἄνθρωπος	The use and nonuse is 48% expected, but the distribution of expected versus anomalous use and nonuse could not be more mathematically random.
9	Ἰσραήλ	The use and nonuse is only 8% expected
10	Δαυεὶδ	The use and nonuse is only 6% expected.
12.5	οὐρανός	No *nomina sacra* are used.
12.5	σταυρός	No *nomina sacra* are used.
12.5	Ἰερουσαλήμ	No *nomina sacra* are used.
12.5	υἱός	No *nomina sacra* are used.
none	σωτήρ	The σωτήρ word family is absent from the text of Matthew.

The first four, Ἰησοῦς, Χριστός, Κύριος, and Θεός, remain in the group exhibiting the highest regularity of usage, consistent with Hurtado's model. The next four, πνεῦμα, πατήρ, μήτηρ, and ἄνθρωπος, form a highly graded middle group with a mixture of expected and anomalous use and nonuse of *nomina sacra*. The next two words, Ἰσραήλ and Δαυεὶδ, barely make it into a third *nomen sacrum* group. Finally, there are no *nomina sacra* forms used in the case of the other four word families that appear in the Matthew text of W: οὐρανός, σταυρός, Ἰερουσαλήμ, and υἱός.*

* I thank Timothy A. Brown for his generous help in checking details in this essay.

Was Codex Washingtonianus A Copy or a New Text?

Dennis Haugh

The Gospel texts in Codex Washingtonianus (W) clearly were produced by the hand of a single scribe, except for the first quire of John. In his study of the Gospel of Mark in W, Larry Hurtado identified and classified 134 "singular," and likely intentional, variants, including a significant proportion of "significant sense changes."[1] Both Hurtado and Henry Sanders, who published the first facsimile and textual commentary on W, agree that the Gospel texts reflect a history of copying.[2] Thus, Codex W presents an intriguing question: Was the original scribe slavishly faithful to a number of exemplars, or did the scribe rather act as a self-conscious redactor, modifying all the Gospel texts to suit the needs of the community who supported the scribal work?

Hurtado's Study of Mark in Codex Washingtonianus

In developing this study, I am indebted to the methodology and conclusions of the previously referenced work of Hurtado. His particular interest was to analyze the textual relationships of Codex W in Mark and also what kind of Markan text W reflects. In particular, he sought to determine whether in Mark Codex W was a major witness for an early stage of the "Caesarean" text.[3] In doing so, Hurtado compared all unique intentional variants in W with the readings of nine other witnesses: A, ℵ, B, D, 𝔓[45], Θ, 565, family 13, and also the Textus Receptus (1873 edition). Hurtado confirmed Sanders's judgment that Codex W has an affinity with the "Western" text in Mark 1–4. But, from some point in Mark

1. Larry W. Hurtado, *Text-Critical Methodology and the Pre-Caesarean Text: Codex W in the Gospel of Mark* (SD 43; Grand Rapids: Eerdmans, 1981), 69–84.

2. Ibid., 87, Henry A. Sanders, *The New Testament Manuscripts in the Freer Collection, Part I: The Washington Manuscript of the Four Gospels* (University of Michigan Studies, Humanistic Series 9/1; New York: Macmillan, 1912), 133.

3. Hurtado, *Text-Critical Methodology,* 1.

5 onward, the textual affinity of W shifts. After measuring the agreement with each of the control witnesses, he found the correspondence between W and representatives of all of the major text-types too weak to align W with any of them. Notably, this includes the so-called "Caesarean" text-type, for Hurtado showed that the levels of quantitative agreement with the chief witnesses of this text-type (Codex Θ and 565) are completely unremarkable. In Mark 5–16, however, Codex W does exhibit an interesting level of agreement with $\mathfrak{P}^{45}$, these two manuscripts of Egyptian provenance perhaps witnesses to a distinctive kind of Markan text favored there.[4]

Because he studied just one of the Gospels, Hurtado left open the question of whether the distinctive readings were the unique work of W's scribe or whether the scribe simply followed an exemplar in which these readings already appeared. To begin to formulate an answer, I have performed two analyses, both relying on Hurtado's work on Mark. My method involves the assumption that a self-conscious redactor of a Gospels codex would produce texts reflecting a single point of view across all the Gospels. In my first analysis, I compared all the unique "intentional" variants in the Gospel of John with Hurtado's list for Mark in W. The second part of the analysis was to observe whether the sort of variants Hurtado classified as "significant sense changes" were reflected also in the Gospel of Matthew.[5] By focusing on "unique" variants (i.e., variants for which we apparently have no other extant witness), I hope to be able to tell whether the unique interests reflected in Mark are also reflected in these other two Gospels. If they are, the case for considering the scribe of W a major editor-redactor is strengthened.

To save the time of the reader who is solely interested in my conclusion, I will say that the Gospel of John does not show the same degree or kind of redactional efforts shown in Mark. Furthermore, the type and number of unique variants in

---

4. Ibid., esp. 24–45, 63–66. I note that the very existence of a Caesarean text-type is a matter of some dispute. Thus the Alands: "When New Testament textual criticism goes beyond these [the Alexandrian or Hesychian, the Koine, and the Byzantine or Lucian text types] to speak of Caesarean and Jerusalem text types the theoretical possibility of these must be conceded.... [Under Eusebius, Caesarea produced many MSS.] ... But the widely acclaimed Caesarean text of the New Testament, we must insist, is thus far purely hypothetical" (Kurt Aland and Barbara Aland, *The Text of the New Testament* [trans. Erroll F. Rhodes, 2nd ed.; Grand Rapids: Eerdmans, 1989], 66).

5. Hurtado (*Text-Critical Methodology*, 69–71) identified fourteen unique variants that he classified as harmonizations of Mark with Matthew. He argued that, because Matthew was the more widely used Gospel and, as first in the Codex, would have been written first by the scribe, harmonization of Mark to Matthew was more likely than the reverse. Therefore, it is possible that my searching for the reflection of unique Markan variants in Matthew is largely a case of confirming Hurtado's own classification system. See Hurtado, *Text Critical Methodology*, 68. It is not clear from Hurtado's explanation of his approach, however, whether he used the text of Matthew in Codex W or a critical edition of Matthew to identify Markan harmonizations to Matthew. In any case, I find the results of my analysis of these data persuasive in their own right.

Mark are not reflected in Matthew. I would conclude, therefore, that the data do not support the notion that the scribe acted as redactor across the Gospels. The countertheory, that the scribe closely followed exemplars, has not been confirmed thereby but certainly still stands.[6] An illuminating sidelight, however, is the discovery of the use of the perfect tense starting in the Johannine passion narrative where other witnesses use the aorist. The reasons why the text of W may prefer the perfect in this section are explored later in this essay.

Comparison of Unique Variants in Mark and John

As noted already, Hurtado identified 134 singular readings that he considered to be deliberate variations from other texts—approximately one for every five verses in Mark. For his study, Hurtado considered "singular variants" to be those "for which no support could be found in Tischendorf's 8th edition or in Legg's apparatus."[7] The categories Hurtado found, and the number of readings in each, were the following:

14	harmonizations, all but one with Matthew and/or Luke
33	changes in vocabulary for idiosyncratic preferences
14	grammatical improvements
7	changes in verbal tense and/or voice
27	changes toward concise expression
10	additions for clarification[8]
18	significant sense changes
11	changes in word order
134	Total Singular Intentional Variants[9]

In light of the purpose of his study, Hurtado was relatively indifferent to the question of whether the scribe was the original author of these readings. Regardless of the immediate authorship, the "changes studied … are still evidence that deliberate and independent changes were made in the textual tradition of Mark

6. I assume that the ultimate confirmation would be the discovery of the manuscripts on which W directly depends. Absent that discovery, the cumulative weight of circumstantial evidence will produce consensus conclusions.

7. Constantinus Tischendorf, ed., *Novum Testamentum Graece* (8th ed.;Leipzig: Giesecke & Devrient, 1869); S. C. E. Legg, *Novum Testamentum Graece: Euangelium secundum Marcum* (Oxford: Clarendon, 1935). Hurtado, *Text-Critical Methodology*, 68

8. Hurtado did not include in this or in any other category either the completion of the Isaiah prophecy in Mark 1:3 or the "Freer Logion," the addition to Mark 16:14. The former is attested in part by a single twelfth- or thirteenth-century Latin manuscript (c) and is not, therefore, technically a singular variant. No comment is made on the omission of the Freer Logion, other than to reference earlier studies of it (Hurtado, *Text-Critical Methodology*, 77 n. 18).

9. Ibid., 69–84.

represented by Codex W.... [T]hey were still intentional changes apparently created with clear editorial purposes in view."[10] That is, Hurtado was not concerned with whether the scribe of Mark in W actually initiated the catalogued intentional variants or not but, instead, with the impact of these variants on the text. In contrast, attempting to identify the authorship of the variants noted here is the question addressed in this essay.

The first step was to duplicate Hurtado's study of Mark in John, enumerating the "singular variants" in W's text of John. This was done by consulting Tischendorf, NA^{27},[11] the 1995 edition of the papyri in John by the International Greek New Testament Project,[12] and the unique readings identified by Sanders.[13] The opening quire of John, 1:1–5:11, produced by another, later scribe, was not analyzed. Furthermore, John 14:26–16:7 is missing from Codex W. Using NA^{27} for versification, there were 662 remaining verses of John in W to be studied.

In these 662 verses, I have identified sixty-four "singular" variants in John. Of these, I have classified twelve as unintentional scribal errors. I detected no common feature among them and have excluded them from further study. The remaining fifty-two variants are shown below by verse and by category.

Singular Intentional Variants in John 5:11 to End
Vocabulary Preferences: 12 (5:15; 12:41; 12:47; 13:38; 16:22; 16:23; 17:26; 19:7; 19:20; 20:1; 20:4; 20:19)
Grammatical Improvements: 9 (5:36; 6:28; 11:10; 13:7; 13:26; 18:18; 20:6; 20:26; 21:14)
More Concise Expressions: 5 (6:60; 10:13; 11:32; 12:9; 19:25)
Expansions for Clarifications: 8 (5:15; 7:14; 10:25; 10:42; 13:38; 17:4; 17:22; 21:15)
Harmonizations: 2 (11:19; 21:17)
Significant Sense Changes: 3 (16:17; 18:17; 21:4–5)
Changes in Verb Tense or Voice: 11 (7:39; 10:25; 14:7; 17:2; 17:8; 18:1; 18:30; 18:39; 19:30; 20:13; 20:30)
Changes in Word Order: 2 (5:21; 5:24)

The incidence of fifty-two singular intentional variants over John's 662 verses is equivalent to one variant for every 12.7 verses, a much lower rate than the one variant for every 5.4 of Mark that Hurtado documented.

10. Ibid., 69.

11. Barbara Aland, Kurt Aland, Johannes Karavidopoulos, Carlo M. Martini, and Bruce M. Metzger, eds., *Nestle-Aland Novum Testamentum Graece* (27th ed.; Stuttgart: Deutsche Bibelgesellschaft, 2001).

12. W. J. Elliott and D. C. Parker, eds., *The Papyri* (vol. 1 of *The New Testament in Greek IV: The Gospel according to St. John;* Leiden: Brill, 1995).

13. Sanders, *Washington Manuscript of the Four Gospels,* 126–28.

In the table below the variants in John are compared with Hurtado's grouping for Mark. In addition to a categorization of the variants themselves, the table shows the percentage of variants in each of the eight categories used (shown in the middle columns). Because it is unlikely that a redactor would be concerned to harmonize John with the Synoptics, harmonizations in John (with the Synoptics) must be, and are, relatively scarce. To normalize the results, the third column shows the frequency of any single type of variant, expressed as the average number of verses per variant type. Thus, Hurtado identified thirty-three variants in which Codex W exercised a singular vocabulary preference in Mark. These thirty-three variants are 25 percent of the total 134 variants. On average, they occur once every twenty-one verses in Mark.

Intentional Singular Variants in Codex W
for Gospel of Mark and John 5:11 to End

	Mark (700 Verses)			John 5:11 to End (662 Verses)		
	Number	%	Frequency	Number	%	Frequency
Vocabulary Preferences	33	25%	21	12	23%	55
Grammatical Improvements	14	11%	48	9	17%	74
Concise Expression	27	20%	25	5	10%	132
Expansion for Clarification	10	7%	68	8	15%	83
Harmonizations	14	11%	48	2	4%	331
Change in Verbs	7	5%	97	11	21%	60
Significant Sense Changes	18	13%	38	3	6%	221
Changes in Word Order	11	8%	62	2	4%	331
Total	134	100%	5	52	100%	13
Verses per Variant	5.2			12.7		

Before studying the results in individual categories, I believe the overall numbers show impressive differences. Over approximately the same number of verses, the text of Mark shows more than twice as many intentional variants, including 2.5 times more "intentional literary variants" (the combination of vocabulary preferences, grammatical improvements, concise expressions, and expansions for clarification) in Mark than in John. Given Mark's reputation for unliterary Greek, this kind of difference is not unexpected.

The two harmonizations in John constitute a smaller percentage of the total intentional variations and occur less frequently than in Mark, only once every 331 verses. Both are clearly internal harmonizations, changing one portion of the text to conform to other references *within John* (11:19, conforming the reference to Martha to the reference to Mary; 21:17, conforming the third verb in the series of questions to Peter to the first two).

In the category of other significant sense changes, Codex W, both in Mark and in John, shows a tendency to dampen criticism of the apostles through deletion of words or phrases.[14] In Mark 8:14, for example, W deletes mention that the apostles forgot to bring bread. A deletion in Mark 10:32 removes mention that the apostles feared. Likewise, in John 21:4–5 the scribe omitted a relatively lengthy section describing how the apostles who had gone fishing did not recognize the risen Jesus standing on the shore. Given the notorious reputation that Mark has for denigrating the role of the apostles, these changes to a more "orthodox" fifth-century view of the apostles are not surprising. It is instructive that in one of the few verses that cite the apostles' bad eyesight Codex W's John goes out of its way to improve their image.

In Mark, W also has two other changes that appear to arise from a desire to make the text less embarrassing or more orthodox. At Mark 3:21 W changes the verb from ἐξέστη, "he is mad," to ἐξήρτηνται αὐτου, "they have become his adherents" (and with Codex Bezae also identifies those who come to seize Jesus as "the Pharisees around him and the rest"). Thus, in Codex W's text of Mark the relatives of Jesus no longer claim that Jesus is mad. The second occurs at Mark 13:33, where W inserts εἴ μη ὁ πάτηρ και ὁ υἵος after ουκ οἴδατε γαρ. The effect is to say that the Father and the Son know the timing of the last days. The variant is all the more interesting in view of the immediately preceding contrary statement (13:32).[15]

The only category in which John has more variants, absolutely and relatively, is "changes in verbs tense or voice." I find some of these to be subtle but powerful modifications of the text. To appreciate this, consider the seven comparable changes recorded by Hurtado for Mark:[16]

---

14. For further discussion of these and other examples in Codex W in Mark, see Hurtado, *Text-Critical Methodology*, 77–80.

15. Ibid., 79.

16. Ibid., 74.

Seven Intentional Changes in Verbs in Mark
5:19 ἠλέηκεν for ἠλέησεν, substituting perfect for an aorist
6:20 ἠπορεῖτο for ἠπόρει, substituting middle/passive for active
[illegible] [illegible] for [illegible], alternative forms for [illegible] pl aorist
9:31 λέγει for ἔλεγεν, substituting (historic) present for imperfect
10:35 αἰτησώμεθα for αἰτήσωμεν, substituting subjunctive middle/passive for subjunctive active
12:10 ἀνεγνώκατε for ἀνέγνωτε, substituting perfect for aorist
16:8 ἔσχεν for εἶχεν, substituting aorist for imperfect

Hurtado comments on these data:

> However clear or obscure the reasons may be today for such changes, the fact is that they were made because a scribe felt that they would be helpful in rendering a passage easier to read and to understand. The only possible exception is the change in 9:31, which substitutes a historic present verb form for an aorist form [sic]. This list of minor changes in verb tense and voice adds to the stock of evidence that the text of W represents a fairly thorough and independent editorial treatment of the Gospel of Mark.[17]

Hurtado thus concludes that, although he sees no pattern in the changes, they do show an intention to improve the text. When compared with the changes in John, the beginnings of a pattern seem to emerge. The eleven instances of intentional changes in verbs in John may be classified as follows:

Eleven Intentional Changes in Verbs in John
five changes in tense from aorist to perfect: 18:1; 18:30; 19:30; 20:13;[18] and 20:30
one change in tense from perfect to aorist: 17:8
five other changes: 7:39; 10:25; 14:7; 17:2; 18:39

It is the relatively high incidence of changes from aorist to perfect tense that catches one's attention. First, I find it intriguing that the first of these appears at the start of John's passion narrative in chapter 18. Second, the impact of changing the tense from aorist to perfect appears significant. In classical Greek, the aorist has the aspect of a "snapshot" of an action that, in the indicative mood, occurred

---

17. Ibid., 74. (Obviously, in Mark 9:31, ἔλεγεν is imperfect, not aorist.)

18. W reads τεθεικασιν where NA[27] has ἔθηκαν. Tischendorf reports two intermediate variants: D and Cyr[h210] have τεθεικαν, whereas X reads τεθεικην. These both appear to be scribal errors, but it is not clear whether the scribes erred in copying the perfect (as seems likely for D and Cyr[h210]) or the aorist. In any event, W still represents a unique reading.

in the past. The perfect, on the other hand, has the aspect of an action in the past that has continuing impact in the present. I find the data especially striking after considering Wallace's statistics on the relative use of the tenses:

Use of Tenses in the New Testament[19]

Aorist	11,606
Present tense	11,583
Imperfect	1,682
Future	1,623
Perfect	1,571
Pluperfect	86

The "alteration" from the aorist to the perfect is even more striking, therefore, given the comparatively less frequent use of the perfect in the New Testament (used only one-seventh as often as the aorist). Morton Enslin found a total of 195 perfects and pluperfects in the Gospel of John (Westcott and Hort's edition), approximately one-eighth of all the perfects in the New Testament.[20] He argued that

> The excessive use of a tense which not only looks at both ends of an action, but which stresses the consequences of this action, is less likely to have been an accident than an evaluation, deliberate or otherwise, by the evangelist, convinced that the effect was still as abiding as when the incident he chanced to be describing took place.[21]

I believe that Codex W's five changes from the aorist to the perfect reflect an expression of the same theological conviction. These five variants are reviewed in detail below. The categories, taken from Wallace, may not be a perfect fit, but they seem reasonable for my purposes.[22]

Effect of Changes from Aorist to Perfect Tense in the Gospel of John

18:1 W uses the perfect tense when describing the disciples and Jesus entering the garden (εἰσελήλυθεν for εἰσῆλθεν). I have classed this a "dramatic perfect," used here perhaps to highlight the dramatic effect of the entry into the garden.

19. Daniel B. Wallace, *Greek Grammar beyond the Basics* (Grand Rapids: Zondervan, 1996), 497.

20. Morton S. Enslin, "The Perfect Tense in the Fourth Gospel," *JBL* 55 (1936): 121 (121–31).

21. Ibid., 121.

22. Wallace, *Greek Grammar,* 574–81.

18:30 There is a significant change from παρεδώκαμεν το παραδέδωκειμεν, as it changes the "handing over" of Jesus by the Jewish leaders from a one-time event to an event with continuing significance in the present, an extensive perfect. I infer that W meant the handing over to be significant for Jews and Christians of the day of the copying of the manuscript.

19:30 This change follows that of 18:30, changing the "handing over" from an aorist to a perfect. This time, however, it is *Jesus* "handing over" his spirit. This too seems to be an extensive perfect. It also conforms the aspect of the "handing over" to the aspect of "It has been finished," τετέλεσται, Jesus' final word.

20:13 As in 18:1, W may be using the perfect, τέθεκασιν, rather than the aorist ἔθηκαν to heighten the dramatic effect. A perfect also makes good sense, as Mary Magdalene would believe that wherever the persons who took Jesus' body put it, the body is still there. Note that it follows οἶδα, a perfect form used with a present sense.

20:30 This seems to be yet another extensive perfect, using πεποίηκεν in favor of ἐποίησεν. W changes the sense from a "snapshot statement" about Jesus' deeds to a statement which includes the sense that these events have meanings and effects extending to the present.

I claim that these five uses of the perfect tense reflect an attempt to heighten the relevance of the last four chapters of John, the passion narrative in particular, for the readers of the text of Codex W. In that sense, the changes do conform to both the tendency of the intentional changes Hurtado noted in Mark and the conviction about the motivation of such tense preferences as noted by Enslin.

Before one accepts this claim, however, two points need to be addressed. First, the extent of this particular type of variant is largely unmatched in Mark. Of the two variants in Mark that show changes from aorist to perfect tense, the first, at 5:19, extends Jesus' mercy to the Gerasene demoniac from a moment in time to a continuing effect. The second, at Mark 12:10, extends the question about whether the chief priests, scribes, and elders (from 11:27) have read the scriptures with continuing effect in their lives. In both cases, the impact of the change is to continue the impact of the event *within* the narrative. The mercy extended to the demoniac continues on; Jesus' opponents may or may not be profiting from the reading of scriptures. Only with great difficulty could one say that the changes from aorist to perfect in Mark extend the impact of the action from *within* the narrative *onto* W's audience. Several of the changes in John, on the other hand, seem to point beyond the narrative to the time of the reader. The two instances of the handing over of and by Jesus and the reference to his deeds have impacts beyond the limits of the narrative world.

Part of the reason for fewer changes of tense in Mark might have to do with Mark's relatively greater use of the imperfect tense. Buist Fanning reported that Mark uses the imperfect 222 times, relatively more frequently than the other Gospel writers.[23] The imperfect carries with it the aspect of seeing the action from the inside.[24] Fanning endorses the view of several Markan exegetes that the greater use of the imperfect and the historic present in Mark reflects a deliberate stylistic choice by the author to render the narrative more vivid.[25]

The second point may be phrased as a question: How can one be sure it would have made any difference to the reader/auditor whether the perfect or the aorist was used? Geoffrey Horrocks's work would seem to deny any relevant difference between the aorist and perfect. He has found evidence of a conflation of the two as early as Menander's late fourth-century B.C.E. dramas and extending with increasing incidence through to Byzantine Greek.[26] Horrocks has numerous examples of the use of the perfect in an aoristic sense—that is, without reference to a present influence of a past action—in the second century C.E., both epistolary evidence from Oxyrhyncus and from *The Shepherd of Hermes.*[27]

When one considers that John probably was completed around the time of both of these texts and that W itself is a late fourth-century manuscript (at the

---

23. Buist M. Fanning, *Verbal Aspect in New Testament Greek* (Oxford: Clarendon, 1990), 253–54. His count excludes, however, the uses of the imperfect of εἰμί and ἔφη.

24. Ibid., 240.

25. Ibid., 255. Fanning cites Cecil Emden, "St Mark's Use of the Imperfect Tense," *ExpT* 65 (1953–54): 146–49; Henry Barclay Swete, *The Gospel according to St. Mark* (3rd ed.; London: Macmillan, 1909), xlix–l; and Vincent Taylor, *The Gospel according to St. Mark* (2nd ed.; London: Macmillan, 1966), 180, 253, 271, 297, 460. Note also that Mark is capable of using the perfect tense as outlined herein. For example, in 11:17 the author contrasts a series of imperfects and aorist (ἐδίδασκεν … ἔλεγεν … κληθήσεται) with a perfect (πεποιήκατε), the intended connotation being that the "moneychangers" did make the temple a "hideout for thieves" (my translation), and it remained so, at least until Jesus threw them out. The use of the perfect in John's passion narrative has some resemblance to the use of tenses in the parallel material in Mark. Taylor points out that in Mark 15:21–27 there are five historic presents and in 15:23–32 three imperfects (apart from ἦν), and only two aorists (one at 15:23 to say that Jesus did not take the myrrh-laced wine and the other at 15:25 to specify when Jesus was crucified). See Taylor, *Gospel according to St. Mark*, 599. Mark's use of tense, one may conclude, seems designed to make the action of the crucifixion immediately present to the audience. The same is likely in John.

26. Geoffrey Horrocks, *Greek: A History of the Language and Its Speakers* (London: Longman, 1997), 53, 118–19. Basil Mandilaras cites the use of an "aorist perfect" by Plato (Basil G. Mandilaras, *The Verb in the Greek Non-literary Papyri* [Athens: Hellenic Ministry of Culture and Sciences, 1973], 224).

27. Horrocks, *Greek*, 96, 116.

earliest), Horrocks's argument would seem to negate the importance of the use of the perfect in Codex W in place of the more widely preferred aorist. To ascertain whether these are "true perfects" or "aoristic perfects" (i.e., perfects whose use is indistinguishable from the aorist), my first step was to consider whether aorist forms of the verbs in question are used elsewhere in John in Codex W. If they are always used in the perfect, then Horrocks's claim that the function of the perfect and aorist is often indistinguishable receives some support. On the other hand, if these verbs are used often in the aorist in the same text where we have uses of the perfect, then the contrary receives support and the choice of the aorist or perfect is more likely deliberate. As the four verbs, παραδίδωμι (used twice), εἰσέρχομαι, τίθημι, and ποιέω, are very common in Koine Greek, it is not surprising that they do indeed have many uses in the aorist in the Gospel of John.[28] I found that the fewest number of aorists in any mood was for παραδίδωμι. The verb itself is used fifteen times in John, but often in the future indicative (as when Jesus speaks of the "handing over" to come), but there are other forms as well.[29] In addition, τίθημι and ποιέω have a few uses in the perfect prior to the passion narrative (e.g., 11:34; 12:18, 37; 13:12). I conclude that the scribe of Codex W assigned distinguishable meaning to the aorist and the perfect of these verbs and chose to use them in these circumstances in the perfect tense.[30]

The understanding of the perfect in New Testament scholarship is not a particularly new problem. Basil Mandilaras proposed three criteria for judging when a perfect was used as an aorist but then promptly discarded two of them (when the aorist is used with the perfect and "when the context denotes no relationship of the past action to present time"), leaving just one: "when there is indication of past time."[31] In other words, Mandilaras concluded that one should not automatically assume that a perfect is used as an aorist when used in close context with an aorist or when there is no clear extension of the past action into the present. Fanning concluded that the second criterion really must be the key to the use of the "true" perfect. The context alone is a prime indicator of whether the perfect is used as a simple statement of past action without consideration of its ongo-

28. Were one to include, and enumerate, the various uses of verb forms based on ἔρχομαι, for instance, one might have hundreds of instances.

29. E.g., future active participle in John 6:64; present active infinitive in 6:71; 12:4; aorist subjunctive in 13:2.

30. In *Verbal Aspect* (303 n. 238) Fanning provides his count of the nineteen verbs that appear most often in the perfect in the New Testament. Of these four verbs, only ἔρχομαι makes the list, standing ninth with twenty-five citations (eight in a compound form). The scribe of W, in other words, would not have had many examples of the use of these verbs in the perfect in New Testament literature, making his own choice to use the perfect forms all the more significant.

31. Mandilaras, *Verb in the Greek Non-literary Papyri*, 225–26.

ing impact. Consider, for example, 1 Cor 15:3b–5a, which Fanning discussed at length: Χριστὸς ἀπέθανεν [aorist] ὑπὲρ τῶν ἁμαρτιῶν ἡμῶν κατὰ τὰς γραφάς καὶ ὅτι ἐτάφη [aorist] καὶ ὅτι ἐγήγερται [perfect] τῇ ἡμέρα τῇ τρίτῃ κατὰ τὰς γραφὰς καὶ ὅτι ὤφθη [aorist] Κηφᾷ. By using this sequence of verbs, Paul clearly asserts that Christ died and was buried once and for all in the past but that his resurrection, which also occurred in the past, has continuing significance, presumably for all of Jesus, Paul, and the Corinthians.[32]

As indicated above, Enslin subscribed to this same approach, emphasizing the context of Johannine perfects. In addition, Enslin pointed out that John's use of the perfect was far more frequent than its use by two important second-century writers, Philostratus (in the *Life of Appolonius of Tyana*) and Justin Martyr (*Dialogue with Typho*). Considering that John used the perfect far more than the Synoptics, written as much as forty years earlier, and more than other literary writers working about forty years later, Enslin concluded that an appeal to vernacular papyri to explain the increased use of the perfect in John was unwarranted.[33]

While the apparent similarity of some of these changes in tense would seem to support the hypothesis that the scribe of Codex W created the intentional variants in both Mark and John, other considerations weigh the other way. For one thing, we should note that there seems to be a general tendency in the Gospel tradition to soften Mark's treatment of Jesus' disciples and family. Therefore, it is not surprising to see later texts, both Mark and John, being modified in line with this trajectory. The change of tense from aorist to perfect in John's passion narrative seems to be a deliberate editorial change that signifies an emphasis on the continuing impact of the passion on W's audience. In so far as there is a lack of evidence of a similar intent in W's Markan passion narrative, it would seem likely that the texts of John and Mark in W were edited by two different persons and that the scribe of Washingtonianus was merely their scribe. That is, it would appear that the scribe of Codex W was more a copyist than an editor in his own right. Discussion of the potential implication of these conclusions will be deferred until the second analysis is completed.

Evidence from Mark's Intentional Changes in Meaning: Are They Reflected in Matthew?

The appendix to this essay lists the eighteen unique, intentional variants in Mark that Hurtado has classified as "significant sense changes." I include in the list the verse, a description of the change, the citation of the Matthaean parallel account, and a

32. Fanning, *Verbal Aspect*, 300–301.

33. Enslin, "Perfect Tense," 126–27.

short note on whether the Matthaean parallel "accepts" Mark's reading or not.[34] If the unique readings in Mark are found in Matthew, this would provide some evidence that the scribe of W imposed a common viewpoint across at least two of the Synoptic Gospels.

We noted above the tendency of W in Mark and in John to avoid embarrassing references to Jesus, his disciples, and his family. As can be seen in the chart, one instance in which Mark's text does this is not reflected in Matthew's parallel. In Mark 8:14 W omits the statement that the disciples had forgotten to bring bread, but Matthew in W includes this statement, along with other major witnesses. In two other cases in Mark where W reflects the desire to improve the image of Jesus' disciples and family—Mark 3:21 (where Pharisees and others say "They have become his adherents" rather than "he is mad") and 10:32 (where W drops the reference to the apostles fearing)—other witnesses also reflect a softening of the language. The parallel to Mark 3:21–30 in Matt 12:46 and the parallel to Mark 10:32 in Matt 20:17–19 reflect a softening of the representation of Jesus' disciples and family and also a good deal of material not derived from Mark.

There are interesting variants in W concerning Jesus in Mark 13:21 and 13:33. Hurtado argued that the intentional variant at 13:21, changing χριστός to κύριος indicates that W's reading reflects a Gentile Christian readership, while χριστός seems to reflect a Jewish-Christian setting "in which 'the Christ' would be much more a topic of discussion."[35] In W, the Matt 24:23–25 parallel continues to use the term χριστός. If Hurtado is correct, then this difference by itself would suggest that the scribe in both Gospels followed his exemplar(s) and was sufficiently unconcerned about these issues to harmonize the two parallel passages. At Mark 13:33, W reads that no one knows the day of the coming of the Son of Man "except the Father and the Son." In Matt 24:36, however, W does not have Jesus make a similar claim.

While the amount of data studied regarding the relationship between Mark and Matthew is less than the data on John and Mark, we nevertheless see evidence supporting the theory that the scribe of W worked from an exemplar in these cases, copying the text of the respective Gospels as it lay before him. There is simply no evidence of a self-conscious redaction attempting to promote a common theological viewpoint in the W texts of Matthew and Mark.

---

34. I acknowledge that this representation of the flow of harmonization may be the reverse of the actual harmonizations. Since the text of Mark serves as the fulcrum for most of this paper, however, it seems easiest to write in this way.

35. Hurtado, *Text-Critical Methodology*, 79.

Summary and Conclusion

The question that formed the genesis of this paper was: Did the scribe who reproduced the Gospel of Mark in Codex Washingtonianus produce the disntictive variants found in Mark, or were these variants in the exemplar from which the scribe copied? To test this hypothesis, we first analyzed the singular, intentional variants in Mark and compared them with the singular, intentional variants in John. There we found that the character of the variants was not similar and that certain of the most noteworthy variants in John, those dealing with changes in verbal tenses, reflected a theological stance that is difficult to track in Mark. Thus, this part of the study was inconclusive.

Our second line of attack was to see whether the unique sense variants in Mark have a "resonance" in Matthew. There we found more complexity. For some variants in Mark that delete embarrassing narrations about the disciples and family of Jesus, there are indications in Matthew of a similar concern, although not the same variants. If we accept Hurtado's comment that the shift from χριστος to κυριος betokens a difference in community ethnicity, then its continued use in Matthew suggests that the Matthean community is not identical to that which produced the text of Mark.

These analyses may not provide a definitive portrayal of the responsibility of the scribe of W in the production of the text. To our original question, however, I would conclude that the probability that the scribe of Codex W was following a copy of Mark that already included the changes noted is significantly greater than the contrary. Further, even if it were to be shown that the scribe did make the changes in Mark, the probability that the scribe did not exercise similar editorial/redactional control over the other Gospels is even greater. Codex W, it appears to me, is a late fourth/fifth-century compilation of unrelated copies of the Gospels by a single scribe in a single codex.[36] Although I am in no position to date the original compilation of these Gospel texts, it is intriguing to speculate whether it might date to the early fourth century and the time of the production of Sinaiticus and Vaticanus. In reconstructing that textual history lies the continuing romance of W.

---

36. This reflects the common dating of Codex W. But cf. Schmid's study of the matter in this volume.

Appendix: Analysis of Whether Significant Sense Changes in Mark Are Reflected in Matthew

Mark	Variant and Implication	Parallel	Matthew in Codex W
3:3	Tells man with cured withered hand to go εκ του μεσου rather than εισ το μεσον. Perhaps scribe thinks Jesus moving man from hostile crowd.	12:9–14	W conforms to bulk of texts.
3:21	Changes εξεστη, "he is mad," to εξηρτηνται αυτου, "They have become his adherents," avoiding a negative reference to Jesus.	12:46–50	W conforms to bulk of texts.
6:5	Jesus changed from εκει to ουκετι ποιησαι δυναμιν. Hurtado speculates that the scribe wanted to smooth out the problem that Jesus promptly heals people. "After this, Jesus was unable to work any miracles 'any longer.'"	13:58	W conforms to bulk of texts.
6:8	Substitutes πηραν for ζηνην. Matt 10:10 uses this very word.	10:10	Could be Markan harmonization with Matthew.
6:11	Changes last word in verse from αυτοις to αυτων, with the consequence that the shaking of dust off the feet is changed from a witness against them to a witness concerning them.	10:1, 7–15	Matthew's judgment is against houses and cities, which are specified.
8:14	Changes επελαθοντο, that the apostles neglected to bring bread, to απελθοντες, omitting the apostles' forgetfulness.	16:5	W conforms to bulk of texts.

9:20	Codex W drops αυτον from the phrase εσπαραξεν αυτον. Hurtado speculates that it is to avoid readers thinking that the spirit is knocking Jesus around rather than the boy possessed by a demon.	17:14–21	In Matthew, no one is thrown on the ground.
9:24	Changes πατηρ του παιδου to πνευμα του παιδαριου, "spirit of a slightly older child." Perhaps wants to save "embarrassment" of the father losing his temper.	17:14–16	Matthew has toned it down anyway so the father λεγων rather than κραξας.
9:49	Codex W changes αλισθησεται, "will be salted" to αλισγηθησεται, "will be polluted." Hurtado (78): "The variant of W is not an accidental misspelling but a thoughtful attempt to make the dark saying meaningful to the reader by the use of the contextual thought. The variant in W might even be called a 'midrashic' or interpretative treatment of the text."	5:13	Matthew in W puts into the future, with εσται. In John, most changes in verbs from aorist to perfect, out of an indefinite time to a time in the past. Here, moving from now to the future.
10:32	W omits εφοβουντο, stating the disciples' fear. The scribe's rationale could have been harmonization with Synoptics, which do not have this in the parallels, or a desire to avoid making the disciples look weak. Hurtado (79): "The scribe perhaps felt that the mention of amazement on the part of the disciples was an understandable and proper attitude in Jesus' presence but that fear was not acceptable."	20:17–19	Matthew's disciples have no reaction to the announcement of Jesus' impending passion.

10:38	Here Codex W changes Ιησους ειπεν αυτοις ("Jesus said to them") to Ιησους αποκριθεις ειπεν αυτω, ("Responding, Jesus said to him"). Hurtado (79): perhaps reflects the tradition that only James suffered martyrdom and not John.		No parallel in Matthew.
12:12	W drops και αφεντες αυτον απηλθον ("leaving Jesus they [his enemies] left"). The scribe may have done so because in the next verse they are still there, asking questions.	21:26–27	In Matthew, no sense that anyone ever leaves. They just fade from view.
12:26	Cleverly, W changes οτι to ει, which seems to be an attempt to make the passage more easily understood.	22:23–33	Issue not arising in the way Matthew frames the discussion.
12:29	Codex W decides to change the Shema! Drops εις. Hurtado (79): "possibly because calling God 'one' seemed meaningless or perhaps at variance with the scribe's conception of the Trinity. The altered phrase reads … 'the Lord God is our Lord,' or perhaps 'the Lord our God is Lord.'"	22: 34–40	Jesus in Matthew does not quote the first part of the Shema.
13:21	Hurtado (79): W changes χριστος to κυριος, perhaps because the term κυριος came to be the more familiar title for Jesus in the circles of intended readers. "The reading also seems to reflect a gentile church situation, while the dominant reading seems to reflect a Jewish-Christian setting in which 'the Christ' would be much more a topic of discussion."	24:23–25	Matthew maintains χριστος in a nomina sacra. If Hurtado is right, it looks very much like Matthew is not made for the same community.

13:33	Famous christological insertion. W inserts ει μη ο πατηρ και ο υιος after ουκ οιδατε γαρ, in what appears to be a move to deflect the charge that Jesus did not know when the parousia would happen. Hurtado (79): the variant is out of character since W generally tries to shorten rather than lengthen, and its intention, if properly described above, is thwarted by a similar statement in v. 32.	25:13–15	W has an insertion as to when the Son of Man comes. But this is a variant with a number of other texts.
14:1	W changes the accomplices of the "priests" from γραμματεις to φαρισαιοι, perhaps reflecting an early Christian view of Jewish rabbis as heirs of the Pharisees.	26:2–5	Matthew has the πρεσβυτεροι conspiring with the αρχιερεις.
14:62	The Son of Man comes not μετα των νεφελων ("on the clouds [of heaven]") but μετα της δυναμεως ("with the power [of heaven]"). The former expression may have seemed a little too puzzling for the scribe.	24:30	The Son of Man comes on clouds.

The Corrections in the Freer Gospels Codex

James R. Royse

In his 1912 *editio princeps* of Codex W (Gregory-Aland 032) of the Gospels, Sanders provided an accurate collation of the manuscript against the Textus Receptus and devoted a dozen pages to the corrections that are found in the manuscript.[1] Shortly thereafter, Goodspeed published, on the basis of Sanders's facsimile, another collation in which a few more scribal corrections were noted.[2] Then, in 1918, Sanders reissued with minor changes his collation volume.[3]

For nearly a century these studies have provided an authoritative basis for any analysis of W, and I have found comparatively few occasions to depart from them substantially, especially from the 1918 publication of Sanders. However, the new color images of the Freer biblical manuscripts made available for this project permit a control and additional precision that were not possible on the basis of the published facsimile. A forthcoming transcription of the entire manuscript by J. Bruce Prior and T. A. E. Brown will be an extremely valuable additional resource for any study of W.[4] Moreover, much new textual evidence has come to

1. Henry A. Sanders, *The New Testament Manuscripts in the Freer Collection, Part I: The Washington Manuscript of the Four Gospels* (University of Michigan Studies, Humanistic Series 9/1; New York: Macmillan, 1912), 28–40.

2. Edgar J. Goodspeed, "The Freer Gospels," *AJT* 17 (1913): 395–411, 599–613; 18 (1914): 131–46, 266–81. Hereafter in this essay, references to "Goodspeed" are to this work, and, if no page number is given, the reference is to his discussion of the reading in question *ad loc.* in his collation.

3. Henry A. Sanders, *The New Testament Manuscripts in the Freer Collection* (University of Michigan Studies, Humanistic Series 9; New York: Macmillan, 1918). Hereafter in this essay, unless otherwise indicated, my references to "Sanders" are to this 1918 volume, and if no page number is given, the reference is to the variant *ad loc.* in his collation. Sanders (ibid., v) comments on Goodspeed's work: "Excellent as the Facsimile Edition is, over-reliance upon it has sometimes led this critic astray, notably in handling erasures. It is not necessary to enumerate the cases nor to note the misprints in his articles. All that is correct has been incorporated in the new edition."

4. J. Bruce Prior and T. A. E. Brown, *The Freer Gospels: Transcription of Washington Manuscript III* (forthcoming). I am very grateful to the editors for their providing me an advance copy

light since the work of Sanders. Accordingly, a fresh look at the corrections present in W, one of the most important Gospels manuscripts of the New Testament, may shed some light on early textual practices.

The Several Hands and Their Corrections

We may begin by separating from W proper (i.e., the main part of the manuscript produced by the original scribe) the first quire of John, which contains John 1:1–5:11a on pages 113–28 of the codex. This is a later (probably eighth-century) replacement quire that bears no relation to the rest of the manuscript and made up for the (presumably) lost original portion. I have included its corrections here for the sake of completeness, but I treat them separately. This quire is regularly cited as W^s. I have designated the original hand as W^{s*} and (following Sanders) the correctors of this portion as "man a" (the scribe of W^s), "man b" (the first corrector in this quire), and "man c" (a second corrector). There are eleven corrections (as already noted by Sanders).[5]

Within W proper Sanders distinguishes four hands: the scribe, a second hand (the διορθωτής), a third hand, and a fourth hand. The activities of the last two hands were limited. By my counts, the original scribe made eighty-five corrections, the second hand made sixty-nine corrections, the third hand made ten corrections, the fourth hand made four corrections, and there remain two corrections that I cannot assign. Also, there are two examples of a correction in two stages (at Matt 24:32a and Mark 10:35), each of which I have counted twice. I follow this classification in the discussion of the corrections here, examining the work of each hand in turn and discussing each of the corrections assigned to that hand.

In order to have one list for reference, I give my list of the 168 corrections in W proper and the eleven corrections in W^s in an appendix at the end of this essay, along with citation of the relevant textual evidence.[6] I have not duplicated this evidence in the following discussion, so the reader should consult the evidence cited in this appendix along with the discussion of the corrections. Note that the

---

of their work, which has been most helpful in my study of W. Three corrections discussed here were first identified by Prior and Brown: Matt 18:31; John 4:8; and Mark 2:25b. References to "Prior" or "Prior and Brown" are to the discussion *ad loc.* in their transcription.

5. Sanders, 38.

6. This material is drawn chiefly from the editions of Tischendorf, von Soden, Legg, the IGNTP, Swanson, NA[27], and Aland's *Synopsis.* In a few places I have confirmed readings by consulting microfilms at the Ancient Biblical Manuscript Center at Claremont, California, and I wish here to express my appreciation for access to that material. At various points I have ignored minor spelling errors in manuscripts (but not, of course, in W itself) as well as readings found only in the versions or Fathers. Following Tischendorf's practice, I use the Greek ς to refer to the Stephanus 1550 edition of the Textus Receptus.

order of citation and discussion throughout is that of the order of the Gospels in W: Matthew, John, Luke, and Mark.

Corrections by the Original Scribe

Sanders counted seventy-eight corrections by the original scribe; my count is eighty-five.[7] Although I have departed from Sanders's assignments of corrections to the various hands rather infrequently, I believe that his remarks on the nature of the original scribe's correcting activity give a misleading impression in two chief respects. First, he supposes that the shift from the scribe's original reading to the correction is often the result of two different choices of reading, where the scribe first followed one reading/exemplar and then changed his mind and followed the other.[8] In fact, in almost all examples I believe that the original reading was a mere slip or oversight and the correction simply restored the reading of the scribe's exemplar. Second, Sanders only rarely observed that in fact many of the corrections by the scribe were made in the course of copying (that is, *in scribendo,* as I shall call it), not during a subsequent check of his work. This aspect of scribal corrections is often ignored.[9]

Sanders identified differences between the first and second hands, and I essentially affirm his observations.[10] We may especially note as a useful criterion that the ε of the original scribe has an extended middle stroke, whereas in the ε of man 2 it is shorter.[11] Sanders also notes that the first scribe's characteristic way of marking a letter for deletion is by placing a supralinear dot over it.[12]

Corrections Made in Scribendo

I believe that as many as twenty-eight of the corrections were made by the original scribe during the course of copying.[13] I set them out with brief comments here.

---

7. Sanders, 28–31 generally (28 for his count of corrections). There is also Luke 6:48, which I find too uncertain to cite.

8. Sanders, 28–29, 31.

9. Corrections *in scribendo* are especially frequent in $\mathfrak{P}^{66}$, and I refer readers to the detailed treatment in my *Scribal Habits in Early Greek New Testament Papyri* (forthcoming). An early study that I have found to be particularly perceptive concerning this aspect of scribal corrections is Erroll F. Rhodes, "The Corrections of Papyrus Bodmer II," *NTS* 14 (1967–68): 271–81.

10. See Sanders, 32.

11. Sanders, 32: the ε of man 2 "has regularly a shorter middle stroke."

12. These dots are found at Matt 17:25; John 10:30; 17:22; 19:9; Luke 6:26; 17:20, 34–37; 19:23; 20:1; 24:14; Mark 10:35; 15:43.

13. I am tempted to include also John 8:44–45, where, however, no one has cited a correction. Here we read (at the end of one line and beginning of another) και ο $\overline{\pi\eta\rho}$ αυτου | εγω δε κτλ. This appears straightforward enough, but in fact αυτου protrudes unusually far into the right margin, and ε of εγω is slightly in the left margin. This last point is hardly unusual, as the

Matt 6:14. I have followed Sanders's first citation of the original reading as υτων, according to which the scribe, as with the scribe of Sinaiticus, at first omitted one α by haplography. Goodspeed read υμων, however, and Sanders subsequently followed him.[14] But I believe that the suggestion of υμων is due to bleed-through from the opposite side of the leaf.

Matt 8:16. The scribe wrote the loop of the α, intending the abbreviation of the more usual singular, but then stopped and wrote τ over that and continued with the abbreviation of the plural.

Matt 12:31. Apparently the scribe at first leapt from βλασφημια **αφεθησεται τοις ανθρωποις** to βλασφημια ουκ **αφεθησεται τοις ανθρωποις**, as in the majority text, and was going to continue on with 12:32. But after completing one line of 12:32, the scribe caught his error, erased the entire line, and then proceeded correctly. The correction was so thorough that the original writing is completely irretrievable. Sanders argued that the original omission shows a relation between W and those manuscripts that read η δε … τοις ανθρωποις and asserted: "It seems quite clear that the parent of W omitted the sentence, but it had been supplied in a marginal gloss, which was not discovered by the copyist of W, until he had written the next following line."[15] But this is an unnecessary hypothesis. It is simpler to suppose that W originally made the same omission by a scribal leap as did a number of other witnesses independently, but then the scribe of W caught the error before proceeding too far.

Matt 18:4. Sanders says that the scribe first wrote του ουρα but erased that and wrote εν τη βασιλ. But this scenario does not seem to fit the remains, and it seems implausible that the scribe began μειζων του ουρανου. In fact, although an

---

scribe often extends a letter into the margin at the beginning of a sense unit. But the overall appearance here makes me think that perhaps the scribe originally omitted αυτου and wrote και ο $\overline{\pi\eta\rho}$ ε and the end of the first line and γω δε κτλ. and the beginning of the following one. Clearly the frequent occurrence of the unmodified ο πατηρ in John might have led a scribe to omit αυτου in v. 44, although no such omission is reported. Also, I believe that there may be some small trace of a letter under the α of αυτου, which resembles the left portion of an ε or ο and which seems not to be explainable as bleed-through from the ειπω (8:55) on the other side of the folio. What I would thus conjecture is that the scribe wrote ο$\overline{\pi\eta\rho}$ ε at the end of the one line (accidentally omitting αυτου) and started the next line with γω, then caught his mistake, erased ε, and wrote αυτου at the end of that line, adding the ε at the beginning of the next line. I note also that in his writing of αυτου the scribe wrote the ο under the bar of the τ, thus saving space as at Luke 19:23 (see below under man 2) and John 12:40 (see note on John 12:40 below). On the other hand, I see that at Mark 7:7 διδασκαλιας extends far into the right margin, but there is no hint of a correction here. Apparently the scribe simply wanted to complete that word on that line and so went beyond his usual margin. Perhaps that is all that has happened at John 8:44–45.

14. See Sanders's initial view in his 1912 collation (147); Goodspeed, 399 (collation) and 279 (n. 1, "υτων is improbable"); and Sanders's assent in his 1918 volume on W (147).

15. Sanders, 29.

original του is fairly clear under the εν, what is seen under the η looks very much like a τ. Then, between the β and α, what is seen looks like an υ. I suppose, thus, that the scribe at first wrote τουτου (or even τουτο ου), having leapt back from μειζων το παιδιον, which would likely have stood (as in W) more or less directly above in the exemplar.

Matt 18:31. This is noted by Prior and Brown only, who cite simply the ι over the ο. I suppose that it is a backward leap from ελθ**οντες δ**ιεσαφησαν to ιδ**οντες δ**ε (as in W and most witnesses, but ιδοντες ουν in ℵ*.cb, B, D, 21; ειδοτες ουν in 33), which the scribe caught immediately.

Matt 19:1. The scribe at first made the accidental backward leap from ορια **της** to απο **της**, which probably stood more or less directly above in the exemplar (as in W). But if so, the correction must have been made *in scribendo*, since the scribe did not continue by repeating και ηλθεν κτλ. Instead, he caught his error at the end of the line or at least after writing λαιας at the beginning of the next line.

Matt 21:30. Sanders (29) says that the scribe first wrote απεκριθη, which was then only partially corrected (i.e., the scribe neglected to change απε- to απο-). But if this is what happened, we must have a correction *in scribendo*. That the scribe first wrote η is clear from the image. The left side of the present ε is vertical rather than curved, and just before the present ι one can see an erased vertical line, which must be the remnant of the original right side of an η. So, the scribe first wrote απεκριθη and at that point caught his error and thus corrected η into ει but failed to look farther back to correct the augment. So we have here an incomplete correction.

Matt 26:41. Goodspeed suggests that εισερχησθε was begun, as seems plausible; presumably the scribe was influenced by ερχεται at 26:40.

Matt 27:4. From an examination of the manuscript, Prior thinks that "the correction of δι to δε is undisputable." I suppose that the scribe began to write οι δ ιπον for οι δ ειπον, thus eliding δε and writing ειπον itacistically. (Note that in 27:6 W has επι for επει.). But before proceeding, the scribe corrected to the fuller writing of each word.

Matt 27:17. This correction is not listed by Sanders, but Goodspeed says, "η first omitted, or written ι, then supplied, or corrected, probably by 1st hand." The existing η is clearly narrower than usual. But it is implausible that it was first simply omitted, since then there would have been too much space between βαραββαν and $\overline{\text{ιν}}$. I conjecture that the scribe started to write βαραββαν ιησουν (or $\overline{\text{ιν}}$), thus omitting the η, but got only as far as ι and the left vertical of η (or of ν) before changing his mind. At that point he altered the existing marks into an η and continued on with the next word. This seems to be at least a possible sequence of scribal moves, since, of course, it is in this verse that we find the startling readings that make the thief's name "Jesus Barabbas" (ιησουν βαραββαν in Θ, 700*, *pc*, Or^{lat}; and ιησουν τον βαραββαν in f^1, *pc*, sy^s, Or^{mss}). In view of the textual agreement in Matthew among W, Θ, 700, and f^1, it seems possible that such a reading was either marked somehow in the scribe's exemplar or at least known to the scribe. But of course it is also possible that the initial slip was merely the omission of η.

John 6:18. Unfortunately, this page is missing from the new images, but the plate in Sanders's facsimile seems to make clear what has happened. After the ρ, the scribe first wrote a straight vertical stroke that could have been intended as an ι or as the left side of an η. I will assume, for the sake of definiteness, that an ι was intended. Immediately, as it seems, the scribe noticed his error, transformed the ι into an ε by adding the horizontal lines, and then continued with το. From the spacing of the letters, it seems to be less likely (although perhaps possible) that the scribe could have made the correction after writing το, and thus we have a correction *in scribendo.* The original reading was simply a sound confusion (ι for ε).[16]

John 9:21. The scribe completed writing τις, the remains of which can be seen fairly clearly. At that point the scribe noticed that he had omitted the preceding η (an inadvertent omission of a short word), erased τις, wrote η τις, and continued.

John 10:17. This is as in John 4:10, where we have a similar instance in W^s. This is presumably a sound error (α for η),[17] since αυτα would not make sense in this context, unless the scribe momentarily thought of the προβατα of 10:15–16.

John 11:7. What has happened here has not, I believe, been described precisely. In his collation Sanders cites a correction by "man 3 (aut 2)" from γωμεν to αγωμεν, but in his discussion (37) he cites this as simply from the third hand and does not see that a change has occurred to μαθηταις as well. However, Goodspeed correctly notes that the α of αγωμεν is written "over ς of μαθηταις and a faint original α" and assigns the correction to "a later (3d?) hand." Prior and Brown, however, state, "Another possibility is that μαθηταις αυτου … was replaced by μαθηται αγωμεν." They also note that the evidence for αυτου is "[a]n erased α followed by the descender of an erased υ." Now, in fact, one can see (I believe) the following traces of erased letters: an α between the α and γ of αγωμεν, an υ between the γ and ω of αγωμεν, and another υ between the μ and ε of αγωμεν. Thus, it seems certain that the scribe originally wrote μαθηταις αυτου (as in many other manuscripts),[18] not μαθηταις γωμεν, as Sanders and Goodspeed thought. But then, it seems to me implausible that the scribe would have continued with εις την ιουδαιαν κτλ., thus deleting αγωμεν. Rather, I would suppose that the scribe noted his error after writing αυτου and so returned to the manuscript to remove

16. See Francis Thomas Gignac, *A Grammar of the Greek Papyri of the Roman and Byzantine Periods* (2 vols.; Testi e documenti per lo studio dell'antichità 55; Milan: Cisalpino-La Goliardica, 1975–81), 1:249–51.

17. Ibid., 1:286, who though calls this interchange "sporadic."

18. On the variations involving αυτου after οι μαθηται, see Hermann Freiherr von Soden, *Die Schriften des Neuen Testaments in ihrer ältesten erreichbaren Textgestalt 1* (Berlin: Duncker, 1902–10), 1431.

the offending αυτου but accidentally changed the noun from dative to nominative as well (even perhaps momentarily thinking of himself as removing σαυτου). This scenario would involve a correction made *in scribendo,* and I suppose that whatever aspects of the α that caused Sanders and Goodspeed to assign it to a later hand result simply from its being a correction. The result is that we have an incomplete correction. The initial error need not have been anything more than a harmonization to general usage by writing αυτου after οι μαθηται.

Luke 6:8. The scribe at first wrote the third-declension accusative χειρα with a final ν, as is commonly found.[19]

Luke 8:2. Although Sanders (37) assigned the correction here to man 3, Goodspeed more plausibly attributed it to man 1; he also stated that εκβεβληκει was originally written, and it seems to fit the remains, whereas Sanders left the matter open. I note at least that the ε has the longer middle stroke characteristic of the original scribe's writing. We seem to have here the influence of Mark 16:9, as also found in a few other witnesses.

Luke 8:21. Note that the stroke proceeding downward to the right from the ρ of προς is in fact the ink from the ρ of καιρον of 8:13 bleeding through from the other side of the folio; it seems to me that the scribe got only as far as αυ before correcting. The original reading seems to be a harmonization to the parallel at Mark 3:33 (where W reads ος δε απεκριθη και ειπεν αυτοις, to which the reading of W* is even closer), a harmonization found also independently in D and a few others.

Luke 8:42. Sanders says, "επνιγονα in ras man 1," and Goodspeed says, "-θλιβ-?" In fact, I believe that after writing συν | ε, the scribe wrote θρ. A circular letter appears between the present ε and π, and then a ρ is faintly visible between the π and ν. The downward stroke of this ρ seems not to be explainable by either bleed-through or cross-printing. Continuing further, one can see remnants of ιβ. Thus, I suggest that the scribe wrote συνεθριβον for συνεθλιβον, substituting ρ for λ.[20] In fact, the scribe got as far as συνεθριβον α before correcting himself, since the remains of an α are visible below the right side of the final ν of the verb, but there is no sign of correction to αυτον. The original reading is, as Sanders notes (30), a (variation of a) harmonization to Mark 5:24, which many scribes could independently have made.

Luke 16:9. Here we can see precisely what the scribe did. After ποιησατε, he wrote the left loop of α and started (from the top) writing the right-hand stroke, but before completing that stroke he noticed his error and reshaped the α into an ε. The initial error was, of course, haplography (ποισατε εαυτοις), perhaps abetted

19. Gignac, *Grammar of the Greek Papyri,* 2:46. The original scribe also wrote χειραν at Matt 12:10 and John 20;25, as noted by Sanders (24).

20. Gignac, *Grammar of the Greek Papyri,* 1:102–7 (the interchange of λ and ρ).

by the common confusion of αυτος and εαυτος. Of course, the agreement with Pseudo-Nilus here can be nothing more than coincidence.

Luke 17:34. The scribe at first omitted 17:35 (as did also the scribes of ℵ, *pc*,1, vg^{ms}), by an accidental visual leap (**αφεθησεται** ... **αφεθησεται**), and wrote the beginning of 17:37 (17:36 [as found in ς^{e}, D, U, *pm*, lat, sy$^{s.c.p.h}$, arm] was evidently not present in the exemplar). But he then caught his error when he came to the end of the line, which also happens to be the end of page 285 of the codex, and deleted και αποκριθεντες λεγου by placing supralinear dots and also marking with quotation marks the beginning and end of the text to be deleted.[21]

Luke 18:16. The scribe started to write ημας, presumably as a harmonizaiton to the context (the two plural verbs), but then altered it to the singular προς εμε. This saying concerning the children occurs three times in the Synoptic Gospels; in the order of W the evidence for προς εμε is:

Matt 19:14	προς εμε ℵ, L, Δ
Luke 18:16	προς εμε W$^{c\ (man\ 1)}$ solus
Mark 10:14	προς εμε W, N

So, the scribe seems to have decided in Luke that προς εμε was the superior reading, and continued it in Mark.

Luke 22:39. The scribe at first made a forward visual leap from εθ**ος** to ορ**ος** των ελαιων, thus starting to write των ελαιων. Then he corrected himself, erasing the τω and writing in the correct words.

Luke 23:21. The scribe started to write σταυρωσον σταυρωσον, the reading found in most witnesses, as must have stood in the exemplar, but then decided midway to omit the second occurrence. Sanders says that the erased letters are "σταυ..," but Goodspeed says merely "σταυ?" This is difficult. It looks to me as though the remains of a "lunate" *sigma*, c, exist just before the present α, having been written very close to the preceding ν. Also, it appears that the erased letters can be seen as far as the space between the present ο and ν of αυτον. If this is so, considerations of space make it likely that the scribe first got as far as σταυρω (as Sanders seems to suggest) before correcting himself. But I cannot identify the remains more precisely. The correction harmonizes to Mark 15:13 (and cf. the one σταυρωθητω at Matt 27:22).

Luke 24:14. The original error here was simply an omission by homoeoarcton (ωμιλουν **π**ρος αλληλους **π**ερι), and then the scribe caught the error just before the end of the line.[22]

---

21. Sanders (26 n. 1), wrote of this instance, "A most interesting case; the scribe himself corrected his mistake after writing three words."

22. Clearly the scribe did not write ωμιλουν περι παντων περι παντων, as Swanson has for W*, and it is uncharitable to suppose, as does the IGNTP, that W* wrote περι παντων προς αλληλους περι παντων.

Mark 2:25b. This correction is cited only by Prior and Brown: "The first ε of εποιησεν is written over the vertical stroke of another letter, perhaps the downstroke of a τ." Certainly another letter was begun, but the downstroke could be either the start of any one of several letters or an ι. I suggest that the scribe, having mistakenly written ο instead of π after ανεγνωτε, momentarily made a forward leap (ανεγνωτε **ο** επ**ο**ιησεν) and was going to continue on with the remaining letters, ιησεν. But after writing the ι, he caught his error, reshaped the ι into an ε, and continued on correctly. (Note that Mark 2:25a was corrected by man 2.)

Mark 4:32. Sanders states: "λαχανων κ in ras man 1 (ḳạị···· prim scr)." It seems clear that the letters λαχανων κ are written over something, but I can make nothing of the remains. I conjecture that the scribe first wrote σπερματων (after παντων των), his eyes having leapt back to the end of 4:31, which lies almost directly two lines above in W. Then, after completing that word, he caught his error, erased it, and continued with λαχανων και κτλ. But many other lapses are certainly possible.

Mark 5:2. Sanders says: "(αν in ras man 1, τ̣· prim scr)." On the one hand, we have here letters bleeding through; the η of κατασκη | νουν (Mark 4:32) is clearly seen to the left of the α of αν, and a κ can be seen between the α and the ν. On the other hand, there is a horizontal line running through the top of the α that cannot be accounted for by anything on the other side (or on the facing page). Also, the loop of the α is elongated more than usual (although not that much more than the one that begins the next to last line on the same page). This horizontal line would be the source of Sanders's "τ̣" as the original letter. (That line was a bit lighter than is found in the τ that begins the preceding line but seems about the same as the one in the middle of the next line.) But then what did the scribe start to write? I believe that it is likely that the scribe became momentarily confused as he ended one line and began another and thus began to duplicate the syllable (i.e., τω) that he had just written, but corrected himself before even writing the second letter. (At least the right side of the N seems to be original.) We would thus have the same phenomenon as we find at the corrections at John 19:9 and Luke 17:20, as well as at John 7:45, where αυ | αυτοις has remained uncorrected. (Alternatively, perhaps we again have a backward parablepsis to the των of αυτων εκ του πλοιου, which would have stood more or less above $\overline{\text{ανος}}$ of the exemplar.) Here the corrected reading is supported by a narrow range of witnesses, and it would be tempting to suppose that some notation of the majority reading (with ανθρωπος after μνημειων) in the exemplar occasioned the confusion, but I do not see how the remains would fit.

Mark 11:15. Sanders says: "ν τω ιερω in ras man 1; prim scr ε τω ιερω." One can see the diaeresis over the original ι and the original ρ distinctly one letter to the left of the ρ in the correction. But the remains under the τ do not seem consistent with an original ω. Goodspeed suggests that ις τα ϊερα was originally written after ε. I suggest, instead, that the scribe first wrote (or at least started to write) εις το ϊερον, as in the earlier part of 11:15 (where D[gr] has εν τω ιερω). The original ι (of εις) was altered into the left vertical of ν, and then the original ς was erased. Where το stood, we now have τ and the left portion of ω. Then, the original ο of ιερον was adapted into ρ; note that the ρ is a bit awkward, and the upper loop is roughly the size of the scribe's ο (as immediately above in ηρξατο). But I do not see anything that indicates that a ν stood under the present ω of ιερω. Thus I suppose that the scribe noticed his error after writing εις το ιερο and at that point made the correction.

Other Corrections (Possibly Later) by the Original Scribe

Besides the twenty-eight corrections made during the course of copying, noted in the previous section, there are the following fifty-seven corrections that were made by the scribe. Of course, some or even all of these might have been made before the scribe proceeded very far in his work, but, equally, they may have been made on a subsequent check of his work.

Matt 4:13. Both spellings are frequent in the tradition (see Tischendorf's note), and W fluctuates (καπερναουμ at Matt 8:5; 11:23; Luke 10:15; καφαρναουμ at the other ten occurrences). It is interesting that the scribe corrects his own spelling at the first occurrence of this name in the manuscript and that both spellings have strong support here. It is tempting to suppose that both readings were marked somehow in the exemplar and that the scribe first wrote one and then decided on the other.

Matt 6:20. The original reading was a sound shift (τ to δ) in two frequently confused words.[23]

Matt 12:46. What the original reading was is completely unclear.

Matt 13:38. The scribe followed the rule of writing a singular verb after the neuter plural τα ζιζανια.[24]

Matt 16:24. Although Sanders (in his collation) and Goodspeed both say that this is man 2, in his discussion (29) Sanders assigns this to man 1. Also, Prior and Brown are, I believe, correct in saying that it is "likely" man 1. Note the extended middle bar of ε, characteristic of man 1. The original reading results from common confusion of αυτος and εαυτος (here αυτον for εαυτον).

Matt 16:25. In his collation Sanders ascribes this to man 2, but he mentions it in his discussion of man 1 (28), whereas Goodspeed does not cite it at all. This is a difficult decision, but I have followed Sanders's ascription to man 1. We have here a simple sound confusion (η for ει),[25] along with the frequent confusion of such forms, as shown in the variation of θελει and θελη earlier in the verse. The corrected form has weaker support than does the original reading but could rep-

---

23. Gignac, *Grammar of the Greek Papyri*, 1:82–83.
24. See BDF §133.
25. Gignac, *Grammar of the Greek Papyri*, 1:240–41.

resent either a shift to the reading of D or an assimilation to απολεσει earlier in the verse (where only ms 28 has απολεση).

Matt 17:19. The original reading is a common sound confusion in the [illegible].[26]

Matt 17:25. Perhaps we have a duplication of εις read initially as οις (– ο ις – ο ιησους). Or perhaps the presence of "Jesus" as subject was so common that its addition was natural. Note that the deleted letters have been marked in two different ways: supralinear dots (man 1) and diagonal lines crossing out the letters (man 2).

Matt 19:9. Writing υμων harmonizes to υμιν earlier in the verse.

Matt 20:12. The shift to the singular αυτον must have been the result of a momentary distraction, perhaps occasioned merely by the ending -ν of the preceding word.

Matt 21:19. Sanders left it open which direction the correction went, but Goodspeed thought that επ was original. Indeed, it seems more likely that the rare reading (επ) was corrected to the usual reading (εν) than vice versa. Moreover, I believe that the diagonal line of the N is secondary; note that in the scribe's original N the diagonal line is lower and has an arc toward the bottom of the line. Here the diagonal line is a bit higher and curves toward the top of the line. The original reading is a harmonization to επ αυτην (or rather, επ αυτης, as in L, W, 157) earlier in the verse. (See note at end of essay.)

Matt 21:32b. The scribe seems to have written the third-person form in harmonization to ηλθεν at the beginning of the verse. If the scribe momentarily took John as the subject of the verb, this might clarify the omission of ουκ before the verb, but the scribe corrected only the verb, leaving the omission of ουκ to be corrected by man 2.

Matt 21:32c. There seems to have been some correction to the final three letters of this verb (not cited by Sanders), but if so the original reading is unclear, as is also what connection there might have been with the correction of the previous occurrence of the verb in this verse.

Matt 22:7. The original reading is harmonized to υβρισαν in 22:6.

Matt 23:37. Here the scribe attempted to shift from the present to the aorist but at first wrote an incorrect form; the correction completed the shift. Perhaps the scribe remembered the aorist at Matt 21:35. The occurrence of this form in Theodoret of Cyrus, as noted by Tischendorf, is curious but I suppose coincidental.

Matt 25:34. Sanders does not cite this, but Prior confirmed Goodspeed's report that η was corrected to α. Indeed, the original η is clearly visible on the image, and the α appears to be from the original scribe. (I take the almost vertical stroke through the lower left of the α to be cross-printing.) The presence of

26. Ibid., 1:264–65.

other *etas* in the vicinity occasioned the error, which the scribe perhaps corrected immediately.

Matt 27:46. Sanders (28) explicitly attributes this to man 1, although in his collation he says man 2, and Goodspeed says "by 2d hand?" I would think that Sanders's explicit citation is less likely to be a lapse than the one in his collation. Moreover, the added ε does seem, with its longer middle stroke, more consistent with man 1. The original reading was simply haplography of ε.

John 10:16. The original omission of this short word seems to have been merely an oversight.

John 10:18. Since the second α is written above the line, it is clear that this was not done *in scribendo*. The original reading is the result of influence from the two earlier occurrences of απο in the verse. Sanders (131) noted that the supplementary quire to John similarly has απο for παρα at John 1:6.

John 10:30. The original reading is harmonized (in diverse witnesses) to 10:29, as von Soden (*ad loc.*) notes.

John 11:24. The original reading was the result of sound confusion (ε to ι).[27]

John 17:22. The first δ is marked in two ways, with a supralinear dot (man 1) and a diagonal line through its bottom right (man 2). The aorist and perfect of διδωμι are frequently confused throughout John, of course (as is seen with δεδωκα and εδωκα later in the verse). But the support from D, Θ, and 157 might be viewed as a shift to a Western reading, although the textual evidence is far from cleanly divided.

John 18:40. The original reading involved two sound confusions (ρρ for ρ and β for ββ) as are found commonly (in both directions) in the occurrences of this name.[28] W has βαρναβας at Mark 15:7 and βαρ | ναβαν at Mark 15:11, both uncorrected (and Mark 15:15 is missing).

John 19:9. The original reading was a nonsense dittography at the end of the line. (Cf. Luke 17:20 as well as John 7:45, where αυ | αυτοις has remained uncorrected.)

Luke 1:6. Perhaps this was merely a sound confusion (η for αι).[29]

Luke 4:36. This was a sound confusion (ε for ει).[30]

Luke 5:25. The original παντων is a harmonization (in diverse witnesses) to Mark 2:12.

Luke 6:1. The scribe (perhaps immediately) caught his error and, rather than simply altering ε to ι, erased ελ and wrote ιλ. This was a sound confusion (ε for ι).[31]

---

27. Ibid., 1:249–51.
28. Ibid., 1:157 (ρ > ρρ), and 162 (one example of ββ > β cited). See also Sanders, 22.
29. Gignac, *Grammar of the Greek Papyri,* 1:248.
30. Ibid. 1:257–59.
31. Ibid., 1:251–56.

Luke 6:26. The original reading is a harmonization, found in diverse witnesses, to 6:25.

Luke 7:30. The original reading results from common confusion of αυτος and εαυτος (here αυτους for εαυτους).

Luke 7:38. The original reading is a harmonization to the three occurrences of αυτου in 7:38.

Luke 7:49. The original reading results from the common confusion of αυτος and εαυτος (here αυτους for εαυτους), but the reading that the scribe ultimately chose seems to reflect the idiom found at Mark 1:27; 9:10; 10:26; 11:31; 12:7; 14:4; 16:3; Luke 20:5; 22:23; John 7:35; 12:19. Here the corrected reading is itself singular.

Luke 8:6. There is bleed-through from καλη και αγαθη (Luke 8:15) from the other side of the folio (p. 238 of the codex). But there are ink marks after the present το that can only be remains of the original reading, although we seem to have cross-printing as well. Goodspeed suggests και δια το (as in א). I am tempted by και τα πε(τεινα), the result of a backward leap to 8:5, but I am unable to fit the extant marks into such a reading. Again, the scribe seems to have caught his error at the end of the line.

Luke 8:7. In his collation Sanders says "man 1 aut man 2," but cites it as man 1 in his discussion (28). Goodspeed says that it is "probably" man 1. Also, in his collation Sanders says that the original letter was ο or ε but in his discussion says that -ξον was corrected; Goodspeed does not decide. I believe that I can see the remains of an ο under the α, and so the scribe originally wrote the second aorist ending.

Luke 8:10. Presumably the reading of W* is the aorist subjunctive, while the correction is the present subjunctive, but the forms of συνίημι show much confusion.[32] See, for example, Matt 13:13 συνιουσιν and συνιωσιν (συνωσιν D, 1424; συνουσιν 579); Matt 13:15 συνωσιν (συνιωσιν C, 2, 33, 1071); and Mark 4:12 συνιωσιν (συνωσιν D*, L, W, 1, 565, 1071, 1424, 1582*). Perhaps the scribe initially harmonized to his reading at Mark 4:12 and Matt 13:15 (but he has συνιουσιν at Matt 13:13).

Luke 10:11a. The reading υμιν is a harmonization to υμιν later in 10:11. The support from D$^{gr\ b}$, Θ, and f^{13} suggests that the correction is away from the Western text (although it is to the reading of D*).

Luke 11:4. Sanders incorrectly states that the second ο of αφειομεν is "in ras[ura]"; it was untouched. What the scribe did was to alter ο to α and ιλ to ει. The original reading looks like a harmonization to the following οφειλοντι (or even a forward leap: αυτοι … παντι οφειλοντι). I suspect that in fact the correction was done *in scribendo*. From whatever cause, the scribe first wrote οφιλ (or even οφιλο), beginning (an itacistic variant of) οφειλοντι. At that point he caught

32. See BDF §94 (2).

his error, erased ο, ε, and ι, and then wrote in the correct text. But it is possible that the correction was made later.

Luke 11:6. In his collation Sanders simply asserts that W* had α... under οδου, but in his discussion (30) he says: "εξ απ corr. by erasing απ and writing οδου. This points to a gloss containing the reading of D d, απ αγρου." What Sanders sees as π, I would see as γ, and I believe that one can see the loop of a ρ between the present δ and ο and its tail extending back below the δ. D's αγρου was thus originally written, and so we have a correction from the D reading to the usual text. Here it seems unlikely that D and W* would independently write απ αγρου,[33] so one must presume that the D reading stood in the exemplar of W, along with the reading of the usual text, one reading as the text itself and the other as a correction. The scribe at first chose the reading of D but then decided on the other.[34]

Luke 13:35. Sanders says that ηξοι was first written; Goodspeed says "ηξσι perhaps," but this would seem to be a misprint. (In fact, ηξθι looks more likely to me, in which case the correction was almost certainly made *in scribendo.*) But what is the cause of the original reading? Here we seem to have visual confusion, as the scribe misread E as Θ or O.

Luke 17:20. Again we have a dittography at the end of a line. (Cf. John 19:9, as well as John 7:45, where αυ | αυτοις has remained uncorrected.)

Luke 18:43. The shift to the aorist harmonizes with the preceding ανεβλεψεν.

Luke 19:23. The deletion marks above the (first) μου are characteristic of the scribe. The change, however, was not done *in scribendo,* since then the scribe would have written μου normally on the next line, whereas he in fact wrote it at the end of the line as a ligature that takes the space of one letter. Presumably the scribe preferred to keep the corrected reading all on one line and so compressed the second μου.[35] But it is not excluded that W* in fact did read μου at both places with N (as the IGNTP cites), and then the deletion of the first μου could have been later, even if by man 1. Since there is no evident explanation for the scribe's original reading from the corrected reading, a deliberate shift from one reading

---

33. The closest parallel would seem to be the description of Simon of Cyrene at Mark 15:21 = Luke 23:26 (and Matt 27:32 according to 33), but this seems very remote.

34. There is further evidence that readings now found in D existed alongside alternative readings in the exemplar (or in some ancestor) of W. An excellent example that Sanders gives (46) occurs at Matt 12:16, where we find: δε ους εθεραπευσεν επεπληξεν αυτοις D, f^1 (-πλησσεν) : και επετιμησεν αυτοις ς, *rell* (επετιμα Θ) : δε ους εθεραπευσεν επεπληξεν αυτοις και επετιμησεν αυτοις W. Here it seems certain that W has combined the other two readings, one of which was in the text, the other noted supralinearly or in the margin. The intention was to indicate a substitution or alternative, but the scribe of W (or possibly an ancestor) made an addition.

35. Similarly, at John 12:40 οφθαλμους occurs at the end of a line, and the second ο is written above the μ "perhaps as a deliberate space-saving measure," as Prior and Brown say. (In any case, no one cites a correction there.) See Sanders (10–11) for the use of such ligatures.

to another seems plausible, although perhaps the most that one can say is that the correction is away from the Alexandrian text.

Luke 20:1. The addition of αυτω is from the parallel at Matt 21:23. The scribe caught his error at the end of the line.

Luke 21:6. The scribe evidently was influenced by the following επι λιθω (which W has *cum* ℵ[c], L, X, Ψ, *f*[1], *f*[13], 33, 157, 579, 892, 1241, 1424, *al*), or perhaps even started to write it by a forward accidental leap.

Luke 22:12. The scribe no doubt intended to reproduce αναγαιον as found in 𝔓[75 vid], ℵ, A, B, D, etc. but first omitted the third α by a sound confusion (ι for αι)[36] and then eventually produced the itacistic variation αναγεον.[37] At Mark 14:15 we find αναγιον unchanged.

Luke 23:9. The original reading was a harmonization to αυτον earlier in the verse.

Luke 23:12. The scribe at first omitted an apparently superfluous article.

Luke 23:34. Sanders says merely that ου is over an erasure, whereas Goodspeed says "of -ων?" An original αυτων seems to me almost certain. It was a harmonization to the plural participle and verb in 23:34b.

Luke 23:43. Sanders says that the scribe formed the lunate *sigma* from an original ι without erasure, whereas Goodspeed says that the *sigma* is "over an erasure (of τ?)." Here it appears that Goodspeed is correct; note that a tiny remnant of the left side of the top bar remains to the right of σοι and (especially) that the top portion of the *sigma* is flatter than is usual for the scribe, indicating that is the remnant of the right side of an original top bar. So if the scribe began with τ, I conjecture that he started to write τημερον, the Attic form of σημερον. Also, if this is the case, it does not even seem required that the correction was made *in scribendo,* although I suspect that the scribe caught it by the end of the line. I have found no parallel to the writing of τημερον within the New Testament tradition.

Mark 1:3. In the long W addition to Mark 1:3, the scribe at first wrote κα for και before a vowel (cf. the corrections at Mark 6:32 and 15:40, as well as the uncorrected examples noted by Sanders, 25).

Mark 6:27. The original reading was a sound confusion (ει for η).[38]

Mark 7:21. The correction could be taken as to the Western reading.

Mark 8:31. The original reading could be a harmonization to the preceding **απο**δοκιμασθηναι or to the parallels (Matt 16:21; Luke 9:22), where απο seems more or less certain. But it is also possible that we have a shift from one reading to another, as Sanders thought, although the evidence does not divide very clearly along known textual lines.

---

36. Gignac, *Grammar of the Greek Papyri,* 1:259–60.

37. The IGNTP incorrectly cites ℵ for αναγαιαν, apparently having confused ms ℵ and ms S, which the IGNTP cites as S and 028, respectively.

38. Gignac, *Grammar of the Greek Papyri,* 1:239–40.

Mark 10:35. This is one of the most puzzling corrections. The mark above the τ must be a mark of deletion, and there is a similar mark on top of the ς; it looks to me as though these (especially the first) were made by the scribe, who indicated the deletion of τες by supralinear dots at the beginning and end only. But then the strong diagonal line through τ looks much more like the scribe's writing than that of man 2, whose lines are much lighter. Indeed, we see such a light line through ε; this would appear to be man 2's work. On the other hand, Sanders (36–37) thinks that the scribe deleted τ only (although this would hardly be sensible), that the second hand then crossed out ες, and that man 3 "again crossed out these two letters, erased the first ε and wrote η." Goodspeed, however, describes all of this as "changed (by 3d hand?)." Sanders's scenario is very complex (and he posits a problematic intermediate stage), but Goodspeed's seems too simple for the variety of marks that we see. I suggest that we have a correction in two stages: from προσελθοντες to προσελθον (by man 1, possibly with man 2's concurrence) and then to προσηλθον (by man 3), where I follow Sanders in the latter ascription. (The η is not well-formed, but that may be the result of its being written over a correction, and it seems to me theoretically possible that it could be the work of any of the first three hands. However, man 4 seems excluded; compare the η at John 6:53.) So what has occurred? As von Soden notes, W (i.e., W^c) is harmonized here to Matt 20:20, with the support of no other witness.[39] With the original reading, the scribe wrote the participle, perhaps expecting a construction as in Mark 6:35 or 10:2 (but not in Matt 20:20). As soon as he saw that a finite verb was not forthcoming, the scribe deleted τες, thinking that he had produced a finite form. It was then left for man 3 to notice that the augment was missing. As Sanders also notes, at this point it is clear that man 3 was not following a manuscript (37). I count this as a correction of both man 1 and man 3.

Mark 14:27. The scribe (like the scribe of ms 300) was perhaps thinking (or looking) ahead to σκανδαλισθησονται in 14:29.

Mark 14:53. This could be a sound confusion (ο for οι),[40] but I think that it is also possible that the scribe momentarily made a forward leap (αρχιερ**εις και**

39. Sanders (36–37) did not notice the influence of Matt 20:20 but says, "The perfect tense of the Old Latin MSS c d f ff_2 [*sic*] r aur, Syr S Sah Bo gives some warrant for the first hand reading." In fact, the present "accedunt" is read by Latin mss k, l, and also vg, while the perfect "accesserunt" is found in a, aur, b, c, d, f, ff^2, i, q, and r^1. Since Mark 10:35 is the only place in the New Testament that προσπορεύομαι occurs, nothing can be deduced from the fact that the Itala and the Vulgate choose to represent it with "accedere," which elsewhere does represent προσέρξομαι. Also, I think that the perfect "accesserunt" as well as the perfects found in $sy^{s.p}$, co, and got (and the imperfects in arm and aeth) are a reasonable representation of the historic present that Mark wrote, and reflect a Greek aorist no more than do Luther's "gingen," the RSV's "came," or the NEB's "approached."

40. Gignac, *Grammar of the Greek Papyri,* 1:199–201.

οι πρεσβυτεροι και οι γραμματ**εις και ο** πετρος) and started to write ο πετρος but then caught his error immediately after writing π and corrected the article.

Mark 15:43. The strong support for both readings here suggests that the scribe was shifting from one reading to another. (Note that at John 19:38, W reads the article where the evidence is also divided.)

We may pause at this point to consider the nature of the corrections by the copyist in the main part of W. Sanders listed twenty places where "the corrections by the original scribe are well-established variant readings. Their appearance as corrections made by first hand seem to indicate that they stood in the parent MS as glosses either between the lines or in the margin, and so were not always seen by the copyist at first."[41] But one can see from the textual evidence that Sanders cites that the support for the original reading is almost always quite scattered. Moreover, most of the original readings are readily explainable as the results of (coincidental) harmonization or other common textual influences. In short, these are hardly a substantial basis for drawing the conclusion that Sanders urged.

But there remain a very few examples where Sanders's hypothesis seems more or less plausible. These are Matt 27:17 (the most conjectural one); John 17:22; Luke 10:11a; 11:6 (what seems the best example); Mark 7:21; 8:31. In these places we have at least some evidence that the parent manuscript of W was marked with corrections and that the scribe first wrote one reading, then decided on the other. Except for the first (very conjectural) example, these corrections were not made *in scribendo*, however, so we may suppose that the scribe, indeed, paused to note an interlinear or marginal correction and changed his text accordingly. But the limited number of such corrections does not suggest that this was very common, and the scattered textual support does not display any clear tendencies of such corrections toward any identifiable text-type.

Corrections by the Second Hand (Man 2)

Sanders (31–36) counts seventy-one corrections by man 2, whom he identifies as the διορθωτής of the manuscript; my count is sixty-nine.[42] Sanders also comments (32), "Quite a number of the corrections by the second hand are either known or natural variants, yet the sum total of such variants is too small to suggest that the διορθωτής regularly compared a second MS." It seems to me that in virtually all of man 2's corrections it is certain that he is simply correcting to the reading of the exemplar, which the scribe had failed to reproduce. Sanders also notes that the second hand's characteristic way of deleting letters is by writing a diagonal line

41. Sanders, 28–29, with a list of these corrections on 28–31.

42. I have not included the three places where the second hand emphasizes deletions by the first hand by marking through the letters: Matt 17:25; John 17:22; Mark 10:35.

through the letters (or at least through a portion of the letters).[43] Additions are sometimes written in the margin, marked with the sign "./." both in the text and in the margin.[44] Substitutions are simply written over the letters to be replaced.[45]

Matt 1:9. There was the original omission of intervocalic γ.[46]

Matt 2:11. The corrector shifted to what is (at least in the New Testament tradition) the more usual spelling.[47] At Rev 1:11 and 2:8, where we have the name of the city, ℵ has ζμυρναν and ζμυρνη, which Tischendorf edits (see his note on 1:11). At John 19:39 D^s and W have ζμυρνης (and ℵ has σζμυρνης). Thus W (and probably D, I suppose) wrote ζμυρν- at both places in the Gospels. The corrector noticed only the one in Matthew.

Matt 2:17. This was an omission by a leap: ιερεμι**ου** του προφητ**ου**.

Matt 3:12. Originally the first σ was omitted from ασβεστω (and B* omitted the other one).

Matt 5:6. The corrector shifted the sound (ω for ο),[48] with support from Θ only. (The scribe adopted the spelling δικαιωσυνη at Matt 3:15; 5:10; 6:33. After that, presumably both the scribe and the corrector were convinced that δικαιοσυνη was correct.) Here the correction is almost singular.

Matt 6:7. This is a simple omission of a short word; perhaps the scribe took οτι as inferential and thus redundant after γαρ.[49]

Matt 7:8. The scribe harmonized to αιτων earlier in the verse.

Matt 7:17. The scribe omitted αγαθον by a visual leap: δενδρ**ον** αγαθ**ον**.

Matt 9:16. The corrector (like the scribe of C) was misled by the preceding ρακους to write αγναφους.

Matt 10:14. The scribe at first chose, as did the scribe of 1194, to write the genitive after ακουση.

Matt 14:24. What originally stood in the manuscript is completely unclear. We seem to have letters bleeding through as well as cross-printing. Yet the β seems certainly to have been corrected. I can only suggest that there is some remnant here of one of the alternative readings to μεσον της θαλασσης ην.

Matt 15:8. Sanders (32–33) discusses this at length, arguing that the exemplar of W had a correction here, with the "Antiochian" εγγιζει … αυτων "inserted above και τοις χειλεσιν με τιμα." The scribe of W took the correction as a substitution rather than an addition and so "did not venture to write it, though he left

43. See Matt 17:25 (already deleted by man 1); 27:55; John 17:22 (already deleted by man 1); Mark 2:25; 3:10; 10:35 (already deleted by man 1).

44. See Matt 2:17; 7:17; 24:24; John 11:9; Luke 12:30.

45. See Luke 6:37; 15:30.

46. Gignac, *Grammar of the Greek Papyri,* 1:71–75.

47. On these alternative spellings, see BDAG, *s.vv.,* as well as Gignac, *Grammar of the Greek Papyri,* 1:121–22.

48. Gignac, *Grammar of the Greek Papyri,* 1:277.

49. Sanders (33), unjustifiably I believe, says the omission "seems due to Coptic influence."

a space for the διορθωτής [i.e., man 2] to use, if he desired." But I am puzzled by the και. In his collation (154) Sanders ascribes to man 2 τοις ... τιμα. But earlier (32) he wrote that "the first hand omitted και τοις χειλεσιν με τιμα, but left some space at the end of the line and the first half of the following line vacant." Indeed, it appears that και at the end of the line (and especially the α) is different from the scribe's writing. So the και was not part of the correction, which the scribe considered a substitution. But if και were part of the scribe's "original" text, that text would have read ο λαος ουτος και τοις χειλεσιν με τιμα, which is not an attested reading. It is also curious that Ω supports the reading of W*. (Was the same marking present in the exemplar of Ω?)

Matt 15:18–19. The scribe made not quite the same leap as did ℵ*, 33^{vid}, bo^{ms}. The latter witnesses leapt from **της καρδιας εξερχ**εται of 15:18 to **της καρδιας εξερχ**ονται of 15:19 and proceeded with ονται διαλογισμοι κτλ. The scribe of W, however, must have made the leap from εξερχε**ται** of 15:18 to εξερχον**ται** of 15:19 (abetted by the general similarity of the words, of course) and then proceeded with διαλογισμοι κτλ. Thus W* wrote the singular verb of 15:18. It is remarkable that the corrector simply shifted the verb rather than restoring the omitted words; clearly he also lost his way in moving back and forth between exemplar and copy.

Matt 19:8. W alone has transposed επετρεψεν, perhaps simply as a stylistic change to move the verb forward in the sentence. However, this placement also agrees with the order of Mark 10:4, where W (with ς, A, *f*^{13}, *pm*) has μωυσης επετρεψε, in place of επετρεψεν μωυσης. While transposing these words, the scribe also omitted υμιν, perhaps by a visual leap: επετρεψε**ν** υμι**ν**. However, I note that at Mark 10:5, the only other place in the Gospels where σκληροκαρδια occurs, W (with D, *f*^{13}, 28, 440, *pc*) also omits υμιν (after εγραψεν, so a similar leap could have occurred); in either location, the omission of υμιν could serve to generalize the applicability of the law. So the changes by W at Matt 19:8 agree in two respects with its text of the parallel at Mark 10:4–5. The corrector restored the omitted υμιν (where the μ and ν show his writing) but not did not change the word order. (Indeed, the only corrections of word order in the codex are at Luke 19:23 and Mark 6:16 [done incompletely].)

Matt 21:32a. The scribe simply omitted one word by oversight, and the corrector restored it.

Matt 22:22. The scribe originally wrote the first aorist ending. The corrector shifted to the much more widely attested form here.[50]

Matt 24:2. The omission of ωδε agrees with Luke 21:6; at Mark 13:2 ωδε is similarly omitted by A, E, F, H, 69, 1506, 2542, *pm*, and lat.

---

50. Sanders (33) comments: "The form in α is characteristic of Egyptian texts and the older parts of W. The omicron forms are universal in the Antioch recension."

Matt 24:24. The omission of μεγαλα in diverse witnesses harmonizes to Mark 13:22, as Tischendorf notes for ℵ. Also, it could also be a visual leap: σημει**α** μεγαλ**α**.

Matt 24:32a. Sanders simply says, "aut littera aut spiritus asper eras," whereas Goodspeed appears correct in judging, "2d hand wrote τ, which has been erased." We thus have here a confusion of gender,[51] as the second hand at first thought that the noun was neuter and so wrote το, but then either he thought better, or a later reader reverted to ο. I count this as a correction of both man 2 and an uncertain hand.

Matt 25:9. The corrector departs from the text to harmonize the adjective to αι. Presumably the scribe of Σ did the same.

Matt 27:55. The original reading could be a sound confusion (η for ου)[52] or, more likely, a syntactical confusion of the correct form of διακονεω.

John 8:12. There is a mark (">") above the α of και, which corresponds to the same mark above the ε of λεγων in the left margin and presumably indicates that λεγων is to replace the phrase και ειπεν, although there is no marking on ειπεν.[53] The original reading was simply an introduction of a very common phrase.

John 11:9. This is a correction of the scribe's simple leap: κοσμ**ου** τουτ**ου**.

John 11:18. The agreement of W* with the "Western" D and sy^{s} is certainly suggestive.

John 11:33. This is probably just an oversight in omitting a short word.

John 16:22. Both readings have weighty support, and the correction is toward both the Alexandrian text and the majority text.[54] Here the use of a second exemplar, or a correction in the exemplar, seems possible.

John 17:24. The scribe's shift to the indicative mood was likely a mere oversight; at Luke 11:54 a similar shift with more support has also been corrected.

John 21:17. προβατια is found at John 21:16 in B, C, 565*, *pc* and at John 21:17 in W$^{c\ (man\ 2)}$, A, B, C, 565, 1582*, *pc*. Why the corrector did not change προβατα at 21:16 is as mysterious as why A wrote προβατα there.

Luke 6:37. The scribe wrote ινα for both occurrences of και ου, as did D, whereas A, Ψ, and *pc* wrote ινα only the first time. The parallel at Matt 7:1 was the source. The corrector noted only the second ινα.

---

51. LSJ, *s.v.*, cites several metaplastic forms, and Gignac, *Grammar of the Greek Papyri*, 2:42, cites a probably third-century example of κλαδον μεγα.

52. Gignac, *Grammar of the Greek Papyri*, 1·217, cites only one example of ου > η.

53. For the difference from the more usual sign for an addition to the text, see Sanders, 32 (and also 35).

54. NA^{27} cites the correction as W$^{v.l}$ because χ is written above the line and ξ is not erased. Although this interpretation is theoretically possible, I believe that the supralinear letter is meant as a replacement, rather than an alternative; see, e.g., Luke 15:30.

Luke 8:49. The original reading is a harmonization by varied witnesses to Mark 5:35.

Luke 9:9. The scribe wrote the neuter instead of the masculine interrogative.

Luke 9:[illegible]. The corrector [illegible] to correct this itacism (αι for ε), as in ms [illegible] independently. (At Acts 21:39, the scribe of D wrote δαιομε for δεομαι.)

Luke 9:52. The original reading results from a common confusion of αυτος and εαυτος (here αυτου for εαυτου, as at Luke 12:47 below), although here the strong support for both readings suggests that another exemplar might have been used as a basis for the correction.

Luke 10:11b. This is an omission of a short word, although the agreement with 𝔓⁴⁵ is suggestive.[55]

Luke 11:49. The corrector shifted from future to present, likely without manuscript support, unless one supposes that the original reading of ℵ was available to the corrector.

Luke 11:54. The original reading was a shift from subjunctive to indicative, in which W* has significant support; at John 17:24 a similar shift where W* is singular has also been corrected.

Luke 12:17. The scribe preferred the construction with the infinitive after ουκ εχω που.

Luke 12:30. The omission of του κοσμου could be a simple oversight, but its occurrence in several witnesses indicates that it is a harmonization to Matt 6:32.

Luke 12:47. The original reading results from common confusion of αυτος and εαυτος (here αυτου for εαυτου), and, as at 9:52, the strong support for both readings suggests that another exemplar might have been used. Sanders correctly remarks that the original reading has "the best and oldest support," while the correction "belongs to the Antioch recension."

Luke 12:50. The original omission of οτου was presumably a mere oversight. The corrector intended to shift to the reading as found in all the early witnesses but wrote π for τ by error.[56] Compare Luke 22:18, where the scribe also erred with οτου.

Luke 15:30. Swanson interprets the supralinear τις (W^c) as an addition to the original reading, thus creating σιτιστευτον, rather than as a replacement for τευ, which would yield σιτιστον. It seems unnecessary to postulate that the corrector wished to read an otherwise unattested word instead of σιτιστον, which is at least found in Matt 22:4 and in various church writers.[57] But it is puzzling that the

---

55. Sanders (34) says that $sy^{s.c}$ agree with W* in the omission, but $sy^{s.c}$ omit the entire phrase εκ της πολεως υμων.

56. Sanders (34): "This mistake tends to confirm the idea that the second hand was inserting hastily written or crowded glosses of the parent MS." But such a hypothesis seems unnecessary to explain a simple error.

57. For σιτιστα at Matt 22:4 G, O, and Σ read σιτευτα, thus writing the more common form. For the LXX, see Edwin Hatch and Henry A. Redpath, *A Concordance to the Septuagint* (Oxford:

corrector intervened in the text only at 15:30 and ignored the same word at 15:23 and 27.[58] Presumably, it was by chance that this occurrence of the word caught his eye,[59] and he then introduced a singular reading.

Luke 16:1. The original reading doubtless reproduced the exemplar, but the corrector thought that he saw the common confusion of αυτος and εαυτος (here αυτου for εαυτου), although here the correction has (as far as I can see) no support, suggesting that the corrector took the initiative to add the letter.

Luke 19:1. The corrector has introduced a reading that is almost singular. Presumably he thought that it was more sensible to say that Jesus went out (from where he was) before he passed through Jericho.

Luke 20:26. Note that here the supralinear letters are barely over the original π but are clearly meant to replace ωπη. Note also the small dots before and after the supralinear letters, as at 22:37. (It is curious that the replacement is γη for ωπη rather than simply γ for ω.) The original reading is presumably a harmonization to the verb at 19:40 (σιγάω occurs at 18:39). But in fact within the Gospels σιγάω occurs only in Luke (9:36; 18:39 [W, B, D, L, P, T, Ψ, *pc;* most manuscripts have σιωπηση]; 20:26), whereas σιωπάω occurs twice in Matthew, five times in Mark, and twice in Luke. So the scribe (like 1009 and 1241) might have preferred the non-Lukan word.[60]

Luke 20:35. The scribe shifted from Luke's repetition of the article (as in Acts 4:2) to the more common αναστασις (των) νεκρων.[61]

Luke 21:5. Perhaps under the influence of the ο earlier in the word, or by a sound confusion (ο for ε or αι),[62] the scribe wrote the aorist ending -ητο.

Luke 21:33. The singular is an attraction to η γη immediately before, or perhaps the scribe took "heaven and earth" as a singular. Here both readings have considerable support.

Luke 21:34. By haplography, the scribe (joined by several others) originally wrote η twice only instead of thrice.

Clarendon, 1897), 1267 (*s.vv.* σιτευτός and σιτιστός); and Joseph Reider and Nigel Turner, *An Index to Aquila* (Leiden: Brill, 1966), 215 (σιτευτός occurs at 2 Kgs 6:13; Isa 1:11; Prov 15:17).

58. At least Δ is consistent, writing its otherwise unknown word σιτευρον at all three verses. (The IGNTP gives no variant at the three occurrences.)

59. Sanders (35) notes the borrowing from Matt 22:4 but then unnecessarily concludes, "the glosses of the parent MS seem to have contained harmonistic additions or corrections."

60. Sanders (35) notes that the original reading might be a "harmonistic error" but also suggests that it "may well have crept into the text under the influence of the early versions with which we find W allied so often." I fail to see how such influence would have produced W*'s reading.

61. Both Swanson and the IGNTP ignore the correction from των to της and cite merely the original omission of εκ.

62. Gignac, *Grammar of the Greek Papyri,* 1:290–91 (e > o), 292 (one example of αι > o).

Luke 22:18. The scribe simply omitted the initial vowel from οτου; the corrector shifted to the reading of the exemplar. Compare Luke 12:50, where the scribe also erred with ωτου.

Luke 22:37. Here τελεσ is written over πληρ, where it is meant to replace πληρω. See also 20:26 for the style of correction with the two dots. As the cause of the original reading Sanders (35) suggests, besides "retranslation from one of the versions," the "harmonistic influence" of Mark 15:28 (as in most witnesses, but not ℵ, A, B, C, D, Ψ). Unfortunately, the folio containing Mark 15:13 (οι δε)–15:38 (εις δυο) is missing from W, although of course the scribe could well have known of that verse whether or not it stood in W. That verse provides a specific source for W*'s reading, although πληρόω is much more common in the Gospels than τελέω, so the original reading might be a harmonization to general usage.

Luke 24:22. This seems to be a sound confusion, resulting in the omission of ρ after ρθ.[63]

Luke 24:34. The original omission was by homoeoteleuton ($\overline{\text{κς}}$ οντως), with some coincidental agreement, and the corrector restored the omitted word.

Luke 24:50. The original omission was by homoeoteleuton (εως εις). Then the scribe, having omitted εις, wrote the genitive βηθανιας appropriately (but the accusative could be used; see LSJ, *s.v.*). The corrector caught both the omisson and the change of case.

Mark 2:25a. The ο was deleted with a line through the letter, and then τι was written above the line. The reading ο is from Luke 6:3, as von Soden notes (*ad loc.*), and the agreement with 700 is likely to be coincidental, as each scribe remembered the Lukan formulation. (And 1082's οτι looks like a conflation.)

Mark 3:10. The correction to αυτω (perhaps influenced by the preceding αυτω) suggests a shift to the Caesarean text (f^{13}), or perhaps the corrector simply thought that the dative was more appropriate (whereas the scribe of B opted for the accusative). There was no shift to αυτω at the parallel Luke 6:19.

Mark 4:17. The scribe wrote the singular verb under the influence of the preceding θλιψεως, διωγμου, and λογον.

Mark 4:31. I would think that the original reading was a sound error (ον to ων,[64] which L made independently) from the reading in ℵ, B, Δ, Θ, 892, and 1071, and man 2 intended to correct to the majority reading but failed to delete ων. So we have an incomplete correction.

Mark 6:14. The scribe wrote αυτου for εν αυτω, perhaps under the influence of the earlier αυτου. But then there was an incomplete correction; the corrector changed the pronoun but neglected to add the preposition, perhaps momentarily thinking that εν was found at the end of ενεργεις.

63. Ibid., 1:107–8 (on omission of ρ, but no close parallels are cited).

64. Ibid., 1:277.

Mark 6:16. At the end of the line the scribe transposed ον εγω from the reading found also in ς, 𝔓^{45}, A, and C, perhaps by oversight but perhaps in order to place the relative pronoun next to the verb. In any case, we again have an incomplete correction; the corrector meant to shift from εγω ον to ον εγω and so inserted the ον before εγω but neglected to delete the following ον.

Mark 6:32. The scribe wrote κα for και before a vowel (cf. the corrections at Mark 1:3 and 15:40, as well as the uncorrected examples noted by Sanders, 25).

Mark 7:15. The original reading is an omission of intervocalic ν.

Mark 8:19. The corrector preferred ει to ι; the shift may show familiarity with the textual tradition found in 𝔓^{45} and D here.

Mark 8:25. The original reading appears to be a harmonization to **ανε**βλεψας in 8:24.

Mark 10:2. Here the scribe preferred the genitive after επηρωτησαν.

Mark 10:36. The με was apparently originally omitted by a leap: θελετ**ε** μ**ε**, as occurred in a few other witnesses.

Mark 12:14. The scribe omitted κηνσον by homoearcton (**κ**ηνσον **κ**αισαρι), and man 2 corrected to the reading of the exemplar. Note that S* made the same leap from within the majority text.

Mark 13:25. The scribe wrote the singular (probably under the influence of the singular του ουρανου in 13:25a), as did two other scribes independently. (W is almost alone with the singular του ουρανου at Matt 3:17 and Mark 1:11, probably influenced by the parallel at Luke 3:22, although at Mark 10:21 W is almost alone in having the plural ουρανοις.)

Mark 14:29. The scribe wrote the frequently attested αλ for αλλ.

Mark 15:40. The scribe again wrote κα for και before a vowel (cf. the corrections at Mark 1:3 and 6:32, as well as the uncorrected examples noted by Sanders, 25), although here we have simply the omission of ι by haplography.[65]

These results for the corrections by the second hand seem consistent with what was seen with those by the original scribe. In a very few places we might think of some shift of textual affiliation: Matt 2:11 (away from D); 4:13; John 11:18; Luke 10:11b; Mark 8:19. But, as noted by Sanders (32), such readings hardly suggest a comparison with another manuscript. It is, of course, possible that the second hand noticed some further corrections marked in the parent manuscript of W that the scribe had missed, but it is equally possible that the second hand was familiar here and there with alternative readings. It seems to me likely, however, that the second hand was simply attempting to conform W to its exemplar at all places (if not always successfully).

---

65. Sanders (34) says: "For the cause of the error compare Sahidic Ⲛ̄ⲒⲰⲤⲎ." Presumably Sanders thinks that the I was omitted after the right vertical of the N and that this omission (not reported by Horner, by the way) somehow found its way into W. (Sanders also invites us to compare 472's ηωση here, as well as 28's ωση at Matt 27:56, although 28 in fact reads ηωση there.)

Corrections by a Second Corrector (Man 3)

Sanders finds eleven corrections by man 3, whereas I count ten.[66] Sanders correctly observes, "These are all natural corrections made by an intelligent reader," noting that the corrections at Matt 24:32b and Mark 10:35 "almost forbid our thinking that he had another text to use for comparison." The only reading that would really suggest comparison with a manuscript is John 8:46, as Sanders notes (37).

Matt 24:32b. Sanders thought that υθ was written over an erasure, presumably because of the coarser forms of those letters. I see no rationale for the shift to ευθυς, which is a singular reading.[67]

John 5:19. The original reading is an omission of intervocalic ν.

John 8:46. The scribe followed 8:45 in omitting δια τι. Rather than inserting δια τι above the line or in the margin, the third hand added the words "by erasing γω [at the beginning of line 28], writing γω δι at end of previous line [line 27] and ατι in the erasure [line 28]" (Sanders, 37).[68]

Luke 4:18. Sanders first cited the original text as τεθρωμενους, but Goodspeed read τεθραμμενους, and Sanders subsequently agreed.[69] I am quite uncertain about this correction, however. The α shows no sign of correction, and the space between ρ and μ is too large for ω, so an original -ρωμ- (as Sanders first had it) is excluded. Yet what appears to be the right loop of an ω does seem to exist under the υ. But it seems exceptionally implausible that the scribe wrote -ραωμ-. So I have hesitantly followed Goodspeed (as did Sanders). The range of readings here is mirrored at Isa 59:6, which is being quoted, where for τεθραυσμενους we find the variants: τεθραμμενους ℵ; τεθρασμενους 93, 565 : τεθραυμενους 62*, 130. We may well have simply a similar range of syntactical confusions at both places,[70] but it seems at least possible that the reading found in W*, 0211, and *pc* is a harmonization to the LXX reading found uniquely in Sinaiticus (but not in Luke 4:18 in ℵ). On the other hand, Goodspeed (280 n. 1 [from 279]) suggests

---

66. See Sanders, 36–37. He includes John 11:7 and Luke 8:2, which I assign to the scribe. And I include Luke 5:37, which he (and Goodspeed) left unassigned.

67. A curious feature involving this word is that W has ευθυς after αρχιερευς in Mark 14:63, perhaps alone (ευθεως is added after διαρρηξας by 124, 565, and 700).

68. Sanders (37) says that it is possible that this correction derives from man 2, who would have been comparing against the exemplar of W and thus noticed the omission, and that "the awkwardness of the writing is due to the depth and roughness of the erasure." For what it is worth, however, the α stands to the left of the erasure, and it seems to me to resemble the α written by the third hand at Luke 4:19 and Mark 11:33. I note also that at Luke 5:33, W, with the support of a few but weighty manuscripts, omits δια τι.

69. See Sanders (1912: 37, 196); Goodspeed, 280 n. 1 (from 279); Sanders (1918: 37, 196).

70. LSJ, *s.v.* θραύω, refers to the readings παρατεθραυμενον and παρατεθραυσμενον at Plato, *Leges* 757E2.

the influence of ανατεθραμμενος a few lines earlier in 4:16,[71] which is perhaps the most straightforward explanation. The correction may be only partial (at any rate, it is toward the majority reading but without the *sigma*).

Luke 5:37. Both Sanders and Goodspeed cite this correction but without assigning it to a hand. Certainly the ο, which is written over the erased λ, is awkwardly formed, yet I believe it is comparable to that of man 3 at Luke 7:3. The original reading is a harmonization, either to Mark 2:22, where απολλυνται is found in W, Θ (απολυνται), and 124 (but απολουνται in ℵ, A, C, D, and *pm* and απολλυται in 𝔓[88], B, 892, and 2427), or to Matt 9:17, where απολλυνται is found in ℵ, B, Θ, f^1, f^{13}, 700, and *al* (but απολουνται in most manuscripts, including W, and απολλυται in D). Despite the complexity of the textual traditions here, it seems that the scribe's present tense is a harmonization, which was noticed by the later reader (perhaps because it is so awkward with εκχυθησεται) and changed to the future tense.

Luke 7:3. The original scribe shifted (ungrammatically) to the dative after ερωτων, corrected by man 3.[72]

Luke 7:22. The scribe first wrote the first aorist ending, and the correction is simply to the form of the second aorist (-ετε from -ατε) that is more widely attested here.

Mark 5:1. The scribe omitted ν before χ.

Mark 10:35. See above under man 1. (I count this as a correction of both man 1 and man 3.)

Mark 11:33. The scribe originally wrote the second aorist ending instead of the correct second perfect ending.

Corrections by the Third Corrector (Man 4)

Sanders ascribes four readings to man 4, as do I. As Sanders says, "These are all corrections by a reader and were not drawn from acquaintance with another MS" (37–38). Thus, the third and fourth hands were simply later readers of the manuscript who noticed a few more or less evident errors or unusual forms. (And man 4 seems to have concentrated his efforts, such as they were, on John 6–9.)

John 6:53. The scribe's omission of one word was surely an oversight.

John 9:6. The scribe wrote υ for ου, influenced by the following τυ.

John 9:23. The scribe wrote the more common ειπον, which was corrected to ειπαν, which here has limited but very weighty support.

Luke 17:1. The scribe skipped one letter (ε = αι) and thus wrote the more common ουδε instead of ουαι δε.

---

71. That is the reading of W, along with ℵ, F[c], L, Θ, Ξ, 0102, f^{13}, 1, 33, 157, 579, 892, *al.* Most manuscripts read τεθραμμενος, although Δ has τεθρεμμενος.

72. Swanson and the IGNTP cite W* for αυτο, but one can see the remains of the outer loops of the ω on either side of the ο. Goodspeed has the correction by man 2.

Corrections by an Uncertain Hand

At two places the simple erasure of a letter cannot be assigned with confidence.

Matt 24:32. Someone (perhaps man 2 himself) erased the ι that man 2 had added here.

Mark 7:22. The erasure of ι is fairly clear (and cited by Goodspeed, although not by Sanders), and the corrector shifts to the Western or Caesarean text.

Classification of the Corrections in the Supplemental Quire (W^s)

Sanders judged that this quire was "slightly older than the rest of the ms" and was thus presumably to be dated to the late fourth century or early fifth century.[73] The usual reference works now give the date of the manuscript as simply fifth century.[74] In the supplemental quire, there are corrections by the first scribe (man a) and two later hands (man b and man c), and Sanders thought that even man c was "not much later" than the writing of the quire.[75] There is no indication that any of the corrections is anything other than the repair of an oversight; in each place the reading of W^{s*} is, as far as I can tell, singular. Sanders himself gives no evaluation of the causes of the original readings.[76]

Corrections by Man a

There are eight corrections by the scribe of this quire. I discuss first those that I take as made *in scribendo* (i.e., by the original scribe in the course of copying).

John 2:16. The scribe started to write μου,[77] making a forward visual leap from **μη** to **μου** οικον on the next line, got as far as μο, then deleted the ο by crossing it out and continued with η. (Here the deletion mark is more horizontal than at 2:24 later on the page and does not extend past the right side of the letter.)

John 2:24. The deletion line here is slightly more horizontal than at 4:22 and also extends on either side of the original letter, while at 4:22 the mark does not cross the inner space.[78] The only assignment of the deletion is by Sanders in his discussion (38), where he ascribes it "certainly" to man a. Here again it seems harsh to credit the scribe with having written οεαυτον. I would suppose that the

73. Sanders, 139.

74. [Ed. note: Cf. Ulrich Schmid's palaeographical study of Codex W in this volume.]

75. Sanders, 38.

76. Sanders (38) lists the readings cited here except for John 4:8 (first noted by Prior and Brown), 4:25 (which, however, he notes in his collation), and 4:47 (where he does not cite a correction at all).

77. Swanson (*ad loc.*) incorrectly has μεη.

78. Swanson's (*ad loc.*) θεαυτον is certainly incorrect.

scribe started to write ο after επιστευσεν, caught his error immediately, marked the ο for deletion, and then continued. But what was the occasion for writing this ο? My only suggestion is that the scribe made a backward visual leap from επιστευσ**εν** to ειπ**εν** ο ι̅ς̅ in 2:22 and thus wrote ο. But that is not a very satisfactory theory.

John 4:10. The mark above the second α is in fact much like the rough breathing at 4:22 (ὁ) or even the less clear rough breathing at 4:12 (ὁς). But it seems uncharitable to believe (as does Swanson) that a scribe intended αυταον, so the other editors take the mark here as indicating a deletion of α. In his collation Sanders says the corrector was "man a aut b" but in his discussion (Sanders, 38) says that man a "certainly" made the deletion. (Goodspeed is noncommittal.) Indeed, I would posit a correction *in scribendo;* the scribe was going to write αυτα but after writing those letters noticed his error and shifted to αυτον by marking (in peculiar fashion) the second α for deletion, and then completed the word by writing ον. But all this is done in a fashion unparallelled elsewhere in the manuscript. (Cf. John 10:17, although different scribes are involved.)

John 4:25. Goodspeed is imprecise in saying that man a first wrote χ̅ρ̅. Prior and Brown correctly observe that the scribe caught his error "before completing the loop on the rho," as is indicated as well by Sanders. It is tempting to think that the occasion for the correction was that χριστος was written *plene* in the exemplar, but I would suppose that it is more likely that the scribe was simply pronouncing the text out loud as he copied and initially started to represent the sound of the word fully.

John 4:47. Sanders cites the text here as simply ιο̣υ̣|δεας. However, although there is much cross-printing and deterioration of the letters, I believe that Goodspeed is correct in proposing, "perhaps corrected from γαλ or γαλι: hand a probably started to write γαλ[ιλεας]." Also, I suppose that the vertical stroke at the end of the line is the original ι. Presumably the scribe at first made a backwards visual leap from εκ **της** to κανα **της** γαλιλεας of 4:46 and caught his error at the end of the line.[79]

I now turn to other corrections that were probably made by the original scribe.

John 3:15. Sanders and Goodspeed see a correction by man b from ζων to ζωην. On the other hand, Swanson thought ζωη was corrected to ζωην. But Prior and Brown correctly note that the letter after ζω shows signs of correction, and this can only be from ν to η. Moreover, Prior and Brown think that the corrector could be man a. Indeed, I believe that whatever (minimal) peculiarities the added ν may have could be explained by its being written supralinearly. (At John 4:36 we find ζων for ζωην uncorrected; see Sanders, 25.)

---

79. It is curious that sy^{c} reads "ex Galilaea in Iudaeam." The rationale for this is presumably that in 4:46 Jesus is already in Galilee and so must have left there in 4:47.

John 3:22. Although Sanders and Goodspeed identified the corrector here as man b, it seems to me that (as in 3:15) it would be expected that a supralinear letter would be smaller and thus that this may be man a. The first reading is likely to be simply a sound error (ε for ει), but of course the scribe may have wanted to write the older form.[80]

John 4:8. This correction was first noted by Prior and Brown. The peculiar shape of the α is, once it is pointed out, evident. This could have been changed by the scribe immediately. (The α is unlike that of man c at John 1:13, and the practice of man b is to cross out the original letter.) The original error was simply a sound confusion (ο for α),[81] perhaps under the influence of the preceding ο.

Corrections by Man b

Sanders (38) assigns the supralinear υ at John 1:33 to the same hand that added one at 4:22. Indeed, the letters appear quite similar. (But Sanders also assigns 3:15 and 3:22 to man b, both of which I assign to man a.)

John 1:33. The original error was a confusion of sounds (ο written for ου,[82] between two occurrences of ο).

John 4:22. The second ο of οοκ is crossed out by a small but clear line on the lower left side, and υ is written above the letter. The original scribe was led by the two *omicrons* in a row into writing a third.

Correction by Man c

There is one further correction in the supplementary quire.

John 1:13. Sanders notes that the first two letters of σαρκος have been written over an erasure and assigns this one correction to man c. The darker ink is striking on this page that has, like the last page of the quire, suffered significant fading, perhaps both having "suffered a similar trauma such as bleaching in the sun," as Prior and Brown suggest. And the α is "both angular and broad," as Sanders observes. There are some ink marks visible under the correction, but I have no hypothesis for what the original reading was.[83]

---

80. Gignac, *Grammar of the Greek Papyri,* 1:257–59 (and 258 on ες for εις).

81. Ibid., 1:286–87.

82. Ibid., 1:211–12.

83. If the correction were by the first hand, of course, one could posit a leap from one θεληματος to the next (as in E*, 96*, 983, and 1573) and a correction *in scribendo.* Note also that B* and 17* omit ουδε … ανδρος by a leap from σαρκ**ος** to ανδρ**ος**.

Other Cited Corrections

Although it is not part of the text, after the subscription at the end of Mark a later hand (Sanders's man 5) has written a note, which then, according to Sanders, has been corrected twice, once by Sanders's man 6 and then by his man 7.[84] Since this is not part of the text of the Gospels, I will ignore whatever corrections have taken place here.

There are sixteen further places where corrections have been cited but that I find too doubtful or unclear to cite. At several of these, even if a correction has been made, what the original reading was remains completely unclear, so it would be impossible to classify the nature of the correction. I provide these with some brief comments.

The following eleven are cited by Goodspeed only. Presumably we can infer from Sanders's silence that he disagrees with Goodspeed's readings.[85]

Matt 19:7. Goodspeed says: "κα perhaps first written for καὶ and ι later added by 1st hand." Prior and Brown think that the letters are simply crowded at the end of the line.

Matt 20:26. Goodspeed (279 n. 1) says that "γενεσθαι is a correction (4th hand?) probably from γινεσθαι."

Matt 24:32. Goodspeed states that the first η of ηδη "seems marked by a point for deletion." He appears to be referring to a very faint smudge visible above the cross bar.

Matt 26:53. Goodspeed says of λεγεωνας: "ι perhaps changed to ε [i.e., the second ε] by 1st hand."

John 5:33. Goodspeed notes the dot above η in τη and adds the comment, "for deletion?" (Could this be crasis: τἀληθείᾳ?)

John 5:34. Goodspeed notes the mark above the ε in δε and remarks "for deletion?" (The mark could be meant to separate the two vowels: εγω δε ου κτλ.)

John 10:24. Goodspeed says that the dot over the first ρ in παρρησια "may be meant to delete it." This is perhaps plausible, but note the dot over the υ of υμιν at the end of the next line. Is that a mark of deletion also?

John 20:5. Of μεντοις, Goodspeed says: "ς marked for deletion by 2d hand?" There is a slight mark through the ς, but it seems more likely to be from cross-printing.

Luke 19:28. Goodspeed says "-ρευετο of ἐπορεύετο probably 1st hand, but over an erasure." The letters πο extend a bit farther than usual into the right margin, and the letters ρευετο appear a bit squeezed together. Also, there is some discoloration in this portion of the page. But I have no suggestion for what the scribe might have written originally.[86]

---

84. Cf. Sanders, 38, 247; Goodspeed, 278.

85. See the reference to Sanders's view of Goodspeed's collation in note 3 above.

86. And with respect to the margin, see my comments on Mark 7:7 in note 13 above.

Mark 5:31. On τις μου, Goodspeed says: "μ erased (or accidentally washed out) so as to read τι σου," and Legg follows him. In fact, we have here some imperfection in the plate in the published facsimile, where there is simply a dark spot about the size of a letter between τις and ου, so Goodspeed's opinion was entirely justified by the visual data available to him. But in the recent images the μ is clear and, as it seems, untouched. The parchment is slightly darker around the μ, but this may be partly due to bleed-through (the μ is more or less directly over εθ of μεθερμηνευομενον in Mark 5:41, as found on the opposite side of the folio). Observe also that there is a wider area of this page that appears somewhat darker and thus evidently has suffered some damage.

Mark 7:21. Goodspeed states, "after γὰρ a letter (α of α|πο?) has been erased." There are two dots of ink after γαρ (one larger, one smaller), but it is difficult to imagine that they could be the remains of an α, since the smaller one is too high on the line. And I see no signs of erasure. So I believe that these dots are simply stray drops of ink. See five lines below, where the dot over the υ of υπερφανια (7:22) is surely accidental.

At five other places both Sanders and Goodspeed cite as corrections what appear to me to be the results of letters bleeding through from the other side of the folio.

Luke 6:48. Sanders was confident that there was a shift of text here, as the scribe started to write τεθεμελιωτο – πετραν of most manuscripts but quickly shifted to δια το – αυτην (as found also in 𝔓$^{75 \text{ vid}}$, ℵ, B, L, Ξ, 33, 157, 579, 892, 1241, 2542, *pc*). However, I see no trace of the τε that Sanders cites: "δια το in ras tamen man 1; τ̣ε̣··· prim scr." (Also, notice that in his discussion [30], he says, "I *seemed* to read τ̣ε̣·· as the original reading" [emphasis added].) Rather, I believe that we have bleed-through from η πως δυνασαι (Luke 6:42) on the other side of the folio. On the other hand, there is some discoloration of the manuscript here, which may be a sign of erasure. But if one wishes to posit a correction, I would propose as a possibility that the scribe, as in 𝔓$^{45 \text{ vid pr. sp.}}$, and 700* (supported by vg^{ms*} and sy^{s}), initially omitted δια το—αυτην by a leap (σαλευσαι **αυτην** … οικοδομησθ**αι αυτην**) and started to write the following ο δε ακουσας.

Luke 20:16. Of τουτους και δωσει here, Sanders says, "τους και δω in ras man 1; αμ̣πε̣λω̣ν̣ος prim scr." But I believe that the appearance of a correction here arises from letters bleeding through from the reverse side.

Luke 23:7. Of ιεροσολυ|μοις Sanders says: "λυμοις in ras man 1." But μοις (beginning a new line) is perfectly clear, so at most λυ is in question, as was seen by Goodspeed, who says that λυ is "by 1st hand over an erasure (of λυ?)." Of course, the scenario that the scribe first wrote λυ, then erased those letters and wrote λυ again is not very persuasive. But presumably Goodspeed came to this suggestion by seeing what appears to be the strokes of an α or λ between the present ο and λ and also what appears to be an υ between the present λ and υ. The only difference, then, would be that the scribe rewrote λυ in a broader fashion.

However, I suggest that what Sanders and Goodspeed take to be the original text below λυ is ρα (of βαραββαν in Luke 23:18) bleeding through from the other side of the folio. That is, the apparent upright of an υ between the present λ and υ is in fact the image of the ρ bleeding through, and the apparent λ between the present ο and λ is in fact the image of the α bleeding through.

Mark 2:19. Of νυμφιοι (a singular reading) Sanders says: "νυμ in ras man 1." But in fact we have letters bleeding through: ανθρ behind νυμ, as can be seen from the other side (from ανθρωπος of Mark 3:1). What is seen under the υ of νυμ is the ρ of the other side.

Mark 2:25. Of μετ αυτου, Sanders says, "εταυτ in ras man 1." But μα (of μαθηταις in Mark 3:9) of the reverse side is bleeding through under τα at least.

Summary

Including these cited corrections would hardly change the general analysis of the correcting activity to be found in W. (Luke 6:48 might provide one more example of a shift from one reading to another.) What we see, therefore, is that most of the corrections emended the initial transcriptional errors of the scribe of W to the text of the exemplar that the scribe was attempting to copy in the first place. Exactly half of the corrections were made by the scribe himself, as he caught his own errors in the course of his copying or during subsequent inspection of his own work. Most of the rest of the corrections were made by a second hand who, likewise, evidently intended to correct W to the parent text. Then two later readers made a few further changes of miscellaneous points that caught their eyes. The corrections made in W^{s} (the replacement first quire of John) are exclusively of minor slips of the scribe of that quire.

In this important codex of the Gospels at least, we see no consistent effort to shift W from one textual tradition ("text-type") to another, nor do we find evidence of any overall redaction of the text under the influence of doctrinal motives. Instead, essentially, Codex W reflects a concern simply to copy with reasonable care.

Appendix: Master List of Corrections in W and W^{S}

Matt 1:9 — εεννη | σεν W* : εγεννη | σεν *prim.* W$^{c\ (man\ 2)}$, ς, *rell*

Matt 2:11 — ζμυρναν W*, D : σμυρναν W$^{c\ (man\ 2)}$, ς, *rell*

Matt 2:17 — του προφητου *om.* W* : του προφητου W$^{c\ (man\ 2)}$, ς, *rell*

Matt 3:12 — αβεστω W* : ασβεστω W$^{c\ (man\ 2)}$, ς, B^{c} (ασβετω B*), *rell*

Matt 4:13 — καφαρναουμ W*, ℵ, B, D, Z, 0233, 33, 700* $^{(?)}$, *pc,* lat(t), co : καπερναουμ W$^{c\ (man\ 1)}$, ς, C, L, Γ, Δ, Θ (καπαρ—) f^{1}, f^{13}, 157, 565, 700$^{c\ (man\ 2\ ?)}$, *rell*

Matt 5:6 — δικαιοσυνην W*, ς, *rell* : δικαιωσυνην W$^{c\ (man\ 2)}$, Θ

Matt 6:7 — οτι *om.* W* : οτι W$^{c\ (man\ 2)}$, ς, *rell*

Matt 6:14	πα | ραπτωματα υτων W*, ℵ* : πα | ραπτωματα αυτων $W^{c\ (man\ 1\ in\ scribendo)}$, ς, ℵ[a], *rell*
Matt 6:20	ουδε W* : ουτε *prim.* $W^{c\ (man\ 1)}$, *rell* : ου 475*
Matt 7:8	αιτων *sec.* W* : ζητων $W^{c\ (man\ 2)}$, ς, *rell*
Matt 7:17	αγαθον *om.* W* : αγαθον $W^{c\ (man\ 2)}$, ς, *rell*
Matt 8:16	πνα (= πνευμα) *scripturus erat* W* *cum* M, Ω, 788 : πντα (= πνευματα) $W^{c\ (man\ 1\ in\ scribendo)}$, ς, *rell*
Matt 9:16	αγναφου W*, ς, *rell* (ακναφου 238, 476, 1071, *pc*) : αγναφους $W^{c\ (man\ 2)}$, C
Matt 10:14	των λογων W*, 1194 : τους λογους $W^{c\ (man\ 2)}$, ς, *rell*
Matt 12:31	τοις ανοις (= ανθρωποις) (*prim.*) | και ος εαν ειπη λογον κατα του υιου | (του ανου κτλ., ut v. 32) *scripturus erat* W* [vid] *cum* X, 579, *l*47, *pc*, a, g[1], l, for : τοις ανοις (= ανθρωποις) | η δε του πνς (= πνευματος) βλασφημια ουκ αφε | θησεται τοις ανθρωποις $W^{c\ (man\ 1\ in\ scribendo)}$, ς, *rell* (η δε του πνευματος *om.* 477, *l*181*; βλασφια E, 1071; τοις ανθρωποις (*sec.*) *cum* ς, C, D, L, Γ, Δ, Θ, 0271, f^{13}, 33, 157, *rell*, it, sy[p.h]; αυτοις F, 71, *pc;* αυτω (b) ff[1], h, sy[s.c], mae, bo[ms] : *om.* ℵ, B, f^{1}, 174, 892, 1424, *pc*, aur, g[2], k, vg, sa, bo, arm, aeth)
Matt 12:46	?? W* : εξω $W^{c\ (man\ 1)}$, ς, *rell*
Matt 13:38	εστι (= εστιν) W* : εισι (= εισιν) *sec.* $W^{c\ (man\ 1)}$, ς, *rell*
Matt 14:24	.... νιζομενον W* : βασανιζομενον $W^{c\ (man\ 2)}$, ς, *rell*
Matt 15:8	εγγιζει μοι ο λαος ουτος τω στοματι αυτων W*, Ω : εγγιζει μοι ο λαος ουτος τω στοματι αυτων και τοις χειλεσιν με τιμα $W^{c\ (man\ 2)}$, ς, C, N, Γ, Δ (*om.* ουτος) 0106, 118, 209, *rell* (εν τω 470; ο λαος ουτος εγγιζει μοι τοις χειλεσιν με τιμα f^{1}) : ο λαος ουτος τοις χειλεσιν με τιμα ℵ, B, D, L, Θ, 073, 084, f^{13}, 33, 579, 700, 892, 1424, *pc*, lat, sy[s.c.p], co, arm, aeth, Cl, Or
Matt 15:18–19	καρδιας εξερχεται διαλογισμοι W* : καρδιας εξερχονται διαλογισμοι $W^{c\ (man\ 2)}$, ℵ*, 33[vid], bo[ms] : καρδιας εξερχεται κακεινα κοινοι τον ανθρωπον εκ γαρ της καρδιας εξερχονται διαλογισμοι ς, ℵ[a], D[2], *rell* (εξερχονται *pro* εξερχεται F, M, Θ, 71, 1194, *al;* και εκεινα Θ, f^{13}, 1071, *al;* εκεινα D, *pc*, c, ff[2], bo; κοινωνει D[*.3], d; και *ante* διαλογισμοι *add.* 579; λογισμοι 71, *pc*)
Matt 16:24	αυτον W* : εαυτον $W^{c\ (man\ 1)}$, ς, *rell*
Matt 16:25	απολεση W*, ς, ℵ, B, C, Γ, *rell* : απολεσει *sec.* $W^{c\ (man\ 1)}$, D, H, L, Δ, 2*, 33, 174, 230, 346, 700* [(?)], 828, 1071, 1424, *al*
Matt 17:19	υμεις W*, 477, *l*181 : ημεις $W^{c\ (man\ 1)}$, ς, *rell*
Matt 17:25	οτε εισηλθεν ο ις (= ιησους) W* : οτε εισηλθεν $W^{c\ (man\ 1\ et\ man\ 2)}$, ς, L, Γ, Δ, 118, 157, 209, 565, 700, 1071, 1424, *rell* : εισελθοντα ℵ[*.cb], 579 : εισελθοντι D : ελθοντα ℵ[ca], B, f^{1}, 892 : οτε ηλθον C, 21, 399, *l*27 : οτε εισηλθον U, 1170, *al*, sy[c] : εισελθοντων Θ, f^{13} : ελθοντων αυτων 33
Matt 18:4	τουτου W* : εν τη βασιλεια $W^{c\ (man\ 1\ in\ scribendo)}$, ς, *rell*

Matt 18:31 δε (οι συνδουλοι αυτου κτλ.) *scripturus erat* W* : διεσαφησαν W^{c} $^{\text{(man 1 in scribendo)}}$, ς, *rell* (εσαφησαν 69)

Matt 19:1 γαλιλαιας *sec.* W* : ιουδαιας W$^{\text{c (man 1 in scribendo)}}$, ς, ℵ^{c}, *rell* (-δεας ℵ*, Θ)

Matt 19:8 επετρεψεν προς την σκληροκαρδιαν υμων W* (προς την σκληροκαρδιαν υμων επετρεψεν 892) : επετρεψεν υμιν προς την σκληροκαρδιαν υμων W$^{\text{c (man 2)}}$: προς την σκληροκαρδιαν υμων επετρεψεν υμιν ς, *rell* (μωυσης *post* υμιν *pon.* D; ημων *pro* υμων 579; εγραψεν 1424)

Matt 19:9 υμων W* : αυτου W$^{\text{c (man 1)}}$, ς, *rell*

Matt 20:12 αυτον W* : αυτους W$^{\text{c (man 1)}}$, ς, *rell* : *om.* 543

Matt 21:19 επ αυτη W*, 692, *l*150* *semel, l*185 (*om.* 945, 990, 1424) : εν αυτη W$^{\text{c (man 1)}}$, ς, *rell*

Matt 21:30 απεκριθη W* : απεκριθεις W$^{\text{c (man 1 in scribendo)}}$: αποκριθεις ς, *rell* (αποκριθης 579)

Matt 21:32a ουκ *om.* W* : ουκ W$^{\text{c (man 2)}}$, ς, *rell*

Matt 21:32b επιστευσατο W* (?) : επιστευσατε W$^{\text{c (man 1)}}$, ς, *rell* (-σαν 1424)

Matt 21:32c επιστευ... W* (?) : επιστευσαν W$^{\text{c (man 1)}}$, ς, *rell*

Matt 22:7 υβρισθη W* : ωργισθη W$^{\text{c (man 1)}}$,ς, *rell*

Matt 22:22 απηλθαν W*, B, D, *pc* : απηλθον W$^{\text{c (man 2)}}$, ς, ℵ, L, Δ, Θ, *rell*

Matt 23:37 λιθοβολησουσα W* : λιθοβολησασα W$^{\text{c (man 1)}}$, Thret (*Interpretatio in quatuordecim epistolas Sancti Pauli,* ad Hebraeos 11:37 [PG 82.769A9]) : λιθοβολουσα ς, *rell*

Matt 24:2 ωδε *om.* W*, g^{1}, r^{1} : ωδε W$^{\text{c (man 2)}}$, ς, *rell* (*post* λιθος *pon.* 047)

Matt 24:24 μεγαλα *om.* W*, ℵ, 273, ff^{1}, r^{1}, vg^{ms}, bo^{ms} : μεγαλα W$^{\text{c (man 2)}}$, ς, *rell* (*post* τερατα *pon.* 28, 300, 1241, 1424, *pc,* bo^{ms})

Matt 24:32a ο κλαδος W* : το κλαδος W$^{\text{c1 (man 2 vid)}}$: ο κλαδος W$^{\text{c2 (man ?)}}$, ς, *rell*

Matt 24:32b εγγυς W* (?), ς, *rell* (ενγυς D) : ευθυς W$^{\text{c (man 3)}}$

Matt 25:9 φρονιμοι W*, ς, *rell* : φρονιμαι W$^{\text{c (man 2)}}$, Σ

Matt 25:34 κληρονομησητε W* : κληρονομησατε W$^{\text{c (man 1)}}$, ς, *rell*

Matt 26:41 εισερ | (χησθε) *scripturus erat* W* : εισελ | θητε W$^{\text{c (man 1 in scribendo)}}$, ς, *rell* (F?) : ελθητε 𝔓^{37}, b, ff^{2}

Matt 27:4 οι δ ι(πον) *scripturus erat* W* : οι δε ειπον W$^{\text{c (man 1 in scribendo)}}$, ς, *rell* (ειπαν L, *f*^{13}, 33)

Matt 27:17 ι(ησουν) *aut* ῑ(ν̄) *scripturus erat* W* (?) : η W$^{\text{c (man 1 in scribendo vid)}}$, ς, *rell*

Matt 27:46 θε W* : θεε *prim.* W$^{\text{c (man 1)}}$, ς, *rell* (*vel* $\overline{\text{θε}}$; θεε μου *unum om.* 482)

Matt 27:55 διακονησαι W* : διακονουσαι W$^{\text{c (man 2)}}$, ς, *rell*

(The corrections in the first quire of John, i.e., W^{s}, which contains John 1:1–5:11a [εν αρχη – αρον τον], are cited at the end of this list.)

John 5:19 αμη W* : αμην *prim.* W$^{\text{c (man 3)}}$, ς, *rell* (ℵ*, 1241, sy^{s}, *om.* αμην *semel,* ℵ^{c} *corr.*)

John 6:18 διηγειρι(το) *scripturus erat* W* : διηγειρετο W$^{\text{c (man 1 in scribendo)}}$, ς, ℵ, A, D, K, Γ, Δ, f^{1}, *rell* (διηγηρετο Θ, 28 : διηγηρετω 579) : διεγειρετο 𝔓$^{\text{28}}$ (διεγε[) B, G, L, U, V, Λ, f^{13}, 1010, 1093, 1170, 1241, *al* : δ̣[ιεγειρ]αṭο vel δ̣[ιηγειρ]αṭο 𝔓$^{\text{75}}$

John 6:53 μη *om.* W* : μη W$^{\text{c (man 4)}}$, ς, *rell*

John 8:12 και ειπεν W* : λεγων W$^{\text{c (man 2)}}$, ς, *rell*

John 8:46 λεγω W$^{\text{* vid}}$: λεγω δια τι W$^{\text{c (man 3)}}$, ς, *rell* (δια τι υμεις *om.* V, 28)

John 9:6 τυ τυφλου W* : του τυφλου W$^{\text{c (man 4)}}$, ς, A, C, K, M, U, X, Γ, Δ, Λ, Π, Ψ, Ω, f^{13}, 28, 157, 579, 700, 1424, *rell,* b, e, f, sy, (bo) : αυτου D, N, 544, 892, 1241, *pc,* lat : *plane om.* 𝔓$^{\text{66}}$, 𝔓$^{\text{75}}$, ℵ, B, L, Θ, 070, 0216^{vid}, f^{1}, 33, 565, *pc*

John 9:21 τις (ηνεωξεν) *scripturus erat* W* : η τις W$^{\text{c (man 1 in scribendo)}}$, ς, *rell*

John 9:23 ειπον W*, ς, 𝔓$^{\text{66}}$, A, K, L, M, N, U, Δ, Θ, Λ, Ψ, f^{1}, 28, 157, 565, 579, 700, 892, 1071, *rell* (*ante* οι γονεις *pon.* X, f^{13}, 249, 330, 1424, *pc*) : ειπαν W$^{\text{c (man 4)}}$, 𝔓$^{\text{75}}$, ℵ, B, D

John 10:16 εκ *om.* W* l : εκ W$^{\text{c (man 1)}}$, ς, *rell*

John 10:17 αυτα W* : αυτην W$^{\text{c (man 1 in scribendo)}}$, ς, *rell* : υπερ των προβατων *pro* ινα παλιν λαβω αυτην 157

John 10:18 απο W*, 157 : παρα W$^{\text{c (man 1)}}$, ς, *rell* (παρ αυτου *pro* παρα του Δ)

John 10:30 ο πατηρ μου W*, Δ, 71, 247, 1279, *l*44, e, sy$^{\text{s.p}}$, co : ο πατηρ W$^{\text{c (man 1)}}$, ς, *rell*

John 11:7 τοις μαθηταις αυτου (αγωμεν) *scripturus erat* W* *cum* A, D, K, Γ, Δ, Λ, Π, 0233, f^{13}, 28, 157, 472, *l*844, *al,* lat (*et* l$^{\text{c (man 2)}}$), sy, co, aeth : τοις μαθηται αγωμεν W$^{\text{c (man 1 in scribendo)}}$: τοις μαθηταις αγωμεν ς, 𝔓$^{\text{6 vid}}$, 𝔓$^{\text{66c}}$, 𝔓$^{\text{75}}$, ℵ, B, L, Θ, Ψ, 0250, f^{1}, 33, *rell,* a, got : αυτοις αγωμεν 𝔓$^{\text{66*}}$, arm : αγωμεν 𝔓$^{\text{45}}$, e, l*

John 11:9 τουτου *om.* W* : τουτου W$^{\text{c (man 2)}}$, ς, *rell*

John 11:18 ως *om.* W*, D, 265, sy^{s} : ως W$^{\text{c (man 2)}}$, ς, *rell*

John 11:24 αναστησιται W* : αναστησεται W$^{\text{c (man 1)}}$, ς, *rell*

John 11:33 αυτη *om.* W*, 1354 : αυτη W$^{\text{c (man 2)}}$, ς, *rell* (μετ αυτης D; συν αυτη 𝔓$^{\text{66}}$, 954, 1424)

John 16:22 εξεται (= εξετε) W*, 𝔓$^{\text{66}}$, ℵ^{c}, A, D, L, N, Θ, Π, Ψ, 33, 157, *l*844, *al,* it, vg^{mss} : εχεται (= εχετε) W$^{\text{c (man 2)}}$, ς, 𝔓$^{\text{22}}$, ℵ*, B, C, Γ, Δ, f^{1}, f^{13}, *rell,* lat

John 17:22 δεδωκας W*, ς, ℵ, B, C, L, X, Γ, Δ, f^{1}, f^{13}, *rell* : εδωκας W$^{\text{c (man 1 et man 2)}}$, A, D, N, U, Θ, Π, Ψ, 047, 157, 248, 482, 489, 544, 579, *l*844, *al,* Cl

John 17:24 θεωρουσιν W* : θεωρωσιν W$^{\text{c (man 2)}}$, ς, *rell*

John 18:40 βαρραβαν W* : βαραββαν W$^{\text{c (man 1)}}$, ς, *rell* (βαρραββαν Θ; βαραβαν 69, 71*, 486; βαραββα *l*184)

John 19:9 και | και W* : | και *sec.* W$^{\text{c (man 1)}}$, ς, *rell*

John 21:17 προβατα W*, ς, ℵ, D, Γ, Δ, Θ, Ψ, f^{1}, f^{13}, 33^{vid}, *rell*, sy : προβατια W$^{\text{c (man 2)}}$, A, B, C, 22, 565, 1582*, *pc* : αρνια Λ, 33

Luke 1:6 πασῃ. W* : πασαις W$^{\text{c (man 1)}}$, ς, *rell* (*om.* 544)

Luke 4:18 τεθραμμενους W* ^{vid}, 0211, 489, *pc* (τεθραμενους 179) : τεθραυμενους W$^{\text{c (man 3)}}$, D^{2}, 1187*, 1542, 2643 : τεθραυσμενους ς, *rell* (τεθραυματισμενους D$^{*.3}$; τεθρασμενους 2613*, *l*181)

Luke 4:36 δυναμε W* : δυναμει W$^{\text{c (man 1)}}$, ς, *rell*

Luke 5:25 πα̅ | των (= παντων) W*, f^{13}, 157, 213, 1604, *l*47, *pc*, a, arm : αυ | των W$^{\text{c (man 1)}}$, ς, *rell* : αυτου ℵ, *l*854 : αυτων παντων 111, 124, 1038, sa^{ms}

Luke 5:37 απολλυνται W* : απολουνται W$^{\text{c (man 3 vid)}}$, ς, *rell*

Luke 6:1 ετελλον W* : ετιλλον W$^{\text{c (man 1)}}$, ς, *rell* (ετειλον 69; ηρξαντο τιλλειν D)

Luke 6:8 χειραν W*, 472, 474, *l*185 : χειρα W$^{\text{c (man 1 in scribendo)}}$, ς, *rell*

Luke 6:26 ουαι υμιν W*, ς, D, Δ, 2, 13, 69, 1424, *pc*, b, r^{1}, sy$^{\text{s.p}}$, co, arm, aeth, Ir^{lat} : ουαι W$^{\text{c (man 1)}}$, 𝔓^{75}, ℵ, A, B, C, L, X, Γ, Λ, Π, f^{1}, 157, 892, *rell* : και ουαι 700

Luke 6:37 ινα W*, D, it, sy^{s}, sa, aeth, Mcion^{T} : και ου *sec.* W$^{\text{c (man 2)}}$, ς, *rell*, lat (και και ου 69)

Luke 7:3 αυτω W*, *l*1056 : αυτον *sec.* W$^{\text{c (man 3)}}$, ς, *rell* (αυτων 2, 346, *l*253, *l*524, *l*859)

Luke 7:22 ειδατε W*, A (ιδ-), f^{13}, (ιδ- 346) : ειδετε W$^{\text{c (man 3)}}$, ς, *rell* (ειδ- ℵ, B, E, F, G, L, Δ, Θ, Λ, f^{1}, 579, *pm;* ιδ- H, K, V, X, Γ, Π, Ψ, 33, 892, *pm*) : οιδατε 483*, 2643 : ειδον υμων οι οφθαλμοι D^{2} (οφθι- D*), e : βλεπετε 69, 1574

Luke 7:30 αυτους W*, 33, 115, 273, 489*, 1606 : εαυτους W$^{\text{c (man 1)}}$, ς, *rell* (σεαυτους 1691) : εις εαυτους *om.* ℵ, D, *pc*, sa, aeth

Luke 7:38 αυτου *tert.* W*, 2766 : αυτης W$^{\text{c (man 1)}}$, ς, *rell* : *om.* 1242*

Luke 7:49 προς αυτους W* : προς εαυτους W$^{\text{c (man 1)}}$: εν εαυτοις ς, *rell* (εν αυτοις Δ) : αυτοις 69*

Luke 8:2 εκβεβληκει W* ^{vid}, 1338, 1424, 1555, 2487, r^{1}, sy^{c} : εξεληλυθει W$^{\text{c (man 1 in scribendo)}}$, ς, ℵ, A, B, C, D, Γ, Δ, Θ, Λ, 0211, *rell*

Luke 8:6 ?? W* : δια το | W$^{\text{c (man 1)}}$, ς, ℵ$^{\text{c et fortasse iam a}}$, *rell* (και δια το ℵ*)

Luke 8:7 απεπνιξον W* ^{vid} : απεπνιξαν W$^{\text{c (man 1 vid)}}$, ς, ℵ^{ca}, *rell* (επνιξαν ℵ*; ανεπνιξον *l*299)

Luke 8:10 συνωσιν W*, f^{1}, 157, 579, 1071, 1424, *pc* : συνιωσιν W$^{\text{c (man 1)}}$, ς, 118, 131, 209, *rell* (ακουσωσιν 2643; ακουωσιν 1047, *l*524)

Luke 8:21 αυ(τοις) *scripturus erat* W* *cum* D, 127, 279, 569, 579, 2643, c, e, Bas : προς αυτους W$^{\text{c (man 1 in scribendo)}}$, ς, *rell* : προς αυτον 𝔓^{75}, b*

Luke 8:42 συν | εθριβον α(υτον) *scripturus erat* W* *pro* συνεθλιβον αυτον *cum* C, L, U, Θ, f^{13}, 28, 33, 157, 472, 892, 1071, *al* (συνεθληβον *l*183; συνεθλιβλον C; συνεθλιγον U, 33; αυτω 1009, *l*1016) : συν

| επνιγον αυτον W$^{\text{c (man 1 in scribendo)}}$, ς, *rell* (απεπνιγον 1573; αυτω 716)

Luke 8:49 απο W*, A, D, Θ, f^1, 472, 700, 1071, 1424, *pc* : παρα W$^{\text{c (man 2)}}$, ς, *rell* (παρ αυτου *pro* παρα του Δ*) : εκ 579, 2643

Luke 9:9 τι W* : τις W$^{\text{c (man 2)}}$, ς, *rell*

Lukc 9:38 δαιομαι W*, Δ, 2* : δεομαι W$^{\text{c (man 2)}}$, ς, *rell*

Luke 9:52 αυτου W*, ς, $\mathfrak{P}^{75}$, ℵ, B, C, D, L, Γ, Δ, Θ, Π, f^1, 33, 69*, 157, 565, 579, 700, 892, *rell* : εαυτου W$^{\text{c (man 2)}}$, A, Λ, Ω, f^{13} (69^{c}), 472, *pm* : *om.* $\mathfrak{P}^{45}$: αυτω 1071*

Luke 10:11a υμιν *prim.* W*, ℵ*, D$^{\text{gr 2}}$, Θ, Λ, f^{13}, 565, 892, 1424, *pc* : ημιν W$^{\text{c (man 1)}}$, ς, ℵ^{a}, D*, f^1, *rell* : *om.* 131, sy$^{\text{s.c}}$ (*et* εκ της πολεως υμων *om.*)

Luke 10:11b υμων *om.* W*, $\mathfrak{P}^{45}$, 892, vg$^{\text{ms*}}$: υμων W$^{\text{c (man 2)}}$, ς, *rell* (υμην 201*; ημων 440)

Luke 11:4 οφιλομεν W*, 2757 (οφει—), 2643 (ωφει—) : αφειομεν W$^{\text{c (man 1)}}$ $\mathfrak{P}^{75}$, ℵ^{c}, A, B, C, D, K, P^{vid}, Γ, Δ, Λ, Ψ, 047, f^{13}, 1, 472, 579, 1187, *al* : αφιεμεν ς, ℵ*, L, X, Θ, Ξ, Π, 070, 33, 118, 131, 157, 209, 892, 1241, *rell*

Luke 11:6 αγρου W$^{\text{* vid}}$, D (*sed* παρεστιν απ *pro* παρεγενετο εξ), aeth : οδου W$^{\text{c (man 1)}}$, ς, *rell* (εξολου 2766)

Luke 11:49 αποκτενουσῑ (= αποκτενουσιν) W*, ς, ℵ^{c}, *rell* : αποκτεινουσῑ (= αποκτεινουσιν) W$^{\text{c (man 2)}}$, ℵ*, X : αποκτενειτε 124, *l*950, c

Luke 11:54 κατηγορησουσιν W*, A, X, Δ, f^{13}, 1071, *pc* : κατηγορησωσιν W$^{\text{c (man 2)}}$, ς, C, Γ, Δ, Θ, Λ, Π, Ψ, f^1, 33, *rell*, lat, vg, sy^{h}, arm (κατηγωρησιας 892$^{\text{c (?)}}$; ευρωσιν κατηγορησαι D, f, sy$^{\text{c.p}}$) : ινα κατηγορησωσιν αυτου *om.* $\mathfrak{P}^{45}$, $\mathfrak{P}^{75}$, ℵ, B, L, 579, 892*, 1241, 2542, *pc*, co, aeth

Luke 12:17 σῡ | αξαι (= συναξαι) W*, Λ, f^{13}, *pc* : σῡ | αξω (= συναξω) W$^{\text{c (man 2)}}$, ς, *rell* (συναξειν 1093)

Luke 12:30 τα εθνη W*, N, Ψ, 40, 63, 213, 482, *al*, l : τα εθνη του κοσμου W$^{\text{c (man 2)}}$, ς, *rell* (του κοσμου *post* επιζητ. *pon.* Γ, *l*299*)

Luke 12:47 αυτου *prim.* W*, $\mathfrak{P}^{45}$, $\mathfrak{P}^{75}$, ℵ, B, D, E*, K, L, X, Θ, Π, Ψ, 070, f^1, f^{13}, 28, 33, 157, 472, 700, 892, 1071, 1424, *pm* : εαυτου W$^{\text{c (man 2)}}$, ς, A, E^{2}, Γ, Δ, Λ, *rell*

Luke 12:50 εως W* : εως οπου W$^{\text{c (man 2)}}$: εως οτου $\mathfrak{P}^{45}$, $\mathfrak{P}^{75}$, ℵ, A, B, D, K, L, Θ, Π, Ψ, 070, f^{13}, 33, 157, 472, 489, 892, 1241, *pm* : εως ου ς E, S, X, Γ, Δ, Λ, f^1, 565, 700, *rell* : εως οτι ου 579

Luke 13:35 αν ηξοι (*vel* ηξθι) οτε W* : αν ηξει οτε W$^{\text{c (man 1 [in scribendo?])}}$, A, N, S, Δ, Λ, Ω, 2, 28, 489^{c} (εξει, εως … ηξει *om.* 489*), 1424, *rell* (ηξη ς, Γ, Ψ, f^1, 565, 700, *pm*) : ηξει οτε D, 047, 2487 : αν $\mathfrak{P}^{45}$, ℵ, M, N, X, Θ, f^{13}, 71, 157, 1071, 1241, 2542, *pc* : *plane om.* $\mathfrak{P}^{75}$, B, L, R, 79, 892, *pc* : οτε K, Π, 265, 489*, 1079, 1219 : αν ηξει οταν 343, 579, 716 : αν ηξη οτι H, 0211, 827, *l*211 : αν ηξη και 1313 c

Luke 15:30 σιτευτον W*, ς, *rell* : σιτιστον W$^{\text{c (man 2)}}$: σιτευρον Δ

Luke 16:1	αυτου *prim.* W*, ς, A, X, Γ, Δ, Θ, Λ, Π, Ψ, *f*^{1}, *f*^{13}, 33, 157, 565, 892, *rell*, lat, sy, sa, bo^{pt} : εαυτου W$^{\text{c (man 2)}}$: *om.* 𝔓^{75}, ℵ, B, D, L, R, 69, 579, 788, 1071, 1241, 2542, *pc*, e, bo^{pt}, arm
Luke 16:9	ποιησα | τε α(υτοις) *scripturus erat* W* *cum* Pseudo-Nil (*Peristeria* 9.6 [PG 79.876A7–8]: ποιήσατε αὑτοῖς) : ποιησα | τε εαυτοις W$^{\text{c (man 1 in scribendo)}}$, ς, ℵ^{a}, A, D, X, Γ, Δ, Θ, Λ, Ψ, 070, *f*^{1}, *f*^{13}, 33^{vid}, *rell*, Ir^{lat}, Cl (εαυτοις *post* φιλους 579, εαυτους H, Π, Ω, *al;* ημιν 1010; υμιν 1215, 1295; υμιν εαυτοις 230, 348, 477, 1216, 1579) : εαυτοις ποιησατε 𝔓^{75}, ℵ*, B, L, R, *pc* : ποιησατε *tantum* 1220*, aeth^{ms}
Luke 17:1	ουδε W* : ουε (= ουαι) δε W$^{\text{c (man 4)}}$, ς, A, X, Γ, Δ, Θ, Λ, Π, *rell*, lat, sy$^{\text{p.h}}$, arm : πλην ουαι 𝔓^{75}, ℵ, B, D, L, Ψ, *f*^{1}, *f*^{13}, 33, 157, 892, 1241, 2542, *pc*, it, sy$^{\text{s.c.hmg}}$, co, arm : πλην ουαι δε 346, 579
Luke 17:20	ποτε | ποτε W* (ποτε πωτε 579) : | ποτε W$^{\text{c (man 1)}}$, ς, *rell* (τοτε 1319*, 1352; οτε 1077)
Luke 17:34	αφεθησεται και αποκριθεντες λεγου | (σιν κτλ., ut v. 37) *scripturus erat* W* *cum* ℵ*, *pc* : αφεθησεται W$^{\text{c (man 1 in scribendo)}}$, ς, ℵ^{a}, *rell* : αφιεται D, K, 063, 116, *pc*, got
Luke 18:16	προς ημ(ας) *scripturus erat* W* ^{vid} : προς εμε W$^{\text{c (man 1 in scribendo)}}$: προς με ς, *rell*
Luke 18:43	ηκολουθησεν W*, 565 (-θεισεν), *pc* (ηκολοθησαν *l*1016) : ηκολουθει W$^{\text{c (man 1)}}$, ς, *rell* (-θη K, Θ, 2, 471, 579, 1071, *l*181, *l*184)
Luke 19:1	εισελθων W*, ς, *rell* : εξελθων W$^{\text{c (man 2)}}$, 0211
Luke 19:23	μου το αργυριον W*, ℵ, A, B, L, Θ, Ψ, 0182, 33, 157, 475, 579^{vid}, 892, 1241, 2542, *l*48, *pc* : το αργυριον μου W$^{\text{c (man 1)}}$, ς, D, Γ, Δ, Λ, Π, *f*^{1}, *f*^{13}, 1071, *rell* : μου το αργυριον μου N : το αργυριον 1012, *l*1127*
Luke 20:1	επεστησαν αυτω | W*, 472, *pc*, sy$^{\text{s.c.p.h}}$, arm : επεστησαν W$^{\text{c (man 1)}}$, ς, *rell* (επετιμησαν 270; *add.* αυτων 1604)
Luke 20:26	εσιωπησαν W*, 1009, 1241 : εσιγησαν W$^{\text{c (man 2)}}$, ς, *rell*
Luke 20:35	των νεκρων W*, 440, 544, 1365, 2643, *pc*, c : της εκ νεκρων W$^{\text{c (man 2)}}$, ς, *rell* (εκ *om.* 60)
Luke 21:5	κεκοσμητο W* : κεκοσμητε (= κεκοσμηται) W$^{\text{c (man 2)}}$, ς, *rell* : κεκαλλωπισται 1241
Luke 21:6	λιθον *prim.* W* : λιθος W$^{\text{c (man 1)}}$, ς, *rell*
Luke 21:33	παρελευσεται W*, C, K, Θ, Π, *f*^{1}, 579, 892, 1241, 1424, *al*, a, e, q : παρελευσονται *prim.* W$^{\text{c (man 2)}}$, ς, ℵ, A, B, D, K, L, N, X, Γ, Δ, Λ, Ψ, *f*^{13}, 33, 157, 565, 700, 1071, *rell*, lat : σαλευθησονται *pc*
Luke 21:34	επιστη ημερα W*, K, V, Δ, *f*^{13}, 440, *pc* (επιστη εφ υμας ενιφνιος ημερα D*; επιστη εφ υμας εφνιος ημερα D^{2}) : επιστη η ημερα W$^{\text{c (man 2)}}$, ς, C, M, X, Γ, Δ, Θ, Λ, Π, *f*^{1}, 33, 346, 565, 700, *rell* (επιστη εφ υμας αιφνιδιος η ημερα ℵ, B, L, R, 77, 157, 579; επιστη εφ υμας η ημερα A, N, Ψ, 16 (ημας) 1071, 1424, 2542, 2643, *pc*)

Luke 22:12	αναγιον W* : αναγεον W$^{c\ (man\ 1)}$, C, 471, 478, 700 (αναγεων 579) : αναγαιον 𝔓$^{75\ vid}$, ℵ, A, B, D, L, Δ, Θ, Π*, 131, 892, 1424, *pm* : ανωγεον ς, X, Γ, f^1, f^{13}, *pm* (ανογεον 047) : ανωγαιον S*, U, Λ, Π², Ψ, Ω, 565, 1582*, *pm* (ανογαιον Y, 1071, *pc*; ανωγαιων 1200) : ανωγεων 69, 157, 1582^c, *al* (ανωγαιαν 34; ανογεων *pc*) : ανωγειων 71
Luke 22:18	εως του W* : εως οτου W$^{c\ (man\ 2)}$, ς, A, D, Γ, Δ, Θ, Λ, Π, Ψ, f^{13}, 565, 700, 1071, 1424, *rell* : εως ου ℵ, B, C^{vid}, F, L, f^1, 157, 579, 892, 2542, *pc* : εως αν 1241 : εως αν οτου E*
Luke 22:37	πληρωθηναι W*, Λ, 124, 262, 482, 1187, *pc*, sy$^{s.c.p}$: τελεσθηναι W$^{c\ (man\ 2)}$, ς, *rell* (τελεσθη *l*80)
Luke 22:39	εθος τω(ν ελαιων κτλ.) *scripturus erat* W* : εθος εις W$^{c\ (man\ 1\ in\ scribendo)}$, ς, *rell* (κατα το εθος *post* ελαιων N)
Luke 23:9	απεκρινατο αυτον W* ^{vid}, Γ, 2*, 579, *l*150, *l*185 *semel*, *pc* : απεκρινατο αυτω W$^{c\ (man\ 1)}$, ς, *rell* (αυτου *l*211; αυτω *om.* 213, *l*184, *l*185 *semel*, *pc*, e, g^1, q, vg^{mss})
Luke 23:12	ηρωδης W*, H, S, U, Θ, Ω, 69, 346, 472, 565, 788, 1582, *al* : ο ηρωδης W$^{c\ (man\ 1)}$, ς, A, D, Γ, Δ, Λ, Π, f^1, f^{13}, 28, 700, *rell*, sy^p, bo, arm (ο τε ηρωδης και ο πιλατος 𝔓^{75}, ℵ, B, L, T, Ψ, 0124, 124, 579, 892, 1071, 1241, 1424, *pc*, lat, sa, bo^{ms}, sy^c, aeth)
Luke 23:21	σταυρωσον σταυρω(σον αυτον κτλ.) *scripturus erat* W* *cum* ς, A, L, X, Γ, Δ, Θ, Λ, Π, Ψ, f^1, f^{13}, *rell* lat (αυτον *om.* 1215*) : σταυρωσον αυτον W$^{c\ (man\ 1\ in\ scribendo)}$, U, 0250, 157, *pc*, it, vg^{ms}, bo^{ms}, arm, aeth : σταυρου σταυρου αυτον 𝔓^{75}, ℵ, B, D² (τον D*), 070
Luke 23:34	αυτων W* : αυτου W$^{c\ (man\ 1)}$, ς, *rell*
Luke 23:43	τη | μερον W* : ση | μερον W$^{c\ (man\ 1)}$, ς, *rell*
Luke 24:14	ωμιλουν περι παντων (των συμβ. κτλ.) *scripturus erat* W* *cum* Λ, 245, 262, 1187*, 1443, 1573, a, b, ff², l, r^1, gat : ωμιλουν προς αλληλους περι παντων W$^{c\ (man\ 1\ in\ scribendo)}$, ς, *rell* : ωμειλουν δε προς εαυτους περι παντων D (c e)
Luke 24:22	ορθειναι W* : ορθρειναι W$^{c\ (man\ 2)}$, 𝔓^{75}, ℵ, A, B, D, K*, L, Δ, Π, 0124, 0211, 1, 1582*, *pc* : ορθριαι ς, K², X, Γ, Θ, Λ, Ψ, f^1, f^{13}, 33, 579, 892, 1241, *rell*
Luke 24:34	ηγερθη ο $\overline{κς}$ (= κυριος) W*, 213, 258*, *l*890, b, e, l : ηγερθη ο $\overline{κς}$ (= κυριος) οντως W$^{c\ (man\ 2)}$, ς, A, K, X, Γ, Δ, Θ, Λ, Π, f^{13}, 33, *rell*, aur, vg, sy^h : οντως *ante* ηγερθη *pon.* 𝔓^{75}, ℵ, B, D, L, P, Ψ, f^1, 157, 579, 1071, *l*844, *l*2211, *pc*, it, vg^{mss}, sy$^{s.c.p}$, co, arm, aeth : οντως *post* ηγερθη *pon.* 66, 1005, 1365
Luke 24:50	εως βηθανιας W*, e (εως βηθανιαν 237, 1279, 1338, 1630, *l*1016 [βιθ—] *pc*) : εως εις βηθανιαν W$^{c\ (man\ 2)}$, ς, A, C³, X, Γ, Δ, Θ, Λ, Π, Ψ, f^{13}, 157, 565, 700, 892, 1071, 1241, 1582^c, *rell* : εως προς βηθανιαν 𝔓^{75}, ℵ, B, C*, L, 1, 33, 579, 1582*, *pc*, a : εις βηθανιαν 5, 118, 131, 209, 1012, *l*524, *l*890 : προς βηθανιαν D

Mark 1:3 κα (*ante* οφθη | σεται) W* : και W$^{\text{c (man 1)}}$: *om.* ς, *rell*

Mark 2:25a ο W*, 700 : τι W$^{\text{c (man 2)}}$, ς, *rell* : οτι 1082

Mark 2:25b ι(ησεν) *pro* εποιησεν *scripturus erat* W* ^{vid} : εποιησεν W$^{\text{c (man 1 in scribendo)}}$, ς, *rell* (εποιεισεν K, σε *super lineam* 69^{c}, 69* *non liquet*)

Mark 3:10 αυτου αψωνται W*, ς, B^{c}, *rell* (αψων C, απτωνται K, U, Θ, Π, 489 *pc*) : αυτω αψωνται W$^{\text{c (man 2)}}$, F, f^{13} : αυτον αψωνται B*, 828 : τουτου αψωνται 476

Mark 4:17 σκανδαλιζεται W* : σκανδαλιζονται W$^{\text{c (man 2)}}$, ς, *rell* (-λισθησονται D)

Mark 4:31 μικροτερον ω̅ (= ων) W*, L : μικροτερος ω̅ (= ων) W$^{\text{c (man 2)}}$: μικροτερον ον ℵ, B, Δ, Θ, 892, 1071 : μικροτερον εστιν D* : μικροτερον *et* εστιν *post* σπερματων M* (μηκρ-), 2, 13, 28, 33, 482, 579, 700, 1424 : μηκροτερον εστιν *et* εστιν *post* σπερματων M^{2} : μικροτερος μεν εστιν D^{2} (μικροτερος *et* εστιν *post* σπερματων ς, C, N, Π, 0107, f^{1}, f^{13}, 157, 565, *rell;* εστιν *post* γης A; μικροτερος εστιν *l*185)

Mark 4:32 σπερματων W* ?? : λαχανων και W$^{\text{c (man 1 in scribendo)}}$ *cum* ℵ, B, C, D, L, Δ, Θ (-νον Θ*), f^{1}, 28, 33, 565, 579, 700, 892, 1071, 1241, 1424, 2427, 2542, *pm* (μειζων *post* λαχανων *pon.* ς, A, E, K, Π, Ψ, Ω, f^{13}, 157, *rell*)

Mark 5:1 τη χωραν W* : την χωραν W$^{\text{c (man 3)}}$, ς, *rell*

Mark 5:2 αυτω | τ(ω) *scripturus erat* W* (?) : αυτω | α̅ν̅ο̅ς̅ (= ανθρωπος) W$^{\text{c (man 1 in scribendo vid)}}$, D, Θ, 565, 700, it, arm, got : ανθρωπος *post* μνημειων *pon.* ς, *rell,* lat : ανθρωπος *om.* 13

Mark 6:14 δυναμεις αυτου W*, 4, 273 : δυναμεις αυτω W$^{\text{c (man 2)}}$, 2, 485*, *l*88 : δυναμεις εν αυτω ς, *rell* : ενεργουσιν εν αυτω *post* δυναμεις *pon.* K, N, Δ, Θ, Π, 1, 13, 33, 472, 565, 579, 1424, *al*

Mark 6:16 οτι εγω | ον W* : οτι ον εγω | ον W$^{\text{c (man 2)}}$: οτι ον εγω ς, 𝔓^{45}, A, C, N, Δ, Π, 0269, f^{13}, 157, 579, 1071, 1424, *rell,* sy^{h}, bo, got : ον εγω ℵ, B, D, L, Θ, f^{1}, 28, 33, 124, 565, 700, 892, 2427, *pc,* latt, sy$^{\text{s.p}}$, arm, aeth : οτι εγω 473* : οτι ον 11

Mark 6:27 φυλακει W* : φυλακη W$^{\text{c (man 1)}}$, ς, *rell*

Mark 6:32 κα (*ante* απηλθο̅ [= απηλθον]) W* : και W$^{\text{c (man 2)}}$, ς, *rell*

Mark 7:15 αυτο ο W* : αυτον ο W$^{\text{c (man 2)}}$, ς, *rell* : αυτον ον 472 : αυτον *et* ο *ante* εισπορευομενον Δ, a, n : αυτον ου 579, *l*184 : αυτον *et* το κοινουν αυτον *pro* ο δυναται αυτον κοινωσαι αυτον B, 2427

Mark 7:21 φονοι W*, ς, *rell* : φονος W$^{\text{c (man 1)}}$, D, 28* : *om.* 28^{c}, g^{1}

Mark 7:22 πλεονεξιαι W*, ς, ℵ, A, B, Θ, f^{1}, f^{13}, 33, *rell,* lat : πλεονεξια W$^{\text{c (man ?)}}$, D, 28, 565, it : *om.* 1515

Mark 8:19 πεντακισχιλι | ους W*, ς, ℵ, C, L, N, Γ, Δ, Θ, f^{1}, f^{13}, 33, 157, 565, 700, 1424, *rell* : πεντακισχειλι | ους W$^{\text{c (man 2)}}$, 𝔓^{45}, A, B, D, 28^{c}, (πενκι— 28*) : επτακισχιλιους 2145

Mark 8:25 ανεβλεπεν W*, Δ, 346, 983 : ενεβλεπεν W$^{c\ (\text{man } 2)}$, ℵ^{c}, B, L, f^{13}, 28, 440 : ενεβλεψεν ς, A, C, M^{2}, Γ, Π, Ω, f^{1}, 33, 1071, *rell* : εβλεψεν ℵ*, Θ, 348, 565, 1093 : ανεβλεψεν F, H, M*, 124, 157, 700, 892, 1424, *pm* : εβλεπεν 244 ; αναβλεψαι D, latt (*et* ωστε *pro* και) : και ενεβλεψεν *om.* 579

Mark 8:31 απο W*, ς, A, X, Γ, Δ, Θ, f^{1}, f^{13}, 28, 157, 565, 579, 700, *rell* : υπο W$^{c\ (\text{man } 1)}$, ℵ, B, C, D, G, K, L, N, Π, Σ, Φ, 33, 473, 489, 892, 1071, 1424, *pc*

Mark 10:2 επηρωτησαν αυτου W* : επηρωτησαν αυτον W$^{c\ (\text{man } 2)}$, ς, A, K, N, X, Γ, Π, f^{1}, f^{13}, 28, 157, 700, 1424, *rell* (επηρωτων ℵ, B, D, L, M, Θ, Ψ, 892, 1071, *pc;* επηρουν C; ηρωτων Δ*;* επερωτων 565; επηρωτουν 472; επηρωτον *l*184; υπηρωτων 579)

Mark 10:35 προσελθοντες W* : προσελθον W$^{c\ (\text{man 1 [et man 2 vid]})}$: προσηλθον W$^{c\ (\text{man } 3)}$: προσπορευονται ς, ℵ^{c}, *rell* ; παραπορ- ℵ*; προπορ- S, Δ, 472, *pc;* προσερχονται 273)

Mark 10:36 τι θελετε ποιησαι W*, Δ, 282, 472, 569, *l*29, *pc* : τι θελετε με ποιησαι W$^{c\ (\text{man } 2)}$, ℵ$^{\text{cb vid}}$, L, 579, 892, 1342, 2427*, *pc* : τι θελετε με ποιησω ℵ^{c}, B, Ψ, 2427^{c}, arm : τι θελετε ποιησαι με ς, A, K, N, X, Γ, Π, 28, 124, 157, 700, 1071, *rell* : τι θελετε ποιησω C, Θ, f^{1}, f^{13}, 565, 1424, *pc* (ποιησωμαι 1082; ποιησομαι *l*184) : ποιησω D : τι θελετε ινα ποιησω 1241, *pc* : ινα ο εαν (v. 35) - δος ημιν (v. 37) *om.* ℵ*

Mark 11:15 εις το ιερο(ν) *sec. scripturus erat* W* ^{vid} : εν τω ιερω W$^{c\ (\text{man 1 in scribendo})}$, ς, *rell* : εν αυτω A : *plane om.* 225 c

Mark 11:33 οιδομεν W* : οιδαμεν W$^{c\ (\text{man } 3)}$, ς, *rell*

Mark 12:14 δουναι καισαρι W* : δουναι κηνσον καισαρι W$^{c\ (\text{man } 2)}$, ℵ, B, C, L, Δ, Ψ, 33, 472, 474, 579, 892, 1241, 1424, 2427, *al*, lat, co, aeth : κηνσον καισαρι δουναι ς, A, N, S^{c}, X, Γ, Π, f^{1}, f^{13}, 157, 700, *rell* : καισαρι δουναι S* : κηνσον δουναι καισαρι 16, 28, aur, c, ff^{2}, q, r^{1}, vg^{mss}, got, arm : καισαρι κηνσον δουναι 7, 1082, 1391 : δουναι επικεφαλαιον καισαρι D, Θ, 565, k, sy$^{\text{s.p}}$: δουναι κηνσον καισαρι a, b, d, i, l, vg : επικεφαλαιον καισαρι δουναι 124 : επικεφαλαιον δουναι κηνσον καισαρι 1071

Mark 13:25 εν τω ουρανω W*, 38, 700 : εν τοις ουρανοις W$^{c\ (\text{man } 2)}$, ς, *rell* : των ουρανων D, K, 115, 1093, 1424, it, co, arm^{mss}, aeth

Mark 14:27 σκανδα | λισθησοντε (= -σονται) W*, 300, 1093 : σκανδα | λισθησεσθαι (= -σεσθε) W$^{c\ (\text{man } 1)}$, ς, *rell*

Mark 14:29 αλ W*, 2*, *l*185 : αλλ W$^{c\ (\text{man } 2)}$, ς, 2^{c}, *rell*

Mark 14:53 ο (*ante* πρεσβυτεροι) W* : οι W$^{c\ (\text{man 1 [in scribendo?]})}$, ς, *rell* : *om.* D, 72

Mark 15:40 και ωση W* : και ϊωση W$^{c\ (\text{man } 2)}$, ς, ℵ*, A, C, K, Γ, Π, 28, 118, 124, 157, 209, 472 (ηωση), 579, 700, 892, 1071, 1241, 1424, 1582^{c}, *rell,* sa, arm, got, aeth^{pp} : και η ιωση Ψ : και ιωσητος ℵ^{c}, D^{gr}, L, Δ^{c} (-

ηβτος Δ*), Θ, 083, 0184, *f*[13], 33, 565, 2427, 2542s*, *l*844, *pc*, k, n, bo : και η ιωσητος B, 131 : και ιωσηπος *f*[1], 1582*

Mark 15:43	ο απο W*, ς, ℵ, A, B*, C, L, Γ, Δ, Θ, Π, Ψ, 083, 0212, *f*[1], *f*[13], 33, 157, 565, 700, 1071, 1424, 2427, *rell* : απο W^c (man 1), B^c, D, 083, 13, 28, 472, 484, 579, 1093, *pc*, bo^pt

The Supplemental Quire (W^s)

John 1:13	.. ρκος W^s* : σαρκος W^s c (man c), ς, *rell*
John 1:33	οτος W^s* : ουτος W^s c (man b), ς, *rell* : ουτως 579 : αυτος A, 954, 1424, 1675, b, e, q
John 2:16	μο(υ) *scripturus erat* W^s* : μη W^s c (man a in scribendo), ς, *rell*
John 2:24	ο εαυτον W^s* : εαυτον W^s c (man a in scribendo vid), ς, 𝔓66, ℵ^c, A[2], K, M, S, U, Y, Γ, Δ, Θ, Λ, Π, Ψ^c, Ω^c, 050, 083, *f*[1], *f*[13], 28, 33, 157, 440^c, 565, 579, 892, 1241, *rell*, sy, Or^s : αυτον ℵ*, A*, B, L, Ψ*, Ω*, 253, 440*, 544, 700, 1071, 1093, *al* : *plane om.* 𝔓75, 579, *pc*, Did (*De Trinitate* 3.29 [PG 39.948A14])
John 3:15	ζων W^s* : ζωην W^s c (man a vid), ς, *rell*
John 3:22	ες W^s* : εις W^s c (man a vid), ς, *rell*
John 4:8	τροφος W^s* : τροφας W^s c (man a vid), ς, *rell*
John 4:10	αυταον W^s* : αυτον W^s c (man a in scribendo vid), *rell* (αυτων 470) : αυτω 472, 1093, 1170
John 4:22	ο οοκ W^s* : ο ουκ W^s c (man b), ς, *rell*
John 4:25	χρ(ιστος) W^s* *scripturus erat* : χ̅ς̅ (= χριστος) W^s c (man a in scribendo), ς, *rell* : χ̅ρ̅ς̅ (= χριστος) D
John 4:47	γαλι | (λεας) *scripturus erat* W^s* vid, ("ex Galilaea in Iudaeam" sy^c) : ιου | δεας (= ιουδαιας) W^s c (man a in scribendo), ς, *rell*

Notes Added in Proof

T. A. E. Brown recently examined Codex W itself and kindly reported to me on the results of his examination of the manuscript as well as of the images at many of the places cited above. From these results I would wish to revise to some degree what I say above, but I will have to reserve further treatment for some later discussion. The most significant change is that at Matt 21:19 no correction has occured at all. Rather, the original reading is επ, and the appearance of a correction arises solely from offset from the facing page. Thus, the paragraph concerning Matt 21:19 should be moved from the discussion of possibly later corrections by the original scribe to the list of other cited corrections, and the counts of corrections should be suitably adjusted.

Brown also indicated that "offset" is a more accurate term than "cross-printing" and that "bleeding through" should be distinguished from "showing through." In my discussion I have used "bleed-through" as a general term for the appearance of letters from the opposite side of the folio. I look forward to the transcription of W by Prior and Brown, where these matters will be more fully handled.

Reassessing the Palaeography and Codicology of the Freer Gospel Manuscript

Ulrich Schmid

Accompanying the initial publication of the famous Freer Gospels manuscript (Freer Gallery of Art, 06.274; Codex Washingtonianus [W], Gregory-Aland 032), its editor, Henry A. Sanders, provided palaeographical and codicological discussions, the results of which have hitherto dominated the perception of Codex W's date.[1] As his main results, Sanders identified two hands that produced the Gospel text. "Scribe A" contributed the first quire of John (see fig. 1), and "scribe B" was responsible for the rest (the main part) of the manuscript (see fig. 2). According to Sanders, five more hands supplied corrections and/or quire numbers, three of which were active on the work of scribe B, whereas two left their mark on the work of scribe A. Finally, three other hands are said to have been involved in a subscription to Mark, which apparently refers to previous owners of the manuscript. The crucial factor in an assessment of the codex's history of composition is the observation that the work of scribe A is represented in a discrete quire. Finally, Sanders dated both scribe A and scribe B to the late fourth/early fifth centuries and proposed that scribe A was the earlier. Although Sanders's dating of scribe B has been accepted in general by subsequent scholars, albeit with a shift of emphasis,[2] there is considerable dissent with regard to his dating of scribe A, the hand of the first quire of John.[3] Part of the problem is due

1. Henry A. Sanders, *The New Testament Manuscripts in the Freer Collection, Part I: The Washington Manuscript of the Four Gospels* (University of Michigan Studies, Humanistic Series 9/1; New York: Macmillan, 1912), 1–40, 134–39.

2. Sanders (ibid., 139): "In determining the date of W most of the evidence thus seems to point to the fourth century, though the beginning of the fifth must still be admitted as a possibility." Cf. Guglielmo Cavallo and Herwig Maehler, *Greek Bookhands of the Early Byzantine Period: A.D. 300–800* (BICSSup 47; London: University of London, 1987), no. 15a, (38): "early v century…, while … the end of the iv century cannot be ruled out completely."

3. Cf., e.g., Kenneth W. Clark, *A Descriptive Catalogue of Greek New Testament Manuscripts in America* (with an introduction by E. J. Goodspeed; Chicago: University of Chicago Press, 1937), 202: "supplied by 8th-C hand"; Frederic G. Kenyon, *The Text of the Greek Bible* (London:

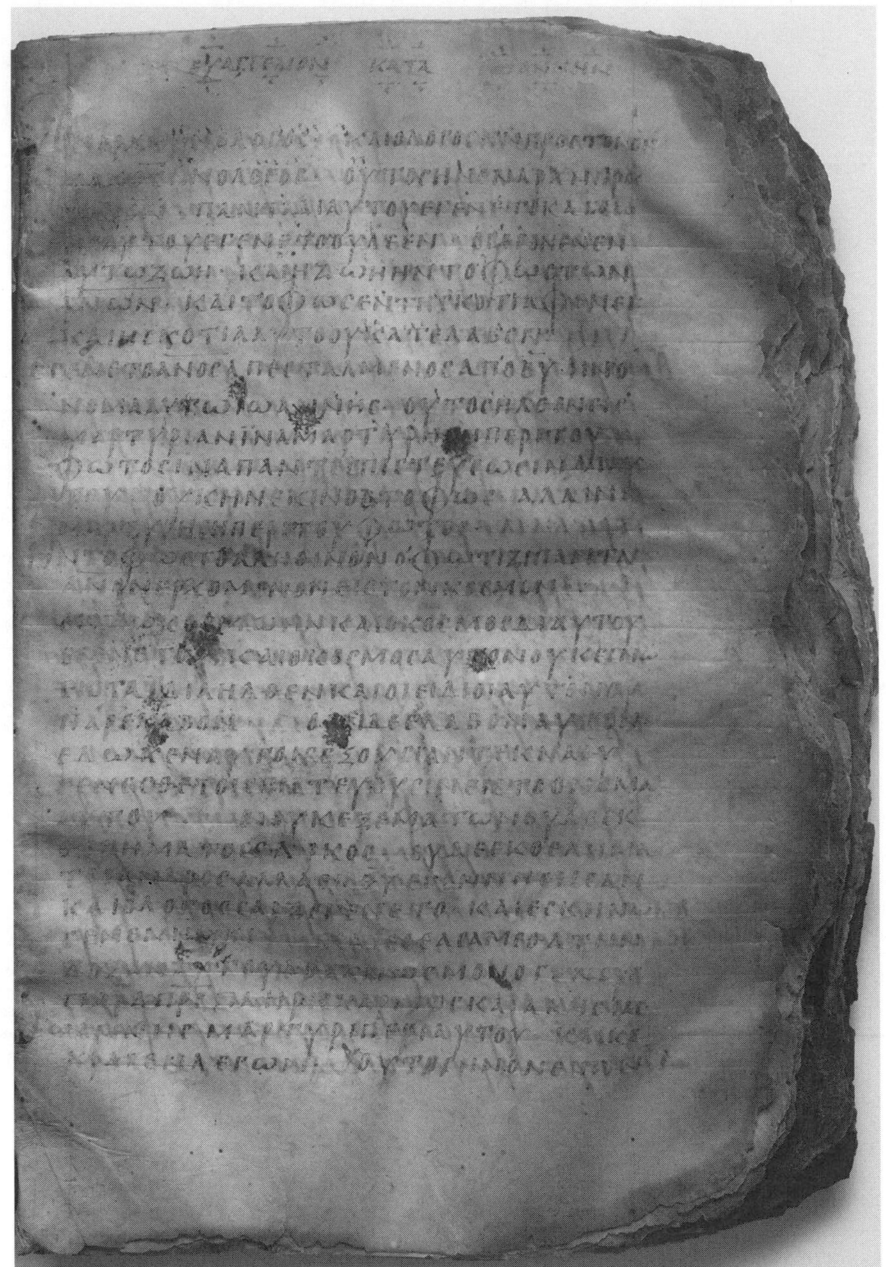

Figure 1: Freer manuscript of John 1:1–15. Freer Gallery of Art, Smithsonian Institution, Washington, D.C.: Gift of Charles Lang Freer, F1906.274 pg. 113. Used by permission.

Figure 2: Freer manuscript of John 5:30–41. Freer Gallery of Art, Smithsonian Institution, Washington, D.C.: Gift of Charles Lang Freer, F1906.274 pg. 130. Used by permission.

to Sanders's peculiar analysis of the prehistory of this quire in relation to the rest of the manuscript.

The aim of this contribution is to review Sanders's analysis of the manuscript's history of composition and to reconsider the dates that are given to it in the light of more recent literature and a century of palaeographical research subsequent to his historic studies.

Codex W's History of Composition

Codex W is among the few Greek manuscripts that give the Gospels in the so-called "Western" order: Matthew, John, Luke, and Mark.[4] One needs to keep in mind, however, that, as in many other early codices, each Gospel in Codex W begins on a new quire. There is clear evidence that the production process deliberately aimed at such a result. Out of the twenty-six quires of the codex, nineteen consist of four folded sheets and five of three sheets; only two quires consist of two sheets, one of these quires terminating the text of Matthew and the other quire concluding the text of Luke.[5] That each Gospel starts with a new quire means that in principle the Gospels could have been assembled in various orderings, and the present order reflects a choice made at the time of the binding of the codex.

Although the first quire of John employs the same basic layout of Codex W (i.e., one column with thirty lines to the page), even a quick glance reveals that it stands apart from the rest of the manuscript, for the hand is markedly different.[6] Closer inspection corroborates that finding. The ruling of these four sheets has been executed differently. Pricking is still visible at the outer margins of the pages, whereas no traces of pricking are visible in the rest of the codex. Also, the form and use of diacritical signs on initial vowels and the orthography are peculiar, in comparison with the remainder of the manuscript. Moreover, I contend that there are good reasons to suggest that the first quire must have been conceived as a supplement from the onset.

Before I offer observations of my own, however, let us consider what Sanders proposed. It is worth quoting him in full. If what follows seems complicated, it is.

Duckworth, 1937; repr., 1953), 101: "a quire added about the 7th century, presumably to replace one which was damaged." Cavallo and Maehler, *Greek Bookhands,* do not comment on the first quire of John.

4. In this arrangement, the two Gospels ascribed to apostles come first (in declining order of length), followed (in declining order of length) by the two ascribed to nonapostolic figures. For a useful summary of various ordering of the Gospels in ancient manuscripts and lists, see Bruce M. Metzger, *The Canon of the New Testament: Its Origin, Development, and Significance* (Oxford: Clarendon, 1987), 295–300.

5. Additionally, the last leaf (i.e., the two pages) of the quire that terminates John is left blank, and the next text, Luke, commences on another quire.

6. See Sanders's convenient samples of letter forms (*New Testament Manuscripts,* 9).

> It is certain that this strange quire was written to fill in a gap, to supply a lost quire. On the last page of it the text is stretched and ends of lines left vacant after each sentence, so as to come out just even.… The three preceding pages were just as plainly crowded, an extra line even being added on each page. It must be admitted that the writer [i.e., scribe A] was both inexperienced and had before him a copy quite different in size of page. Yet with all his care to make his quire come out even he omitted nearly a verse at the end. This not only emphasizes the difference in form of the MSS from which and for which he was copying, but proves conclusively that one was not the parent of the other. In other words, he was not copying an injured or wornout quire, but was restoring a lost one; he was not copying a definite quire, but was striving to arrange in a quire a certain amount of text. His task was to copy as far as the words κραβαττον σου και περιπατει of 5,12, but he stopped with the same words in verse 11. This might have been an omission in the parent text and be explained as due to like endings, but the fact that the omission falls exactly at the end of the quire seems sufficient proof that it was first made in copying this inserted quire. Exactly the same omission is noted by Tischendorf with the words '*Ceterum* Γ Λ* *al*[6] *b om versum 12, quippe transilientes a* και περιπατει ad και περιπατει.' This explanation is, of course, possible, but exactly the same words are omitted by the jump from κραβαττον to κραβαττον, which we know took place in W. I can not avoid the conclusion that the error had a common origin, and therefore all others having it are indebted to W, or rather to the first quire of John in W. The omitting MSS are Γ Λ* 54*, 57, 64, 68, 357, Old Latin b, and Syr S. Of these we have seen above (p. 128), that Γ and Λ were related to W in the first quire of John at least, while the fifth century MSS b Syr S show a closer relationship to all the uncorrected parts of the W text. Yet if the mistake was original in W, the date of this quire must be before the fifth century, while the whole MS would have to be still earlier, if a lost quire of it was replaced by the quire under discussion. A date for the whole MS earlier than the second half of the the fourth century seems impossible. Furthermore the fact that Γ and Λ show a closer affiliation to W in the first quire of John than in the rest of the MS implies that the parts were not yet united when the ancestor of Γ and Λ did the borrowing.[7]

It is appropriate to pause for a moment to tease out the specific reasoning involved in Sanders's theory regarding the place of the first quire of John within the history of the entire manuscript.

(1) The first quire of John has been designed to contain an exact amount of text up to κραβαττον σου και περιπατει in 5:12.

(2) The exemplar of which this quire originally formed a part was different in form and size from Codex W.

7. Sanders, *New Testament Manuscripts*, 135–36.

(3) The scribe of the first quire of John accidentally omitted 5:12, by visually leaping from the περιπατει at the end of 5:11 to the opening words of 5:13. Thus, the resulting omission of 5:12 in Codex W occurred in the process of transcribing the supplemented quire.

(4) The omission of John 5:12 in this first quire makes it the likely parent of all the other known witnesses that also omit that verse (Γ Λ* 54*, 57, 64, 68, 357, Old Latin b, and Syr S).

(5) Because of the age of the Latin and Syriac witnesses (fifth century) displaying this same omission, the first quire of John, therefore, has to be earlier than the fifth century, "while the whole MS [for which the quire was originally prepared] would have to be still earlier, if a lost quire of it was replaced by the quire under discussion."

(6) "The fact that Γ and Λ show a closer affiliation to W in the first quire of John than in the rest of the MS implies that the parts were not yet united when the ancestor of Γ and Λ did the borrowing." That is, the parent of Γ and Λ was not Codex W; it was another manuscript for which the first quire of John was originally intended as a replacement quire.

Let us take a critical closer look at Sanders's views. Conclusions 1–3 are inferences drawn upon evidence from the different parts of W alone. Although they tend to go beyond the extant manuscript, in that a description of the exemplar used for the first quire of John is included, nevertheless the key points of departure in Sanders's theory are solely observations of phenomena in Codex W. Conclusions 4–6, on the other hand, build on evidence gathered from other textual witnesses. These conclusions include not only judgments on genealogical relationships between W and other witnesses but also inferences drawn from the dates and/or textual data of these other witnesses. These inferences are then exploited to unravel the datings and successive stages of W's composition history, specifically the combination of the first quire of John with the rest of the manuscript. We can, however, hardly fail to note that conclusions 4–6 introduce considerable tension into the overall picture of W's history of composition.

The problem is mainly due to difficulties in reconciling various matters logically and chronologically. For clarity, I itemize the specific features that combine to raise questions about Sanders's theory.

(1) Codex W (including the present first quire of John + the rest of John) is not earlier than second half of the fourth century.

(2) The first quire of John + the rest of John for which it was prepared became the parent text of the fifth-century Old Latin b and Syr S, which would require that this copy of John must be prior to the fifth century, even considerably earlier allowing for the wear that required the replacement of the first quire of John.

(3) The first quire of John in W (and the manuscript for which it was originally prepared) also became the parent text of Γ and Λ. But this was at a time

when the first quire of John had not yet been joined with the rest of John in Codex W.

In sum, according to Sanders, W in its present form could not have been itself the actual parent manuscript that generated in other witnesses the omission of John 5:12. Instead, the present first quire of John in W was originally prepared as a replacement quire for a *previous* copy of John. Sanders found what he regarded as corroborating evidence for this theory.

> The quire number θ is written exceptionally low for this MS and a careful examination with a good lens revealed the reason. In the place above the quire number the parchment, though badly decayed, shows plain signs of an erasure. I have not been able to read an erased quire number on this spot, even with the aid of hydro-sulfide of ammonium, and the decayed state of the parchment prevents further attempts. However, on an excellent negative of this page, secured four years ago, both Professor Bonner and I have read independently a small angular alpha under the erasure. This accords exactly with all the other points noted. The quire was once the first quire of a MS and so suffered more severely from wear. The MS probably did not include Matthew and may have contained only John. After the original first quire had been lost or worn out, the present quire was written to complete it. The MS seems not to have been well bound, for the last page of the quire has suffered from wear almost as much as the first page.… Yet the quire as a whole was in such good condition, when W was copied, that it was taken over into the new MS. Presumably it is not much older than the rest of the MS.[8]

8. Sanders, *New Testament Manuscripts,* 137. "This is not impossible in ancient MSS. Sometimes they were repaired when the newly added portion equaled the old in amount, as in Codex Aesinus of the Agricola of Tacitus (tenth and fifteenth centuries)" (ibid., 137 n. 1). Codex Aesinus is indeed an interesting example. This miscellaneous manuscript was finally prepared by Stefano Guarnieri, a fifteenth-century humanist, and it contained Dictys's *Ephemeris belli Troiani,* Tacitus's *Agricola,* and *Germania* (cf. Cesare Annibaldi, *L'Agricola e la Germania di Cornelio Tacito nel MS. Latino N. 8 della Biblioteca del Conte G. Balleani in Jesi* [Città di Castello: Lapi, 1907]; idem, *La Germania die Cornelio Tacito* [Leipzig: Harrassowitz, 1910]; Rudolf Till, *Handschriftliche Untersuchungen zu Tacitus Agricola und Germania mit einer Photokopie des Codex Aesinas* [Berlin-Dahlem: Ahnenerbe-Stiftung Verlag, 1942]). Of the three quaternions covering the two small works of Tacitus, Guarnieri himself transcribed two; the third quaternio was taken over from a Carolingian manuscript of Tacitus's *Agricola.* Guarnieri not only modeled his own handwriting according to the Caronlingian *quaternio,* but he also tried to produce a page layout broadly similar to the ninth-century manuscript, i.e., two columns. The number of lines per page, however, ranges from 26–30 in the parts transcribed by Guarnieri, whereas the Caronlingian *quaternio* has 30 lines throughout. Strangely enough, one more double sheet from the Carolingian manuscript originally containing the end of Tacitus's *Agricola* has been washed off, integrated within the third *quaternio,* and rewritten by Guarnieri.

Thus, according to Sanders, the present first quire of John in Codex W originally was written to supplement an otherwise lost manuscript, which we may refer to as "X." This manuscript X subsequently suffered from some sort of disintegration and/or wear, as a result of which its supplemented first quire of John ended up being used to save the scribe of what is now Codex W from having to copy John 1:1–5:12. I set out below a visual layout of this theory.

X

(subsequently loses first quire of John)

X^{def} (then supplemented with new quire of John {=A})

A+ X^{def} (= pre-fifth century, lacking John 5:12, influences Latin b Syriac S, and ancestor of Γ and Λ; suffers wear and disintegration)

A (taken over into newly copied MS {B})

A+B = W (4/5th century)

Thus, we are asked to accept a series of defects and supplementations that twice resulted in conveying exactly the same error (omission of John 5:12). In the first case, the scribe of A, when producing a supplemental quire up to the words κραβαττον σου και περιπατει of 5:12, stopped short at the very same words of 5:11. In the second case, the scribe of B, whose responsibility must have been to start transcribing with the words κραβαττον σου και περιπατει of 5:11, similarly marred his work by mistaking the final words of A as the end of John 5:12. Because of alleged differences in textual affiliation between the supplemental quire and the rest of John's Gospel in W, the second error cannot be viewed as a simple rehearsal of the first error, due to copying a defective exemplar. Thus, both omissions of John 5:12 must be conceived as independent from each other.

But this scenario stretches one's imagination too far. Apart from the chronological problems, we face a serious difficulty with the internal logic of Sanders's scenario. On the one hand, the omission of 5:12 has to be genealogically significant in order to allow for Sanders's musings about textual history and dates to stand reasonably firm. That is, Sanders's theory depends upon ascribing all omissions of 5:12 in textual witnesses to an original and influential omission. In order to be genealogically significant, however, errors/readings should not be likely to have arisen several times independently. But, ironically, Sanders's scenario presupposes exactly that, for he posited that the allegedly genealogically significant omission of John 5:12 not only happened twice independently but even twice within a highly complicated (largely conjectural) textual history of one and the same manuscript.[9]

The safest way to deal with the problems as outlined seems to be to reject Sanders's theory of Codex W's history of composition. The omission of John 5:12 in W cannot be shown to have any bearing on the omission of the same verse in other textual witnesses. Instead, this is simply one of many instances of the sort of visual leap from one word or phrase to the same word or phrase that one finds often in manuscripts. One cannot rightly build a genealogical connection of textual witnesses on a single variant that could easily have arisen more than once coincidentally. Thus the date of those other witnesses cannot be used as termini ante quem for dating the various parts of W or of a postulated partial-precursor manuscript.

Further Questions

Before we turn to discuss the dates of the two parts of Codex W in the next section of this essay, we must consider three more of Sanders's observations that might raise questions regarding the prehistory of W's first quire of John. Sanders noted the erasure of the original quire number that was given to this quire, the exceptional wear of the first page of this quire, and the signs of wear on the last page of the quire. However, there are several factors that need to be taken into account in judging what these data mean.

We should note that Sanders provided evidence that the manuscript has been rebound at least once, and perhaps several times.[10] It is unfortunate that we have no clearer information on the important issue of whether the replacement of the first quire of John in W and the repair of quires IΓ and KΓ took place at the same time or in multiple successive stages, and, if the latter, which one came first. There might even be more indicators of rebinding. For example, Sanders referred to "compass points pricked in the parchment" (which were made preparatory to ruling the pages for copying), even where they are no longer visible.[11] Since compass points are only visible in the first quire of John and nowhere else, one might even ask whether they are not there because of damage to the edges or perhaps because of trimming the edges in rebinding.

Regarding the putative erasure of an original quire number of the replacement quire of John, we would need to know which hand wrote the first quire number. But Sanders did not venture a guess. Recall that he could not read it

---

9. As an aside, Sanders's scenario as outlined makes B (the main part of W, 25 quires) technically a supplement to A (the first quire of John), in that he proposes that B took over the layout of A.

10. Sanders, *New Testament Manuscripts,* 6.

11. Ibid., 7.

from the original of the manuscript itself but thought that he could do so in a photograph. Unfortunately, I cannot assess his claims about the erasure and the supposedly earlier quire number (*alpha*) with the limited means at my disposal. I suggest the possibility, however, that the earlier quire number, *alpha,* could stem from a point in Codex W's history when it was taken apart for the purpose of replacing its initial quire of John. At that point, this replacement quire of John received a number that later was considered wrong, either because of a simple mistake while transcribing the quire (e.g., the scribe of the replacement quire simply added a quire number without thinking) or through misperception or confusion with respect to the "original" Western order of W prior to taking it apart for supplementation. That is, perhaps the person responsible for putting the quires back in order simply started numbering with the new quire, taking it for the opening quire out of a vague, but wrong, recollection of the unusual order of Gospels in W.

The exceptional wear of the first page of that quire is somewhat balanced by another observation concerning the blots on the opening pages of all the Gospels. The opening page of Matthew has twenty of these blots; John has sixteen, Luke five, and Mark four. These blots apparently stem from oil lamps or candles. This may indicate a special use for those opening pages over time, perhaps to show them to curious visitors to the place where the codex was stored and perhaps held as "an object of interest or peculiar sanctity" (as Sanders suggested).[12] In any case, the opening pages of the first two Gospels most severely suffered from blots and wear, reflecting more frequent attention to these pages.

We should also note the parchment quality of the first quire of John. Sanders observed, "In the first quire of John the parchment is all of sheepskin and seems to be of somewhat different character. it is regularly a little thicker, but more worn and decayed."[13] Moreover, on the last page of the quire, there is heavy cross-printing from the opposite page (due to moisture), which further contributes to the appearance of wear.

The Dating of W

In addition to his assessment of Codex W's composition history, Sanders dated the manuscript, based on palaeographical examination of it. Almost in passing, he affirmed that the owners' notes at the end of W are in "fifth-century semi-cursive hands."[14] However, he did not substantiate this claim. Moreover, semicursive hands are not easily dated. Thus, we leave these subscriptions aside

12. Ibid., 134–35.
13. Ibid., 5.
14. Ibid., 2.

and concentrate on the book hand(s) of W itself. In so doing, we follow the lead of Sanders and subsequent palaeographical analyses of the Freer Gospels.[15]

The script of Codex W has been characterized as "a sloping pointed majuscule."[16] A systematic historical analysis of the developments of that kind of script has been offered by Lameere,[17] partly building on the work of Sanders. In an attempt to describe and date one of the Homeric manuscripts that he discusses, Lameere starts with two papyri of the *Iliad* that are confidently datable to the beginning of the third century,[18] one of which was also used by Sanders.[19] At the opposite end of the time scale, Lameere situates many examples of the sloping majuscule, also called "slavonic," out of which the Uspenskij-Psalter of 862 C.E. is the most well known manuscript.[20] In short, the development of the script is placed between the third and ninth centuries, and the Freer Gospels, together with two papyri containing works of Menander (one of which is PSI 126), are considered as marking the transition between the third-century beginnings of this style and the later sixth/seventh-century examples, W assigned a fifth-century date.[21]

Cavallo and Maehler offer an attempt to break down the many examples of sloping pointed majuscule across these several centuries into "three different, although related, types."[22] It must be said, however, that they do not use any of the early dated manuscripts that Lemeere has brought to the fore to make their case.

---

15. I have consulted (in addition to Sanders) the following important publications that discuss the Freer Gospels within a historical perspective of the development of the scripts involved: William Lameere, *Aperçus de paléographie homérique* (Les publications de scriptorium 4; Paris: Édition Erasme, 1960); Guglielmo Cavallo, *Ricerche sulla maiuscola biblica* (Firenze: Le Monnier, 1967); Cavallo and Maehler, *Greek Bookhands;* B. L. Fonkič and F. B. Poljakov, "Paläographische Grundlagen der Datierung des Kölner Mani-Kodex," *Byzantinische Zeitschrift* 83 (1990): 22–30.

16. Cavallo and Maehler, *Greek Bookhands,* 4. Lameere (*Aperçus de paléographie homérique,* 178) called it "écriture littéraire penchée vers la droite." Fonkič and Poljakov ("Paläographische Grundlagen," 23) use the expression "rechtsgeneigte ogivale Majuskel ('Spitzbogenmajuskel')," which is basically a combination of the previous expressions.

17. Lameere, *Aperçus de paléographie homérique,* 178–81. Cavallo, *Ricerche sulla maiuscola biblica,* 119 considers Lameere's analysis authoritative.

18. Lameere, *Aperçus de paléographie homérique,* 178, cites P. Oxy. 223 and Papyrus Florence 108. The datings of these two can be secured because of the dated nonliterary texts on the verso and on the recto respectively.

19. Sanders, *New Testament Manuscripts,* 137–39, fig. Va = Papyrus Florence 2.108. Cf. Domenico Comparetti, ed., *Papiri fiorentini: Papiri letterari ed epistolari* (vol. 2 of *Papiri Greco-Egizii;* Milan: Hoepli, 1911), no. 108.

20. Lameere, *Aperçus de paléographie homérique,* 180–81.

21. Domenico Comparetti, ed., *Papiri greci e latini* (Publicazioni della Società Italiana per la Ricerca dei Papiri Greci e Latini in Egitto 2; Firenze: Tipografia Ariani, 1913). A plate of this manuscript can be found in Cavallo and Maehler, *Greek Bookhands,* pl. 15b.

22. Cavallo and Maehler, *Greek Bookhands,* 4.

However, Cavallo and Maehler confidently date the Freer Gospels slightly earlier than PSI 126, which they consider "early v century."[23] Fonkič and Poljakov, on the other hand, heavily rely on the dated examples from the ninth century. In their view, this evidence allows one to single out a certain group of manuscripts written in sloping pointed majuscule of a so called "palästinischer Duktus," because of the many examples that can be traced to a Syro-Palestinian origin.[24] Within this group they single out an early subgroup that includes the Freer Gospels and the Cologne Mani-Codex,[25] tentatively dating the latter to the eighth century.[26]

We now turn to evaluate the cases in some greater detail. Two points should be noted from the outset, however. First, palaeography should not be considered hard science. At the heart of it lies a lot of experience and an eye trained to spot similarities and dissimilarities between various examples of similar types of script, in order to identify a specific type of hand by describing and tracing its developments in the course of time. Second, Sanders and certainly Lameere, Cavallo, and Maehler have looked at more Greek manuscripts with a trained eye than the present writer. For the purpose of this study, therefore, I shall not introduce new evidence beyond the examples that have been discussed up to 1990. Instead, our focus is on building upon the previous work by closely following the reasoning employed for the various datings that have been presented for key manuscripts. We proceed in two steps. First, we concentrate on the early-date position, which includes Sanders, Lameere, and Cavallo and Maehler; then we evaluate the later-date approach as favored by Fonkič and Poljakov.

Early Dating

As a start, it seems appropriate to look first at the examples that Sanders used. It is interesting to note that he starts with examples of sloping script on parchment. His first example is P. Cair. 10759. This manuscript contains parts of the *Gospel of Peter*, the *Apocalypse of Peter*, and parts of *1 Enoch*, and it was written by three different hands.[27] Hands b and c, responsible for transcribing the *Enoch* portion

---

23. Ibid., 38.

24. Fonkič and Poljakov, "Paläographische Grundlagen," 24–26. For an example of a "Palestinian 'sloping pointed majuscule,'" see Cavallo and Maehler, *Greek Bookhands*, 120, pl. 55c.

25. P. Colon inv. 4780. See Ludwig Koenen and Cornelia Römer, eds., *Der Kölner Mani-Kodex: Abbildungen und diplomatischer Text* (Bonn: Habelt, 1985), and the beautiful images at http://www.uni-koeln.de/phil-fak/ifa/NRWakademie/papyrologie/Manikodex/mani.html.

26. Fonkič and Poljakov, "Paläographische Grundlagen," 27. They do not explicitly date the Freer Gopels. However, by their association of W with the Cologne Mani-Codex, by implication they also date W to the eighth century. The main topic of their study, however, was the "Kölner Mani-Kodex."

27. For specimens of all three hands, see Cavallo and Maehler, *Greek Bookhands*, pls. 41a–c. Relevant editions of the mentioned texts are listed there as well. In addition, a recent edition

of the manuscript, were discussed by Sanders.[28] In his view, hand b "though written carelessly with a broad pointed pen, bears considerable resemblance in forms of letters to the first hand of W."[29] In his view, however, hand c

> bears a much closer resemblance to the hands of W.... The ease, grace, and slope of the hand remind one strongly of the first hand of W, but the shapes of many of the letters, notably γ ε κ μ σ and ω, are far closer to hand a (first quire of John). I see no reason for not considering the two hands of the Enoch fragment contemporary. It has been dated in the sixth century, but though both hands are somewhat more developed types than the hands of W, I should not place the date later than the end of the fifth.[30]

Sanders's second example was P. Berol. 9722, a fragment of Sappho, of which he says: "the writing both in slope and forms of letters is a close parallel to hand 1 [?] of W. The ornamental dots on such letters as κ γ τ υ are, however, much more pronounced and frequent, thus approximating hand a [i.e., the first quire of John] of W."[31] Based on the impression that P. Berol. 9722 is said to be the remainder of a parchment roll rather than a codex, Sanders argues for an early date "(third or fourth century)."[32] With his next example, P. Rylands 53 (though bearing "no close resemblance to any of the hands above discussed"), Sanders makes the point that there must have existed a number of early sloping majuscule hands on parchment that "have no connection with the later Slavonic uncial, but are parallels to or imitations of the sloping papyrus hand of the second to fifth centuries."[33] Having posited that, he then moves on to examples on papyrus. The example he especially focuses on is P. Florence 2.108, a dated manuscript from the mid-third century. Of this manuscript Sanders observes,

> The writing is the characteristic sloping uncial, which we have been discussing, and is even more noteworthy since it has heavy ornamental dots on the letters γ χ υ and rarely τ as in hand a of W [= first quire of John]. Also the ξ and ω have

---

of the writings attributed to St. Peter with plates of the relevant portion of the Cairo papyrus should be mentioned: Thomas J. Kraus and Tobias Nicklas, eds., *Das Petrusevangelium und die Petrusapokalypse: Die griechischen Fragmente mit deutscher und englischer Übersetzung* (Berlin: de Gruyter, 2004).

28. Sanders also gives specimen of both hands (see his pls. III + IV). I use the designations b (= 41b) and c (= 41c) for ease of reference with the Cavallo-Maehler numberings.

29. Sanders, *New Testament Manuscripts,* 137.

30. Ibid., 137–38.

31. Ibid., 138. An image of the Sappho fragment can be found in Cavallo and Maehler, *Greek Bookhands,* pl. 39b.

32. Sanders, *New Testament Manuscripts,* 138.

33. Ibid.

> similar decidedly early forms. Heavy ornamental dots are no more a mark of late date than the sloping hand. Both are early, if not frequently combined.[34]

From Sanders's discussion we learn that he must have felt the need to argue against two basic and accepted assumptions that would point toward a later dating of W: (1) sloping uncials on parchment are to be aligned with the later Slavonic majuscule rather than with earlier sloping scripts found among the papyri, and (2) ornamental dots are indicative of a later date.

We now move on to Lameere's analysis of the sloping pointed majuscule, with special emphasis on the two points argued against by Sanders. Regarding Sanders's first point, that the sloping pointed majuscule hand derives from an early provenance, we find Lameere evidently siding with Sanders. Papyrus Florence 2.108 is among Lameere's first examples for the "écriture littéraire penchée vers la droite" from the Roman period. Regarding Sanders's view of the significance of ornamental dots, we have to delve into Lameere's analysis of the hand found in Gand, Bibliothèque de l'Université no 75 (P. Oxy. 1817).[35] In a detailed description of the horizontal stroke of the letter *tau*, Lameere describes small hooks at both ends as part of one single stroke of the pen rather than decorative strokes added to the ends of the bar. He pays special attention to this observation, because it underlines the rapid flow of the hand, frequently starting the left hook from an upward position with a downward curve to the left, whereas the right hook is sloped downward to the right.[36] That would imply some distinction regarding the way ornamental dots are executed in detail. Thus, a closer look at ornamental dots seems warranted.

We will return to that issue shortly. At present, however, I would like to introduce another feature Lameere comments on, namely, the contrast between thin and thick strokes. For P. Oxy. 1817, he contends that this contrast is not always very visible, though clearly present seen in the thinner horizontal stroke of π and the horizontal middle stroke of ε.[37] In the analysis of Lameere, we note acceptance of Sanders's positing of an early origin of the pointed majuscule hand, whereas his view about the ornamental dots receives qualification. Lameere emphasizes that ornamental dots have to be judged by the way they are executed. Moreover, Lameere brings another point to the fore, namely, the contrast between thin and thick lines.

We now move on to Cavallo and Maehler, who from the outset recognize that the origins of the sloping pointed majuscule go back even to the second century C.E., although it is only from the late fourth century onward that "it becomes dis-

---

34. Ibid., 138.

35. A specimen photo is in Cavallo and Maehler, *Greek Bookhands*, pl. 28a.

36. Lameere, *Aperçus de paléographie homérique*, 177.

37. Ibid.

tinguishable from the numerous other forms of sloping script of Late Antiquity."[38] As did Lameere, Cavallo and Maehler place the Freer Gospels together with PSI 126 in the fifth century, considering the former to be earlier than the latter. Let us also note how they handle the examples adduced by Sanders. Lameere did not deal with P. Cair. 10759, but Cavallo and Maehler give the following assessment of the hands in this manuscript:

> The script of hand b is a bold sloping majuscule of a rather crude type, represented in the v century by P. Vindob. G 2314 (17b); for the hand of the Cairo codex, however, a considerably later date is suggested by its heavier design and the more marked contrast between thin and thick strokes. Moreover, the form of B [*beta*] with its baseline drawn out to the left suggests a date not before the late vi century. Lastly, the sloping majuscule of [hand] c, of the same type as that of [hand] b and equally crude, shows a very advanced stage in the development of this script in the way that heavy and fine strokes are contrasted and in its use of prominent ornamental roundels at the ends of the thin lines. All this points, with little margin of error, to a date for the Cairo codex near the end of the vi century.[39]

We note that Sanders and Cavallo and Maehler agree in characterizing both hands of the Cairo *Enoch* fragment as a more developed stage of the sloping majuscule than the script(s) of W.[40] In their dates for P. Cair. 10759, however, they differ by roughly a century. Whereas Sanders focused on the forms of letters and the general impression of the ductus, Cavallo and Maehler give fuller indicators regarding the development of the script. We note especially several points from their analysis: (1) a "marked contrast between thin and thick strokes," (2) "the form of B with its baseline drawn out to the left," and (3) "use of prominent ornamental roundels at the ends of the thin lines." The Sappho fragment (P. Berol. 9722) is discussed by Cavallo and Maehler, together with the Homer papyri (P. Berol. 11754 + 21187). They comment,

> These fragments are an example of the type of "sloping majuscule" which also occurs in PSI 126 (15b) and P. Oxy. 1817 (28a), but are later in date. The pronounced and artificial contrasts in the thickness of the strokes, the frequent use of ornamental roundels at the ends of horizontal strokes and fine diagonals

38. Cavallo and Maehler, *Greek Bookhands*, 4.

39. Ibid., 90. The letters a, b, and c in their statement refer to specimens listed here as nos. 41a, 41b, and 41c.

40. It should be noted again that, apart from Sanders, none of the other mentioned scholars engaged in dating the first quire of John found in the Freer Gospels. Hence, their characterizations and dates for W only refer to the hand that has written the remaining twenty-five quires, i.e., the main hand in W.

> … are all factors which suggest a date not earlier than the middle of the vi century.[41]

We note again a significant difference in date for the appearance of a sloping majuscule on parchment. The difference is at least two hundred years between Sanders's view (third or fourth century) and the judgment of Cavallo and Maehler (second half of sixth century). In assessing Sanders's view, however, we should note that he had been misled by the original editor of P. Berol. 9722, W. Schubart, who later "withdrew as untenable his original assumption … that the leaves formed a parchment roll."[42] In short, two of Sanders's prime examples of early (pre-500 C.E.) parchment codices that also contain sloping majuscule hands employing ornamental dots (P. Cair. 10759 and P. Berol. 9722) are to be considered inappropriate for making Sanders's case for a fourth/fifth-century dating of W.

Unfortunately, neither Lameere nor Cavallo and Maehler discuss the script of Sanders's last example, P. Florence 2.108. In what follows, I shall partially fill in that void by especially focusing on the first quire of John. Finally, equipped with the observations and standards set forth by Lameere and Cavallo and Maehler, I will even venture to reassess the dating of the main hand of the Freer Gospels.

The sloping script of P. Florence 2.108 appears less developed than the two hands of W. The thickness of the individual strokes hardly varies. Despite being a sloping script, the proportions of the hand of P. Florence 2.108 are different. This is especially apparent with the vertical strokes of Φ, P, and Y. In P. Florence 2.108, they only very slightly extend below the baseline. Also, there is a marked difference in the proportions of Φ. Both hands of W usually place the two roundels that are attached to the vertical stroke in the middle of the stroke with a tendency toward the upper part of it, whereas P. Florence 2.108 has an inclination to the lower part of the vertical stroke. Furthermore, there are differences in the T. In P. Florence 2.108 the vertical stroke does not often not meet the bar right in the center, but much more to the right, which has the effect that the left part of the bar is remarkably longer than the right part. This might be partially due to the ornamental dots that are sometimes found on the left wing of the bar. These ornamental dots, however, do not appear to be crafted with much emphasis. In shape they rather appear like blots of ink, although they are, of course, intentional and not accidental slips of the pen.

This is in marked contrast to the hand of the first quire of John in the Freer Gospels, to which Sanders especially related the ornamental dots in P. Florence 2.108. Without any doubt, there are significant differences between the two. In the first place, the hand of the first quire of John always, not "rarely," places orna-

41. Cavallo and Maehler, *Greek Bookhands*, 86.

42. Ibid., 86. Thus the Sappho fragment originally belonged to a codex.

mental dots on both ends of the T. Furthermore, many of the ornamental dots employed by the hand of the first quire of John appear as if cut into the manuscript, displaying sharp edges (see, e.g., the ornamental strokes on the upper end of the descending leg of the A and the Λ and the two strokes on both upper ends of the T. This feature is particularly characteristic of the T. In this letter the ornamental dots are two vertical strokes executed with the broad side of the pen. Thus, the crossbar of the T consists of three strokes performed with two extra pen lifts, a feature not evident in P. Florence 2.108. In conclusion, although being a sloping majuscule, P. Florence 2.108 should hardly be called "pointed." Therefore, I reject this manuscript as contributing anything positive to dating the hand of the first quire of John in the Freer Gospels.

Let us now turn to consider the main scribal hand of W. Although Sanders's examples (P. Cair. 10759, P. Berol. 9722, and P. Florence 2.108) are now considered to be either invalid or considerably later than he had thought, the dating of W's main hand appears (surprisingly?) stable, as reflected in the views of Lameere (fifth century) and especially Cavallo and Maehler (fourth/fifth century). In what follows, however, I want to reconsider views of the date of W's main hand in light of the descriptions by Lameere and Cavallo and Maehler of what they consider to be sixth-century hands.

I suggest that Lameere's analysis of the hand of P. Oxy. 1817 applies to W's main hand with only very minor modifications. Granted, differences between Lameere's description of P. Oxy. 1817 and the evidence from W can be found in the formation of the letters M[43] and Ω.[44] Much more often, however, there are similarities between the two hands.[45] It is especially interesting to note that the formation of the horizontal stroke of the T in P. Oxy. 1817, as described by Lameere, is a complete match with the main hand of W.[46] Moreover, the main scribe of Codex W betrays a greater tendency to vary the thickness of strokes. In

---

43. Lameere (*Aperçus de paléographie homérique,* 177) hints at the size of the M in P. Oxy. 1817, with its profoundly curved middle stroke, when compared to the narrower forms of the rounded letters B, E, θ, O, and Σ. In contrast, the main hand of W exhibits some variation regarding the letter M. Usually, however, the two vertical strokes of the letter M are not as far apart from each other as in P. Oxy. 1817, though some horizontally extended versions can be found as well.

44. Ibid., 177: "Enfin, les deux panses de l'omega, sont de grosseur inégale et se situent à des niveaux différents: l'une et l'autre sont anguleuse, mais la panse du côté gauche est moins ouverte et la pointe inférieure de la panse du côté droit se situe à un niveau supérieur à celui de la pointe inférieure de la panse du côté gauche." The Ω in W is shaped on the basis of two bottom curved strokes, like the bottom half of an angular *omicron,* followed by a vertical stroke. All three strokes descend from the same top line level. This is in marked contrast to P. Oxy. 1817, where the middle stroke descends from a much lower level than the two outer strokes.

45. Compare Lameere's description of the formations for A, Δ, and Λ, as well as the size of I (ibid.).

46. See ibid.

addition to the thinner horizontal strokes in the Π and E, similar to what Lameere noted in P. Oxy. 1817, we might add the thinner horizontal strokes in the H and the baseline of the Δ.

In sum, judging by Lameere's description of a mid-sixth century sloping majuscule hand that I regard as very similar to the main hand of W, I can find no reason to date W earlier than P. Oxy. 1817. To be sure, Lameere did not attempt to provide any reasons for dating W to the fifth century, and, obviously, had he done so, he would have specified further details in support of this view. However, the little exercise that I have conducted yields at least some insights into the complicated matter of dating hands.

We now turn to Cavallo and Maehler, who give a short characterization of W's main hand in comparison with PSI 126:

> a [= W] and b [= PSI 126] show typical features which link them directly to hands of the iv century, in A, B, E, O, Ω in particular. However, there is a certain artfulness in the tracing of the letters, and the shapes of certain letters, especially in b, where Δ often appears in a slightly slanting position … which is more common from the beginning of the vi century.[47]

Although they mention some letters that exhibit "typical features" linking them to hands of the fourth century, unfortunately we are not told more exactly what these features are. Nor is there any indication as to whether the authors consider these to be features of fourth-century sloping majuscule hands or fourth-century hands in general. We may tentatively hark back to previous descriptions of sloping hands found in Cavallo and Maehler in order to find possible hints to evaluate their contention regarding W and PSI 126.

Most suitable seem to be their examples listed as 2a (= P. Herm. Rees 4) + 2b (= P. Chester Beatty XI) and 11a (= P. Oxy 2459) + 11b (P. Vindob. G 19815). The first pair are dated to the early half of the fourth century, the second pair to the later half of the fourth century. I offer some detailed comparisons of specific letters. If we study carefully the shape of the *alpha,* for instance, we observe some slightly curved diagonals in Codex W.[48] This is a feature also found most obviously and markedly in their hand 2a and to a lesser extent in 2b and 11a+b. However, in these hands the diagonals only rarely extend to the baseline, which gives the letters a cursive appearance, especially in cases where they are tied to the following letter. This is certainly not true with W! To the forms of the beta we shall return later.

Concerning the shape of the letter *epsilon,* we observe predominantly narrow angular forms in Codex W. The letters are formed with a vertical stroke (inclined

---

47. Cavallo and Maehler, *Greek Bookhands,* 38.

48. Cavallo and Maehler (ibid., 10) observe a "markedly curved diagonal" in P. Herm. Rees 4.

to the right, of course) that extends almost to the baseline and then takes a turn to the right ending in a hook that sits solidly on the baseline. The upper part of the letter is formed by an appended hook starting from the upper end of the vertical stroke to the right. Both hooks usually involve thinner parts due to the change of direction of the pen stroke from vertical to horizontal. The medium horizontal stroke usually extends farther to the right than the upper and lower hooks, sometimes touching the left part of the following letter. With the possible exception of this last feature, it is hard to tell what would exactly constitute a direct link between Codex W's form of the E and hands of the fourth century. In most cases, the E in Cavallo and Maehler's 2a+b and 11a+b has a rounder appearance. This might be due to the fact that they do not contrast thin and thick strokes.

It is also not clear what links to fourth-century hands one might posit regarding the shape of the O in Codex W. The sloping pointed majuscule is characterized by narrow angular forms of round letters. This is exactly what we find in Codex W and the examples such as P. Cair. 10759 and P. Oxy. 1817 from the sixth century and beyond. We may note, however, that such forms are not found in the earlier examples noted by Cavallo and Maehler, their 2a+b (P. Herm. Rees 4 + P. Chester Beatty XI). Concerning the shape of the Ω, compared with the main scribal hand in Codex W, the shapes of the letter in Cavallo and Maehler's 2a+b are much rounder, and the Ω in 11a+b resembles more the letter as found in P.Oxy. 1817. In sum, on the basis of comparison of the aforementioned letters, it is not obvious to the present writer how a link of Codex W to fourth-century hands can be established.

We may now turn to examples of sloping pointed majuscule discussed by Cavallo and Maehler and ascribed a later date than Codex W. The first example is P. Vindob. G 2314 (= Cavallo and Maeher's 17b), of which they say that its type of hand "is that of the 'Freer Gospels' (15a) but also shows a certain contrast between thin and thick strokes [of letter forms], something which is found in some examples of 'sloping majuscule' from the later v century onwards."[49] This may be true, but it only gives us an approximate date for the Freer Gospels in relation to P. Vindob. G 2314. In itself, this does not enable us to assign either of these two manuscripts firmly to the fifth century. There are, however, the two examples from the sixth century already noted, P.Oxy. 1817 and P.Cair. 10759, and these might also be relevant for assessing the main hand of Codex W. It is unnecessary, however, to rehearse here the matters discussed earlier in this essay. For our purpose here, I would like to highlight two features noted by Cavallo and Maehler that are, according to them, indicative of a later date and that are also prominent in W.

49. Ibid., 42.

The first feature has been mentioned already in discussing P.Oxy. 1817: "sharp, pointed ends of the verticals that descend below the baseline."[50] Although this feature is only a relative indicator, with regard to a second feature Cavallo and Maehler venture a confident chronological dividing line: "the form of [the letter] B with its baseline drawn out to the left suggests a date not before the late vi century."[51] I point out that this is also the characteristic way that the B is rendered by the main hand of Codex W. Moreover, it is also present in the hand of the replacement first quire of John. If this form of the *beta* is as crucial as Cavallo and Maehler suggest, then the date of Codex W moves later than that commonly assigned, perhaps down to the late sixth century.

Late Dating

Let us now turn to further reasons to consider such a later dating for Codex W, focusing on the import of a study by Fonkič and Poljakov. It should be emphasized again that Fonkič and Poljakov arrived at a later date for Codex W by reassessing the date of the Cologne Mani-Codex. Because of the similarities between one of the two hands of the Mani-Codex and the main hand of W, the two manuscripts are usually dated in tandem.[52] To be more precise, because it was discovered subsequent to the publication of Codex W, the Cologne Mani-Codex was initially dated with reference to the date that had been given to Codex W. As a result, a different date for the Mani-Codex inevitably calls into question the usual date of Codex W.

Fonkič and Poljakov start their case by presenting the dated examples of what they call "rechtsgeneigte ogivale Majuskel (sog. 'Spitzbogenmajuskel') palästinischen Duktus."[53] These include Sin. gr. NE Meg. Perg. 12 + Sin. gr. 210, datable to 861/62 c.e.,[54] and St. Petersburg, Public Library grec. 216 (Uspenskij-Psalter), datable to 862 C.E.[55] In addition to these two, they refer to many more

---

50. Ibid., 64.

51. Ibid., 90.

52. Koenen and Römer (*Der Kölner Mani-Kodex*, xiii) wrote, "Buchstabenform und Schriftduktus des zweiten Hauptschreibers [sc. des Kölner Mani-Kodex] sind der Haupthand des neutestamentlichen Codex Washingtonianus (W; IV/V Jahrh.; s. Anm. 1) zum Verwechseln ähnlich … man möchte sagen, sie haben beim gleichen Lehrer gelernt."

53. Fonkič and Poljakov, "Paläographische Grundlagen," 23.

54. Dieter Harlfinger, Diether Reinsch, Joseph A. M. Sonderkamp, and Giancarlo Prato, *Specimina Sinaitica: Die datierten griechischen Handschriften des Katharinen-Klosters auf dem Berge Sinai. 9.–12. Jahrhundert* (Berlin: Reimer, 1983), 13–14, pls. 1–4.

55. Specimens of this famous manuscript can be found in Viktor Gardthausen, *Griechische Paläographie* (2nd ed.; Leipzig: Veit, 1913), 2:143; and Wilhelm Wattenbach, *Scripturae Graecae Specimina in usum scholarum…, Schrifttafeln zur Geschichte der griechischen Schrift* (4th ed.; Berlin: Grote, 1936), pl. 10.

examples of the same type of hand. According to Fonkič and Poljakov, apart from the sloping script, other characteristic features are in the forms of the A, Δ, Z, P, Υ, Φ, Ψ, Ω, and also the X. Moreover, they state, "Zur Hervorhebung von Überschriften dienen hierbei Sonderzeichen, die entweder kurze horizontale Striche oder andere recht einfache Kombinationen darstellen."[56] This last matter seems interesting, because it includes decorative elements in conjunction with superscriptions. Nevertheless, in its present form the statement is much too broad to provide a basis for a precise date of a manuscript. Short horizontal strokes, usually in pairs, one above and one below the first and last letters of each (longer) word of a superscription are most common in biblical majuscule manuscripts from early on, so it is not surprising to find them also in Codex W.[57]

Despite mentioning letters that are said to exhibit characteristic features, Fonkič and Poljakov do not tell us what exactly these features are. Therefore, we must rely on somewhat circumstantial evidence. Fortunately, we have a reasonably detailed description of the script of Sin. gr. 210, the manuscript that serves as Fonkič and Poljakov's first dated example of the "rechtsgeneigte ogivale Majuskel (sog. 'Spitzbogenmajuskel') palästinischen Duktus."[58] After describing the verticals of the P, Υ, Φ, and Ψ, which descend below the baseline, Harlfinger, Reinsch, Sonderkamp, and Prato say,

> Rho ist unten oft geöffnet, im Kappa sind die beiden schrägen Striche von der Senkrechten gelöst; das Epsilon zeigt nicht selten eine vom übrigen Körper getrennte und bisweilen auf einen Punkt verkürzte Zunge; im Chi ist der von links nach rechts hinabführende Strich sehr dick, der von rechts nach links dagegen dünn, gebogen und mit einem Apex am oberen Ende versehen.[59]

These features are also found in the script of the Uspenskij-Psalter and in Paris Suppl. Graec. 693.[60] Thus, they appear in a representative sample of the sloping pointed majuscule style from the ninth century. But (with the possible exception of an occasional slightly disjointed *kappa*) Codex W does not exhibit these features. However, Fonkič and Poljakov join Codex W with Vat. Graec. 2200, the Cologne Mani-Codex, and the Psalter fragment Λa from the Freer Gallery to form a group of earlier representatives of that "Palestinian" type of hand

---

56. Fonkič and Poljakov, "Paläographische Grundlagen," 26.

57. Cf. Chester Beatty Papyrus II (P 46), Cod. Vat. graec. 1209 (03), Brit. Lib., Royal 1 D. VIII (02).

58. Harlfinger, Reinsch, Sonderkamp, and Prato, *Specimena Sinaitica*, 14.

59. Ibid.

60. Specimens of both manuscripts appear in Guglielmo Cavallo, "Funzione e strutture della maiuscola greca tra i secoli VIII–XI," in *La Paléographie grecque et byzantine* (Paris: CNRS, 1977), 115, pls. 5+6.

dated to the eighth century.[61] Yet this appears rather unconvincing. Judged by the description of Sin. gr. 210 above, as given by Harlfinger, Reinsch, Sonderkamp, and Prato, the Psalter fragment also exhibits exactly the same features as the dated examples from the ninth century. But Codex W and the Cologne Mani-Codex clearly stand apart, even from Vat. Graec. 2200, based on the forms of the letters noted above. So, looking at Codex W (and even at the Cologne Mani-Codex for that matter) in light of the dated examples of the sloping pointed majuscule of the ninth century does not provide a satisfactory perspective for deciding about a correct date, at least not yet.

Concluding Remarks

The aims of this paper were to review Sanders's reconstruction of Codex W's history of composition and also Sanders's dating of W in the light of more recent palaeographical discussion. It should be clear that Sanders's proposed history of the copying of Codex W is not very convincing because it is too complicated and based on inconsistent logic. However, having said that, it should also be remembered that there remain questions about the original quire number of the replacement quire of John, which, apart from Sanders and Professor Bonner (a contemporary of Sanders) no one hitherto has been able to read. Moreover, we need a serious codicological analysis that is geared to identifying and chronologically locating previous bindings and assessing the apparently different forms of the ruling of the pages. Therefore, the time is not yet ripe for a definitive new history of composition for Codex W, except for the tentative conclusion that the present first quire of John is later than the rest of the manuscript. Consequently, the first items on my wish list would be multispectral photos of crucial pages of the Freer Gospels and a new codicological analysis.

With regard to Sanders's dating of Codex W, the results of our inquiry are even less reassuring. The examples with which Sanders compared Codex W in 1912 are dated differently today, as can be seen by comparison with Cavallo and Maehler's judgments. In itself, that renders Sanders's dating inconclusive and outdated. Yet at the same time Cavallo and Maehler more or less stick to the same date for Codex W, the early fifth century (late fourth century not totally excluded). It remains unclear to me, however, what the reasons were for them to do so. I am even more puzzled in the light of judgments about various letter forms from Codex W that are said to be indicative of a later date (late sixth century), but, curiously, only when found in other manuscripts. Comparing Codex W and the Cologne Mani-Codex to dated ninth-century manuscripts, Fonkič and Poljakov appear equally unconvincing in their analysis. They simply use too broad a brush,

61. For a specimen of Vat. Graec. 2200, see Cavallo and Maehler, *Greek Bookhands,* 120, pl. 55c; for a specimen of the Freer Psalter fragment, Cavallo, *Ricerce,* pl. 109.

and their argument lacks sufficient precision of evidence. A new and comprehensive palaeographical study of the various types of sloping pointed majuscule is certainly needed. Moreover, the other hands in Codex W (correctors and owners) merit further serious analysis as well. Only after all the evidence is taken into account will we be able to get a better understanding of the dates and history of this precious and unique artifact in New Testament and Byzantine manuscript studies. As I noted early in this essay, however, palaeography is not a hard science. Therefore, employing "hard science" might be necessary ultimately to settle the questions considered here. Thus, the last item on my wish list is a state-of-the-art radiocarbon dating of the two parts of the Freer Gospels.

The Scribal Characteristics of the Freer Pauline Codex

Thomas A. Wayment

Since the publication of the *editio princeps,* the Freer codices, particularly Codex I (Washington MS IV; Gregory-Aland 016; van Haelst 507), the Pauline Epistles codex, have received surprisingly little sustained scholarly attention.[1] In fact, Elliott includes in his bibliography of New Testament manuscripts no specialized studies of Codex I.[2] Henry A. Sanders offered a fairly comprehensive analysis, although now dated, of the Pauline codex. Without duplicating the work of Sanders, in this

1. Henry A. Sanders, *The New Testament Manuscripts in the Freer Collection, Part II: The Washington Manuscript of the Epistles of Paul* (University of Michigan Studies, Humanistic Series 9/2; New York: Macmillan, 1918; repr., New York: Johnson, 1972). The Freer Pauline codex was acquired in a heavily damaged state, essentially a lump of parchment, with only corners of codex pages left. These had to be separated painstakingly and with very rudimentary technology involving deft use of a table knife! Portions of eighty-four leaves survive, of an estimated 208 to 212, whose original dimensions were ca. 20 x 25 cm and about thirty lines per page. It is copied in a decorative and skilled hand usually dated to the sixth century. Only portions of a few lines per page are extant, and some lines are very difficult to read on account of the blackening of the parchment, probably through water damage in the course of the centuries during which it lay somewhere in Egypt. Portions of the following texts survive as components of what was a copy of the Pauline corpus (in this order): 2 Corinthians, Galatians, Ephesians, Philippians, Colossians, 1 Thessalonians, Hebrews, 1 Timothy, 2 Timothy, Titus, Philemon.

2. A bibliography of plates and/or physical descriptions of Codex I include J. K. Elliott, *A Bibliography of Greek New Testament Manuscripts* (SNTSMS 109; 2nd ed.; Cambridge: Cambridge University Press, 2000), 58; Caspar R. Gregory, *Das Freer Logion, Versuche und Entwürfe* (Leipzig: Hinrich, 1905), 23; Marie-Joseph Lagrange, *Critique textuelle: La critique rationnelle* (Paris: Gabalda, 1935), 468–69; Kenneth W. Clark, *A Descriptive Catalogue of Greek New Testament Manuscripts in America* (Chicago: University of Chicago Press, 1937), 205–6; William H. P. Hatch, *The Principal Uncial Manuscripts of the New Testament* (Chicago: University of Chicago Press, 1939), xxxi; Joseph van Haelst, *Catalogue des papyrus littéraires juifs et chrétiens* (Paris: Sorbonne, 1976), 507; Guglielmo Cavallo, *Ricerche sulla maiuscola biblica* (Studi e testi di papirologia 2; Florence: Le Monnier, 1967), 88–93, 100, 104, 113, 123.

essay I will look at the scribal characteristics of Codex I based on the new electronic images of the manuscript.[3]

Although many early Christian texts were likely copied through the process of dictation in a scriptorium, the more recent trend in scholarship has been to propose a model of personal dictation, in which a scribe read the text out loud, remembered it, and then copied it down.[4] This method, it is argued, could also produce phonetic corruptions of the text, which, when coupled with regional orthographic variation, would explain the confusion of homophones present in many New Testament manuscripts. It does, however, seem difficult to imagine that a scribe could read a short passage and then immediately write it down, during the process consistently confusing certain homophones, unless that scribe's Greek was relatively weak. It seems more likely that a scribe who, for example, had the ability to harmonize a given Gospel text to its Synoptic parallels or to know the wording of an Old Testament quotation would have the ability to correctly identify and remember the spelling of a few words at a time. Some random confusion and transposition would occur, such as the confusion of γγ for νγ, but consistent confusion of homophones seems unlikely.[5]

Differentiating the work of the scribe from that of the lector would help determine with a greater degree of accuracy the text of the exemplar, as well as those readings that were introduced during copying by a reader (ἀναγνώστης).[6]

---

3. See Peter Head, "Some Observations on Early Papyri of the Synoptic Gospels, Especially Concerning Scribal Habits," *Bib* 71 (1990): 240–47; idem, "The Habits of New Testament Copyists: Singular Readings in the Early Fragmentary Papyri of John," *Bib* 85 (2004): 399–408; Ernest C. Colwell, "Scribal Habits in Early Papyri: A Study in the Corruption of the Text," in *The Bible in Modern Scholarship* (ed. J. P. Hyatt; Nashville: Abingdon, 1965), 370–89; republished as "Method in Evaluating Scribal Habits: A Study of P45, P66, P75," in idem, *Studies in Methodology in Textual Criticism of the New Testament* (Leiden: Brill, 1969), 106–24; James R. Royse, "Scribal Habits in the Transmission of New Testament Texts," in *The Critical Study of Sacred Texts* (ed. W. D. O'Flaherty; Berkeley: Graduate Theological Union, 1979), 139–61; idem, "Scribal Tendencies in the Transmission of the Text," in *The Text of the New Testament in Contemporary Research: Essays on the Status Quaestionis: Festschrift Bruce Metzger* (ed. B. Ehrman and M. W. Holmes; Grand Rapids: Eerdmans, 1995), 239–52.

4. Colwell, "Scribal Habits in Early Papyri"; David C. Parker, "A 'Dictation Theory' of Codex Bezae," *JSNT* 15 (1982): 97–112; Alphonse Dain, *Les Manuscrits* (Paris: Belles Lettres, 1949), 20–22; Colin H. Roberts, "Books in the Graeco-Roman World and in the New Testament," in *Cambridge History of the Bible* (ed. Peter R. Ackroyd; 3 vols.; Cambridge: Cambridge University Press, 1970), 1:49–50, 65 (48–66).

5. See T. C. Skeat, "The Use of Dictation in Ancient Book Production," *Proceedings of the British Academy* 42 (1957): 179–208; also Francis T. Gignac, *Phonology* (vol. 1 of *A Grammar of the Greek Papyri of the Roman and Byzantine Periods;* Milan: Cicalpino–La Goiardica, 1976), esp. 191–93.

6. Bruce M. Metzger, *Manuscripts of the Greek Bible: An Introduction to Greek Paleography* (New York: Oxford University Press, 1991), 21–22.

However, as is common in textual studies, the singular readings, itacisms, and other changes to the text of the exemplar that were introduced by a lector are, without the further development of critical methods to differentiate between the two, lumped together with the changes made by the scribes of the same manuscript. If, for example, a scribe was unable to distinguish differences between the written text of the exemplar and phonetic changes introduced by the lector, then the lector in those instances became a factor as significant as the scribe, or in some ways even a more significant factor, for textual alteration. However, if the scribes were well versed in the text, then they could have corrected the text read out by a lector or made slight adjustments according to memory as it was dictated, thereby making the scribe a more influential factor.

Another significant factor in dictated texts is the pronunciation of the lector. In instances where the scribe and lector spoke with a similar accent or in the same dialect, it is unlikely that the scribe would mentally be able to correct certain peculiarities in pronunciation of the lector. However, in instances where their pronunciation was different, there would be a greater likelihood that that the scribes might recognize changes and make corrections. In Codex I, the scribe appears to have failed to allow for the accent of the lector, but fortuitously the lector appears to have changed with the beginning of the Epistle to the Ephesians, thus providing one means of differentiation between the singular readings introduced by the lector and those introduced by the scribe. A third factor also influenced the text of this manuscript, a later corrector (διορθωτής) whose influence is minor and easily identifiable through paleographical analysis. The corrector, however, did not make any identifiable changes to the orthography of the manuscript based on the exemplar. Although it is uncertain how the process of reading back a manuscript and correcting it was carried on, it is possible that in reading the text out loud the scribe would read the text in the same accent as that of the corrector, which would make differences between the exemplar and copied text difficult to identify.[7]

Codex I provides a glimpse into the peculiarities of a dictated text and, unlike the majority of manuscripts, enables us to detail some of the distinctive traits of both the scribe and the lector.[8] In order to appreciate fully the importance of the singular readings in Codex I, it is imperative to distinguish, where possible, between those readings that have been introduced into this manuscript during its copying and subsequent transmission and those that originate from the textual exemplar. After isolating those singular readings that result from the dictation and copying of the manuscript, only a very small handful of readings emerge

---

7. Skeat, "Use of Dictation," 179–91.

8. For a discussion of some of the issues associated with dictated texts, see Barbara Aland and Kurt Aland, *The Text of the New Testament* (trans. Erroll Rhodes; Grand Rapids: Eerdmans, 1995), 286.

that can be considered genuine (deliberate) textual variants. A similar conclusion can be reached by studying the scribal habits of the scribe who produced a given manuscript, but in instances where there is a single hand scribal peculiarities and habits are more difficult to discern.

Sanders did not propose a dictation theory for Codex I and probably rejected the dictation theory outright. After the publication of Skeat and Milne's *Scribes and Correctors of the Codex Sinaiticus*, in which they proposed a dictation theory for portions of Sinaiticus, Sanders responded in print by rejecting their claims.[9] Even though Skeat continued to defend his position in subsequent publications, Sanders showed no signs of having ever entertained the idea.[10]

The Lector

Accuracy in distinguishing the two types of changes made to the text mentioned above would enable us to some degree to characterize the text of the exemplar and the text created through the process of dictation/copying. In a groundbreaking study, Colwell compared the work of the scribes of 𝔓45, 𝔓66, and 𝔓75 as to the ways they copied their respective texts and found marked differences. He judged that the scribe of 𝔓45 wrote by looking at the exemplar and copying "three to five words at a time," essentially copying out short phrases, whereas the scribe of 𝔓75 copied individual letters.[11] The two approaches in reproducing their respective manuscripts led to very different results in the quality and consistency of text, with the scribe of 𝔓75 creating a considerably larger number of nonsense readings. On the other hand, the scribes of 𝔓45 and 𝔓66 generally produced a text more free of nonsense readings and with fewer misspellings, the changes they made being predominantly the rearrangement of word order.

The scribe of Codex I, as did those of 𝔓45 and 𝔓66, copied the text in short phrases, probably in small sense units of about five words at a time. In fact, examples of readings resulting from homoeoteleuton, homoeoarcton, parablepsis, and dittography are almost completely missing.[12] The scribe of Codex I was able to hear and mentally work through or adjust the text before he wrote it,

9. H. J. M. Milne and T. C. Skeat, *Scribes and Correctors of the Codex Sinaiticus* (London: British Museum, 1938). Cf. Henry A. Sanders, "Review of *Scribes and Correctors of the Codex Sinaiticus*," *AJP* 60 (1939): 486–90.

10. For a favorable review of Milne and Skeat, see Eric G. Turner, "Review of *The Use of Dictation in Ancient Book-production*," *JTS* 10 (1959): 148–50. Skeat defended his position in "Use of Dictation." R. Sheldon MacKenzie, "The Latin Column in Codex Bezae," *JSNT* 6 (1980): 58–76, applied dictation theory to Codex Bezae. Parker, "Dictation Theory," later discounted his findings.

11. Colwell, "Scribal Habits in Early Papyri," 381.

12. Some potential examples are 2 Cor 8:6, where the scribe or lector confused προενήζασθε (8:10) with προενήρζατο; 2 Tim 4:9 (dittography); and Heb 12:9 (parablepsis).

thus significantly reducing the number of nonsense readings in the manuscript.[13] Indeed, the preserved portions of this manuscript contain only one or two nonsensical readings.[14]

Those few singular readings that were introduced into the text through parablepsis, which are probably the result of the lector and not the scribe, are Col 2:17–18, where fifteen words are omitted; 1 Thess 2:15, where four words are omitted; and 2 Tim 4:8, where three words are omitted. At 1 Tim 2:1 ἐντύξεις is omitted, and at Heb 10:27 ζῆλος is omitted, which may represent an omission either by the scribe or the lector.[15] A careful lector, whose sole focus was the accurate reading and enunciation of the text, would produce relatively few skips resulting from parablepsis and likely very few or even no errors from homoeoteleuton and homoeoarcton.[16]

I propose that several commonalities of the singular readings confirm the oral background of the text (i.e., copying from a lector's reading), while also preserving evidence that there may have been a change in lector partway through the copying. That text shows consistent and repeated confusion of homophones, the most common of which are ει for ι (53 times), ε for αι at the end of words (28 times), ι for ει at the end of words (11 times), αι for ε (7 times), ἐάν for ἄν (2 times), and ἡμῶν for ὑμῶν (2 times).[17] Some of these singular readings could be attributed to regional orthographic peculiarities of the exemplar, which had itself probably originated in Egypt. However, such a solution cannot account for the itacisms resulting from probable auditory confusion where the consonants are visually dissimilar. For example, the scribe heard χ for κ, χ for ξ, and ξ for ζ. In each instance the confusion resulted in the creation of an unintelligible written text but a reasonably clear vocalized text. A practiced scribe, such as the one who wrote Codex I, would have corrected the majority of the confused readings, had he seen them in the exemplar, and it seems unlikely that he would have confused the spelling so consistently between reading the text aloud himself and copying it down. Moreover, at Heb 9:18 the scribe copied down ἐνκεκένισται rather than ἐγκεκαίνισται, mistaking the spelling of the verb because of the way it was

13. Cf. James R. Royse, "The Treatment of Scribal Leaps in Metzger's *Textual Commentary*," *NTS* 29 (1983): 545.

14. It may well also be the case that scribes could request the lector to reread a line.

15. These figures are based on the text of NA^{27}.

16. A similar conclusion was reached by Skeat, "Use of Dictation," 206.

17. The scribe also confused the following homophones one time each: ει for η, ε for ει, α for η, ου for ο, ε for η, ε for ο, η for ι, η for ει, ι for ε, χ for κ, χ for ξ, and ξ for ζ. Some of the confusion should perhaps be attributed to scribal/visual error, such as the confusion of ε for ο, but the majority of these singular readings are the result of mishearing and not visual alteration. Sanders's calculations were quite different because he based his on the Westcott and Hort text and may have used some of a restored text (based on Westcott and Hort) when doing his calculations (*Washington Manuscript of the Epistles of Paul*, 257–58).

pronounced and not because of any visual confusion between the letters ν and γ or ε and αι. Some of the confusion in the pronunciation of vowels was probably a result of historical shifts in pronunciation, but some of the changes were probably also a result of accent.[18]

Sanders attributed the complete text of Codex I to the work of single scribe, noting here and there some evidences of a second hand correcting minor orthographic mistakes.[19] Based on my examination of the manuscript, I found this assessment to be essentially true, but what went unnoticed in the original description is that the number of "singular" textual variants increases dramatically after Galatians. To give specific figures, in the fifty-eight folios that appear before Galatians, there are only eight singular readings, whereas the number increases to 131 singular readings in the remaining 109 folios.[20] The fragments do become significantly larger between folios 49 and 159, but even so the number of singular readings per extant line of text is markedly different in the two sections.

An exact comparison of the singular readings in the two sections is made more difficult because of the fragmentary nature of the manuscript, which contains relatively few complete lines of text for any portion of it. Therefore, a comparison of itacisms per line or inch of visible text would appear to be the most accurate means of making the comparison.[21] On the one 139 lines extant in the first fifty-eight folios, there is less than one singular reading for every fifteen lines of text, whereas, randomly taking 139 lines in the second half of the manuscript, there is an average of one singular reading for every seven lines of text; if the average is taken from the book of Hebrews, it is dramatically higher.[22] The simplest solution would be to look for the hand of a second scribe somewhere in the manuscript after Galatians, but paleographical analysis reveals that the codex is the work of a single scribe.[23]

---

18. Metzger, *Manuscripts of the Greek Bible,* 22; Royse, "Scribal Tendencies," 240; Aland and Aland, *Text of the New Testament,* 286.

19. Sanders, *Washington Manuscript of the Epistles of Paul,* 258.

20. "Singular" readings are identified here as those not found in any of the following: NA^{27}; Oscar Leopold von Gebhardt, *Novum Testamentum Graece: Recensionis Tischendorfianae Ultimae Textum cum Tregellesiano et Westcottio-Hortiano* (Leipzig: Tauchnitz, 1881); Hermann von Soden, *Die Schriften des Neuen Testaments* (Göttingen: Vandenhoeck & Ruprecht, 1913); and Reuben J. Swanson, *New Testament Greek Manuscripts: Variant Readings Arranged in Horizontal Lines against Codex Vaticanus* (Wheaton, Ill.; Tyndale House, 2003).

21. Colwell, "Scribal Habits in Early Papyri," 373–74.

22. These calculations are based on the new Multi-Spectral Images (MSI) done by the Institute for the Study and Preservation of Ancient Religious Texts (ISPART) at Brigham Young University. See Thomas A. Wayment, "Two New Textual Variants from the Freer Pauline Codex (I)," *JBL* 123 (2004): 737–40.

23. Sanders, *Washington Manuscript of the Epistles of Paul,* 258; this assessment as well has been confirmed through the use of the ISPART digital images of Codex I.

An alternate solution to the dilemma, one that can account for the differences in the two halves of the manuscript and the strong evidence that this codex was completed in a scriptorium through dictation, is to suggest that somewhere after Galatians, probably at the beginning of the Epistle to the Ephesians, the lector changed, not the scribe. In the first portion of the manuscript, errors are limited to the confusion of a few homophones (ε for αι, ἀν for ἐάν, ἡμῶν for ὑμων, and ι for ει). In the first portion of the codex, there are also numerous words and constructions that are written correctly but that are confused in the second half, such as the almost ubiquitous confusion of unaccented ι and ει, of final ε and αι in third-person-singular constructions.

Singular Readings in Codex I: The Scribe

Having attempted to account for the influence of the lector, it is now possible to consider the singular readings that originated either with the scribe or from the text of the exemplar. In some instances it may be possible to differentiate between scribe and exemplar, but for the most part there is no means of separating the two completely. Also, the process yields very few singular readings that have a potential claim to being part of the larger body of variants considered in New Testament textual criticism.

In a few instances the scribe presumably rearranged the word order of the text of the exemplar. If the text was read aloud, then it is easy to see how a scribe would mentally reorder the text if he were copying it down in short phrases. There are six surviving examples of such changes to word order, four of which are these: αὐτῷ δίδωσι (1 Cor 15:38), μεν ἐπιστολαὶ (2 Cor 10:10), ἄλλος δοκεῖ (Phil 3:4), and τὸ ἅγιον αὐτοῦ (1 Thess 4:8).[24] In the first instance, the scribe simply transposed the direct object of a transitive verb, a change that may have been triggered from similar usage elsewhere in the New Testament (cf. Eph 4:7; 1 Pet 1:21). Although the construction is not uniquely Pauline, its usage is manifest elsewhere in the New Testament. Similarly, the likely change of word order from τὸ πνεῦμα αὐτοῦ τὸ ἅγιον to τὸ πνεῦμα τὸ ἅγιον αὐτοῦ demonstrates that the scribe was probably influenced by his familiarity with the common construction τὸ πνεῦμα τὸ ἅγιον, rather than by an exemplar containing a rearranged word order.

Additionally, in 1 Tim 1:1 and 2 Tim 1:1 the scribe inverted the construction, χριστοῦ ἰησοῦ, probably because of his familiarity with the formulation "Jesus Christ." Given that the scribe worked by copying phrases after hearing them read out loud, it is more likely that the few changes in word order were simply the result of slight confusions between what was heard and what was subsequently written

24. At 1 Cor 15:38, the scribe dropped the final *nu* from διδωσιν because it was followed by a word beginning with a consonant.

down. That the number of changes to word order is limited to six instances attests to the carefulness of the scribe.

One other instance of the transposition of word order may demonstrate that the scribe was copying down text in longer units, perhaps remembering as many as eight words at a time. The phrase in question (Heb 10:17) reads, καὶ τῶν ἁμαρτιῶν αὐτῶν καὶ τῶν ἀνομιῶν αὐτῶν, which the scribe of Codex I wrote as, καὶ τῶν ἀνομιῶν αὐτῶν καὶ τῶν ἁμαρτιῶν αὐτῶν. The shift does nothing to change the meaning of the phrase but, instead, may be a partial harmonization to the wording of the Greek text of Jer 38:34 (31:34 MT).[25] Another small variant appears at 2 Cor 3:16 (not a singular reading), where the scribe records δ' ἄν instead of δὲ ἐὰν. This change in text may result from auditory confusion where the scribe failed to recognize the elision of the vowels, but, as in the Hebrews passage, it may also reflect the influence of phrasing from the Old Testament passage (Exod 34:34 LXX) that is echoed in 2 Corinthians here.

On a number of occasions the scribe altered the case of a noun. These changes all originate in the second portion of the manuscript. At Eph 4:18 the scribe changed the dative plural (ἐν αὐτοῖς) to a dative singular (ἐν αὐτῷ), which also changes the antecedent of the pronoun from ἔθνη (4:17) to θεοῦ (4:18). This subtle change in the pronoun produced a dramatic shift in meaning. Instead of reading "being alienated from a life in God because of the ignorance which is in them," one reads that they were "alienated from a life in God because of the ignorance that is in him." At 1 Thess 3:12 the accusative τὴν ἀγάπην replaces the dative singular. Περισσεύω requires a dative object, and therefore the reading τῇ ἀγάπῃ is correct. But in constructions where the proposition εἰς is used, the case of the object is the accusative (cf. 2 Cor 4:15). It is possible that the scribe mentally altered the case of the noun through attraction to the preposition εἰς. A similar occurrence likely took place at 2 Thess 1:1, where the preposition ἐν requires the dative but, through attraction to the noun, κυρίῳ was changed to a genitive κυριοῦ. Finally, at Heb 4:12 the scribe replaced the genitive plural ἐνθυμήσεων with the genitive singular ἐνθυμήσεως.[26]

Clearly, the scribe was well versed in Greek and readily declined the nouns in these instances accurately, while in the process creating several new singular readings. A result of his expert knowledge of Greek is that the text contains very few nonsense readings, and only occasionally did the scribe make a change that dramatically or significantly altered the meaning of the text. None of the examples listed above has any strong claim to being an early reading; in each example the changes appear to have been introduced by the scribe.

---

25. The relevant wording of the Rahlfs LXX at Jer 38:34 = ἵλεως ἔσομαι ταῖς ἀδικίαις αὐτῶν καὶ τῶν ἁμαρτιῶν αὐτῶν οὐ μὴ μνησθῶ.

26. Herbert W. Smyth, *Greek Grammar* (rev. ed.; Cambridge: Harvard University Press, 1984), §268; for this usage in particular in New Testament Greek, see BDF §182(5).

The instances of genuine errors are limited to a very few. The final sigma is missing from μερισμοῖς at Heb 2:4, which the corrector also ignored. At Heb 5:7 the scribe introduced the nonsense reading ικεισιας instead of ἱκετηρίας and at Heb 6:2 wrote βαπτισθενν instead of βαπτισμῶν. The scarcity of such nonsense readings is surprising. With a hand copied text, the percentage of nonsense readings (as a percentage of copyist-attributable variants) can number as high as 40 percent (𝔓[66]) and as low as 10 percent (𝔓[45]).[27] Exact figures for the majority of New Testament manuscripts are lacking, but all things considered, the scribe of 𝔓[45] was relatively careful in copying, while the scribe of 𝔓[66] appears to have been less so. Therefore, using Colwell's study of 𝔓[45], 𝔓[66], and 𝔓[75] for comparison, if the errors introduced into the text by the scribe of Codex I approach a percentage similar to that of 𝔓[45], the most careful of the three scribes, then the work of the scribe of the Freer codex could be considered equally careful.

If orthographic differences are excluded, in Codex I the ratio of nonsense readings in comparison to the total number of singular readings is less than one in twenty.[28] Comparatively, the scribe of Codex I was extremely careful in copying, even though the scribe produced a relatively high number of orthographic variants. If the copyist of this manuscript made an error of any sort, the newly created error almost always makes sense, rather than disrupting the flow of the text. This reflects the scribe's facility in Greek and also strongly indicates that the text was transmitted through dictation.

Potentially Early Variants in Codex I

Given the carefulness of the scribe in copying the text and the scribe's proclivity to reproduce a text that made sense, the following singular readings could be considered potentially early and important for the reconstruction of the New Testament text. At 1 Cor 15:38 the scribe included the article with ἴδιον, perhaps harmonizing the text to other similar usages in the Pauline corpus (see 1 Cor 3:8). However, although ἴδιον with the article is the preferred construction in the Pauline letters, the possessive adjective without the article is also attested (1 Cor 7:7).[29] The occasional dropping of the article is not surprising, but, given Paul's preference for including the article, it may well be the article originally appeared here. In his study of scribal habits, Dain states that the most common scribal

27. Colwell, "Scribal Habits in Early Papyri," 374–75. See also James R. Royse, "Scribal Habits in Early Greek New Testament Papyri" (Th.D. diss., Graduate Theological Union, 1981), for the most thorough analysis of relevant features of early New Testament papyri. Regrettably, it has still not yet been published.

28. Nonsense readings are defined as those that cannot be found in a lexicon or do not make sense in the context of the sentence.

29. BDF §286.

errors are these: (1) homoeoteleuton, (2) homoeoarcton, and (3) the omission of short words. Therefore, it is plausible that the reading of Codex I here is potentially early.[30]

At Phil 2:2 the text of Codex I reads, "fulfill my joy that you may *all* be likeminded." The addition of πάντες here may be the result of a scribal gloss that envisions the kingdom of God thriving in utopian harmony. This reading could be construed as a harmonization to Phil 1:7, which has the φρονεῖν and πάντων in close proximity. But, if so, the scribe certainly was adept at his work. In a similar vein, the scribe replaced διδασκαλίᾳ in 1 Tim 5:17 with ἀλήθεια. "Teaching" is likely the earlier reading, and, at some point likely prior to Codex I and its exemplar, a scribe substituted the one term for the other, both of which are employed somewhat synonymously in this epistle.[31] The extended context of 5:17 clarifies the nature of the teaching being referred to here, although when copying out longer texts, phrases and ideas tend to be viewed in greater isolation. Perhaps, therefore, the scribe inserted a clarifying noun. Although this reading cannot be traced definitively to the hand of the scribe of Codex I, it is possible that it was introduced during the copying process. But the stronger likelihood is that it originated from the exemplar.

In one instance the scribe replaced an adjective with a synonym, ἀγαθοῖς in place of καλοῖς (1 Tim 6:18). In the standard Pauline corpus, the use of ἀγαθόν with ἔργον is preferred (Rom 2:7; 13:3; 2 Cor 9:8; Phil 1:6; 2 Thess 2:17), whereas the adjective καλόν with ἔργον is attested only in the letters commonly referred to as "deutero-Pauline" or as originating from a Pauline school in the mid to late first century C.E. (1 Tim 3:1; 5:10, 25; Tit 2:7, 14; 3:8, 14; Heb 10:24). The use of ἀγαθός with ἔργον is, however, attested and therefore cannot be used to determine the originality of this reading (cf. Eph 2:10; Col 1:10; 1 Tim 2:10; 5:10; 2 Tim 2:21; 3:17; Tit 1:16; 3:1; Heb 13:21). The nearness of τὰ ἔργα τὰ καλὰ in 1 Tim 5:25 may argue for the choice of adjective in 1 Tim 6:18 by the author, but ἀγαθοῖς is equally plausible.[32]

At Heb 10:7 the scribe included the reading ἠβουλήθησαν (a phonetic corruption of the aorist ἐβουλήθησαν) after θέλημά σου. The scribe or lector was certainly mentally harmonizing the quotation with LXX Ps 39:9 (40:9 MT), which contains the reading ἐβουλήθην, but either scribe or lector inadvertently changed the third-person singular to a third-person plural.

At 2 Tim 1:10 the text of Codex I reads θεοῦ instead of χριστοῦ ἰησοῦ. A shift from God to Christ Jesus would be simple to explain as an instance of scribal

---

30. Dain, *Les Manuscrits*, 43–44; Colwell, "Scribal Habits in Early Papyri," 376 n. 6.

31. For διδασκαλία, see 1 Tim 1:10; 4:1, 6, 13, 16; 6:1, 3. For ἀλήθεια, see 1 Tim 2:4, 7; 3:15; 4:3; 6:5.

32. Michael W. Holmes, "The Case for Reasoned Eclecticism," in *Rethinking New Testament Textual Criticism* (ed. David Alan Black; Grand Rapids: Baker, 2002), 77–100.

clarification of the text, but the opposite is more difficult to explain. A possible explanation seems to be that the lector conflated 2 Tim 1:8–9 with 1:10, and, seeing θεοῦ in these earlier verses, harmonized 1:10 with them.[33] It is obvious, with the insertion of θεοῦ, that the passage still refers to the saving work of Jesus Christ, and therefore the reading should at least be included in the critical apparatus of the Greek New Testament (as it is in the apparatus of NA^{27} edition at this point). Whether it is original is nearly impossible to tell, since it can be accounted for and dismissed on the same grounds.

Conclusion

The trend of New Testament textual criticism over the past several decades has been to lean away from the suggestion that manuscripts were widely copied through dictation in scriptoria. Dictation theory, however, may aid in explaining the appearance of certain types of textual variants and singular readings, which otherwise would be attributed to the scribe. When it can be shown that a text was copied through dictation, it is important, where possible, to differentiate between the work of the scribe and lector. One important reason for doing so is that readings that can accurately be traced to the lector can in turn reveal something of the exemplar being used in the dictation process. Furthermore, readings that can be attributed to the scribe alone can be isolated and explained in their historical context rather than being conflated with the larger body of potential early textual variants. Knowing that a reading originated in North Africa in the sixth century, for example, with Codex I, would in turn provide details about the church in that locale in that specific time period. Admittedly, we are a long way off from being able to describe the transmission history of the New Testament writings with such detail, but as the field continues to progress the potential to explain in greater detail the process through which New Testament texts were copied is appealing. Theory requires that the subject be given consideration with respect to specific textual examples.

The scribe of Codex I produced an accurate and carefully recorded text. The scribe was an excellent penman and formed letters with great skill and consistency. The greatest obstacle in the transmission process was phonetic confusion of unaccented vowels. Rarely was there any confusion of consonants, although the homophones ξ ζ, χ presented some confusion. Only in a few instances did the scribe create a nonsensical reading, being careful to decline nouns and conjugate

33. The term σώτηρ is dominantly used with reference to God in the Pastoral Epistles (1 Tim 1:1; 2:3; 4:10; Tit 1:3; 2:10; 3:4; cf., however, Tit 1:4; 3:6), so a scribe may simply have been influenced here by this more typical reference to *God* as "Savior." It is also just possible that the scribe intended to refer to Jesus as "God" in preferring the latter term here. At least from early second-century texts onward, Christians could refer to Jesus as "God."

verbs accurately to their context. Given the carefulness of the scribe and the apparent accuracy of the dictation process for this text, the few singular readings that do exist have a greater claim to have originated in the scriptorium's exemplar. In the larger context of textual criticism, these singular readings hold the same claim to originality that the exemplar can claim, and only in a few instances is there evidence that the exemplar contained additional potential early readings.

Manuscript Markup

Timothy J. Finney

Introduction

The potential of computing in relation to biblical manuscripts is largely unrealized. Granted, the infrastructure to allow manuscript texts and images to be shared through computer networks is already in place. However, digital versions of the texts and images are few and far between. Moreover, those that exist do not conform to a common standard, thereby frustrating any effort to construct a great archive of biblical manuscripts.

The change from print to computer media is well under way. One can compare it to the shift that began in the mid-1400s, when the movable-type printing press was introduced to Europe. In that momentous development, the biblical text was the first to enter the new paradigm. Even so, the Greek New Testament had to wait over fifty years until Erasmus threw together his edition, based on the manuscripts he had close to hand. Nowadays, the texts of many Bible versions are available online. However, the manuscripts on which these rest remain locked in dusty corners, almost as inaccessible as when Tischendorf set out on his quest to bring them to light in the nineteenth century.

Biblical manuscripts and the texts that they contain are of enormous importance. They are the basis of the biblical text, yet we have neglected to translate them into the computer medium. One could despair of ever reaching the goal of digitizing the manuscripts, for the scale of the task is so huge that even a single-minded prodigy such as Tischendorf would find it impossible. The task is, nevertheless, achievable by combined effort. However, to avoid another Babel, we *must* agree on common methods. With agreed standards, we will be able to create a great archive of our biblical manuscript heritage. Without common standards, digital renditions of the biblical manuscripts will continue in their present state of disarray, and a unified collection will remain an impossible dream.

As one step toward the goal of a collective online archive of biblical manuscripts, this essay outlines a method for transferring the texts of biblical manuscript (as opposed to their images) into the computer medium. It will use as a case study the Epistle to the Hebrews as found in the Freer manuscript of Paul.

Markup Fundamentals

"Markup," or transcription, might be described as the process of interpreting that which is symbolically depicted (the verbal form is "mark up"). To ground this definition in the context of biblical manuscripts and computers, "transcription" is conversion of scribal handwriting to text in a computer, with "metadata" (often described as data about data) adding interpretations of the text.

Being human productions, manuscripts exhibit much variety. What we choose to mark up might depend on convention or on our individual preference. In any case, when planning a markup project, it is essential to keep in mind the eventual purposes of the marked-up documents. What needs to be included is governed by what needs to be done with the documents afterwards.

There is nothing absolute about markup. It really is an exercise in interpretation and in choosing to include what is thought most useful. The choosing should be done carefully. Besides obsolescence, a potential danger for transcriptions is complexity. Including too much markup inspired by a particular interpretation of what the text is makes the transcription less useful to those who view the text differently. We seek, therefore, a common basic framework that includes the fundamentals but allows others to pin their interpretations upon it.[1]

What, then, are the fundamentals involved? Some of these relate to the manuscripts and the purpose for which we want to use them, whereas others relate to the markup system that we aim to create. What is it about manuscripts that matters the most? Artistic embellishments matter to an art historian. Format, writing material, and construction matter to a codicologist. But it is the *words* that matter for traditional text-critical purposes, which focus on establishing a text and unraveling the history of its transmission. Therefore, we are concerned with who wrote what when and, perhaps, why.

Words are made of letters, and one could place the focus of a transcription there, being careful to classify each letter's style, ink, state of preservation, and so on. But if our main concern is the words and not the letters, then digital manuscript editions would do well to have words as their primary focus. This is not to say that spelling is unimportant. In fact, orthographic variation among the manuscripts contains information that can be extracted using means such as multivariate analysis to help understand the history of the text. It is a mistake, therefore, to level the spelling (ignoring itacisms) at the transcription stage. However, as fewer of the eventual users of a transcription or its derivative works will be interested in scribal habits, the edition should retain the orthography but allow it to be hidden from view. That is, one should be able to switch between a

---

1. Paul Eggert, "Text-Encoding, Theories of the Text, and the 'Work-Site,'" *Literary & Linguistic Computing* 20 (2005): 425–35.

smoothed text that uses conventional and standardized spelling and a crude text that faithfully reproduces scribal quirks.

Integrity is another essential. This is particularly true of the biblical text, where the words matter at many levels. What we seek for each manuscript is no less than a "canonical" text—an authoritative transcription that can be used as the launching point for all subsequent work. In order to become authoritative, the text first has to be accepted by its audience. To help this happen, it needs to be open to peer review and correction. The transcription should, therefore, live within a versioning system that keeps track of each alteration and that, if necessary, allows the history of the digital text to be reconstructed.

Perhaps the most important aspect of integrity is the ability to admit doubt. On the one hand, it is a common error of readers to assume that the reading text of an authoritative edition is beyond reasonable doubt. On the other hand, editors struggle with how to convey that this is not the case at all. In printed transcriptions, they use sublinear dots and similar devices to indicate uncertainty at the letter level. However, the extent and nature of the doubt thus conveyed is notoriously unclear.[2] The same is true of the quaint *vid.* used to signal doubt at the word level. We would do well to end this uncertainty about uncertainty once and for all. The transition to computer-based transcriptions provides the perfect opportunity to do so.

In cases where multiple manuscripts of the same writing exist, it is natural to want to compare them. Computers possess an innate aptitude when it comes to comparison. However, the current generation of computers is mindless and therefore requires a series of guideposts to stay on track when comparing biblical manuscript texts. The conventional book, chapter, and verse divisions of the Bible provide a useful frame of reference for collation purposes.

Other essential elements of a good markup system are openness and utility. A design that requires proprietary systems to compose, interrogate, or reconfigure transcriptions is destined for obscurity, as noted by Eggert.[3] Markup involves a lot of work, so any planning that will help make the transcriptions "future-proof" is worth the effort. I am well-acquainted with the problem of obsolescence, having spent five years transcribing the thirty or so papyrus and uncial Greek manuscripts of the Epistle to the Hebrews known at the time I did the work.[4] I used a markup system that was then a reasonable choice but is now obsolete. It is likely that my own analysis, using collation programs I had to write for the purpose, is the only use to which these transcriptions will ever be put.

---

2. Herbert C. Youtie, "Text and Context in Transcribing Papyri," *Greek, Roman, and Byzantine Studies* 7 (1966): 251–58.

3. Eggert, "Text-Encoding."

4. Timothy J. Finney, "The Ancient Witnesses of the Epistle to the Hebrews" (Ph.D. diss., Murdoch University, Western Australia, 1999). Online: http://purl.org/tfinney/PhD.

To avoid the demise of its products, a transcription system should integrate well with readily available, reasonably priced, and established text editors for composition, query languages (e.g., XQuery) for interrogation, and transformation languages (e.g., XSLT) for presenting the transcriptions in common media formats such as HTML and PDF. The system should not impose unreasonable demands upon transcribers. It should be easy to learn, easy to use, and robust. It should make common tasks straightforward and deal with ambiguity in a well-defined manner. These requirements are especially apt in a technically challenged field such as biblical studies.

One fundamental aspect of a good transcription remains to be mentioned. A transcription is not complete unless it includes a bibliographic description of its subject. This might include the manuscript's name, date, provenance, contents, present location, shelf number, details of who performed the transcription, a record of alterations, and so on.

Data Structures and Abstractions

Computer scientists use data structures and abstractions to represent real objects as digital entities. Before launching into a transcription exercise, it is worth looking at what kinds of data structures and abstractions are needed to convert marks on a manuscript into bytes on a computer disk. The data model used as the basis of a transcription system must be capable of representing the text of a biblical manuscript. Otherwise, insurmountable problems may be encountered during the transcription phase.

What Is a Transcription?

Descartes arrived at *cogito ergo sum* after seeking a statement about reality that could not be challenged. What would be an equally unassailable definition of a transcription? I suppose that the simplest definition is "a sequence of words." If that were all a transcription is, then it would be easy to come up with an adequate data structure to represent it. However, the reality is not so simple. For one thing, a word can appear in various guises. For another, there can be parallel sequences of words within a single manuscript, as when a corrector has been at work. Finally, there is uncertainty. The words that compose a transcription may be subject to doubt. Whatever the cause, the presence of uncertainty creates a dilemma: the very foundation of our transcription data structure—the text itself—is shifting sand. A more general definition is therefore "a set of sequences of words, where the contents of each sequence may be subject to doubt."

Words

Words are abstractions, Platonic ideals. There are many physical renditions of a word, no two the same in every detail. In manuscripts, words have variable spelling and diacritics. In a computerized transcription, a text is a sequence of words and punctuation, and words are sequences of letters and diacritics that are themselves represented as sequences of bytes.[5] The computer architecture necessary to enter characters is not trivial. Until recently, text was entered using a single byte per character. There are, however, only 256 combinations of eight bits, so this is the maximum number of characters that can be accommodated by a single-byte encoding system. Due to the limited number of code points, it is necessary to use the same ones to represent letters from different scripts. Thus, code point 97 decimal (61 hexadecimal) is rendered as "a" in a Roman font but may also represent α in a Greek font or א in a Hebrew font.

Unicode uses multiple bytes to represent individual characters.[6] It has code points for every script used in biblical manuscripts, with each alphabet assigned its own block of code points. Roman letters are assigned one range of code points (the same as used in the single-byte system), Greek letters another, and Hebrew letters yet another. Each letter has its own code point. So, for example, Roman "a" is assigned 97 decimal as before, but Greek α is assigned 945 decimal (3B1 hexadecimal), and Hebrew א is assigned 1488 decimal (5D0 hexadecimal).

Unicode is the best system to use for encoding the characters in biblical manuscripts. A practical problem remains, however. What does one do to enter the characters? Modern operating systems are Unicode-compliant and provide various means for entering Unicode, including switchable keyboard mappings and direct code point entry. With switchable keyboards, a user can choose one keyboard mapping to enter, for example, Roman characters and another to enter the Greek or Hebrew text of a given manuscript. Direct entry, which involves entering the numerical code for each character, is only practical if a few characters need to be transcribed. It is therefore not suitable for transcribing whole manuscripts.

Unicode provides two ways to deal with diacritics. One, precomposed characters, incorporates a letter and its diacritics in a single code point. The other, combining diacritical marks, employs separate code points for the letter and its diacritics. For example, code point 1F00 hexadecimal is defined as "Greek small letter alpha with psili." The same letter and breathing can be formed by following the letter α (3B1 hexadecimal) with a combining smooth breathing mark (313 hexadecimal). Both approaches result in an *alpha* with smooth breathing being

5. A byte is a sequence of eight binary digits, or bits.

6. Unicode Consortium, "About the Unicode Standard." Online: http://www.unicode.org/standard/standard.html.

displayed in a Unicode-compliant system. The approach that renders diacritics and alphabetic letters separately would seem the best for transcribing biblical manuscripts—it allows the transcriber to treat letters and diacritics individually if, say, a letter is well preserved but its diacritics are not.

Moving back to words, when collating the substantive (i.e., orthographically leveled) texts of a collection of manuscripts, it is first necessary to convert each word and punctuation mark to an ideal form. To do this, a standard orthography has to be specified for *every* word and punctuation mark of the manuscript! Does this mean that the transcriber has to type in twice as many characters? Fortunately, biblical manuscript texts are sufficiently uniform to allow partial automation of this task. A program could be written that uses a standard text to supply orthographic equivalents for most of a manuscript's words. It would track the manuscript text using book, chapter, and verse milestone markers and supply matching words at most points. However, the program could be confounded and would fail wherever the manuscript text diverges from the standard text, requiring a human to fill in the missing parts. Other strategies are possible, but none is perfectly reliable. For example, a look-up table that compares a manuscript word with, say, all the words in the *Thesaurus Linguae Graecae* might select the wrong equivalent, especially if the manuscript word has particularly eccentric spelling, is poorly preserved, or lacks the diacritics that are sometimes required to choose the correct lexical form.

Punctuation is a different matter. There is such a variety of forms and scribal practice that it is unsafe to supply equivalents from a standard text. Even spaces may function as punctuation in some *scriptio continua* manuscripts.[7] Faced with this difficulty, one could emulate Procrustes and specify a single equivalent for all punctuation, stretching or chopping all of the pauses to one size.

Who Wrote What When?

A manuscript text can be the work of more than one scribe and is often altered by one or more correctors. Consider the analogy of a string made up of differently shaded segments, with each shade corresponding to a particular scribe or corrector, as in figure 1.

Stretches of text affected by more than one hand can be represented as parallel segments between points of divergence and convergence. This is an example of a very general data structure called a "graph," which may be defined as a set of nodes connected by arcs.[8] If the editor can identify which hand is responsible for

7. Frederic G. Kenyon, ed., *Pauline Epistles: Text* (suppl. to fasc. 3 of *The Chester Beatty Biblical Papyri: Descriptions and Texts of Twelve Manuscripts on Papyrus of the Greek Bible*; London: Emery Walker, 1936), xiv.

8. I use the term "graph" in the formal sense used by mathematicians and computer scientists. For more details, see Paul E. Black, ed., *Dictionary of Algorithms and Data Structures* (US National Institute of Standards and Technology). Online: http://www.nist.gov/dads/.

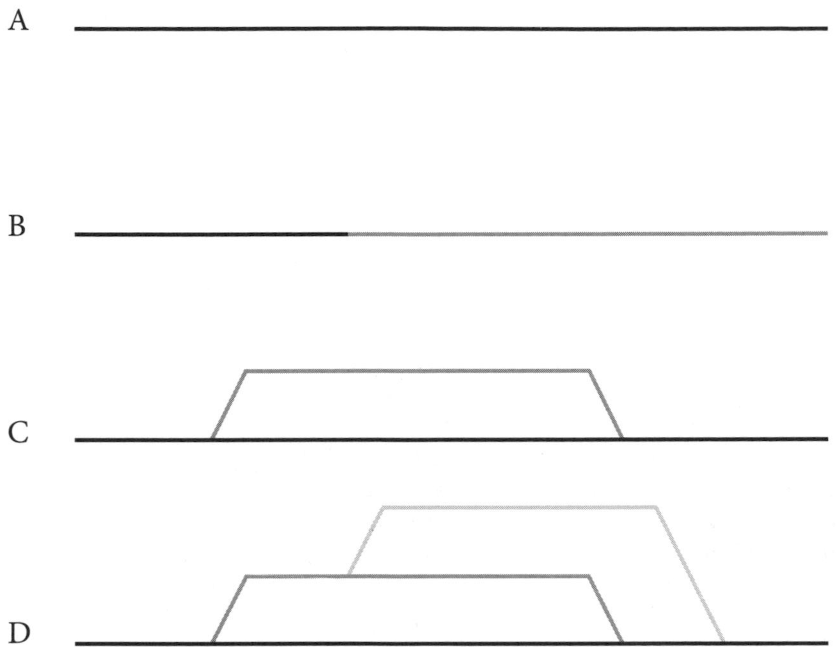

Figure 1. String analogy of scribes and correctors. (A) The work of a single hand. (B) The first part is copied by one hand, the second by another. (C) Part of the first hand's text has been corrected by another hand. (D) As in (C), but a third hand has corrected some of the second hand's corrections, then continued on to correct some of the first hand's text.

which piece of text, the manuscript can be represented by a graph, each arc (i.e., segment) being associated with one hand.

The Text Encoding Initiative (TEI) guidelines constitute a well thought out and practical transcription system.[9] However, due to the underlying data model, there are inherent limitations to what the system can be used to represent. The guidelines employ Extensible Markup Language (XML) to describe objects. The data structure underlying XML is a "tree"—a hierarchy of nodes and subnodes beginning with a single root node and spreading out to "leaf" nodes, which have no subnodes.[10] Consequently, editors wishing to use the TEI guidelines will encounter problems when they want to transcribe nonhierarchical data structures such as the one shown in figure 1 (D).

---

9. C. M. Sperberg-McQueen and L. Burnard, eds., *TEI P4: Guidelines for Electronic Text Encoding and Interchange* (Oxford: Text Encoding Initiative Consortium, 2002).

10. See Black, *Dictionary,* for definitions of all these terms.

Despite this limitation, the guidelines are very rich in features relevant to manuscript markup. They are widely used for markup within the humanities, so it is unwise to abandon them, in spite of this difficulty. Indeed, there are a number of ways to create TEI-conformant transcriptions that can deal with the problem. One uses a mechanism called "stand-off" markup, which has the effect of converting the tree structure of XML into the graph structure required to represent properly the features of a typical biblical manuscript.

When a number of scribes and correctors have worked on a manuscript, the question of "who wrote what when" becomes important. Such a manuscript consists of multiple layers, with each successive scribe and corrector superimposing text on what is already there. Each layer is a sample of the respective scribe or corrector's "exemplar" (whether that be an actual manuscript or simply the corrector's preferred reading of the text). Analysis of the layers therefore allows us to plot the course of textual development.

In order to separate the layers, an editor must first separate the work of each scribe and corrector. The editor must also determine the order in which they worked, and dates for each may be guessed as well. In addition, each of these steps is subject to uncertainty. When it comes to the order of scribes and correctors, the nature of the uncertainty becomes complex. The question of "who wrote what when" must be asked at every place where multiple layers of text exist, and it must be asked as many times as there are layers. Getting the answer wrong at one layer will affect the validity of any assertions made about subsequent layers.

Uncertainty

Since the biblical manuscripts preserve a message that deals with the high ideal of truth, it is apt to be truthful when recording what they contain. Every aspect of a transcription is subject to uncertainty, from the letters themselves to who wrote them, to when they were written, to what words they represent. It is necessary, therefore, to be able to describe the uncertainty associated with any aspect of a transcription. This can be achieved with a linking mechanism that allows a description of uncertainty to be associated with every uncertain element of the transcription.

A linking mechanism is only part of the overall solution. There also needs to be a useful convention for describing the degree of uncertainty. The editor could use a probability value such as "0.46." However, this gives a false sense of precision to what is usually a judgment. Forensic language such as "beyond reasonable doubt" is more appropriate. Even so, it is helpful for the reader to know what range of probabilities to associate with a description of uncertainty. This can be achieved by selecting a number of categories to express editorial confidence. Each category has a forensic description and an associated confidence interval (i.e., range of probabilities).

In general, the fewer the categories, the more repeatable but imprecise the description. At the other end of the spectrum, the inclusion of more categories makes a more expressive system, but separate editors will concur less often concerning which category is appropriate to describe the uncertainty of a particular feature.[11] A binary system is the most repeatable and least expressive. Its categories are "beyond reasonable doubt" and "not beyond reasonable doubt." If the first category is associated with a confidence interval of greater than 0.95, then the other category has a probability range of less than or equal to 0.95. There are, however, many other possibilities. The following tables present this binary system along with my suggestions for three-level and four-level schemes. The probability levels that delimit each category (e.g., 0.95, 0.50, 0.05) are arbitrary. Nevertheless, they are not without justification. The values of 0.95 and 0.05 are commonly used in the context of confidence intervals. If, for example, I assert a confidence level (C) of greater than 0.95, I am saying that I expect to be right in at least nineteen out of twenty instances. This is a high enough level of confidence to associate with "beyond reasonable doubt."

Another reason for using these particular probability levels is that there are roughly twenty letters in the alphabets of the subject matter. Therefore, assigning a confidence level of 0.05 or less to a particular letter is roughly equivalent to saying that it could be any letter. Finally, a probability of 0.50 represents an even chance, a choice between two equally commendable possibilities.

Table 1. Two levels

Code	**Confidence interval**	**Description**
2–A	0.95 < C <= 1.00	Beyond reasonable doubt.
2–B	0.00 < C <= 0.95	Not beyond reasonable doubt.

Table 2. Three levels

Code	**Confidence interval**	**Description**
3–A	0.95 < C <= 1.00	Beyond reasonable doubt.
3–B	0.05 < C <= 0.95	The most commendable of up to twenty possibilities.
3–C	0.00 < C <= 0.05	Very doubtful.

Table 3. Four levels

Code	**Confidence interval**	**Description**
4–A	0.95 < C <= 1.00	Beyond reasonable doubt.
4–B	0.50 < C <= 0.95	The more commendable of two possibilities.
4–C	0.05 < C <= 0.50	The most commendable of between two and twenty possibilities.
4–D	0.00 < C <= 0.05	Very doubtful.

---

11. Timothy J. Finney, "Uncertainty in Text, Markup and Beyond" (2005). Online: http://purl.org/tfinney/uncertainty/uncertainty.html.

The last of these is comparable with the four-level scheme used to grade the editors' confidence in readings selected for the text of the United Bible Societies *Greek New Testament.*[12]

Frame of Reference

A common frame of reference is required to allow convenient access to the parts of a transcribed manuscript text. The biblical text already has a suitable referencing system: verse, within chapter, within book. If every transcription of a given biblical text incorporates this scheme, then a particular verse in a particular transcription can be readily extracted. The same allows an array of transcriptions to be aligned for machine collation.

This is not the only reference system that might be considered. There is also line within column, column within folio, and folio within quire. The editor cannot know beforehand which scheme a given reader prefers, so both must be incorporated. These two reference schemes cannot coexist as hierarchies in a markup system such as TEI XML because their transition points do not coincide. However, they can coexist if the respective hierarchies are indirectly marked using empty "milestone elements." This is another case where it is necessary to use a graph instead of a tree when representing the data of a biblical manuscript.[13]

The transition points in these reference schemes are sometimes ambiguous. Surprisingly, the location of a verse division can vary between authorities. For example, there are places where the verse divisions of the Textus Receptus and the United Bible Societies *Greek New Testament* do not coincide. Consequently, the editor must use the division points of one and only one authority and inform readers of the choice. Similarly, quire, folio, column, and line numbers are subject to uncertainty, as when a manuscript is fragmentary. In such cases, all the editor can do is make a best estimate and inform the reader concerning the nature and degree of doubt associated with the estimate.

Stand-Off Markup

A typical biblical manuscript contains one or more sets of words, word dividers, and punctuation comprised of individual symbols that we shall call "characters." Each set represents the work of one scribe or corrector. The characters, the words,

12. Barbara Aland, Kurt Aland, Johannes Karavidopoulos, Carlo M. Martini, and Bruce M. Metzger, eds., *The Greek New Testament* (United Bible Societies 4th rev. ed.; Stuttgart: Deutsche Bibelgesellschaft, 1993), 3*.

13. Again, I use terms familiar among those who work in computing. See definitions in Black, *Dictionary.*

and the time-order of scribes and correctors may be subject to doubt. How might an editor deal with this structure and include annotation as well?

In one approach, which I shall call "inline" markup, the markup is interspersed with the transcription. This technique is compact and economical but does not cope well with concurrent hierarchies of the sort noted above. Another approach, "stand-off" markup, superimposes interpretation upon a skeletal transcription, using a pointing mechanism. Each item in the transcription is provided with an identifier that allows it to be associated with relevant markup.

Example 1. Inline versus Stand-Off Markup

Inline markup of a simple phrase with several annotations might look like this:

```
<w>The</w><w>cat</w><w>sat</w><w>on</w><w>the</w><w>mat
</w><note>This word may be "rat."</note><c type="punct">.
</c><note>This sentence is often used in examples.
</note>
```

In stand-off markup, the skeletal transcription would look like this: (Any suitable naming convention can be used for identifiers such as `xml:id="aaaa"`; the one shown here leaves plenty of room to insert additional items.)

```
<w xml:id="aaaa">The</w>
<w xml:id="bbbb">cat</w>
<w xml:id="cccc">sat</w>
<w xml:id="dddd">on</w>
<w xml:id="eeee">the</w>
<w xml:id="ffff">mat</w>
<c type="punct" xml:id="gggg">.</c>
```

Interpretive markup is then placed in another part of the transcription:

```
<milestone unit="sentence" n="1" synch="aaaa"/>
<note target="aaaa" targetEnd="gggg">This sentence is
often used in examples.</note>
<certainty target="ffff" locus="First letter." degree="3-
B"/>
<note target="ffff">This word may be "rat."</note>
```

In either technique, scribes and correctors can be treated individually, and the work of each can be transcribed separately. Alternatively, one transcription can be used for all. If so, however, corrections of the kind shown in fig. 1 (D) will cause problems with inline markup because they do not "nest" hierarchically (i.e., the one does not go within the other in a hierarchical relationship). By contrast, stand-off markup has no trouble coping.

Example 2. Handling Nonhierarchical Structures

It seems that the first hand wrote, "The cat sat on the mat"; a second changed this to "The cat pounced on the mat"; and a third altered the text to "The cat pounced upon the rat."

```
<w xml:id="aaaa">The</w>
<w xml:id="bbbb">cat</w>
<w xml:id="cccc">sat</w>
<w xml:id="ccdd">pounced</w>
<w xml:id="dddd">on</w>
<w xml:id="ddee">upon</w>
<w xml:id="eeee">the</w>
<w xml:id="ffff">mat</w>
<w xml:id="ffgg">rat</w>
<c type="punct" xml:id="gggg">.</c>
```

The text of each hand is specified as a group of links that point to the words themselves:

```
<linkGrp xml:id="h1">
<ptr type="word" target="aaaa"/>
<ptr type="word" target="bbbb"/>
<ptr type="word" target="cccc"/>
<ptr type="word" target="dddd"/>
<ptr type="word" target="eeee"/>
<ptr type="word" target="ffff"/>
<ptr type="punct" target="gggg"/>
</linkGrp>
<linkGrp xml:id="h2">
<ptr type="word" target="aaaa"/>
<ptr type="word" target="bbbb"/>
<ptr type="word" target="ccdd"/>
<ptr type="word" target="dddd"/>
<ptr type="word" target="eeee"/>
<ptr type="word" target="ffff"/>
<ptr type="punct" target="gggg"/>
</linkGrp>
<linkGrp xml:id="h3">
<ptr type="word" target="aaaa"/>
<ptr type="word" target="bbbb"/>
```

```
<ptr type="word" target="ccdd"/>
<ptr type="word" target="ddee"/>
<ptr type="word" target="eeee"/>
<ptr type="word" target="ffgg"/>
<ptr type="punct" target="gggg"/>
[illegible]
```

This approach has the pleasing side effect of simplifying machine collation. A collation program need only compare the unique identifiers to decide whether two texts are the same at a particular place. Otherwise, it would need additional logic to distinguish between actual and spurious alignment where the same word is repeated in a section of text.

There still remains the question of what to do if the editor is not certain of which scribe wrote what. When it comes to alterations, an error of markup in an earlier stage invalidates the markup of later stages. I do not know how to deal with this Gordian knot. For now, it must suffice to note occasions when there is uncertainty of this kind and to present alterations in whatever order seems most consistent with the evidence.

Application

So much for theory. What follows is a transcription case-study with the Epistle to the Hebrews in the Freer manuscript of Paul as subject. TEI XML is employed for the purpose, using inline rather than stand-off markup. This denies the benefits of stand-off markup but also saves the drudgery of supplying each word and punctuation mark with a unique identifier. If the need ever arose, it would be reasonably straightforward to generate a stand-off markup equivalent from the inline transcription.

The TEI guidelines provide such a rich set of tags that it is unlikely any two transcribers working in isolation would mark up a manuscript transcription in precisely the same way. A "guide to local practice" focused on biblical manuscripts would encourage consistency of markup within the field. I previously wrote a short guide on manuscript markup using TEI Lite, a scaled-down version of the full TEI tag set.[14] Subsequently, the *EpiDoc* guide has been created in an effort to standardize epigraphic markup.[15] I have consulted both of these guides, along with the full TEI guidelines, in order to compose a TEI XML rendition of Henry Sanders's 1918 edition of Codex I (016). This digital document, named

14. Timothy J. Finney, "Converting Leiden-Style Editions to TEI Lite XML" (2001). Online: http://www.tei-c.org/Sample_Manuals/leiden.html.

15. Tom Elliott, ed., *EpiDoc: Epigraphic Documents in TEI XML*. Online: http://epidoc.sourceforge.net/.

U16.xml, provides examples of how to mark up various phenomena encountered in this manuscript.[16] For the sake of brevity, it is confined to the text of the Epistle to the Hebrews in Codex I.

A Lightning Introduction to XML

An XML document consists of a tree comprised of nodes (i.e., branching points). There are various kinds of nodes, with "element" and "text" nodes being frequently encountered types. Element nodes may contain other element nodes, text nodes, or nothing at all. An empty element node or text node is a leaf of the tree—a terminus of branching. Each element may possess attributes, which serve either for identification or to qualify the element's meaning.

Which elements and attributes are allowed where can be specified by a "schema." Armed with a schema and an XML "validator," an author can check whether his or her document conforms to the rules contained in the schema. For example, one could write a schema that includes a rule allowing that page elements may contain line elements but not vice versa. A document that contained a page element within a line element would not be validated in this schema. My XML transcription of Codex I obeys the rules of the Text Encoding Initiative's schema and is, thus, a TEI XML document.

An XML document can be reconfigured using XSLT (extensible stylesheet language transformation). A common transformation is from XML to HTML (hypertext markup language), which can be displayed with a web browser. The appearance of the HTML may be further controlled with CSS (cascading stylesheets). A new language named XQuery allows collections of XML documents to be "interrogated" in order to extract data. One can hardly imagine the research potential of an XML database loaded with a large collection of consistently marked up biblical manuscript transcriptions. Given such a database, it would be possible to write XQueries to investigate relations among texts, analyze trends that occur across texts (for example, from earlier to later correctors), and so on.

A "transform" (U16.xsl) and stylesheet (U16.css) have been written to produce an HTML document (U16.html) from my XML transcription (U16.xml). All these files are available from the SBL web site, where they can be viewed with a web browser.[17]

16. As a programmer, I have an aversion to beginning a file name with a numeral. I therefore prefer the "U" (for "uncial") prefix over the conventional "0."

17. See http://www.sbl-site.org/Resources/Resources_ManuscriptMarkup.aspx. Anyone who wishes to write and process XML, XSLT, CSS, and XQuery files is well advised to do so within an adequate XML development environment. I use an Ubuntu Linux operating system and the oXygen XML editor for file preparation and processing.

The Header

The following is a basic TEI XML file.

Example 3. A basic TEI XML file:

```
<TEI xmlns="http://www.tei-c.org/ns/1.0">
<teiHeader>
<fileDesc>
<titleStmt>
<title>
<!-- supply a title -->
</title>
</titleStmt>
<publicationStmt>
<p>
<!-- supply publication information-->
</p>
</publicationStmt>
<sourceDesc>
<p>
<!-- supply information about the source -->
</p>
</sourceDesc>
</fileDesc>
</teiHeader>
<text>
<front>
<!-- front matter goes here -->
</front>
<body>
<p>
<!-- the body goes here -->
</p>
</body>
<back>
<!-- back matter goes here -->
</back>
</text>
</TEI>
```

The “root element” (<TEI>) branches into two “child elements,” one for the “header” (<teiHeader>) and one for the text itself (<text>). The header contains information about the transcription: details such as its title, the authority under which it is published, the source from which it was transcribed, and other items necessary for a useful bibliographic characterization. TEI XML includes a manuscript description module that can be used in the header and elsewhere. The transcription file (U16.xml) shows how the header can be used to include metadata for a biblical manuscript.

TEXT

The <text> element branches into <front>, <body>, and <back> elements. The <front> is intended for prefatory matter; the <back> is for appendices and the like. The main text goes in the <body>. Apart from a transcription of the biblical text itself, a printed edition of a biblical manuscript might include an introduction, apparatus, notes, bibliography, perhaps even a translation. Digital renditions of these parts may be put in the <front> and <back>, or they may be included as labeled divisions of the <body>. Whether for good or bad, both of the previously mentioned guides take the latter approach.

Example 4. Divisions of the <body>

```
<body>
<div type="description">
<p>A description would go here.</p>
</div>
<div type="transcription">
<ab xml:id="some.id.scheme">
The transcription goes here.
</ab>
</div>
<div type="whatever">
<p>Add whatever divisions required.</p>
</div>
<div type="bibliography">
<p>A bibliography would go here.</p>
</div>
</body>
```

My transcription of Codex I includes descriptive material in the <sourceDesc> element of the header, although this material could have been placed in a <div type="description"> instead. Purists may argue that a rich header is preferable to a multifaceted body. However, working with the TEI header is sometimes challenging, making the less-constrained environment of divisions within the <body> more attractive.

The transcription itself has a dedicated division and is placed within an <ab>, which the TEI guidelines describe thus: "(anonymous block) contains any arbitrary component-level unit of text, acting as an anonymous container for phrase or inter level elements analogous to, but without the semantic baggage of, a paragraph."[18] Many biblical manuscripts are fragmentary. As a consequence, they do not begin or end at canonical boundaries. The anonymous aspect of the <ab> therefore makes it suitable for holding fragments. The element is also useful for splitting a long transcription into convenient segments, such as individual books.

Milestones

As noted already, at least two reference systems apply to each biblical manuscript. One system is the modern biblical book, chapter, and verse scheme; the other specifies manuscript, quire, folio (or page), column, and line. As mentioned before, these cannot be represented as concurrent hierarchies in an XML document. They can, however, be included by using empty "milestone" elements. There are two varieties. One type is the generic <milestone>, whose `unit` and `n` attributes specify the kind of division and its value. The other type is comprised of dedicated elements for widely encountered divisions such as page (<pb>) and line (<lb>) breaks. Here are the first few lines of the text of Hebrews in Codex I, showing the use of milestones. Quire and page numbers are as given by Sanders. Column numbers are redundant in a one-column manuscript and are therefore omitted.

Example 5. Milestone Elements

```
<milestone unit="quire" n="ΚΓ"/>
<pb n="101"/>
<gap reason="not transcribed"/>
<ref target="images/F1906_275_105.jpg">
<pb n="105"/>
</ref>
<milestone unit="bk" n="Hebrews"/>
<fw>ΠΡΟΣ ΕΒΡΑΙΟΥΣ †</fw>
<lb n="1"/><milestone unit="ch" n="1"/><milestone
unit="vs" n="1"/><supplied>ΠΟ</supplied>ΛΥΜΕΡΩΣ ΚΑΙ
ΠΟΛΥΤΡΟΠΩΣ<lb n="2"/><supplied>ΠΑ</supplied>ΛΑΙ Ο
<abbr type="ns">ΘΣ</abbr> ΛΑΛΗΣΑΣ ΤΟΙΣ ΠΑΤΡΑΣΙΝ
```

18. Sperberg-McQueen and Burnard, *TEI P4*, ch. 35 ("Elements").

The text of Hebrews begins on page 105, but the corresponding quire begins at page 101. Consequently, milestones are inserted for quire KΓ, page 101, and page 105, with a <gap> showing by means of its reason attribute that the intervening text has not been transcribed. Another milestone marks the beginning of the text of Hebrews, and an <fw> ("forme work") contains the running title. An <lb> marks each line break, and <milestone>s mark chapter and verse breaks.

Leiden Conventions

Printed editions of biblical manuscripts employ the Leiden conventions, a system developed by papyrologists to indicate doubtful and illegible text, lacunae, additions, deletions, and so forth in their transcriptions.[19] The following table gives a TEI XML equivalent for each category of these conventions. Its descriptions are taken from the concise summary included in recent volumes of the *Oxyrhyncus Papyri.*

Table 4. Leiden to TEI markup conversions

Leiden	**TEI**	**Description**
α̣β̣γ̣	<unclear cert="doubtful">αβγ</unclear>	"The letters are doubtful, either because of damage or because they are otherwise difficult to read."
...	<unclear cert="unread">...</unclear>	"Approximately three letters remain unread by the editor."
[αβγ]	<supplied>αβγ</supplied>	"The letters are lost, but restored from a parallel of by conjecture."
[...]	<gap reason="lost" extent="3"/>	"Approximately three letters are lost."
θ(εο)ς	θ<expan>εο</expan>ς	"Round brackets indicate the resolution of an abbreviation or a symbol."
[[αβγ]]	<del>αβγ</del>	"The letters are deleted in the [manuscript]."
`αβγ´	<add place="above line">αβγ</add>	"The letters are added above the line."

19. "Essai d'unification des méthodes employées dans les éditions de papyrus," *Chronique d'Égypte* 13–14 (1932): 285–87.

<αβγ>	<corr>αβγ</corr>	"The letters are added by the editor."
{αβγ}	<sic>αβγ</sic>	"The letters are regarded as mistaken and rejected by the editor."

In the Leiden conventions, supplied text is enclosed in square brackets. A letter with even the slightest remnant belongs outside square brackets; if illegible, it is replaced with a bare dot. By contrast, the TEI guidelines define <supplied> as text supplied by the transcriber or editor in place of text which cannot be read, either because of physical damage or loss in the original or because it is illegible for any reason. Thus, the conventions and guidelines differ in their treatment of illegible letter remnants. In order to make the two systems compatible, it is necessary to restrict use of the <supplied> element to cases where the text is entirely lost and to use <unclear cert="unread">...</unclear> where a trace remains but is illegible.

Anyone who bothers to compare my transcription with the equivalents shown above will notice alternative markup choices made. For example, I encode nomina sacra abbreviations thus: <abbr type="ns">θς</abbr>, instead of θ<expan>εο</expan>ς. This reiterates the point that in the world of TEI there is often "more than one way to do it" (borrowing a favorite chant of Perl programmers). This seems, however, to go against the entire thrust of this article, that the field of biblical studies would benefit from a unified approach to the digital publication of its primary sources. How shall we extract ourselves from this dilemma? The solution lies in generalization. The last five equivalents shown above are special cases of the general solutions shown below.

Alternatives

Pairs of elements contained within a <choice> element allow alternative views of the text to be encoded.

Table 5. The <choice> Element

Description	Example	Comments
Scribal abbreviation	<choice> <abbr type="ns">θς</abbr> <expan>θεος</expan> </choice>	The type attribute can be used to indicate the kind of abbreviation (e.g., ns for *nomina sacra,* kc for και *compendia,* fn for final ν overlines, and sc for other scribal contractions).

Editorial correction	<choice> <sic>βαιβεαν</sic> <corr>βεβαιαν</corr> </choice>	The scribe's erroneous text is enclosed in the <sic> element, and the modern editor's correction goes in the <corr>.
Orthographic normalization	<choice> <orig>κριττονος</orig> <reg>κρειττονος</reg> </choice>	The scribal original goes in the <orig> element, and the modern editor's "regularized" version is placed in the <reg>.

These examples take a whole-word approach to the alternatives. An encoder may prefer to work at the letter level, producing markup such as the following: β<choice><sic>αι</sic><corr>ε</corr></choice>β<choice><sic>ε</sic><corr>αι</corr></choice>αν.

Alterations

Printed editions rely on an apparatus to indicate which scribe wrote what. The TEI guidelines provide a corresponding set of elements that should be used in conjunction with <add> and <del> when encoding corrected manuscripts.

Example 6. Apparatus Element

```
<app>
<rdg varSeq="1" hand="h1">
<del><unclear cert="unread">..</unclear><lb n="4"/
>ΔEN</del>
</rdg>
<rdg varSeq="2" hand="h1">
<add>OY<lb n="4"/>ΔEN</add>
</rdg>
</app>
```

This example, taken directly from the transcription of Codex I, shows how the readings, their sequence, and the scribe or scribes responsible for writing them are recorded using the <rdg> element along with its varSeq and hand attributes. (I use the "h" prefix for "hand" instead of the traditional "m" for *manus*.) A line-break milestone is recorded in each reading. This allows a mindless computer to get the formatting right, regardless of which reading is selected for presentation.

Annotation

Notes can be recorded in a separate division, with pointer (<ptr>) elements in the text referring to them. A more straightforward approach includes annotation at the place to which it refers.

Example 7. Note Element

```
ΚΑΤΕΠΑΥΣΕΝ<note><bibl>Sanders [1918, 296]</bibl> has
κατευπασεν by mistake.</note>
```

Images

The TEI guidelines focus on encoding texts and do not have much to say about images. Nevertheless, it is very useful to be able to include a reference to an image, as in the case of a suggested revision of Sanders's transcription at Heb 5:7. A picture is worth a thousand words; there is little point trying to describe some feature when the reader can be shown it.

Example 8. Referencing an Image

```
A <ref target="images/F1906_275_113_1492.jpg">narrow-
band image</ref> of this page shows no sign of αυτον in
the margin.
```

This illustrates how advantageous high-quality manuscript images can be. Gone are the days of pouring some fatal tincture on a manuscript in the hope of revealing its faded text. Now one can use digital cameras to produce images in narrow bands of infrared or ultraviolet, as well as visible light. The narrow-band images of the Freer manuscripts produced in the last few years are a wonderful example.

The <ref> element of U16.xml is transformed to the "anchor" (<a>) element of U16.html using the XSLT transform U16.xsl. Pointing a browser to the HTML document (U16.html) then allows one to see the transcription and to follow its links to images. A CSS stylesheet (U16.css) causes the HTML to be formatted in the same manner as a printed edition, except that supplied text is colored grey and doubtful text is underscored with a dotted line. (In printed editions, there is just one sublinear dot per doubtful character.) One could instead use different colors to highlight doubtful and supplied text. It is possible to emulate fully the print conventions of square brackets and sublinear dots. However, to do so would introduce these characters into the mix. Consequently, selecting a section of text would pick up the spurious characters as well.

Other Phenomena

Not every phenomenon encountered in biblical manuscripts is covered here. If an encoder requires further guidance, he or she should consult the TEI guidelines. There is also an active TEI development community that has a dedicated Internet discussion list (TEI-L@listserv.brown.edu). The list members have an illustrious history of providing helpful answers to enquirers with encoding questions.

What Next?

An encoded set of parallel texts can be subjected to a number of analytical techniques, including phylogenetic and multivariate analysis. The first seeks to reconstruct a "family tree" of manuscripts just as phylogenetic analysis of DNA sequences seeks to trace genetic relationships. The second technique involves statistical analysis of the variations among a group of parallel texts to discover relationships among its members. These techniques can reveal much if used in an appropriate manner, and both have already been applied to biblical manuscripts. However, not much has been said on whether it is appropriate to use the techniques.

An important question in this respect is, What proportion of the manuscripts do we have? Taking Greek New Testament manuscripts of the Pauline Epistles as a case in point, about fifteen remain from the time before Constantine. Given that the population of the Roman Empire was about fifty million, it is possible to obtain a rough estimate of the number of copies that would have been produced during this era. Assuming that Greek-speaking Christians constituted 10 percent of the population by 300 C.E. and that there was one manuscript of the Pauline Epistles per one thousand Christians, there would have been about five thousand of these manuscripts when Constantine became emperor. We thus arrive at a survival rate in the region of fifteen per five thousand, or 0.3 percent. Even if this estimate is off by a factor of ten in either direction, the fact remains that we have a very small remnant of the entire textual picture.[20]

I suspect that phylogenetic analysis will produce questionable results under these circumstances. By contrast, a multivariate technique named multidimensional scaling (MDS) is quite robust against loss of data and remains a viable exploratory tool.

---

20. Those interested in a slightly more sophisticated treatment may wish to look at my manuscript-copying simulation program: Timothy J. Finney, "MSS: A Manuscript Copying Simulation" (2002). Online: http://purl.org/TC/downloads/simulation/.

Multidimensional Scaling

Given a set of distances between an array of points, MDS produces a spatial configuration or map. In general, the number of dimensions required for a perfect representation is one less than the number of points but can under certain circumstances be fewer. For example, four points may form the vertices of a tetrahedron, which requires three dimensions to represent. However, the points may lie in a plane (two dimensions), along a straight line (one dimension), or in the same place (zero dimensions). Also, a reasonable appreciation of the configuration can be obtained by taking a two-dimensional projection of the higher-dimensional reality.

The results of a collation of parallel texts can be converted to a matrix that shows the similarity of each pair of texts as a proportion of readings in which they agree. Each similarity can then be converted to a "distance" by subtracting it from one. In this way, the minimum distance between a pair is zero and the maximum one. A distance matrix can be fed directly into a scaling program to produce a two-dimensional map.[21]

Figure 2 is a map of substantive variations—those that affect the meaning of the text. The sigla represent different manuscripts and versions: Gregory-Aland numbers have "P" (papyrus), "U" (uncial), and "M" (minuscule) prefixes; "UBS4" stands for the text of the United Bible Societies fourth edition, "TR" for the Textus Receptus. The axes point along directions of maximum variation, with the first axis subsuming more variation than the second. As might be expected, Codex I (`U16`) is "closer" to texts such as 𝔓[46], Alexandrinus (`U2`), and Claromontanus (`U6`) than to "Byzantine" texts such as minuscule 2815, which is one of those used by Erasmus for his 1516 edition of the Greek New Testament. It is not surprising that the Textus Receptus also lies among the Byzantines and that the UBS text is "near" to 𝔓[46].

Things get more interesting when orthographic variations are subjected to the same analysis, as in figure 3. This time the UBS text lies in virtually the same place as the Byzantine texts, which makes sense because it has their spelling. Other texts, Codex I included, keep their distance. The fact that the same basic configuration occurs in both substantive and orthographic maps points to an inherent cause, something that is in the texture of both data sets. But what could this be? I think that the answer is related to geography. If so, maps of orthographic variation serve as a clue to the geographical origins of the constituent manuscripts. We know that Codex I and 𝔓[46] were recovered from Egypt, and the orthographic map places them "near" each other as well. Perhaps Streeter was right after all, and the history of the New Testament text is best understood in terms of local texts.

---

21. Finney, "Ancient Witnesses."

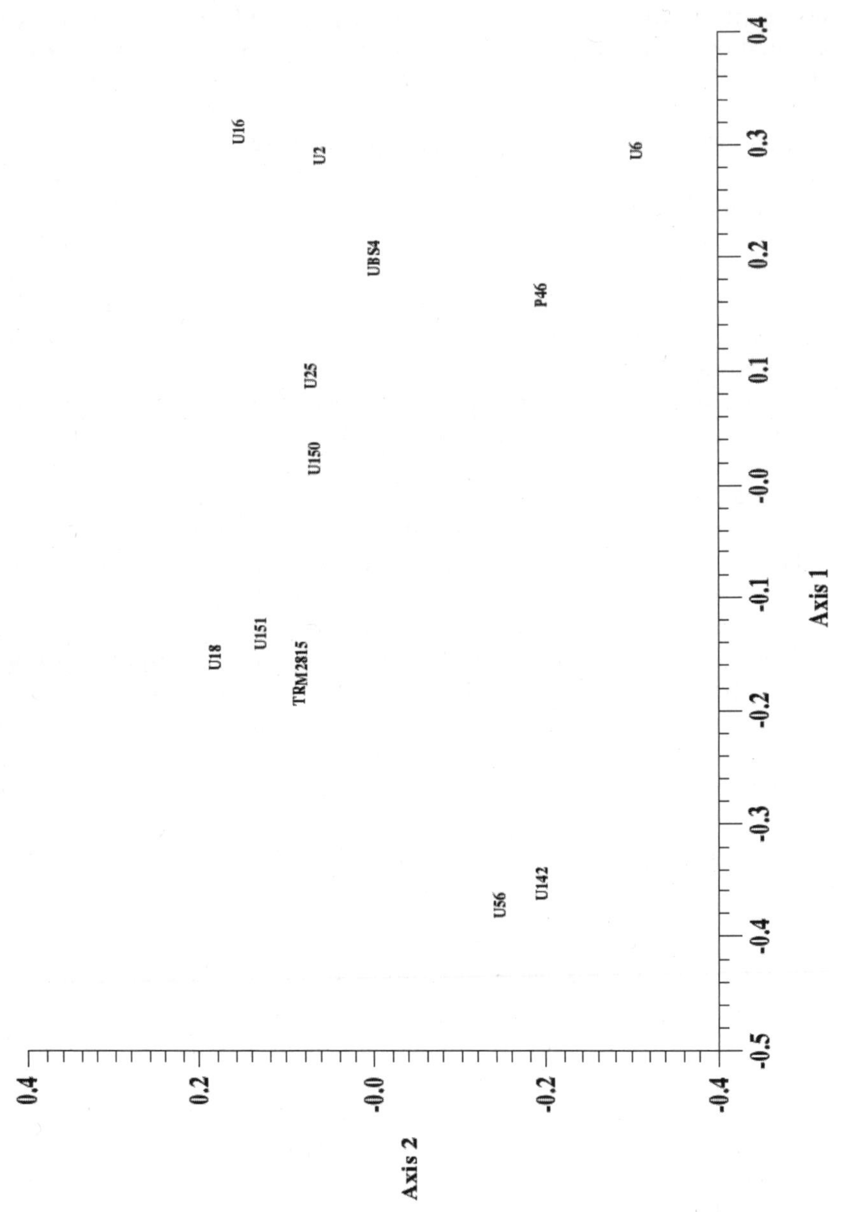

Figure 2. MDS map for Codex I (substantive variations)

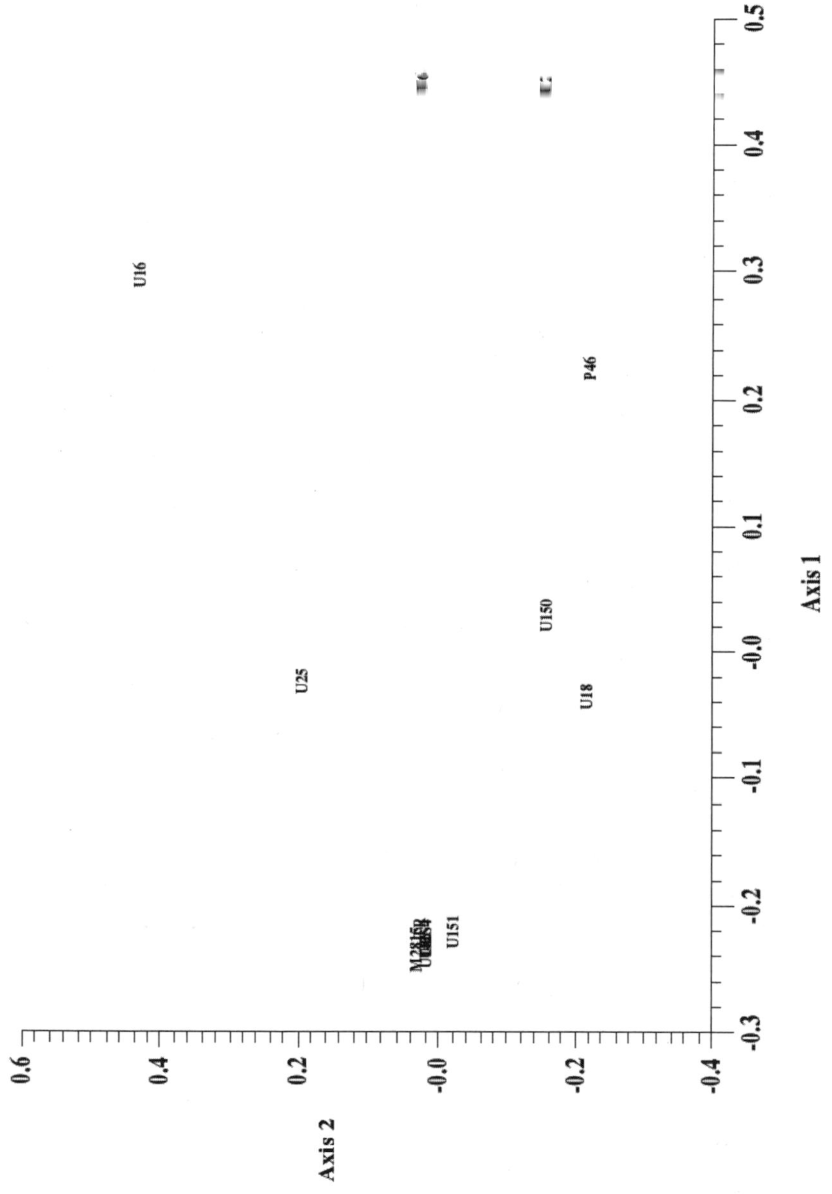

Figure 3. MDS map for Codex I (orthographic variations)

Select Bibliography

Aland, Barbara, Kurt Aland, Johannes Karavidopoulos, Carlo M. Martini, and Bruce M. Metzger, eds. *The Greek New Testament*. United Bible Societies. 4th rev. ed. Stuttgart: Deutsche Bibelgesellschaft, 1993.

Aland, Kurt. *Biblische Papyri: Altes Testament, Neues Testament, Varia, Apokryphen. Vol. 1 of Repertorium der griechischen christlichen Papyri*. Berlin: de Gruyter, 1976.

Aland, Kurt, Barbara Aland, Klaus Wachtel, and Klaus Witte. *Die synoptishen Evangelien 2: Das Matthäusevangelium*. Vol. 4 of *Text und Textwert der griechischen Handschriften des Neuen Testaments*. Berlin: de Gruyter, 1999.

Aland, Kurt, and Barbara Aland. *The Text of the New Testament*. Translated by Erroll F. Rhodes. 2nd ed. Grand Rapids: Eerdmans, 1989.

Aland, Kurt, and Hans-Udo Rosenbaum. *Kirchenväter-Papyri, Teil 1: Beschreibungen*. Vol. 2 of *Repertorium der griechischen christlichen Papyri*. Berlin: de Gruyter, 1995.

Allegro, John. *The Dead Sea Scrolls: A Reappraisal*. 2nd ed. Harmondsworth: Penguin, 1964.

Ampoux, Christian-Bernard. "Le texte évangélique de Césarée et le type de texte 'Césaréen' des Évangiles." *Filologia Neotestamentaria* 12 (1999): 3–16.

Annibaldi, Cesare. *La Germania di Cornelio Tacito*. Leipzig: Harrassowitz, 1910.

———. *L'Agricola e la Germania die Cornelio Tacito nel MS. Latino N. 8 della Biblioteca del Conte G. Balleani in Iesi*. Città di Castello: Lapi, 1907.

Ayuso, Teofilio. "¿Texto arrecensional, recensional o prerecensional?" *Estudios Biblicos* 6 (1947): 35–90.

———. "¿Texto Cesariense o precesariense? Su realidad y su trascendencia en la critica textual del Nuevo Testamento." *Bib* 16 (1935): 369–415.

Baedeker's Egypt. 4th ed. Upper Saddle River, N.J.: Prentice Hall, 1990.

Baines, John, and Jaromír Málek. *Atlas of Ancient Egypt*. New York: Facts on File, 1984.

Bell, H. Idris, and H. Thompson, "A Greek-Coptic Glossary to Hosea and Amos." *JEA* 11 (1925): 241–46.

Belzoni, G. B. *Belzoni's Travels: Narrative of the Operations and Recent Discoveries in Egypt and Nubia*. Edited by A. Siliotti. London: British Museum, 2001.

Black, David A., ed. *Linguistics and New Testament Interpretation: Essays on Discourse Analysis.* Nashville: Broadman, 1992.

Black, Paul E., ed. *Dictionary of Algorithms and Data Structures.* US National Institute of Standards and Technology. Online: http://www.nist.gov/dads/.

Blass, Friedrich, and A. Debrunner. *A Greek Grammar of the New Testament and Other Early Christian Litarature.* Translated and edited by Robert W. Funk. Chicago: University of Chicago Press, 1961.

Boak, Arthur E. R. "The Building of the University of Michigan Papyrus Collection." *Michigan Alumnus Quarterly Review* 66 (1959): 35–42.

———. "Dimê." *AJA* 36 (1932): 522–23.

———, ed. *Soknopaiou Nesos: The University of Michigan Excavations at Dimê in 1931–32.* Ann Arbor: University of Michigan Press, 1935.

Bouriant, Urbain. "Fragments du texte grec du livre d'Énoch et de quelques écrits attributés à saint Pierre." Pages 93–147 in *Mémoires publiés par les members de la mission archéologique française au Caire 9.* Cairo: Mission archéologique française au Caire, 1892.

Bowen, Gillian E. "The Fourth-Century Churches at Ismant el-Kharab." Pages 65–85 in *The Dakhleh Oasis Project: Preliminary Reports on the 1994–1995 to 1998–1999 Field Seasons.* Edited by Colin A. Hope and Gillian E. Bowen. Oxford: Oxbow, 2002.

———. "The Small Church at Ismant el-Kharab, Ancient Kellis." *Bulletin of the Australian Centre for Egyptology* 11 (2000): 29–34.

Breasted, James H. *A History of Egypt from the Earliest Times to the Persian Conquest.* 2nd ed. New York: Bantam, 1964 (1905).

Brown, Scott G. *Mark's Other Gospel: Rethinking Morton Smith's Controversial Discovery.* Waterloo, Ont.: Wilfred Laurier University Press, 2005.

Brunk, Thomas. "'The House That Freer Built.'" *Dichotomy* 3/4 (1981): 5–53.

Capasso, Mario, and P. Davoli, eds. *New Researches on the Fayyum: Proceedings of the International Meeting of Ehyptology and Papyrology, Lecce, June 8–10, 2005.* Forthcoming

Carlson, Stephen C. *The Gospel Hoax: Morton Smith's Invention of Secret Mark.* Waco, Tex.: Baylor University Press, 2005.

Caton-Thompson, Gertrude, and E. W. Gardner. *The Desert Fayum.* 2 vols. London: Royal Anthropological Institute of Great Britain and Ireland, 1934.

Cavallo, Guglielmo. "Funzione e strutture della maiuscola greca tra i secoli VIII–XI." *La Paléographie grecque et byzantine.* Paris: CNRS, 1977.

———. *Ricerche sulla maiuscola biblica.* Firenze: Le Monnier, 1967.

Cavallo, Guglielmo, and H. Maehler. *Greek Bookhands of the Early Byzantine Period, A.D. 300–800.* Bulletin of the Institute of Classical Studies Supplement 47. London: University of London, 1987.

Charlesworth, Scot D. "*Nomina Sacra* as Windows on Textual Authority and Compartive Transmission of Canonical and Non-canonical Gospels in the

Second Century." Paper presented at the Annual Meeting of the Society of Biblical Literature, Philadelphia, 2005.

Clark, Kenneth W. *A Descriptive Catalogue of Greek New Testament Manuscripts in America.* Introduction by E. J. Goodspeed. Chicago: University of Chicago Press, 1937.

Clark, Nichols. "Charles Lang Freer: An American Aesthete in the Gilded Era." *American Art Journal* 11 (1979): 54–68.

Comfort, Philip Wesley. *Encountering the Manuscripts: An Introduction to New Testament Paleography and Textual Criticism.* Nashville: Broadman & Holman, 2005.

———. "Scribes as Readers: Looking at New Testament Textual Variants According to Reader Reception Analysis." *Neot* 38 (2004): 28–53.

Comparetti, Domenico, ed. *Papiri Greco-Egizii. Papiri Fiorentini.* Vol. 2. Milano: Hoepli, 1911.

Crum, Walter Ewing. *A Coptic Dictionary.* Oxford: Oxford University Press, 1939.

———. "Un psaume en dialect d'Akhmim." Pages 73–76 in *Orient grec, romain et byzantin,* vol. 2 of *Mélanges Maspero.* Cairo: Institut français d'Archéologie orientale, 1934.

Curry, David P. "Charles Lang Freer and American Art." *Apollo* 118/258 (1983): 169–79.

Davoli, Paola. "Excavations at Soknopaiou Nesos (Dime) El-Fayyum." *Egyptian Archaeology* 25 (2004): 34–36.

———. "New Excavation at Soknopaiou Nesos: The 2003 Season." Pages 29–39 in *Tebtynis und Soknopaiu Nesos: Leben im römerzeitlichen Fajum.* Edited by S. L. Lippert and M. Schentuleit. Wiesbaden: Harrasowitz, 2005.

Dawson, Warren R., and Eric P. Uphill. *Who Was Who in Egyptology.* 3rd ed. London: Egypt Exploration Society, 1995.

Dennison, Walter. *A Gold Treasure of the Late Roman Period From Egypt. Part 2 of Studies in East Christian and Roman Art.* University of Michigan Studies, Humanistic Series 12/2. New York: Macmillan, 1918.

Depuydt, Leo. *Catalogue of Coptic Manuscripts in the Pierpont Morgan Library.* Leuven: Peeters, 1993.

Depuydt, Leo, and David A. Loggie. *Catalogue of Coptic Manuscripts in the Pierpont Morgan Library.* 2 vols. Corpus of Illuminated Manuscripts 4, 5. Oriental Series 1, 2. Leuven: Peeters, 1993.

Diebner, Bernd, and Rodolphe Kasser, eds. *Hamburger Papyrus bil. 1: Die alttestamentlichen Texte des Papyrus bilinguis 1 der Staats- und Universitätsbibliothek Hamburg.* Geneva: Cramer, 1989.

Eggert, Paul. "Text-Encoding, Theories of the Text, and the 'Work-Site.'" *Literary & Linguistic Computing* 20 (2005): 425–35.

Ehrman, Bart D. "Intentional Fallacies: Scribal Motivations and the Rhetoric of Critical Discourse." Paper presented at the Annual Meeting of the Society of Biblical Literature, Atlanta, 2003.

———. “Methodological Developments in the Analysis and Classification of New Testament Documentary Evidence.” *NovT* 29 (1987): 22–45.

Elliott, Tom, ed. *EpiDoc: Epigraphic Documents in TEI XML.* Online: http://epidoc.sourceforge.net/.

Elliott, W. J., and David C. Parker, eds. *The New Testament in Greek IV: The Gospel According to John.* Leiden: Brill, 1995.

Enslin, Morton S. “The Perfect Tense in the Fourth Gospel.” *JBL* 55 (1936): 121–31.

Epp, Eldon J. “Text-Critical, Exegetical, and Social-Cultural Factors Affecting the Junia/Junias Variation in Romans 16:7.” Pages 227–91 in *New Testament Textual Criticism and Exegesis: Festschrift J. Delobel.* Edited by Adelbert Denaux. BETL 161. Leuven: Leuven University Press/Peeters, 2002.

———. *The Theological Tendency of Codex Bezae Cantabrigiensis in Acts.* SNTSMS 3. Cambridge: Cambridge University Press, 1966.

“Essai d’unification des méthodes employées dans les éditions de papyrus.” *Chronique D’Égypte* 13–14 (1932): 285–87.

Fahlman, Betsy. “Wilson Eyre in Detroit: The Charles Lang Freer House.” *Winterthur Portfolio* 15/3 (1980): 257–70.

Fanning, Buist M. *Verbal Aspect in New Testament Greek.* Oxford Theological Monographs. Oxford: Clarendon, 1990.

Fee, Gordon D. “Codex Sinaiticus in the Gospel of John: A Contribution to Methodology in Establishing Textual Relationships.” *NTS* 15 (1969): 23–44.

———. “The Use of the Definite Article with Personal Names in the Gospel of John.” *NTS* 17 (1970–71): 168–83.

Fenollosa, Ernest F. “The Collection of Mr. Charles L. Freer.” *Pacific Era* 1/2 (1907): 57–66.

Field, Fridericus. *Origenis Hexaplorum quae supersunt.* 2 vols. Oxford: Clarendon, 1875. Repr., Hildesheim: Olms, 1964.

Finney, Timothy J. “The Ancient Witnesses of the Epistle to the Hebrews.” Ph.D. diss. Murdoch University, Western Australia, 1999. Online: http://purl.org/tfinney/PhD/.

———. “Converting Leiden-Style Editions to TEI Lite XML.” 2001. Online: http://www.tei-c.org/Sample_Manuals/leiden.html.

———. “MSS: A Manuscript Copying Simulation.” 2002. Online: http://purl.org/TC/downloads/simulation/.

———. “Uncertainty in Text, Markup and Beyond.” 2005. Online: http://purl.org/tfinney/uncertainty/uncertainty.html.

Fonkič, B. L., and F. B. Poljakov. “Paläographische Grundlagen der Datierung des Kölner Mani-Kodex.” *Byzantinische Zeitschrift* 83 (1990): 22–30.

Frederick G., ed. *The Chester Beatty Biblical Papyri: Descriptions and Texts of Twelve Manuscripts on Papyrus of the Greek Bible.* 16 vols. London: Emery Walker, 1932–58.

Freer, Charles Lang. Charles Lang Freer Papers, Freer Gallery of Art and Arthur M. Sackler Gallery Archives, Smithsonian Institution, Washington, D.C. Gift of the Estate of Charles Lang Freer. Abbreviated as CLFP.

Freer Gallery of Art and Arthur M. Sackler Gallery. "Charles Lang Freer: A Finding Aid to His Papers at the Freer Gallery of Art and Arthur M. Sackler Gallery Archives." Freer Gallery of Art and Arthur M. Sackler Gallery Archives, Smithsonian Institution, Washington, D.C. No pages. Online: http://www.asia.si.edu/archives/finding_aids/freer.html.

Frey, Jörg. "Zu Text und Sinn des Freer-Logion." *ZNW* 93 (2002): 13–34.

Gardner , Iain, ed. *Kellis Literary Texts.* Oxford: Oxbow, 1996.

———. Kellis *Literary Texts II.* Oxford: Oxbow, forthcoming.

Gardner, Iain, Anthony Alcock, and Wolf-Peter Funk, eds. *Coptic Documentary Texts from Kellis.* Oxford: Oxbow, 1999.

Gardthausen, Viktor. *Griechische Paläographie.* 2nd ed. 2 vols. Leipzig: Veit, 1913.

Goodspeed, Edgar J. "The Detroit Manuscripts of the Septuagint and New Testament." *The Biblical World* 31/3 (1908): 218–26.

———. "Notes on the Freer Gospels." *AJT* 13 (1909): 597–603.

Gottheil, Richard, and William H. Worrell. *Fragments from the Cairo Genizah in the Freer Collection.* University of Michigan Studies, Humanistic Series 13. New York: Macmillan, 1927.

Greenlee, J. Harold. *Introduction to New Testament Textual Criticism.* 2nd ed. Peabody, Mass.: Hendrickson, 1995.

Gregory, Caspar R. *Das Freer-Logion.* Leipzig: Hinrichs, 1908.

———. "Vier neue biblische Handschriften." *Theologisches Literaturblatt* 29/7 (1908): 73–76.

Grenfell, Bernard P., Arthur S. Hunt, and David G. Hogarth. *Fayûm Towns and Their Papyri.* London: Egypt Exploration Fund, 1900.

Grenfell, Bernard P., Arthur S. Hunt, et al., eds. *The Oxyrhynchus Papyri.* 69 vols. London: Egypt Exploration Society, 1898–.

Grossouw, Willem. *The Coptic Versions of the Minor Prophets: A Contribution to the Study of the Septuagint.* Rome: Pontifical Biblical Institute, 1938.

Gunther, Ann C. *A Collector's Journey: Charles Lang Freer and Egypt.* Washington, D.C.: Freer Gallery of Art, 2002.

Guth, Christine. "A Tale of Two Collectors: Hara Tomitaro and Charles Freer." *Asian Art* 4/4 (1991): 29–49.

Haaker, K. "Bemerkungen zum Freer-Logion." *ZNW* 63 (1972): 125–29.

Haelst, Joseph van. *Catalogue des papyrus littéraires juifs et chrétiens.* Paris: Sorbonne, 1976.

Haines-Eitzen, Kim. *Guardians of Letters: Literacy, Power, and the Transmitters of Early Christian Literature.* New York: Oxford University Press, 2000.

Halliday, M. A. K., and Ruqaiya Hasan. *Cohesion in English.* London: Longman, 1976.

Harlfinger, Dieter, Diether Roderich Reinsch, Joseph A. M. Sonderkamp, and Giancarlo Prato. *Specimina Sinaitica: Die datierten griechischen Handschriften des Katharinen-Klosters auf dem Berge Sinai.* 9.-12. Jahrhundert. Berlin: Reimer, 1983.

Harnack, Adolf von. "Neues zum unechten Marcusschluß." *TLZ* 33 (1908): 168–70.

Hasitzka, Monika R. M., ed. *Neue Texte und Dokumentation zum Koptisch-Unterricht.* Vienna: Hollinek, 1990.

Havemeyer, Louisine W. "The Freer Museum of Oriental Art." *Scribner's Magazine* 73 (1923): 529–40.

Hedley, P. L. "The Egyptian Texts of the Gospels and Acts." *Church Quarterly Review* 118 (1934): 23–39, 188–230.

Helzle, Eugen. "Der Schluß des Markusevangeliums (Mk 16, 9–20) und das Freer-Logion (Mk. 16, 14 w), ihr Tendenzen und ihr gegenseitiges Verhältnis: Eine wortexegetische Untersuchung." Ph.D. diss., Tübingen University, 1959.

Hendriks, Wim. "Brevior lectio praeferenda est verbosiori." *RB* 112 (2005): 567–95.

Hengel, Martin. *The Four Gospels and the One Gospel of Jesus Christ.* London: SCM, 2000.

Herodotus. *The Histories.* Translated by Aubrey de Sélincourt. Harmondsworth: Penguin, 1954.

Hobbs, Susan. "A Connoisseur's Vision." *American Art Review* 4 (August 1977): 76–101.

———. "The Little Known Side of One Great American Collector." *Smithsonian* 7 (January 1977): 50–57.

Horrocks, Geoffrey. *Greek: A History of the Language and Its Speakers.* London: Longman, 1997.

Hurtado, Larry Weir. "Codex Washingtonianus in the Gospel of Mark: Its Textual Relationships and Scribal Characteristics." Ph.D. diss., Case Western Reserve University, 1973.

———. *The Earliest Christian Artifacts: Manuscripts and Christian Origins.* Grand Rapids: Eerdmans, 2006.

———. *Lord Jesus Christ: Devotion to Jesus in Earliest Christianity.* Grand Rapids: Eerdmans, 2003.

———. "The Origin of the *Nomina Sacra:* A Proposal." *JBL* 117 (1998): 655–73.

———. "P45 and the Textual History of the Gospel of Mark." Pages 132–48 in *The Earliest Gospels: The Origins and Transmission of the Earliest Christian Gospels—The Contribution of the Chester Beatty Gospel Codex P45.* Edited by Charles Horton. London: T&T Clark, 2004.

———. *Text-Critical Methodology and the Pre-Caesarean Text: Codex W in the Gospel of Mark.* Studies and Documents 43. Grand Rapids: Eerdmans, 1981.

Hyvernat, Henri. *A Checklist of Coptic Manuscripts in the Pierpont Morgan Library.* New York: privately printed, 1919.

James, T. G. H. *Excavating in Egypt: The Egypt Exploration Society, 1882–1982.* Chicago: University of Chicago Press, 1982.

Jaworski, Adam, and Nikolas Coupland. *The Discourse Reader.* London: Routledge, 1999.

Jeremias, Joachim. "2. The Freer Logion." Pages 248–49 in vol. 1 of *New Testament Apocrypha.* Edited by W. Schneemelcher. Translated by R. McL.Wilson. Rev. ed. 2 vols. Louisville: Westminster John Knox, 1991.

Jerome, Thomas S. *Aspects of the Study of Roman History.* Edited by John G. Winter. New York: Putnam's, 1923.

Jobes, Karen H., and Moises Silva. *Invitation to the Septuagint.* Grand Rapids: Baker, 2000.

Johnstone, Barbara. *Discourse Analysis.* Oxford: Blackwell, 2002.

Kasser, Rodolphe. *Livre des Proverbes.* Papyrus Bodmer 6. Louvain: Secrétariat du CorpusSCO, 1960.

Kelsey, Francis W. Francis W. Kelsey Papers, Bentley Historical Library, University of Michigan, Ann Arbor. Abbreviated as FWKPapers.

Kelsey, Francis W. Francis W. Kelsey Records, Kelsey Museum Archives, Bentley Historical Library, University of Michigan, Ann Arbor. Abbreviated as FWKRecords.

Kenyon, Frederic G. "B.—Graeco-Roman Egypt, 1907–8." *Archaeological Report: Egyptian Exploration Fund* (1907–1908): 47–48.

———. *Handbook to the Textual Criticism of the New Testament.* 2nd ed. London: Macmillan, 1912.

———. *Our Bible and the Ancient Manuscripts.* New York: Harper & Row, 1958.

———. *Recent Developments in the Textual Criticism of the Greek Bible.* Schweich Lectures of the British Academy 1932. London: Oxford University Press, 1933.

———. *The Text of the Greek Bible.* London: Duckworth, 1937. Repr., 1958.

———, ed. *Isaiah, Jeremiah, Ecclesiasticus.* Fasc. 6 of *The Chester Beatty Biblical Papyri:* London: Emery Walker, 1937.

———. *Pauline Epistles: Text.* Supplement to fasc. 3 of *The Chester Beatty Biblical Papyri: Descriptions and Texts of Twelve Manuscripts on Papyrus of the Greek Bible.* London: Emery Walker, 1936.

Koenen, Ludwig, and Cornelia Römer, eds. *Der Kölner Mani-Kodex: Abbildungen und diplomatischer Text.* Bonn: Habelt, 1985.

Kraus, Thomas J., and Tobias Nicklas, eds. *Das Petrusevangelium und die Petrusapokalypse: Die griechischen Fragmente mit deutscher und englischer Übersetzung.* Berlin: de Gruyter, 2004.

Lagrange, M. J. "Le Group dit Césaréen des Manuscrits des Évangiles." *RB* 38 (1929): 481–512.

———. "Le papyrus Chester Beatty pour les Évangiles." *RB* 43 (1934): 5–14.

Lake, Kirsopp, and Silva Lake. "De Westcott et Hort au Pére Lagrange et au-dela." *RB* 48 (1939): 497–505.

———. *Family 13 (The Ferrar Group): The Text according to Mark with a Collation of Codex 28 of the Gospels.* Studies and Documents 11. London: Christophers, 1941.

Lameere, William. *Aperçus de paléographie homérique.* Les publications de scriptorium 4. Paris: Édition Erasme, 1960.

Lane, Edward William. *Description of Egypt.* Edited by Jason Thompson. Cairo: American University in Cairo Press, 2000.

Lawton, Thomas, and Linda Merrill. *Freer: A Legacy of Art.* Washington, D.C.: Freer Gallery of Art, 1993.

Layard, Austen Henry. *Discoveries in the Ruins of Nineveh and Babylon: With Travels in Armenia, Kurdistan and the Desert.* London: Murray, 1853.

———. *Nineveh and Its Remains: With an Account of a Visit to the Chaldæan Christians of Kurdistan and the Yezidis or Devil-Worshippers; and an Inquiry into the Manners and Arts of the Ancient Assyrians.* 2 vols. London: Murray, 1849.

Lepsius, Karl Richard. *Denkmäler aus Aegypten und Aethiopien.* 6 vols. Berlin: Nicolai, 1849–56.

Leuven Database of Ancient Books. Online: http://ldab.arts.kuleuven.be/.

Louie, Richard. *Freer Gallery of Art.* Washington, D.C.: Freer Gallery of Art, 1983.

MacCoull, Leslie S. B. "Greek and Coptic Papyri in the Freer Gallery of Art." Ph.D. diss., Catholic University of America, 1973.

MacDonald, Margaret F., Patricia de Montfort, and Nigel Thorp, eds. *The Correspondence of James McNeill Whistler, 1855–1903.* Including Georgia Toutziari, ed., *The Correspondence of Anna McNeill Whistler, 1855–1880.* Online edition, Centre for Whistler Studies, University of Glasgow, 2003. Online: http://www.whistler.arts.gla.ac.uk/correspondence.

Mandilaras, Basil G. *The Verb in the Greek Non-Literary Papyri.* Athens: Hellenic Ministry of Culture and Sciences, 1973.

Mansfield, Howard. "Charles Lang Freer." *Parnassus* 7/5 (1935): 16–18.

Martin, J. R. "Cohesion and Texture." Pages 35–53 in *The Handbook of Discourse Analysis.* Edited by Deborah Schiffrin, Deborah Tannen, and Heidi Ehernberger Hamilton. Oxford: Blackwell, 2001.

Martin, Victor. *Papyrus Bodmer II: Évangile de Jean, Chap. 1–14.* Cologny-Genève: Bibliotheca Bodmeriana, 1956.

———. *Papyrus Bodmer II: Évangile de Jean, Chap. 14–21.* Cologny-Genève: Bibliotheca Bodmeriana, 1958.

Martin, Victor, and Rodolphe Kasser. *Papyrus Bodmer XIV–XV: Evangiles de Luc et Jean.* Cologny-Genève: Bibliotheca Bodmeriana, 1961.

Mechlin, Leila. "The Freer Collection of Art: Mr. Charles L. Freer's Gift to the Nation, to Be Installed at Washington." *Century Magazine* 73 (January 1907): 357–68.

Merkel, H. "Appendix: The 'Secret Gospel' of Mark." Pages 106–9 in vol. 1 of *New Testament Apocrypha.* Edited by W. Schneemelcher. Translated by R. McL. Wilson. 2 vols. Rev. ed. Louisville: Westminster John Knox, 1991.

Merrill, Linda, ed. *With Kindest Regards: The Correspondence of Charles Lang Freer and James McNeill Whistler, 1890–1903.* Washington, D.C.: Freer Gallery of Art, 1995.

Metzger, Bruce M. *The Canon of the New Testament: Its Origin, Development, and Significance,* Oxford: Clarendon, 1987.

———. *Chapters in the History of New Testament Textual Criticism.* Grand Rapids: Eerdmans, 1963.

———. *Manuscripts of the Greek Bible: An Introduction to Greek Palaeography.* Corrected Edition. New York: Oxford University Press, 1991 (1981).

Metzger, Bruce M., and Bart D. Ehrman. *The Text of the New Testament: Its Transmission, Corruption, and Restoration.* 5th ed. New York: Oxford University Press, 2005.

Meyer, Agnes E. *Charles Lang Freer and His Gallery.* Washington, D.C.: Freer Gallery of Art, 1970.

———. "The Charles Lang Freer Collection." *Arts* 12/2 (1927): 65–82.

Milik, J. T. *Ten Years of Discovery in the Wilderness of Judaea.* Translated by J. Strugnell. SBT 26. London: SCM, 1959.

Montevecchi, Orsolina. *La papirologia.* Milan: Vita e Pensiero, 1988.

Morey, Charles R. *East Christian Paintings in the Freer Collection.* Part 1 of *Studies in East Christian and Roman Art.* University of Michigan Studies, Humanistic Series 12/1. New York: Macmillan, 1918.

Müller, C. Detlef G. "Apocalypse of Peter." Pages 620–38 in vol. 2 of *New Testament Apocrypha.* Edited by W. Schneemelcher. Translated by R. McL.Wilson. 2 vols. Rev. ed. Louisville: Westminster John Knox, 1991.

Nestle, Eberhard. *Introduction to the Textual Criticism of the Greek New Testament.* Translated by W. Edie. London: Williams & Norgate, 1901.

Nunan, David. *Introducing Discourse Analysis.* London: Penguin English, 1993.

Nordenfalk, Carl. "The Beginning of Book Decoration." Pages 9–20 in *Essays in Honor of Georg Swarzenski.* Edited by Oswald Goetz. Chicago: Regnery, 1951.

———. *Studies in the History of Book Illumination.* London: Pindar, 1992.

Oriental Institute, The. "The 1905–1907 Breasted Expeditions to Egypt and the Sudan: A Photographic Study." Online: http://oi.uchicago.edu/OI/MUS/PA/EGYPT/BEES/BEES.html.

Paap, A. H. R. E. *Nomina Sacra in the Greek Papyri of the First Five Centuries A.D.: The Sources and Some Deductions.* Leiden: Brill, 1959.

Pack, Roger A., *The Greek and Latin Literary Texts from Greco-Roman Egypt.* Ann Arbor: University of Michigan Press, 1965.

Papiri greci e latini. Publicazioni della Società Italiana per la Ricerca dei Papiri Greci e Latini in Egitto 2. Firenze: Tipografia Ariani, 1913.

Parker, David C. *Codex Bezae: An Early Christian Manuscript and Its Text.* Cambridge: Cambridge University Press, 1992.

Pliny. *Natural History.* Translated by J. Bostock and H. T. Riley. 6 vols. London: Bell, 1898.

Porter, Stanley E. "Discourse Analysis and New Testament Studies: An Introductory Survey." Pages 14–35 in *Discourse Analysis and Other Topics in Biblical Greek.* Edited by Stanley E. Porter and D. A. Carson. JSNTSup 113. Sheffield: Sheffield Academic Press, 1995.

———. *Idioms of the Greek New Testament.* 2nd ed. Sheffield: JSOT Press, 1994.

Porter, Stanley E., and D. A. Carson, eds. *Discourse Analysis and Other Topics in Biblical Greek.* JSNTSup 113. Sheffield: Sheffield Academic Press, 1995.

Prior, J. Bruce, and T. A. E. Brown. *The Freer Gospels: Transcription of Washington Manuscript III.* Forthcoming.

Pyne, Kathleen. "Portrait of a Collector as an Agnostic: Charles Lang Freer and Connoisseurship." *The Art Bulletin* 78/1 (1996): 75–97.

Racine, Jean-François. *The Text of Matthew in the Writings of Basil of Caesarea.* SBLNTGF 5. Atlanta: Society of Biblical Literature; Leiden: Brill; 2004.

Rahlfs, Alfred, and Detlef Fraenkel. *Verzeichnis der griechischen Handschriften des Alten Testament.* Vol. 1. Göttingen: Vandenhoeck & Ruprecht, 2004.

Read-Heimerdinger, Jenny. *The Bezan Text of Acts. A Contribution of Discourse Analysis to Textual Criticism.* JSNTSup 236. London: Sheffield Academic Press, 2002.

Read-Heimerdinger, Jenny, and Stephen H. Levinsohn. "The Use of the Definite Article before Names of People in the Greek Text of Acts with Particular Reference to Codex Bezae." *Filologia Nuevo Testamento* 5 (1992): 15–44.

Reed, Jeffrey T., and Stanley E. Porter, eds. *Discourse Analysis and the New Testament: Approaches and Results.* Sheffield: Sheffield Academic Press, 1999.

Rhoades, Katharine N. "An Appreciation of Charles Lang Freer." *Ars Orientalis* 2 (1957): 1–4.

Richards, W. Larry. *The Classification of the Greek Manuscripts of the Johannine Epistles.* SBLDS 35. Missoula, Mont.: Scholars Press, 1977.

Roberts, Colin H. *Manuscript, Society and Belief in Early Christian Egypt: The Schweich Lectures of the British Academy 1977.* London: Published for the British Academy by the Oxford University Press, 1979.

Robinson, J. A., and M. H. James. *The Gospel according to Peter and the Revelation of Peter.* 2nd ed. London: Clay & Sons, 1892.

Sâlih, Abû. *The Churches and Monasteries of Egypt and Some Neighboring Countries.* Translated by B. T. A. Evetts and A. J. Butler. Oxford: Oxford University Press, 1895.

Sanders, Henry A. "Age and Ancient Home of Biblical Manuscripts in the Freer Collection." *AJA* 13/2 (1909): 130–41.

———. *Facsimile of the Washington Manuscript of Deuteronomy and Joshua in the Freer Collection.* Ann Arbor: University of Michigan, 1910.

———. *Facsimile of the Washington Manuscript of the Four Gospels in the Freer Collection.* Ann Arbor: University of Michigan, 1912.

———. *Facsimile of the Washington Manuscript of the Minor Prophets in the Freer Collection and the Berlin Fragment of Genesis.* Ann Arbor: University of Michigan, 1927.

———. "Four Newly Discovered Biblical Manuscripts." *The Biblical World* 31/2 (1908): 82, 138–42.

———. "The Freer Psalter." *The Biblical World* 33/5 (1909): 290, 343–44.

———. "New Manuscripts of the Bible from Egypt." *AJA* 12/1 (1908): 49–55.

———. *The New Testament Manuscripts in the Freer Collection, Part I: The Washington Manuscript of the Four Gospels.* University of Michigan Studies, Humanistic Series 9/1. New York: Macmillan, 1912.

———. *The New Testament Manuscripts in the Freer Collection, Part II: The Washington Manuscript of the Epistles of Paul.* University of Michigan Studies, Humanistic Series 9/2. New York: Macmillan, 1918.

———. *The Old Testament Manuscripts in the Freer Collection, Part I: The Washington Manuscript of Deuteronomy and Joshua.* University of Michigan Studies, Humanistic Series 8/1. New York: Macmillan, 1910.

———. *The Old Testament Manuscripts in the Freer Collection, Part II: The Washington Manuscript of the Psalms.* University of Michigan Studies, Humanistic Series 8/2. New York: Macmillan, 1917.

———. "A Papyrus Manuscript of the Minor Prophets." *HTR* 14 (1921):181–87.

———. "Proceedings of the Thirty-Ninth Annual Meeting of the American Philological Association Held at Chicago, Illinois, December, 1907." *Transactions and Proceedings of the American Philological Association* 38 (1907): xiii.

Sanders, Henry A., and C. Schmidt. *The Minor Prophets in the Freer Collection and the Berlin Fragment of Genesis.* New York: Macmillan, 1927.

Schmidt, Carl. "Die neuen griechischen Bibelhandschriften." *TLZ* 33/12 (1908): 359–60.

Schneemelcher, Wilhelm, and C. Maurer. "The Gospel of Peter." Pages 216–27 in vol. 1 of *New Testament Apocrypha.* Edited by W. Schneemelcher. Translated by R. McL.Wilson. 2 vols. Rev. ed. Louisville: Westminster John Knox, 1991.

Scrivener, Frederick H. A. *A Plain Introduction to the Criticism of the New Testament.* 4th ed. 2 vols. London: Bell & Sons, 1894.

Smith, Morton. *Clement of Alexandria and a Secret Gospel of Mark.* Cambridge: Harvard University Press, 1973.

———. *The Secret Gospel: The Discovery and Interpretation of the Secret Gospel according to Mark.* New York: Harper & Row, 1973.

Snyman, A. H. "Discourse Analysis: A Semantic Discourse Analysis of the Letter to Philemon." Pages 83–99 in *Text and Interpretation: New Approaches in the Criticism of the New Testament.* Edited by Patrick J. Hartin and Jacobus H. Petzer. NTTS 15. Leiden: Brill, 1991.

Soden, Hermann Freiherr von. "Ein neues 'herrenwort,' aufgehalten als Einfügung in den Schluk des Markusevangeliums." *Die Christliche Welt* 22/20 (1908): 482–86.

———. *Die Schriften des Neuen Testaments in ihrer ältesten erreichbaren Textgestalt.* Vol. 1.1. Göttingen: Vandenhoeck & Ruprecht, 1913.

Sperberg-McQueen, C. M., and L. Burnard. *TEI P5: Guidelines for Electronic Text Encoding and Interchange.* Draft rev. ed. Text Encoding Initiative Consortium. Online: http://www.tei-c.org/P5/.

Sperberg-McQueen, C. M., and L. Burnard, eds. *TEI P4: Guidelines for Electronic Text Encoding and Interchange.* Oxford: Text Encoding Initiative Consortium, 2002.

Strabo. *The Geography.* Translated by H. C. Hamilton and W. Falconer. London: Bell, 1913.

Streeter, Burton Hillman. *The Four Gospels: A Study of Origins, Treating of the Manuscript, Sources, Authorship, and Dates.* London: Macmillan, 1926.

———. "The Washington MS and the Caesarean Text of the Gospels." *JTS* 27 (1926): 144–47.

———. "The Washington MS. of the Gospels." *HTR* 19 (1926): 165–72.

Swain, George R. *Photographs of the Washington Manuscripts of the Psalms in the Freer Collection.* Ann Arbor: University of Michigan, 1919.

Swanson, Reuben J. *New Testament Greek Manuscripts: Variant Readings Arranged in Horizontal Lines against Codex Vaticanus.* 4 vols. Sheffield: Sheffield Academic Press, 1995.

Swete, Henry B. *Two New Gospel Fragments.* Cambridge: Deighton, Bell, 1908.

———. *Zwei neue Evangelienfragmente.* Bonn: Marcus & Weber, 1908.

Thackeray, Henry St. J. "A Papyrus Scrap of Patristic writing." *JTS* 30 (1929): 179–90.

Till, Rudolf. *Handschriftliche Untersuchungen zu Tacitus Agricola und Germania mit einer Photokopie des Codex Aesinas.* Berlin: Ahnenerbe-Stiftung Verlag, 1942.

Till, Walter, *Die Achmîmische Version der zwölf kleinen Propheten.* Hauniae: Gyldendal, 1927.

Tischendorf, Constantine von. *Codex Sinaiticus: The Ancient Biblical Manuscript now in the British Museum.* 8th ed. London: Lutterworth, 1934.

———. *When Were Our Gospels Written? An Argument by Constantine Tischendorf with a Narrative of the Discovery of the Sinaitic Manuscript.* New ed. London: Religious Tract Society, n.d.

———, ed. *Novum Testamentum Graece.* 8th ed. 2 vols. Leipzig: Giesecke & Devrient, 1869.

Tomlinson, Helen N. "Charles Lang Freer: Pioneer Collector of Oriental Art." 4 Vols. Ph.D. dissertation, Case Western Reserve University, 1979.

Traube, Ludwig. *Nomina Sacra: Versuch einer Geschichte der christlichen Kürzung.* Munich: Beck, 1907. Repr., Darmstadt: Wissenschaftliche Buchgesellschaft, 1967.

Turner, Eric G. *The Typology of the Early Codex*. Philadelphia: University of Pennsylvania Press, 1977.

Ulrich, Eugene. *The Dead Sea Scrolls and the Origins of the Bible*. Grand Rapids: Eerdmans, 1999.

Unicode Consortium, The. "About the Unicode Standard." Online: http://www.unicode.org/standard/standard.html.

University of Chicago Library. "Photographic Archive, Middle East Department, University of Chicago Library." Online: http://www.lib.uchicago.edu/e/su/mideast.

Vaganay, Léon, and Christian-Bernard Amphoux. *Initiation à la critique textuelle du Nouveau Testament*. 2nd ed. Paris: Cerf, 1986.

VanderKam, James, and Peter Flint. *The Meaning of the Dead Sea Scrolls*. New York: HarperCollins, 2002.

Voss, David O. "Is von Soden's Kmd Kr a Distinct Type of Text?" *JBL* 57 (1938): 311–18.

Wallace, Daniel B. *Greek Grammar beyond the Basics: An Exegetical Syntax of the New Testament*. Grand Rapids.: Zondervan, 1996.

Warner, Langdon. "The Freer Gift of Eastern Art to America." *Asia* 23/8 (1923): 164–67.

Wattenbach, Wilhelm. *Scripturae Graecae Specimina in usum scholarum…, Schrifttafeln zur Geschichte der griechischen Schrift*. 4th ed. Berlin: Grote, 1936.

Wessely, Carl, *Griechische und Koptische Texte theologischen Inhalts*. Vol. 4. Leipzig, 1914. Repr. Amsterdam: Hakkert, 1967.

Westcott, B. F., and F. J. A. Hort. *Introduction to the New Testament in the Original Greek*. New York: Harper & Brothers, 1882. Repr., Peabody, Mass.: Hendrickson, 1988.

Worrell, William H. "Francis Willey Kelsey." *Dictionary of American Biography*. Edited by D. Malone. New York: Scribners, 1933.

Worrell, William H. *The Coptic Manuscripts in the Freer Collection, Part I: The Coptic Psalter*. University of Michigan Studies, Humanistic Series 10/1. New York: Macmillan, 1916.

———. *The Coptic Manuscripts in the Freer Collection, Part II: A Homily on the Archangel Gabriel by Celestinus, Archbishop of Rome, and a Homily on the Virgin by Theophilus, Archbishop of Alexandria, from Manuscript Fragments in the Freer Collection and the British Museum*. University of Michigan Studies, Humanistic Series 10/2. New York: Macmillan, 1923.

Youtie, Herbert C. "Text and Context in Transcribing Papyri." *Greek, Roman, and Byzantine Studies* 7 (1966): 251–58.

Ziegler, Joseph, ed. *Duodecim prophetae*. 2nd ed. Göttingen: Vandenhoeck & Ruprecht, 1967.

———. *Ezechiel*. 2nd ed. Göttingen: Vandenhoeck & Ruprecht, 1977.

———. *Isaias*. 5th ed. Göttingen: Vandenhoeck & Ruprecht, 1983.

Contributors

Kent D. Clarke is Associate Professor of Religious Studies at Trinity Western University, Langley, British Columbia, Canada. His primary areas of specialization include the New Testament text and canon, biblical hermeneutics and theology, biblical Greek languages, eighteenth-century Enlightenment thought, and nineteenth-century biblical criticism.

Malcolm Choat is an Associate Lecturer in the Department of Ancient History, Macquarie University, Sydney, Australia. He is part of the project on Papyri from the Rise of Christianity in Egypt, in the Ancient History Documentary Research Centre, Macquarie University. His expertise lies particularly in papyrology and Coptic and Greek paleography.

Kristin De Troyer is Professor of Hebrew Bible in the Claremont School of Theology and Professor of Religion in Claremont Graduate University, Claremont, California. She is an internationally recognized specialist in the study of the textual history of Greek translations of the Hebrew Bible.

Timothy J. Finney wrote a Ph.D. dissertation on the computer-assisted transcription, collation, and analysis of the papyrus and uncial manuscripts of the Epistle to the Hebrews. He currently works as a programmer for the Electronic Imprint of the University of Virginia Press.

Dennis Haugh is a Ph.D. student in the joint Denver University and Iliff School of Theology doctoral program, Denver, Colorado.

Larry W. Hurtado is Professor of New Testament Language, Literature, and Theology in the University of Edinburgh and Director of the Centre for the Study of Christian Origins, Edinburgh, Scotland. His research interests include New Testament text criticism and the wider import of early Christian manuscripts for the study of Christian origins.

J. Bruce Prior (Ph.D.) is an independent scholar who is co-editor with T. A. E. Brown of recently completed transcriptions of the Freer Gospels Codex and the Freer Deuteronomy-Joshua Codex to be published in 2006.

Jean-François Racine is Assistant Professor of New Testament in the Jesuit School of Theology at Berkeley/Graduate Theological Union, Berkeley, California. His prior research includes a major study of the Gospel quotations in Basil of Caesarea.

James R. Royse is Professor of Philosophy at San Francisco State University. His previous research includes study of the scribal characteristics of early New Testament papyri.

Ulrich Schmid completed his doctorate at the University of Münster and his *Habilitation* at Bielefeld. He is a researcher on the Principio Project (transcriptions of manuscripts of the Gospel of John in connection with the International Greek New Testament Project), in the Centre for Editing Texts in Religion, University of Birmingham, Birmingham, England.

Thomas A. Wayment is Associate Professor of Ancient Scripture at Brigham Young University, Provo, Utah. He earned a Ph.D. in New Testament at the Claremont Graduate School. His research interests include Christian origins, textual criticism of the New Testament, and early Christian heresies.

Index of Modern Authors and Authorities